Dead Last

THE TRIUMPH OF CHARACTER, PASSION, AND TEAMWORK IN EDUCATION

Stephen Wallis

TRILOGY CHRISTIAN PUBLISHERS

TUSTIN, CA

Trilogy Christian Publishers

A Wholly Owned Subsidary of Trinity Broadcasting Network

2442 Michelle Drive

Tustin, CA 92780

Dead Last: The Triumph of Character, Passion, and Teamwork in Education

Rights Department, 2442 Michelle Drive, Tustin, CA 92780.

Trilogy Christian Publishing/TBN and colophon are trademarks of Trinity Broadcasting Network.

For information about special discounts for bulk purchases, please contact Trilogy Christian Publishing.

Trilogy Disclaimer: The views and content expressed in this book are those of the author and may not necessarily reflect the views and doctrine of Trilogy Christian Publishing or the Trinity Broadcasting Network.

Manufactured in the United States of America

10 9 8 7 6 5 4 3 2 1

Library of Congress Cataloging-in-Publication Data is available.

ISBN: 978-1-63769-574-6

E-ISBN: 978-1-64769-575-3

Contents

To Nick, Alex, Thad, and Stella

true all-stars each,

who inspire me, fill me with pride, and always make me smile.

With love,

Papou

Good habits formed at youth make all the difference.

—ARISTOTLE

If this book revolves around any one meaningful message,
it is that the soul of any school is its character,
what the Greeks called ethos,
without which meaningful teaching and learning
cannot—will not—take place.
—Stephen Wallis

Preface

I retired a few years ago, having spent over three decades in the field of education, the first few years as a high school English teacher, several years as a high school administrator in various settings, and the last few years as principal of a Baltimore-Washington area in-crisis middle school, one beset with disrespectful, disruptive, frequently violent student behavior; low test scores; poor teacher morale; little to no active parental engagement among a large segment of the school community; and abject parent frustration on the part of those who were caring and actively involved in their youngsters' lives.

I see friends now and then from my past, dear friends from my old neighborhood or from my time serving in the U.S. Army. It's interesting to hear them talk about how they remember my speaking about schools and my desire to become a teacher, because as a youngster attending high school and receiving average grades, I never considered myself a particularly stellar student. School deserved a higher priority than many of us in the neighborhood gave it. While I was not a disruptive student at all, my friends and neighborhood were a bit hard scrabble.

Families generally were composed of hard-working parents, some of whom were actively involved in the lives of their children, other parents not so much. While some mothers worked outside the house, others, like mine, were stay-at-home moms. I was fortunate to have a pretty terrific mom, who remains my personal hero today. She and my dad had seven children, with their first boy having died as a young child. They divorced when I was very young, and while there was little spare money, we never felt poor. So I grew up with six women in a three-bedroom house with *one* bathroom, a challenge at times. My dad lived in Washington, D.C., and while he played an intermittent role in our lives, I think it's fair to say that he was generally absent from the family scene.

I felt we were otherwise pretty much an ordinary family. I recall that a good bit of clothes washing was done by hand and hung out to dry on a backyard clothesline. Metal insulated boxes on front home porches were a reminder of a time when milkmen would routinely drop off bottles of milk to homes without refrigeration. My mom would send me to the store almost daily to pick up food. Instead of computer games, most of our games were played outside. Kids were found playing capture the flag, hide-and-seek, swinging hula hoops, and skipping or jumping rope. We often played in the street, since traffic was light and never an issue. For hours on end, boys played football or a form of baseball called line ball, where each ball hit was determined to be a single, double, triple, or home run, depending on how far or what line in the dirt was reached.

A brain tumor would later claim my mom's life at a young fifty-four years of age, a shocking and terribly sad time for her children. I would be drafted into the United States Army not six months later, when most of my friends had already been drafted and were serving in the U.S. military. At the snap of a finger, my lifestyle was altered, and I was in army basic training boot camp, along with some 350 other recruits, anywhere from seventeen to twenty-six years of age, with various levels of education. I would be tapped by those in command to be among five squad leaders "responsible" for seeing that our company graduated combat basic training some three months later. I recall lying in my bunk one evening, thinking that I had graduated from high school with a mediocre education, and though I was on a par with the majority of my peers, I could have derived more from my schooling had I applied myself meaningfully at the time.

Following combat basic training, everyone awaited "orders" for the next duty assignment. All of us were convinced we were heading for advanced infantry training in Louisiana. Our time in boot camp included physical, mental, and emotional training and testing. We were assigned an MOS—a Military Occupation Specialty—and mine was in the area of administration and data analysis. My next assignment had me posted to Fort Dix, New Jersey, for several months, working with the Adjutant General's Office. My commanding officer inquired of my interest in serving as an officer and asked if I might have an interest in attending West Point Military Academy. I was a "strac" solider—a term used to describe one as competent, dependable, proud, and confident, someone who believed in duty; I was also shocked. While I was proud to be thought of so highly, I eventually declined, perhaps due to naivete, immaturity, or just poor judgment. Whatever the reason, I continued working in solid stead at Fort Dix until many of us received our follow-up orders, assigning us to the "Overseas Replacement Station" and heading to Europe.

We received a short amount of time for "leave," and I made my way to the Pentagon to request reassignment to Southeast Asia, where my friends had been fighting. I believed that America, in fact, was there for the right reasons. I reasoned that I could collect combat pay, and I was confident that with my duties, I would safely return—more mature, more "educated," and with some reasonable savings accumulated. It was not to be. I was told directly, "Soldier, the answer is no; we've enough men with your MOS in 'theatre,' and your skills and talents are needed in another part of the world, supplanting NATO forces." I replied, "Yes, sir," of course, and was on my way.

The United States has always had military troops stationed throughout the world, both in wartime and in peacetime. While I am among those called Vietnam-era veterans, I served my specific tour of duty in Heidelburg, in what was then called West Germany (as opposed to Russian-controlled East Germany), with both countries divided by the Berlin Wall. Our work was important, our military duty station between Patton Barracks and Campbell Barracks in Heidelburg-Rohrbach was second to none, and the German citizens living within close proximity always seemed supportive and appreciative of our service. My tour of duty afforded me the opportunity to travel throughout Germany, including in communist East Germany, by way of Checkpoint Charlie, the Berlin Wall crossing point between East Berlin and West Berlin during the Cold War—as well as western Europe, usually with three army buddies, and on one occasion, with my dad. I considered the travels unique opportunities to see, among other places, Italy, France, Switzerland, the Netherlands, Luxembourg, and Portugal. One memorable experience was using a three-day pass to travel to Austria, where we were awakened early one morning from our tents by a goat herder and the sound of bells ringing from the necks of his goats grazing in the Alps over top the Von Trapp estate in Salzburg. While serving overseas, a few of us were fortunate to play competitive football during our tour of duty, and the team compiled a strong win-loss record.

On the eve of my military discharge, one of the officers in my unit, knowing where I was from, informed me of a scheduled NFL free agent/walk-on tryout. I thanked him and said that while I felt I could hold my own and handled the ball well, my speed was not at that level of play. As he looked askance at me, I immediately thought, *Okay, not much sense in annoying him, I enjoy the sport, and I should see*

this as among those opportunities that would broaden my life experience.
So I said, "Alright, thank you, sir; I'll spare no effort." Upon my discharge from the U. S. Army in the early 1970's, I started working on
my college degree. Indeed, I also capitalized on the opportunity and
showed up on the appointed day at George Mason University for a
walk-on tryout session with the Washington Redskins, where coaches sized up everyone in attendance, releasing many of the candidates
within minutes of the 7 a.m. camp start. The day would give them an
opportunity to review overall physical fitness, including one's agil-
ity, strength, and speed, hoping they'd find the next Herb Mul-key (a
speedy kick returner from a previous similar walk-on tryout). While
running and completing a successful post pattern, Coach George
Allen yelled, "Nice grab there, 87"—the jersey number I wore at the
time. I thanked him and proceeded to grind it out for the remainder
of the day. It was late afternoon when wide receiver Charley Taylor
was among those assistants holding stop watches for our 40-yard
dash time trials. My 4.9/5.0 time didn't cut it, as I knew it'd have to be
closer to 4.5 to show promise. Nonetheless, it was a rewarding, enjoyable experience; I gave it my best shot and felt I had kept the promise
to my former lieutenant-colonel colleague to "spare no effort."

With my military service behind me, I continued to work in earnest on my undergraduate degree. I read a newspaper article at the
time regarding a shooting incident at an area high school that took
the life of a student, and after doing some research, I found that a
number of schools exhibited a kind of instability that I believed undermined their mission. I felt that schools, even then, did not appear
orderly and purposeful, that such a loose environment, left unat-
tended, could well become chaotic. So I wrote an op-ed piece on the
matter that saw publication in a Washington, DC area newspaper.
Interesting that nearly fifty years ago, when I wrote that op-ed piece,
I was somehow dialed in on the importance of an appropriate teach-

ing-learning environment, the need to be purposeful and to connect with one another, as well as the paramount role that character could and should play in every schoolhouse.

I was attending college on the G.I. Bill and living in an apartment. I was also a volunteer firefighting officer with a local Washington, D.C., area engine company. I thought I could use some additional income, and I knew retired firefighters who drove school buses to supplement their retirement; firefighters already had the requisite driver's license to operate large vehicles. Eureka! I arranged my university classes to be the middle of the day and the evenings, allowing me to earn extra money driving a school bus in the mornings and afternoons, when I would occasionally drop off my last group of kids—mostly black—park the bus, and play basketball with them for an hour or so. The bus lot supervisor was impressed that I kept the cleanest school bus in the area (I would frequently turn a fire hose on it), knew I was a young veteran attending college, and offered the idea of my keeping the bus at the end of my morning run, needing only to return it at the end of the day. I'd drive it to the university campus, where it sat parked outside the athletic fieldhouse, campus officials assuming it was for a student field trip. That bus saved me the cost of a university student parking pass the entire time I attended the University of Maryland.

Along the way, I encountered a particularly gifted college English professor, who sparked in me a palpable interest in teaching English. I believed I could make a meaningful contribution to present-day schools and likely could teach English to youngsters better than I thought I had been taught. I decided to major in English, and after graduating and considering other careers, including law, television broadcasting (in which I was offered a job), the Secret Service, and professional firefighting (because of my familiarity with the fire service), I chose teaching high school English...and I loved it. The idea of teaching was something I saw as noble, and I wanted to support, connect with, and commit to my students that we were in this thing together—that they would, in fact, learn to think, to speak, and to write well. Each year I was able to ensure that I had a broad array of student levels, from those who had always struggled, to the average student, as well as those who were smart and talented ("gifted and talented," they were called). All of them touched me immeasurably throughout those years, and so many years later, it continues to be a delight to encounter some of them in person or on social media.

I spent several years in the classroom, and along the way I developed an interest in public school administration. I felt I could make a meaningful contribution in that area, affecting education policy in a broader fashion. I believed I could lead a school better than what I observed was happening in various communities, so I started my trek through the administrative maze, including obtaining a university master's degree and spending years as an assistant principal, serving various diverse populations. I developed an acute, if not, passionate interest in education, teaching, and learning, and I was actively involved in American schooling, writing for think tanks, assisting state legislators on education policy, testifying and participating in shaping education policy before the state legislative assembly, as well as providing testimony before the United States Congress. I was later asked to take on a uniquely challenging assignment, taking the helm of a particularly troubled school in Columbia, Maryland, as cited in the opening paragraph.

This is not so much a how-to guide, as it is a description of the kinds of decisions made and actions we took in a particular school setting to reverse its decline, increase student achievement, and be nationally recognized for its success. I emphasize the word we—this would include students, staff, parents, and the wider business community—because it was they who believed in me, took my lead, felt the passion, worked hard, and were every bit part of bringing about our success.

Schools can be vastly different in the way of curricula and course options, after-school and extra-curricular activities, facilities, athletic fields, and their art & music program offerings; each school community can also present unique challenges. I'd like the readers of this book to come away with a renewed perspective on ideas, thoughts, suggestions, and policy prescriptions that just might work in their own school communities.

There are successful schools that dot the American landscape; this is a story about one of them: a come-from-behind, academically failing, disruptive, frequently violent school setting that came to believe in itself to become a State Character School of the Year, cited among the top schools in the Virginia–Washington, D.C.–Maryland Metropolitan area, and later designated a National School of Excellence.

*Students don't care how much you know
until they know how much you care.*

—Unknown

Acknowledgments

I'm a fortunate guy and most appreciative of the love and support from my family—Eric and Piper Wallis, grandson Thad and granddaughter Stella; Amanda and Jim Buckler, and grandsons Nick and Alex—for their caring, support, and endorsement throughout this lengthy process.

My heartfelt appreciation to my wife, Elaine—my partner in everything—for her support, forbearance, and encouragement, enduring lengthy days and nights while I worked on this project. I am fortunate to have such a soulmate, who always lent an ear on ideas and issues I was mulling over, and who graciously read the manuscript, providing her insights along the way.

Special thank you to Piper Furbush Wallis, for her thoughtful and creative perspective on the various questions I had on the book publishing process.

I express my love and appreciation to my grandson Alex Buckler, one of sharp mind and wit, always readily providing clarity and assistance in discussions of and compiling statistics within the book.

This book is a product of over three decades spent in an education career that saw my life enriched by my association with several thousand students, their parents, and teaching staff colleagues, from my early years as a high school English teacher to the many years I served various school communities as a high school administrator, and later as principal of a hard luck school that is the soul of this book. I appreciate and thank each of you, one and all, for the many ways you enriched my life. As such, this book is an homage—a tribute— to each and every one of you.

To George "Bud" Rossiter, more a brother than brother-in-law, now deceased, and a onetime stalwart of a teacher and school administrator. I remain appreciative of his love, loyalty, and unending support!

My thanks and appreciation to those, who were supportive of this project and graciously reviewed the book manuscript, whose comments were collectively invaluable. These reviewers would include Patricia Almquist, a first-rate professional teacher and instructional leader, whose excellence in the classroom, intelligence, and caring provided insightful perspectives on teaching and learning. Special thanks, as well, to Al Tucci, former teacher and recognized top-shelf school district human resources leader, for his thoughtful and reasoned frame of reference on issues, including American culture and education, someone who always believed I should write a book one day.

I am lovingly and respectfully appreciative of my mom and dad, Katherine and Charles Wallis, and I express my love and gratitude to my sisters Junie, Dolores, Carolyn, Florence Marie, and Patti because they are part and parcel of who I am today and, well, they're my sisters and would likely be annoyed if I failed to mention their names.

I also want to thank Laura Waters, Juanita Robinson, and Gloria Rockmore—many years all fearless community education advocates and tireless supporters of me, my philosophical viewpoint on American school leadership, and my perspective on the importance of and the requirements for meaningful teaching and learning.

I am grateful to Reid Buckley—novelist, columnist, founder of a school of public speaking, and a terrific supporter, who always felt that my life's work as a school principal had me performing "God's work."

I express my gratitude to Robert Moffit—Senior Fellow at The Heritage Foundation and a seasoned veteran of a quarter-century in Washington policymaking, who saw "determination and a reasoned passion" in a long-ago op-ed I penned, offering me the opportunity to write what turned out to be a chapter in the Heritage Foundation–published book *Making America Safer,* to work with members of the United States Congress on national education reform proposals, and to appear before the United States Senate Committee on Government Affairs hearings, providing expert testimony on the role schools can play in the effort to combat crime and violence, and in the process, cultivate an appreciation of character, compassion, dignity, and respect throughout American communities.

My sincere thanks and appreciation to Trilogy Publishing staff, all of whom were professional and competent through all aspects of the book publishing production process. I respected the knowledge and insights of those in the areas of design, review, copy editing, and cover design, as well as the expertise of those in page design, printing preparation, distribution, and marketing. I remain grateful.

Introduction

If this book revolves around any one meaningful message, it is that the soul of any school is its character, what the Greeks called *ethos*, without which meaningful teaching and learning cannot—will not—take place.

Many throughout the United States look at the seeming precarious state of national and international affairs and believe, as I do, in the importance of renewing our commitment to the philosophy and tenets of our country's founding. In doing so, I wonder about the role the declining state of American education has played in our current condition.

We look at our social and cultural state of affairs and find too many Americans devoid of basic knowledge, from their math facts and both oral and written skills, to a lack of knowledge of history—American or otherwise. Company managers regularly complain about job candidates' inability to express themselves.[1] That should be no surprise, as many high school and college graduates lack both hard and soft skills—from writing proficiency; public speaking; and data analysis to critical thinking and problem-solving; paying attention to detail; and understanding leadership, communication, and listening; as well as the importance of interpersonal connections, etiquette, and teamwork.[2] The dearth of workplace talents makes it all the more difficult for graduates to find, much less to hold, the jobs that are increasingly based on knowledge and information. Folks on both sides of the political spectrum, young and old, have bemoaned the continued overall abysmal state of American education.

We have our share of successful schools throughout the country. It is fair to say, however, that American K-12 education annually lags behind the educational systems of many other industrialized nations. Why is it that so many schools appear chaotic, "graduating" students year after year bereft of the most basic skills, much less the ability to think critically?

This is a story of a hard-luck public school that occupied the low end of the achievement scale for years, a school that many teachers felt was not a place where they wanted to teach, a school abhorred by many parents, a number of whom actively sought out other schools or education locales in the effort to provide their youngsters with a better education. Such dreadfully poor-performing, disruptive school environments can undergo remarkable transformation, when there are underlying values that revolve around character and a tireless, near-monomaniacal emphasis on self-discipline, quality instruction, continuous improvement, making connections with one another, and establishing partnerships—day after day, year after year. It's a story about hope; about grit, fortitude, determination, caring, passion, perseverance, and teamwork evidenced by students, staff, and parents. It's a story about character.

While located in what is considered an otherwise wealthy county in the Baltimore-Washington, D.C. corridor, considered a top-rated school system, some members of the Harper's Choice Middle School (HCMS) staff and community stated that they felt the school was ignored, because of the unfavorable condition of the school's environment and its poor academic performance. Whatever the case, I viewed it as the quintessential public school, a majority-minority school serving students of various races, ethnicities, and socioeconomic levels, a kind of "United Nations," running the gamut from well-to-do single-family homes to low-income apartments and condominiums, and the majority of those students qualified for free or reduced lunch. I wanted to know precisely where our foreign-born youngsters hailed from, and I found that the student body represented countries and nationalities from Puerto Rico, Mexico, El Salvador, Ghana, Liberia, Iran, Nigeria, Ethiopia, Taiwan, Vietnam, Honduras, and China.

The school was also described as "dead last" in conversations with teaching staff, parents, and school district officials. It was among those schools replete with disruptive student behavior, including widespread bullying and thievery; failing state academic test scores; low staff morale; racial unrest; and parent dissatisfaction with school and school district administrators. However, it later rose to become a State Character School of the Year, cited among the top schools in the Virginia–Washington, D.C.–Maryland area, and later designated a National School of Excellence, only to return later to an unfavorable academic condition. How does such a transformation occur? And how is it that, once a school has overcome its hard luck and achieved success, it can find itself yet again at the bottom of the barrel?

The turnaround started with my belief that schools must revolve around character. In the case of Harper's Choice, it became the soul of the school, from which decisions would be made regarding students, staff, the instructional program, parents, and the wider community. This specific quality will be a recurring theme throughout the book. I will also devote extended analysis or commentary to hot button issues in American K-12 education, some of which will appear as chapters in the book. These are exceedingly important topics that figured prominently in our school's success or are of pivotal import to the success of American education today: *character*, without which organizations simply cannot reach their optimum level of success;

leadership, a cornerstone in any orchestrated successful endeavor; *school safety and security*, a topic I could well have made the first chapter, given its critical importance; the resegregation and poisonous racial narrative that is *wokeness and critical race theory*; the *achievement gap*, that persistent performance disparity among groups, the elimination of which is arguably the holy grail in education; *parents and schools*, a linchpin in a youngster's school success; *school choice*; and *vocational-technical education*.

I spent a career in public school teaching and administration. I was passionate about the profession, and I sought to ensure that students enjoyed attending school every day, that their parents believed in and felt good about the school their kids were attending, that teachers and staff enjoyed getting up in the morning and coming to work each day, and that the wider business community respected the school serving the community and felt confident that we were producing good citizens and, perhaps, future company employees. I believe such came under my specific purview, and I was going to do everything within the scope of my position to make that happen, to advance the teaching profession, and maybe even save some lives.

I have only my extensive experience and modest observations to offer. I would like the reader to gain a glimpse of what it is like to run a busy demographic school, a term I use to describe my statistical view of a school community, this school community: multicultural ethnicities, a wide variance in community member education levels, income distribution, marital status, criminal behavior and police activity, social services casework load, and parent-school involvement.

This school's busy demographic presented students carrying emotional baggage, with an array of challenges, including pregnancy; involvement in the juvenile justice system, with some youngsters required to wear ankle bracelets; as well as those affected by family turmoil and disruption. As such, there were any number of folks in and out of the school building on a daily basis. They might be county or state social services staff, psychologists, court-appointed individuals representing the student or parent, parent(s) arriving with an attorney, family services representatives, and the like.

I would like the reader to understand the day-to-day challenges of such school communities, and to take from this book suggestions that might well prove successful in a school serving your community. If we continue to share "what works," perhaps larger percentages of people—including students, parents, teachers, school officials, and legislators—will find it within themselves to transform the plethora of failing, disruptive, and violent schools into educational settings promoting first-rate teaching, exemplary student behavior, outstanding student academic achievement, and active parent participation and support throughout our country.

The reader will note that I will sometimes place quotation marks around a word or phrase and, depending on the context, it likely implies that I do not, in that specific case, agree with the meaning of the word as normally used.

The book clarifies how character, grit, traditional values, respect, and a no-nonsense attitude trump the typical education orthodoxy of appeasement, identity politics, and excuses. It's a book about a hard-working staff—ordinary people having accomplished something special, something extraordinary— and in the process, found in themselves—students, staff, and parents— a kind of rebirth, a new beginning in how they began to look at themselves to become more purposeful, more meaningful in the lives of others. In that vein the book provides useful insights for any organization or corporation on the power of character, passion, and teamwork to obtain maximum results.

Research studies, my professional teaching career, media reports, and the assessment of scholars on the condition of American education inform a point of view and critique made throughout this book of schools, educators, students, parents, and legislators, as well as the suggestions I offer for consideration. Having said that, I am as appreciative as I am humbled of the rewarding and edifying experiences I enjoyed as a professional high school English teacher, school administrator, and school principal. I hope the following pages adequately express that sentiment and that the reader takes away some equally edifying insights as to how best to improve K-12 education for our youngsters, our families, and for a stronger, more robust America.

Where mediocrity is the norm,
it is not long before mediocrity becomes the ideal.

—A. N. Wilson

1

Current Condition of American Schools

Among the reasons I believe this book is important is the continuing state of American education—its disappointing mediocre to poor international standing, the appallingly high number of failing schools throughout the country, the disruptive atmosphere cataloged almost daily in the American news media, and the manner in which school systems have all but destroyed vocational education in this country. Add to this the current backlash across the country to what is called "wokeness" in our schools—blatant activism with regard to gender ideology and racially divisive training and curriculum that passes for education in many schools. These ills have resulted in widespread dismay among classroom teachers, students, parents, and America writ large. It is no secret that our schools are viewed as lackluster, and the statistics generally bear this out year after year. Throughout my tenure in this profession, I was periodically reminded of the quote attributed to English writer and newspaper columnist A. N. Wilson: "Where mediocrity is the norm, it is not long before mediocrity becomes the ideal."

There are any number of variables that account for the various upticks and downticks in schooling metrics; teaching and learning can be complex, and generally, no single reason can explain education trends, positive or negative. Having said that, we should be honest and recognize where we are before we can appropriately employ best practices that will begin to shore up and advance our system of K-12 education.

The National Assessment of Education Progress (NAEP), commonly known as the "Nation's Report Card," reports that the country's student scores are flat, and average scores on both the ACT (American College Testing, a readiness assessment for high school achievement and used for college admissions) and the SAT (Scholastic Assessment Test, a reasoning test measuring reading, writing, and mathematics levels, also used for college admission) are down.[1]

Many "educrats"—local, state, and national education officials, legislators, and policy wonks—boast about our country's high school graduation rate, but that figure—and these folks know this—does not provide the public with an accurate picture of the state of our schools.

In fact, it becomes particularly troublesome when unethical, at times, criminal behavior is involved in the various statistics provided to the American public. It is entirely appropriate to ask if the various data on American schools conveyed to the public are, indeed, accurate at all. It's healthy to question and examine information presented to the public. Why? See the chapter titled "Character."

Let's focus, for the moment, on information and data presented frequently to the general public with respect to school graduation rates and take at face value the graduation statistics presented to the American public. A 2012 U.S Education Department report cites an 80 percent graduation rate, and in October 2016, officials touted an all-time high of 83 percent in the 2014–2015 school year.[2]

This is problematic for two not-so-minor reasons. First, that 80 percent graduation rate still leaves one in every five students walking away without a high school diploma, some 1.2 million students annually, or nearly seven thousand students a day. About 25 percent of high school freshmen fail to graduate from high school on time. These statistics rank the United States twenty-second out of twenty-seven developed countries.[3]

Second, what is not mentioned too widely of the 80 percent high school graduation rate is that nearly 60 percent of college/university freshmen discover that, while they were eligible for college entrance, they were not at all prepared for postsecondary studies.[4] These students learn that they must take remedial courses in English and mathematics, which do not earn them college credits. They realize quickly that the gap between college eligibility and college readiness is huge. Only 19 percent of students graduate on time from public universities; the graduation rate is only 36 percent at flagship research public universities. There are a number of reasons for this failure to graduate on time, among which is the issue of remediation.

The National Center for Public Policy and Higher Education says, "Increasingly, it appears that states or post-secondary institutions may be enrolling students under false pretenses. Even those students who have done everything they were told to do to prepare for college find, often after they arrive, that their new institution has deemed them unprepared. Their high school diploma, college-preparatory curriculum, and high school exit examination scores did not ensure college readiness." The paper goes on to say, "This huge readiness gap is costly to students, families, institutions, and taxpayers, and is a tremendous obstacle to increasing the nation's college attainment levels."[5]

How costly is it? Nearly two million students each year commence college in remediation, and only one in ten of those remedial students will even graduate from college. Each additional year a student attends a four-year university is, on average, $22,826 for that cost of attendance (including tuition and fees, room and board, books and supplies, transportation, and other expenses); couple this expense with lost wages of $45,327, and you've got a total of $68,153, on average, for each one of those students, according to a Complete College America Report.[6] Further, a report from researchers at Education Reform Now (ERN), a nonpartisan, nonprofit organization, found that enrolling in remedial coursework during the first year of college costs students and their families nearly $1.5 billion a year in out-of-pocket expenses.[7] Again, they are receiving remedial assistance for skills, concepts, and subjects that should well have been mastered in their K-12 education. The ERN research study cites the following:

> Forty-five percent of those students came from middle- and upper-income families. Not only does college remediation cut across all income levels, but it's also common across all types of post-secondary institutions. Nearly half—43 percent—of remedial students were enrolled in public four-year colleges or private two- and four-year colleges. The other 57 percent were enrolled in public community colleges.

The report's co-author said:

> We have long studied how our country's elementary and secondary schools have under-served low-income students and students of color, but inadequate academic preparation does not end with students and schools from low-income communities. The problem is much more widespread. Inadequate high school preparation, as reflected by post-secondary remedial course enrollment, is also a middle class and upper-class problem and has real out-of-pocket financial consequences for all.

The report went on:

> One in four college freshmen pays on average an extra
> $3,000 and borrows nearly an extra $1,000 for remedial
> coursework in the first year of college. However, students
> from families in the top income quintile that attend more
> expensive private nonprofit four-year colleges pay on av-
> erage an extra $12,000 for remedial classes.

While under-prepared students average two remedial courses
each during their first year, higher-income students at expensive
private nonprofit four-year colleges take more remedial classes than
lower-income students at those same colleges, suggesting these
schools enroll many lower-achieving but higher-income students.
Full-time students seeking bachelor's degrees that take remedial
courses in their first year are 74 percent more likely to drop out of
college. Those who do graduate take 11 months longer than non-re-
medial students, requiring additional living expenses and delaying
earnings.[8] Peter Cunningham, executive director of Education Post,
which commissioned the study, said, "High schools are not rigorous
enough. Higher standards have raised the bar, but we need to hold
schools accountable for meeting those standards."[9]

School systems bluster of readying students for college and careers and getting students into college, when they would be well advised to focus on creating a culture for teaching and learning in every
classroom, in every schoolhouse, substantively enhancing efforts to
provide these students with the knowledge and skills needed to complete satisfactorily their certificates or degrees.

National polling always cites education and schools as among
the most important topics to Americans. The condition of American

schooling remains important and relevant. After all, our country's economic outlook—and our future economic success—are inextricably connected to the health of our nation's schools. Among the public, as well as those whose business it is to study and research American schooling, there is general agreement that our schools continue to fail our youngsters. It's all the more disappointing, given the local, state, and national reform efforts that were an outgrowth of the 1983 landmark report, *A Nation at Risk: The Imperative for Educational Reform*, created during the administration of President Ronald Reagan. As a young school administrator, I recall the report's sobering assessment:

> Our nation is at risk. Our once unchallenged preeminence in commerce, industry, science, and technological innovation is being overtaken by competitors throughout the world. This report is concerned with only one of the many causes and dimensions of the problem, but it is the one that undergirds American prosperity, security, and civility.
>
> We report to the American people that while we can take justifiable pride in what our schools and colleges have historically accomplished and contributed to the United States and the well-being of its people, the educational foundations of our society are presently being eroded by a rising tide of mediocrity that threatens our very future as a Nation and a people.
>
> What was unimaginable a generation ago has begun to occur—others are matching and surpassing our educational attainments.
>
> If an unfriendly foreign power had attempted to impose on America the mediocre educational performance that

exists today, we might well have viewed it as an act of war.
As it stands, we have allowed this to happen to ourselves....
We have, in effect, been committing an act of unthinking,
unilateral educational disarmament.

Our society and its educational institutions seem to have
lost sight of the basic purposes of schooling, and of the
high expectations and disciplined effort needed to attain
them.[10]

When the issue of U.S education quality is discussed, there are
those on both sides of the topic who have their share of recrimina-
tions and criticisms, but let us look at how far we've come since the
Nation at Risk report. The 1983 report highlighted that 13 percent of
seventeen-year-olds could not read, that our performance on international tests was mediocre to poor, that student achievement was
falling on standardized tests, and that there was a sharp increase in
the number of students requiring remedial instruction in colleges.
Further, our armed forces and businesses throughout the country
expressed dismay that they felt they had to offer remedial training of
recruits and employees.

Over thirty years later, having spent billions of dollars on American education, we find that 19 percent of this country's high school
"graduates" cannot read. In fact, 14 percent of the adult population
in the United States—that's thirty-two million folks—cannot read,
and 21 percent of adults who can read do so below a fifth-grade level,
according to the U.S. Department of Education and the National Institute of Literacy.[11]

We continue to find ourselves showing uninspiring performance
on international tests that compare us with the rest of the industrialized world. The Organization for Economic Cooperation and Development (OECD) conducts a triennial survey of fifteen-year-old

students to determine if they have acquired key knowledge and skills essential for full participation in modern societies. The worldwide assessment, called Programme for International Student Assessment (PISA), focuses on mathematics, reading, and science, as well as an "innovative domain," and in 2015, the domain was collaborative problem-solving. It assesses not only what kids know, but how well students can extrapolate what they've learned and apply that knowledge in unfamiliar settings. The approach reflects the fact that modern economies reward individuals not so much for what they know, as much as what they can do with what they know. The assessment is meant to "offer insights."

The 2015 PISA Results in Focus Report places the United States below twenty-four other nations in their "Snapshot of Performance in Science, Reading, and Mathematics."[12] The OECD correctly cites knowledge as the "driver of productivity and economic growth." Students graduating from school must know stuff—meaningful things—and there will continually be a renewed focus on the role of information, technology, and learning in economic performance. Today's societies are, in fact, knowledge-based economies, and the way we teach and learn, today and tomorrow, must be geared to, and in sync with, that idea.

The National Assessment of Educational Progress—as cited earlier, "The Nation's Report Card"—is the largest nationally representative and continuing assessment of what America's students know and can do in various subject areas. The percentage of American students at or above NAEP proficiency in key academic subject areas declines as they matriculate through our K-12 education system. Except as otherwise noted, the following reflects the percentage of students at or above 2019 NAEP Proficiency in key academic subjects:[13]

	Grade 4	Grade 8	Grade 12
Civics:	27%	23%	24%
Geography:	21%	27%	20%
Mathematics:	40%	34%	25% (2015 NAEP)
Reading:	37%	36%	37% (2015 NAEP)
Science:	38%	34%	22%
U.S. History:	20%	18%	12%

It should be no surprise that a growing number of companies find it inordinately difficult to hire workers with the hard skills (teachable abilities or skill sets that are easy to quantify, e.g., foreign language proficiency, a degree or certificate, typing speed, machine operation, computer programming) and soft skills (people or interpersonal skills, e.g., communication, flexibility, leadership, teamwork, and time management) needed to perform various jobs.[14]

What is the effect on our American workforce, our ability to innovate, to produce, to manufacture? The Manpower Group 2018 Talent Shortage Survey of nearly forty thousand employers in forty-three countries and territories finds that more employers than ever are struggling to fill open jobs, citing a global average of 45 percent of companies reporting talent shortages. The survey points out that 46 percent of America's largest companies report critical talent shortages.[15]

What I have shared thus far with the reader provides a review of the less-than-stellar academic findings that make up American K-12 education. I will share findings and a perspective on the safety and security aspect of our schools and the deleterious effect of this issue on the daily lives of our teachers, our school-age youngsters, and their families.

Having looked at the academic performance of our American youngsters, it follows, then, that every schoolhouse must provide an appropriate school culture—one that values and cultivates teaching and learning—if teaching excellence and outstanding student academic performance are to flourish. That only occurs when character is recognized as the soul of the school. Therein lies the rub; far too many school communities at the K-12 and university levels (including educators, school and university officials, local school board members) seemingly fail to grasp an understanding of this quality, much less recognize the importance—the crucial importance—that character plays in administering a top-shelf school or university community that provides a first-class education to America's students. While that should be found appalling to many, it is not all that surprising. I recall a conversation years ago that William Bennett, former director of the Office of National Drug Control Policy under President George H.W. Bush, had with a Detroit judge, who often asked his defendants, "Didn't anyone ever teach you right from wrong?" Often, they responded, "No, no one has ever taught me that ever."

My years of experience as a public school teacher, administrator, and principal have proven time and again that among the pivotal reasons for this country's flat, failing academic performance revolves around the lack of decorum, if not uncivilized behavior, that is all too evident in our school classrooms, corridors, athletic venues, and communities. Worse, the response from school officials and politicians to disrespectful, disruptive, violent school behavior typically has been partial, cosmetic, and ad hoc. I have both commented on and have published writings on this scourge for the better part of my over three decades in the education profession.

In a 2015 nationally representative sample of youth in grades 9 through 12:

- 7.8 percent reported being in a physical fight on school property in the twelve months before the survey.

- 5.6 percent reported that they did not go to school on one or more days in the thirty days before the survey because they felt unsafe at school or on their way to or from school.

- 4.1 percent reported carrying a weapon (gun, knife, or club) on school property on one or more days in the thirty days before the survey; that's over two million students carrying weapons while attending school!

- 6.0 percent reported being threatened or injured with a weapon on school property one or more times in the twelve months before the survey; that's some three million students who were threatened or injured by another carrying a weapon in school!

- 20.2 percent reported being bullied on school property, and 15.5 percent reported being bullied electronically during the twelve months before the survey. We're talking over ten million students who, when attending school, were bullied, intimidated, and made to feel less than human.[16]

On the issue of bullying alone, a number of research organizations cite that, "160,000 students stay home from school every day because of bullying." A Cyberbullying Research Center survey revealed that 18.5 percent of students (some 4,750,000 students) have skipped school at some point in the last year "because of bullying" at school. Some 600,0000 students claim that they've stayed home from school "many times."[17] Further, 10 percent—or 2,750,000 students surveyed—said they had stayed home from school because of bullying online. This issue of bullying alone has an enormous deleterious effect on student achievement.

Students are not the only victims of intimidation or violence in schools. The National Center for Education Statistics (NCES) periodically reports on the condition of American schooling. Its *Indicators of School Crime and Safety* (last updated June 2014) cites key findings, among which are the following:

Teachers are subject to threats and physical attacks, and students from their schools frequently commit these offenses. The School and Staffing Survey from NCES asks schoolteachers whether they were threatened with injury or physically attacked by a student from their school in the previous twelve months. During the 2011–2012 school year, 9 percent of schoolteachers—some 279,000 educators—reported being threatened with injury by students from their school, a percentage that was higher than the percentages of teachers who reported being threatened with injury in 2003–2004 and 2007–2008. Further, the percentage of teachers reporting that they had been physically attacked by a student from their school in the 2011–2012 school year was 5 percent—that's 155,000 educators—a percentage higher than in any previous survey year.

That same year, I recall the *Philadelphia Inquirer's* investigative series ASSAULT ON LEARNING, in which it was reported that in one year "690 teachers were assaulted; in the five years prior, 4,000 were." The newspaper reported that in Philadelphia's 268 schools, "on an average day 25 students, teachers, or other staff members were beaten, robbed, sexually assaulted, or victims of other violent crimes. That does not include thousands more who are extorted, threatened, or bullied in a school year."[18] It is a sad commentary that throughout the year, one may read in a daily newspaper of similar disruptive, violent behavior playing out regularly in far too many school districts across America.

Private schools are not immune to such incorrigible behavior. Three percent of private school teachers—15,000 educators—report being physically threatened by students, and 3 percent—another 15,000—report having been physically attacked by their students.[19] These are statistics that do not include the thousands of other school staff (secretaries, teacher and student aides, cafeteria workers, custodial and maintenance workers, bus drivers, etc.) who work in schools throughout the country and face this kind of criminal behavior while at work every school year. This kind of workplace atmosphere is heinous and intolerable, and we as a country are capable of providing a better service to our citizenry.

The result is the human toll that school communities experience up front and close, as record numbers of teachers decide it's time to quit, causing instability for the industry due to the impact on student performance and costing U.S. schools $7.3 billion in losses every year, according to the National Commission on Teaching and America's Future.[20] Teachers who leave the profession cite a host of reasons, among which are "challenging physical conditions, unmanageable class sizes, emotional stress, working 10–15 hour days and weekends, ineffective administrators, and no support for discipline problems."[21] More on this issue later in the book.

My perspective on the issue of students' disrespectful behavior and school disruption has been shared on any number of occasions throughout my tenure in education, whether expressed in published research and national periodicals or when speaking before community groups or in radio/television interviews. The fact is that student disruptive behavior affects the many thousands upon thousands of well-behaved students in every grade level, youngsters who are mature, responsible, caring, and respectful.

We can hardly assert the need to "set rigorous standards," as has been said time and again by many, and then ignore the primary reason that such standards are unachievable. Like a common thief, poor student behavior steals learning and achievement potential from our students. That pervasive disrespectful behavior is such a powerful obstacle to learning is frequently unacknowledged and unaddressed by public school officials and local boards of education. Yet teachers openly complain that they often are able to teach only two-thirds of course content because of the inordinate time spent managing behavior in the classroom. A Northwest Regional Educational Library research report based on work sponsored by the U.S. Department of Education Office of Educational Research and Improvement cites that "approximately one-half of all classroom time is taken up with activities other than instruction, and discipline problems are responsible for a significant portion of this lost instructional time."[22] Successful students in many schools feel that their hard-earned accomplishments come in spite of the rampant bad behavior of peers, evidenced daily in classrooms, auditoriums, gymnasiums, and school corridors.

School attendance is involuntary in every state of the Union, so taxpayers have a right to expect state and local officials to do their duty and provide their children a safe environment in which to learn. In too many schools, they do not. Teachers have a right to teach, and students have a right to learn, free from violence, harassment, gutter language, and other verbal abuse and disruption. For economically disadvantaged parents and students who are practically denied a choice of educational options, making it more difficult for them to escape failing and violent schools, the obligations of state and local officials take on an even greater urgency.[23]

Student disruption, after all, is a product of school culture, that philosophical foundation of norms and beliefs—academic and social—that informs every aspect of a school's daily operation. When character is at the heart of your business, your company—in this case, our schools—you can see in word and action sundry examples of honesty, integrity, effort, hard work, perseverance, and other core ethical values on display in and around the school campus. Such will cultivate what I call an appropriate teaching-learning culture. However, when the policies governing behavior are weak or inconsistently enforced, the mission of schooling becomes amorphous, and sensible expectations are eroded. The culture in these schools is ruled by an insidious silent—or not-so-silent—chaos, and a laundry list of behavior problems emerges—the "dissing" of peers and adults, bullying, routine disregard of school rules because any corrective action taken (if any at all) is weak and ephemeral, disregard for proper dress, pushing, fighting, alcohol and drug activity, tardiness, inappropriate sexual displays, truancy, indifference to class participation, routine use of vulgar language—often with no corrective behavior or consequences. It is as though such schools are waiting until youngsters are at the edge of the cliff before they take action. The wake-up call for too many officials is a tragedy that might, otherwise, have been averted.

In the book *Making America Safer*, Edwin Meese and Robert Moffit argue that "failing to recognize the close relationship between school discipline and criminal behavior and believing that we can achieve a safer society on the cheap add up to a prescription for failure. Citizen interest, involvement, and support—expressed in terms of devotion of time, energy, and resources—are making the difference in those communities around the country where the crime rate is being reduced."[24]

Such is precisely a not-so-minor prescription for turning around failing schools that communities across this great land would be wise to recognize. Indeed, I will clarify for the reader just how our emphasis on a shared partnership figured prominently in transforming a once-failing academic institution into a thriving, robust school of excellence.

Successful schools emphasize goals, expectations, and the 4 Rs—including RESPECT—and they are perceived by those who attend and work in them as welcoming venues of learning, warmth, caring, and accomplishment. The culture of success in these schools is infectious, and where that is the case, the teaching staff project it, students know that they can and are expected to achieve mastery of instructional objectives, and parent satisfaction is off the charts. I insisted that our school would see character at its core, from which every decision, every action, would emanate. There are such schools that dot the American landscape, but they differ from the many because their school climate is based firmly on a high regard for study, dignity, hard work, and achievement. Ours would become such a school.

Former Obama administration Education Secretary Arne Duncan estimated that 82 percent of America's public schools were not passing the test in educating our children (meaning the number of schools failing to meet No Child Left Behind proficiency goals)—82 percent.[25]

Many schools continue to be saddled with a widespread lack of decorum and civility, the wholesale disappearance of courtesy and manners; as such, we should not be surprised at the disappointing standing of American K-12 education. Add to this unfortunate commentary that a host of school communities throughout the country have elected, as cited earlier, to compound the challenges outlined in this chapter by allowing government and activist politics to engineer social or political outcomes in American schools, a topic I will touch upon in a later chapter. Where such nonsense is allowed to exist, schools are unable to impart to our youngsters the academic skills and knowledge required to be successful in the 21st century.

Just as I never tolerated such foolishness for years as a classroom teacher and high school administrator, I knew that such ill behavior and poor decision-making that would vitiate teaching and learning would not be the case at this school where I would be its principal, and I needed specific reassurance that I would not be undermined, that I would be given the appropriate latitude to make decisions that might or might not be in agreement with my various constituencies, be they staff, students, parents, politicos, school headquarters folks, or the media. Absent that reassurance, I would respectfully decline taking the helm of that school community.

2

Character

Character is the soul of man; it enhances and gives meaning—substance—to an individual. Being honest, loyal, respectful, responsible, humble, compassionate, and fair seem almost outmoded, if not, unfashionable in today's sometimes seemingly egocentric world. All the more reason, in my view, that we inculcate in our young an understanding of the principles concerning the distinction between right and wrong, or good and bad behavior. Aristotle wrote that good habits formed in youth make all the difference. Moreover, as expressed by former Secretary of Education William J. Bennett, author of *The Book of Virtues*, moral education is the training of heart and mind toward the good.

Our sixteenth president, Abraham Lincoln, was often cited among those who stood for honesty and integrity, character traits that kept him in solid stead, as he led our country through one of the most trying periods of its history, including the Civil War.

The idea of shaping and role modeling character creates loving, caring, responsible, and respected families. It fosters respectful and successful institutions, indeed, whole communities that, in turn, make for a better society. My sense is that character has to be at the core of any individual and any institution, in this case, the schoolhouse. It's been said that there is nothing more influential, more determinant, in a child's life than the moral power of quiet example.

For children to take morality seriously, they must be in the presence of adults who take morality seriously, and with their own eyes, they must see adults take morality seriously.[1]

As we teach, as we learn, as we interact daily with students, staff, parents, and the community, we have to be about developing character. This is not to be confused with the wrongheaded, foolhardy emphasis on self-esteem that many educators, parents, and school systems have mistakenly emphasized over the years. Indeed, one's self-concept is important, but I am talking about developing the mental and moral qualities distinctive to an individual, and we have the opportunity to do so with every singular interaction we have daily within the school setting. When such occurs, we build better, stronger individuals, whose sense of self-esteem is far more likely to be cultivated and part of their emotional makeup as they continue to matriculate through their years of schooling.

Character comes from the Greek word *ethos*, the guiding beliefs or ideals that characterize a community, a nation, an ideology. Those guiding beliefs—particularly for a community's school principal—should revolve around principles of right and wrong, dignity, fairness, and the recognition that everyone within the school and community matters, regardless of one's position. Whether you are a student, parent, educator, custodian, cafeteria worker, secretary, or bus driver, each is uniquely important, and I would like to think that everyone having worked with, for, or around me would be able to say objectively that I held in high esteem their position, their contribution, and their opinion on any decision, policy, or issue at hand.

Among the myriad questions and comments I received over the years as principal of Harper's Choice Middle School were two that revolved around why I chose to accept the responsibility of leading such a failing school, as well as how on earth I was able to transform such a horrible school environment into such a wonderful place to work, where students, their parents, and the staff were totally committed to excellence.

I chose to accept the offer because of the challenge, really. The superintendent, who at the time had recently arrived in the area from New York, told me it was a particularly challenging request that he was making of me, involving a school that parents and school system staff said was "in crisis," "failing and out of control," a "powder keg," and was "dead last" in every statistical category. He continued that he felt he could not ask anyone else, that he had reviewed my résumé and experience, talked to school board and community members who knew me, and felt that I was the "absolute right choice," and asked if I would think about the offer.

The second question regarding how I was able to transform the school from one that was failing, disruptive, and violent to one that revolved around respectful behavior, teaching-learning excellence, and active parental involvement was understandably a popular question. To be certain, such a challenge is not accomplished solo. Rather, the turnaround was due to the solid efforts of many—staff, students, parents, and the wider business community—all of whom invested a great deal of faith, trust, and confidence in my leadership, and I was not about to let them down. What I had observed was unacceptable, and I personally knew that I had the mental acuity, know-how, and stamina that would outgun any obstacle; in all matters in and out of the classroom and about the school community, I simply would not accept what had been business as usual.

The transformation would require more than the hard work of the school community. I knew this would require a change in the culture, and such a challenge would require an anchor, one that would prove almost spiritual as the days, weeks, months, and years passed. Character and the mantra that followed from it would prove to be that anchor of support, guidance, a kind of lodestar. Character became an integral, if not central aspect of the school landscape, ensuring that every decision I made for that school and the surrounding community would emanate from the heart, the soul of the school—its character.

Staffing one's school is of critical importance, and I was fortunate in working with and hiring the very finest individuals, who knew their subjects and were committed to working with me in dramatically changing the entire school culture to one that saw professional teaching excellence and successful student academic performance as standard fare.

I use the term *school culture* often throughout this book. I tend to describe it each time, as if to hammer home the pivotal importance such plays if schools are to be successful. As I talk about teaching, learning, and school reform, I am referring to an *appropriate school culture* or an *appropriate teaching-learning culture*, that philosophical foundation of norms and beliefs—academic and social—that informs every aspect of a school's daily operation. Such a positive culture emanates from the building's character and is at the heart of every successful school.

If you agree that character, in and of itself, is a vitally important trait in an individual, and if you can see why it would play a major role in how a company, corporation, university, school, or school system conducts itself, absorb for a few minutes the astounding lengths to which a sampling of education institutions—completely devoid of any sense of character, any degree of propriety, virtue, scruples, and honor—have willfully gone to deceive you, the American public.

Research and a review of newspaper and television exposés reveal a startling number of times when individual schools and school systems have deliberately submitted incorrect statistics, including graduation rates and test scores, for public review.

In the case of K-12 education, school officials frequently pound their chests, boasting of high graduation rates, even in light of continued mediocre to poor student performance in reading and mathematics on the National Assessment of Educational Progress.[2]

A review of investigations from Atlanta and New York to schools in Maryland and Washington, D.C., cite documentation and staff accounts of administrators, "guidance counselors," and other staff members using questionable and flat-out unethical methods to satisfy calls to raise graduation rates. Previous and current investigations reveal that these "educators"—school and central office headquarters staff—knew, should have known, and in many cases, actively participated in fraudulently inflating grades and/or softening grading scales, doctoring records, changing test scores, and using what they call "credit recovery programs," allowing students to take abbreviated versions of the actual courses that these students had failed due to extensive truancy or their individual failure to participate, engage in, and complete course assignments. Educators, including school principals, told investigators that such was standard operating procedure, that school system headquarters administrators were well aware of what was going on.

You might think that such reprobates masking as stand-up school officials and classroom teachers throughout the country are automatically fired and made to find other work; you would be wrong. Sometimes those who practice such fraudulent behavior are held accountable, as in the Atlanta Public Schools years-long cheating scandal, where school district administrators and teachers received jail sentences for being involved in altering, fabricating, and falsely certifying test answers. The former state attorney general who investigated the scandal stated that there were [imagine] "cheating parties," erasures in and out of the classrooms, and teachers who were told to make changes to student answers on tests.[3] The superintendent, who

received more than $500,000 in "performance bonuses," was await-
ing criminal trial for her alleged participation, when she died before
trial.[4]

However, a number of school officials and educators frequently
are not at all held accountable, and some of these administrators,
principals, and superintendents—if anything is done at all—are
prodded to retire, while others (superintendents, under whom such
unethical, fraudulent, and illegal activity was or is standard operating procedure) reportedly receive "contract extensions." Laughably,
others find work as "adjunct professors" at universities and are paid
to head up school "leadership" programs, ostensibly to "train" young
professional educators, those who are studying to earn a master's degree and hoping one day to lead a school themselves.

An investigative report found that grade marks for some 5,500
students in a Maryland public school system were altered days before
graduation.[5]

Yet another investigation found that students in Washington, D.C., were marked absent more than one hundred days—one
marked absent 151 days—yet each still received a diploma. We know
through research that missing 10 percent (approximately eighteen
days) of the school year negatively affects a student's academic performance. Fully half of the "graduates" in this high school missed
more than three months of the school year with unexcused absences;
one in five students was absent more than they were present, missing more than 90 days of the 180-day school year. Internal school
documents obtained by investigators show that 164 students received
diplomas, "smoke and mirrors," teachers say, and among those 164
students were those, they state, who literally could not read or write.
As though all of this were not horrible enough, teachers tell investigators that the assembled crowd on "graduation night" was seen as
"triumphant," with screaming family and friends snapping photos

and cheering over the fact that every graduate had applied and had been accepted to college.

What these folks fail to grasp is that a school system fails those very students—indeed, the entire school community—when recognizing and giving plaudits to those who did not earn them. Whether students, staff, or administrators, the system went out of its way to make people feel good rather than recognize them for an actual accomplishment. They didn't understand or didn't care that, when you give individuals something for nothing, you rob them of their dignity and sense of self-worth.

The irresponsible, neglectful attitude of so many "parents" of regularly truant students, of not understanding or caring to understand that their irresponsible behavior makes it less likely that their youngsters will ever succeed, is shameful. They choose to ignore the already difficult job of today's classroom teachers, who want to build their child's academic skills and progress but cannot when so many large numbers of students are truant for most of the academic year.

What is absent from such reports is the fact that this sort of irresponsible parent and student behavior is a slap in the face to the many responsible parents and students throughout the country. In this specific case, there were twenty-three exceptional students, each of whom had perfect attendance, youngsters whose parents or guardians generally found themselves in the same social and economic predicament as all the other parents and guardians. These families chose a different path as they lovingly, caringly, and responsibly ensured that their children accepted responsibility daily for learning, a wonderful first step toward a successful life...and successful they surely will be.[6]

Our K-12 schools are not alone. Colleges and universities have conducted themselves similarly. In the case of universities, they have reported inflated SAT scores and high school rankings of their incoming freshmen, each angling for prestige to "stand out in a crowded market." Regarding those colleges and universities that have been found guilty of fraudulent statistics, an editor with *Inside Higher Ed*, a media company and online college and university publication, stated there is a widespread feeling that this goes well beyond those that have been caught or have come forward.[7] An article in *The Atlantic* follows up on five of the schools that have been implicated, stating that Tulane University, Bucknell University, Claremont McKenna College, Emory University, and George Washington University are just the schools that got caught:

A survey of 576 college admissions officers conducted by Gallup last summer for the online news outlet *Inside Higher Ed* found that 91 percent believe other colleges had falsely reported standardized test scores and other admissions data. A few said their own college had done so.

For such a trusted report, the *U.S. News* rankings do not have many safeguards ensuring that their data is accurate. Schools self-report these statistics on the honor system, essentially.

U.S. News editor Brian Kelly told *Inside Higher Ed*'s Scott Jaschik, "The integrity of data is important to everybody.... I find it incredible to contemplate that institutions based on ethical behavior would be doing this." But plenty of institutions are doing this, as we noted back in November 2012 when GWU was unranked after being caught submitting juiced stats.[8]

Much of the information that schools and universities make available to parents and to the general public is not independently verified, making it impossible to know for certain if the reported data are accurate and a true reflection of our schools and institutions of higher education.

If you care enough about something, if you go about an area of interest, or in this case, your profession with intellectual curiosity and passion with the idea of continually improving what you and your school community can do, you have to shake your head in abject frustration and sadness that such abysmally poor behavior is standard fare in too many American schools. The White House, the secretary of education, legislators, educators, parents, businesses, and those with an interest in our youngsters and the country's future need to look with a jeweler's eye at American education and our entire country's social structure.

The unscrupulous actions cited in these investigations are but a cursory review of magazines, newspapers, and television news broadcasts that reveal a passel of fraudulent and unethical behavior on the part of those associated with various K-12 schools, school districts, and universities, not unlike the unprincipled and corrupt actions found too often in politics and the corporate world. You find that many of these incompetents share a common characteristic: Each seemingly disregards any concern for the principles of right and wrong behavior, of being high-minded, honorable, and decent.

Each of us is fallible, and no one has a lock on being noble at all times. It would appear fair to say that we'd be a nobler, stronger, and better society if more of us understood the pivotal importance of character and proceeded to be role models for and inculcate in our children an understanding of virtue, dignity, compassion, morality, respect, and law-abiding behavior.

I knew and felt in my heart that if my students and I, our staff, parents, and the wider business community were going to achieve greatness in this school community, it would be because of an insistence on character being the soul of the school, that when we—together—understood, appreciated, and began to exemplify character traits such as trustworthiness, respect, courage, responsibility, fairness, caring, and citizenship, then and only then would we be able to achieve any goal we set before us.

3

Principal's Arrival and Initial Impression

School districts generally try to operate in an organized fashion, as they should well be expected to do, but some operate in a more comprehensive, more competent fashion than others. Each system has a philosophy revolving around preparing students for college and the world of work. They have curriculum guides for their teaching staff, and they provide a teacher-pupil ratio in accordance with local priorities and budget constraints. The Harper's Choice Middle School community boasts a multicultural demographic, with a good portion of students receiving free and reduced meals (a federal measurement of poverty) and a fair number of the students living in government Section 8 subsidized housing. In contrast, Harper's Choice is located in a school district touted among the best in the nation, which is why so many parents found it appalling that a school—their school—would be allowed to become so "foul," so "dysfunctional" (their words); further, they felt that the incompetence and irresponsibility were shared between the school administration and staff, as well as school district headquarters officials who, they maintained, ignored their pleas year after year.

Be that as it may, I believe the district had a generally organized and solid instructional delivery program, at the time called the "Comprehensive Plan for Accelerated School Improvement."[1] All schools in the district could avail themselves of the resources available regarding their particular school's improvement. It would appear to be a reasonable expectation that a community's school officials would be on top of and aware of the values that underscore successful schools, the researched high-level practices that propel schools, and the kind of professional development that ought to be in place to meet school goals.

So, what happened, and what is happening today in such schools throughout the country that allow so many students, teachers, and parents to feel—for months, sometimes years—that their voices, their opinions, and their feelings do not count, to the point that they feel "stuck" (a familiar refrain used in parents' letters to school officials, presented to me by the community on my arrival) and resentful of having to send their children to such failing school environments?

What is it that makes the difference between having to send your child to a failing school or one that is professionally sound on all fronts, one that is vibrant, warm, inviting, and successful, no matter your zip code? To discover these answers, I invite you to read on.

It was mid-July when I arrived to take the helm, as principal, having been asked to take the position only days earlier. As I mentioned previously, when I was offered the position, I informed the superintendent that, if I were to accept this challenge, I would need his full support. I had to be given the latitude to make decisions that, at times, likely would not be in concert with those of quite a few school system headquarters folks, staff members and/or their union reps (although I would always operate within the parameters of the teachers union–school system negotiated agreement), parents, students, and likely, some legislators. He looked at me for a moment and then spoke only two words: "Alright, done."

As I pulled up to the parking lot that first day, I surveyed the grounds and the immediate area surrounding the school; it struck me that it was not unlike what I would have seen in a more urban, blighted setting. This was odd to me, given the school's location—situated in a suburban area of one of the richest counties in the nation. I drove slowly through the campus grounds, getting out at times to walk about, taking in what appeared to be a sad, if not depressing and unwelcoming school, an embarrassment, frankly, given the positive reputation of the school district. The grounds were unkempt, with trash strewn about the grass and parking lot areas, including beer cans, broken glass, liquor bottles, condoms, and a spent syringe needle. There was no landscaping to speak of, and the grass and weeds needed to be cut. I noticed a vehicle at the end of the lot that looked beaten up and abandoned. The flagpole at the entrance to the school building stood bare, with no American flag flying. The parking lots and sidewalks were broken up and in need of attention, and the school building itself had various cracked or broken windows. Two separate exterior doors were kept partially open, with empty, crushed soda cans between the door and frame to prevent them from latching, and there was graffiti on the building and on the rear pavement area, where, I would learn, physical education classes regularly conducted their outside activities.

Instead of entering the building, I returned to my car, put it in reverse, and drove directly to the school district's lawns and maintenance department, where I spoke to the director and some of the staff members. They were salt-of-the-earth, terrific, professional "can do" guys I had known and worked with for years. We had always enjoyed a mutual admiration, as I respected the good job they'd done for me on any number of occasions at the various high schools where I'd worked and they remarked, on occasion, how much they respected the work I did and how much they held me in high esteem.

When I arrived that day, I explained that I had just taken the helm of Harper's Choice. They weren't particularly happy for me, explaining how much they thought the school was out of control, how the administration and staff seemed not to care about the place, and how, because of that, they'd put their efforts—rightly or wrongly—into other schools and grounds throughout the district. It is a fact, by the way, that you can obtain a clear picture of how a school is run and how well it is operating by chatting it up with school district grounds and maintenance staff—they are in and out of the schools on a daily basis, and they see and hear quite a lot over a period of time. So they were quite familiar with the school, its setting, and the environment in which I would soon find myself working daily.

We chatted for a while, and I asked one of the guys about his mom—a special lady with whom I had worked when I was a high school administrator and she was on staff in the kitchen. She always appreciated my presence in the cafeteria, occasionally thanking me for audibly reminding students in line to remember their manners and to say, "Thank you," or "Yes, ma'am," or "Have a nice day!" to the kitchen staff and generally holding the kids to a respectful standard, a considerable challenge and growing more so with each passing year. The cafeteria ladies always treated me well—which meant they always gave me generous servings and extra fries. I told the maintenance guys that I'd like to schedule an appointment for them to come out and walk the grounds of Harper's Choice with me, to discuss ideas of how we might make the place presentable. They promptly agreed, a few of them remarking that they were particularly familiar with that building site and grounds and would have some ideas for me when we met.

I returned to the school campus that would be teeming with faculty and staff in a few short weeks, as they all returned from summer break. As I parked the car, I noted a wooded area with homeless individuals standing adjacent to the school building. There were males who looked to be in their thirties, forties, and fifties milling about an encampment, with a tarp suspended among the tree branches, mattresses on the ground, and a spent campfire in the center of their position. This was an area between the school and the community shopping center, directly next to a sidewalk used during the school year by kids going to and from school. While I can sympathize with those who find themselves in such dire straits, it seemed bizarre to me that such an encampment was permitted to exist in such close proximity to a school. Interestingly, I'd soon learn there was a county police substation located in that very shopping center, which made the homeless loitering site seem even stranger to me.

Shaking my head, I walked up to the building, through the entrance, and into the school's main office, where a few staff members were standing about, appearing skeptical of the guy just entering. "Hello," I said with a smile. "I'm Stephen Wallis, the principal." I sensed a palpable feeling of tension and discontent among the few staff members in the office area. Some appeared curious, and others appeared not particularly elated to see me, but that was alright. My persona as a school administrator was known, and a reputation followed it; I believe it's fair to say it was generally positive with most folks. That said, there were any number of times when I had needed to invoke a suspension of a student or hold as unsatisfactory the performance of certificated and non-certificated staff, some of whom were related to family, friends, or colleagues who were on staff at Harper's Choice. I had also published some writings, including opinion-editorial newspaper pieces, on education topics, and not everyone agreed with my position on the issues. This at times caused a bit of consternation among some folks at school headquarters and in various corners throughout the district. However, if local Baltimore newspaper and radio accounts were any indication, the vast majority of the public agreed with my position on the issues.

I enjoy people, am sensitive to the concerns and needs of others, and I conduct myself with a professional demeanor. I expect the same of my teaching staff, and I believe that parents should be equally courteous and professional, and should send their children to school prepared, courteous, and ready to learn. So, I understood the initial apprehension on the part of some, particularly those whom, I would come to learn, were themselves unsatisfactory teachers and had felt, up to my arrival, that they had always been on *easy street*, with no particular sense of accountability.

I smiled and shook the hand of the secretary sitting outside the principal's office, a terrific lady who would continue as Principal's Secretary, the title accorded the position by the school district human resources department. She was still nursing a facial wound from an assault received from a student involved in an altercation on a school bus at the close of the previous school year. I shook my head, saying to myself, *Game on!* When I entered my office, I was surprised to see the desk turned around, facing a rear wall and window; the secretary stated that the previous occupant had preferred that arrangement. That struck me as emblematic of the overall condition of the school I'd inherited. The walls were painted a pale pink, which I would soon have repainted a more suitable color, and several cardboard boxes were on the floor, the contents of which should have been more appropriately stored in a locked cabinet. I turned the desk around so that I was facing anyone at my door; that small mundane act felt symbolic—that the times, they were a-changin'.

I was well aware that the last few years had been particularly troublesome for this school community, and everyone was coming off of a particularly tumultuous year with considerable tension among staff, students, parents, former school administration, and the board of education. The sundry of issues included poor student academic performance, reflected in abysmal state test scores; disrespectful, disruptive student behavior; considerable school debt; community discord; widespread bullying; racial strife; repeated thefts; disgruntlement among staff; involuntary transfer of staff; an administration that parents felt was ineffective and indifferent to their concerns; and few parents who bothered to step foot on the grounds, much less take an active role.

Add to the mix a considerable amount of work that needed to be accomplished before the opening of the school year, including the interviewing and hiring of important certificated and non-certificated staff, including Spanish, mathematics, reading, social studies, special education, and technology education teachers, as well as a guidance department secretary. I mentioned "special education" as among the teaching positions that needed to be filled: Harper's Choice Middle had a number of special needs youngsters—some with emotional disabilities—and they had caring teachers who were among the best a principal could have on staff. I would think about those youngsters as we worked hard to realize a calmer, more robust, and steady teaching-learning climate for all.

In addition to hiring staff members, school manuals needed to be read, edited, and updated with current school system policies; a host of physical plant work needed to be accomplished in various areas of the building; and I would need to decide the type and coordination of professional development activities that I'd want in place the first week that staff returned. As if that were not enough, my only administrative colleague would be a new assistant principal, who would cut her teeth on a particularly challenging school setting—generally not ideal. Further, I was advised that she would not be reporting for another two weeks or so, which was just about when the teaching staff would also be returning—unbelievable. I would soon place a telephone call to her so I could introduce myself, as well as ask if she might be able to report earlier so we could better prepare for the impending school year.

I requested copies of the school's staffing sheet, its bookkeeping reports, the latest state department of education academic performance report (which detailed the school's poor reading, writing, and mathematics performance), and the building's school improvement plan, if there was any. I spent time poring over department- and grade-level lists of teachers, budget and accounting entries, and both statewide and individual school performance data; my secretary said she would have to spend more time looking for any such school improvement plan. I would study the various instructional and non-instructional positions needing to be filled, review various résumés at the school district headquarters human resources office, and ask that appropriate interviews be scheduled as soon as possible. Looking over the school's budget, I found that the school was several thousand dollars in arrears, the majority of the debt being owed to the state governor's office, more specifically, the lieutenant governor's office, through which a grant had been considered for the school. Coincidentally, I received a telephone call that day from the governor's office regarding the issue.

Amazingly, the state governor's office had released the funds after a request was made by this school's previous administration, I was advised, but the state said they had released the funding against their better judgment, because the former principal's request had the approval of his director. They said that the school had not completed its application requirements, and no money should ever have been released. Furthermore, according to the governor's office staff, it turned out that the school had mishandled its expenditures, paying funds to unauthorized staff members for activities not approved within the funding application guidelines. The bottom line was that the state wanted the funds returned. As though the school's academic, instructional, poor student behavior, physical plant, and grounds-keeping challenges were not enough, I wound up spending a protracted, inordinate amount of time repaying our debt to the state, using PTA assistance, fund-raising activities, and years-old contacts in the school system district finance office.

That afternoon, I also took a call from a school system director who was not all that enamored with my taking the helm of the school; she wanted me to meet with her posthaste. I interjected with a quick discussion of the several-thousand-dollar debt the school owed to the state, regarding the previous principal's funding request that she herself had approved. She said she didn't want to discuss that issue, stating, "And besides, the school system isn't in the business of bailing out schools." I stated that her approval had been, in my view, an unwise and costly mistake, but that I would take care of it. I further informed her that I was inundated with work at the time and was unable to see her that afternoon. I stated I would be happy to suggest another day and time, and that I was sure she understood; she did not. She remained brusque, and I told her I needed to attend to other matters, that she should address any concerns about me or the issues with the superintendent. She hung up the phone. I would hear from her again at the start of the school year.

The state department of education had designated this school a so-called School Improvement Unit (SIU), not a particularly proud distinction. SIU schools were those that repeatedly failed their school communities and year after year were not able to make adequate yearly academic progress, known throughout school systems as AYP.[2] All schools are expected to meet AYP, and they do so by achieving all of the targets, or Annual Measurable Objectives (AMOs), in a particular year. Nineteen group and subgroup checks for AMOs must be met for a school to achieve AYP, and elementary, middle, and high schools must meet the 95 percent participation requirement. I would ensure that the goals we set for this school would allow us to focus on achieving AYP and more.

Among the more important roles of school principals is that of ensuring that every staff member is an ideal fit for their school community. Each year, staff throughout the county have the opportunity to make application to be transferred to a specific school. I was looking to see who might be interested in working at Harper's Choice before I began looking outside the county. However, the folder I was given had not a single request to transfer to this school, which I found telling.

I was informed that some staff previously had been hired and placed at the school by the school district human resources department. I put an end to that procedure, as I wanted to know exactly who was going to teach a specific course and grade level to ensure that the youngsters and the academic department were getting a quality teacher. I generally look for someone who is personable, and I ask myself if I would mind this particular individual teaching my own children or grandchildren. My taking the time to sit and confer with candidates is as much an interview of me, allowing prospective staff to decide if they want to work with me and under my leadership. I want to glean from the interview that they know and have a passion for their subject area and/or grade level, that they enjoy working with and around youngsters, and that they are comfortable with their peers and working with other staff members. I want to know that they believe *all children can learn*—that not all will learn at the same rate, and that some will not be as bright as others, but that every child can learn—and I want to know that teaching candidates believe this and realize they can make a difference in the lives of their students, by moving students to think critically and examine facts, look for evidence, ask questions, and support whatever argument they are making. Many in the profession, certainly school administrators, frequently cite the importance of critical thinking, yet many of their schools reveal school settings that are anything but conducive to consistent teaching and learning, indicating they know nothing about an appropriate academic setting, much less anything remotely close to critical thinking. Such would not be the case anymore at Harper's Choice Middle School; we would exhibit quality teaching, and our students would begin to learn higher-level thinking skills.

As the school year progressed, the assistant principal would handle some of the hiring, with final approval occurring only after she and I discussed the final two choices among the candidates.

In time, this would not be as crucial, as I developed trust that my assistant principal was comfortable in her job, familiar with the character of the school, and knew how important hiring staff was to our school's success. In fact, she would become a competent and trusted school administrator.

Minutes later on that summer afternoon, a couple parents, one of whom had served as the previous year's PTA president, knocked on my door, asking if they could introduce themselves. They proceeded to share with me a blue folder containing documentation detailing the passel of problems and concerns that had plagued the community for years, including many letters written by staff, parents, business owners, and school system central office staff. Both of the parents before me said they were tired of dealing with the stress, informing me that no one, as yet, had volunteered any interest in the role of PTA president—not a good start for the impending school year, I thought to myself. They went on to make clear their displeasure with the previous school administration, the lack of communication, and the continuing low test scores. They decried what they viewed as the inconsistent quality of teaching, and they registered repeated concerns regarding rampant disrespectful student behavior and violence on the school grounds, as well as on the way to and from school daily, having frequently reported threatening behavior to the police. They alluded to equally poor behavior observed from time to time on the part of some of the students' parents. All the while, they were holding up letter after letter written by various parents and politicos, sharing their abject frustration with the situation, as well as their complete exasperation—bitterness really—concerning the vapid responses they had received from school system headquarters staff and board of education members over the last couple years. I sat there listening to their complaints for well over an hour, letting them vent, and giving them what they appeared to need...an attentive ear from someone they thought—they hoped—could be their answer regarding change for the better.

When they had completed their diatribe, I shared my background and experience with them and made clear that I understood their frustration and their disgust, that I shared their disappointment that such a predicament had been allowed to take hold and fester for so long, and that I simply would not tolerate such behavior from anyone...student, staff, or parent. I advised them that the newly hired superintendent had informed me that he had a different take on school system accountability, that he had never permitted such incompetence on his watch, and that he had no intention of doing so now. After reviewing my résumé and having spoken with board members and staff, he had asked me to take this school's principal-ship only days earlier, placing full faith and support in my ability to turn things around, and I assured them I had no intention of disappointing him or the two of them. I pledged that the school, from that day forward, would begin to appear dramatically different to them.

As they were leaving, they appeared relieved, though I am sure they were cautiously optimistic. I walked them out, clarifying that if they or others had any questions about any issue, the community need only contact this administration directly.

I remained outside for a few minutes, thinking about the school community setting that I consented to lead and how my combination servant-transformational leadership style could best kick-start a meaningful turnaround. I was this school's instructional leader, and I would focus on serving my constituents in a manner that I hoped would bring out the very best in our students, our staff, and the wider community. It was a matter of duty, and together, I reasoned, we would effect a positive turnaround in the way of high-level teacher instruction, student academic and behavioral performance, and parent satisfaction. I would entertain nothing less.

I would lead by example. Given the school's history, the task before us was formidable, for certain. Leaders answer to the communities they serve. How they conduct themselves provide insight into how they think and what they value. I would unequivocally give this .
school community my best effort, my heart and soul, with a laser focus on teaching excellence and quality student behavioral and academic performance. I hoped and believed the community would see me as reliable, resolute, and reasonable, because I was confident, I knew what I was doing, and I was sincere. We would soon enough see how things would shake out.

At that point a politico and his wife walked up to the school entrance way to meet me, and we chatted for several minutes. The gentleman said he and "others" were concerned about the school and the "change"—I assumed he meant my taking the helm—and he hoped there wouldn't be "mass suspensions." I stated politely that the "concern" on his part and that of the "others" might better have been expressed years earlier, possibly avoiding the school's receiving a failing

rating. I informed him that suspension from school was but a frac-
tion of a comprehensive school discipline program, that it was only
a piece—a necessary piece—but still only a piece of a whole array of
disciplinary interventions and alternatives considered in providing a
safe, secure, and comprehensive education to a community's youngsters. While I couldn't predict outcomes with any measure of certain-
ty, I stated that if numbers of suspensions went up, so be it. What
I could state to them unequivocally was that we could all expect an
eventual diminution of ill conduct—including disrespectful, disruptive, and violent student behavior, which would then trigger a drop
in the need for disciplinary measures, including suspensions. More
importantly, they can expect an increase in overall successful student
behavioral and academic performance. This positive change would
play out when the community began to understand the important
role that character would play in the school's daily operations. We
shook hands, and I asked the couple to stop by again in the future.

I returned to my office and continued to do a fair amount of reading, familiarizing myself all the more with the school, the community, the issues, and any areas of a positive nature that I might wish
to continue to run with the next school year. I would also occasionally pick up and read through what I called the "horror file"—the blue
folder presented to me earlier by the parents. In it, I saw a school
newsletter to parents, poorly formatted, which had red proofreading
and editing marks throughout the document. The proofreader—a
parent—was properly incensed that such would be sent out to the
community by the school administration. Among the parents' concerns, of course, was how little to nonexistent, in their opinion, communication was, and to receive such a poorly written communique
was a bit much for this individual, an active community business
member. The corrected document had been returned to the school,
along with the parent's scathing remarks. You can picture me shak-

ing my head. It so happened that I had noted over the years, with increasing regularity, the number of school administrators—from school system superintendents to building-level school-based administrators—who could not write well, nor were they comfortable speaking fluently with the public, an observation that I always thought was a disappointing commentary on the profession.

Three additional parents, active supporters of the school, dropped in, saying (loudly enough for me to hear) to my secretary, "We thought we'd come by and meet our new principal." They were pleasant, warm, and engaging, and they made it clear that they had been "unhappy, angry really, with the school and school system." We discussed their criticisms, which were identical to those expressed earlier to me by other parents. They hammered on the problem of poor student behavior and "how much craziness is tolerated by the whole staff," one offering, "there's some teachers here that need to get their act together, if you ask me." Our discussion included the multicultural make-up of the community, which led to the topic of race. I noted of interest that the two women of color made it clear that they and their friends do not call themselves "African-American," saying, "We're Americans who happen to be black, one continuing, "I don't really know anything about Africa." They both shared that, "Actually, the community would be better if everyone felt that way about themselves." *Amen to that,* I said to myself. I informed them that I fully expected to see a far more positive academic year from here on out, that it would require a positive attitude and equally hard work from all of us. They agreed, and we each shook hands. It turned out that they would be among our school's most active boosters, supporting our school, in and out of the classroom for the years their children attended Harper's Choice.

I was also interested in becoming familiar with the building and the operation of the physical plant itself. I wanted to meet the building custodial chief, who had spent several years at this school site. I asked my secretary to provide him with a pencil and notepad as he entered my office. We chatted for a while, and I asked if he had time to take a stroll about the building and grounds. It was a frank discussion. He felt things were generally fine; I didn't. While I had only just arrived, my initial impression was unsatisfactory. I shared what a professional workplace, in my view, should look like, that I would expect the windows to be cleaned every day, with particular attention given to the school's entrance area. It was important that students, staff, and community members entered a clean building, one that made a good first impression. I shared that when we were expected to produce a first-rate education for the students, it began by ensuring that the lawn, landscaping, and entrance areas looked clean, sharp, and presentable. Doors would be secured daily, and the front entrance would be the only way into this building from the outside from that day forward.

He was taken aback, informing me that he had been at this school site for years and everyone thought things were fine. I told him I thought that was shocking, given what we were observing together, that if he and his staff planned to be there much longer, everyone would need to develop a new perspective and get on board with it quickly. I inquired about any outstanding work that still needed to be accomplished before the opening of school, and he responded, "We're doin' the best we can." I asked him to touch base with my secretary, and later, with the assistant principal on her arrival, and work with them to ensure that all work requests were being processed and checked off as having been completed. He could start with ensuring that any graffiti was removed as soon as possible. Further, I asked him to advise the remaining custodial staff that I would like to meet with them the following morning, that I'd like to chat with all of them and continue walking the building and grounds with him and his entire team. I thanked him for his time and said I was looking forward to the upcoming school year; he wasn't, I'm certain.

I returned to the school's Main Office and found a lady waiting to see me, a black female in her sixties, dressed casually and wearing a smile as she said, "Mr. Wallis, welcome to Harper's Choice. My name's Juanita Robinson, and I've been a member of this community for many years. I'm pleased to know what I think I know about you." I smiled back, thanked her, and invited her into my office to chat things up. It turned out she'd be among the nicest, the most generous, the most hardworking, and among the biggest supporters that a guy could have in this job, each and every year I held the position. She worked for a church and the local community center. She tended to the poor and the not-so-poor, and virtually everyone in and outside of the community knew "Ms. Juanita." If a child was having emotional difficulty, if a family needed extra time to pay their utility bills, if someone needed a bed for the night, or if a local or state politician needed a favor, Ms. Juanita was their go-to person. She loved the various schools in the community; in her opinion, "The way they run all these schools ain't right. Kids are out of control, too many teachers and administrators don't seem to care, and the kids are out late at night tearing up the neighborhood." She went on the say that she did some research on me and had talked to people she knew—parents, teachers, and businesspeople—folks who also had worked with me over the years at different schools in the district. She took out a folder in which she had kept an old *Baltimore Sun* op-ed piece that I had written on how schools handle—or do not handle—disrespectful, disruptive student behavior. It had caused a stir at the time and was discussed on radio, television, and among politicos (including the state's governor, who invited me to share a radio program with him, after which came an offer to take an associate superintendent position in neighboring Baltimore City). Ms. Juanita said she'd enjoyed reading the piece and was happy to hear that the guy coming to Harper's Choice was the author of the piece she'd kept for so many years.

We wound up chatting and walking about the campus grounds for an hour; she knew the area well and pointed out locations known for drug dealing, bullying, and loitering. We shook hands at the end of our meeting and agreed that we'd be partners for a long time, with her telling me I could count on her assistance. Given our conversation, I asked her if she might be able to round up some eight to ten people, perhaps folks who had some time available on a day off, perhaps retirees or grandparents, but individuals who were reasonably fit, alert, and wanted something to do that would benefit the community. My idea was to have adult pairs be a kind of quiet presence on the various trails leading to and from the school into the community. I would work on purchasing two-way radios, and I'd also request that police be more visible in the area before and after school, asking them to get out of their patrol cars, check out the trails, and feel free to touch base with the school's adult volunteers. She loved the idea and was excited, saying she was confident that she could assemble some people, all of whom would meet with me and our local beat police officer for an orientation and information session. Further, I said that they'd be called "Citizens on Patrol" (COPs), and I would make sure that each received a shirt to wear that would identify them as a bona fide school volunteer. Each would have pen and tablet to note any concerns, and I, too, would make it a point to be outside each and every day and find time to touch base with the volunteers.

Ms. Juanita displayed a great smile when we parted, and she proved to be a die-hard supporter until the day she died, just a few years ago. I felt blessed to know her, and I remain thankful that she was able to witness the total and complete turnaround of our school community. God bless Ms. Juanita!

I returned to the building feeling a bit tired—emotionally and physically—as I took everything in. I read through some additional files for a few more minutes and put still more reading materials together to peruse at home. I was looking forward to returning home and "hittin' the garage"—my expression for working out with some weight-training exercises and going for a jog, something I'd been doing regularly ever since my armed forces discharge thirty-some years earlier.

I left school that day with a clear image in my mind of what I planned to do and the results I wanted for this specific school community. I was committed to these results and would see it through!

4

Preparing for Opening Day

The following morning I provided breakfast snacks and met with the custodial team; coincidentally, the school district custodial manager, whom I had known for years, happened to stop by, so I invited him to spend time with us. This time would allow us to get to know one another, and I advised them that, either now or later in the day, they should feel free to think about, take note of, and advise me of any concerns they might have, including making any requests they felt would allow them to perform their jobs more successfully. We discussed various issues for several minutes. We would continue talking as we toured the building and outside grounds, stopping first in the school cafeteria, which was among the topics cited by parents in letters from the "horror file." The parents had good reason to be dismayed: The cafeteria floor was dirty, and the walls all needed cleaning and/or painting. I informed the custodial staff of my disappointment, particularly because this was where children ate their lunches daily, and it seemed dismissive to me that not enough care was given to ensure that a clean, attractive, and safe eating area was available each day to every child attending the school.

We continued walking. There were outdated notices on some walls, pen and pencil scrawls on other walls, and a bulletin board that was barely hanging outside the guidance office area. As I continued to critique the interior of the building, they appeared aware of the meaningful role custodians would be expected to play at Harper's Choice. We talked about the host of work proficiencies that would need to be in place: elbow grease–like cleaning and maintenance of walls and floors, including sweeping, vacuuming, mopping, stripping floors, waxing, buffing, and where appropriate, polishing. Restrooms would need to be scrubbed and sanitized daily, as well as restocked with any necessary supplies.

As employees whose responsibilities required their working intermittently inside and outside the building daily, they needed to recognize the serious role they played in securing the grounds and the school building. I mentioned the broken-down vehicle in the corner of the lot that looked abandoned, but they knew nothing. Asked about the homeless area close to the school building, they had no information, saying "we keep our distance from those guys." I inquired about the flagpole and asked why no flag was flying at full mast. One of them explained, "Somebody cut the rope two or three years ago, so it ain't been up since."

I went on to clarify the importance of ensuring that every bit of trash—interior or exterior—was picked up promptly, and then reiterated my view that every window was to be cleaned, and if cracked or broken, work orders were to be processed to repair them immediately. Each school custodian typically had a custodial closet full of tools, cleaners, and other equipment for which he/she was responsible. Much like it's important to make one's bed first thing each day, I asked them to consider a similar routine at the workplace, making sure each closet was clean, organized, and stocked with needed supplies, including disinfectants and cleaning agents, and that all equipment/tools were in good working condition. I shared with them that such a routine had stuck with me since 1970, the year I was drafted into the U.S. Army. Making one's bed was of paramount importance in the military—the very first accomplishment of the day. Years later retired navy admiral William H. McRaven would author a book about this very idea, saying, "If you make your bed every morning, you will have accomplished the first task of the day. It will give you a small sense of pride and it will encourage you to do another task and another and another. By the end of the day, that one task completed will have turned into many tasks completed. Making your bed will also reinforce the fact that little things in life matter. If you can't do the little things right, you will never do the big things right."[1]

We walked and talked for over an hour, until I asked them to join me in what turned out to be the music choir classroom. We sat for a bit, and I purposely took a few minutes to share the gist of a theory that I'd employed for years in various facets of my professional and private life, one I thought might be unfamiliar to them: The Broken Windows Theory.[2] It goes something like this:

Originally conceived by Philip Zimbardo, a Stanford University social psychologist, the Broken Windows Theory found prominence in the criminological work of social scientists James Q. Wilson and George L Kelling, and it was instrumental in the positive turnaround of crime statistics in New York City under former mayor Rudy Giuliani and his police commissioner at the time, William Bratton. In short, the research consisted of leaving an unlocked and damaged vehicle in two locations: the Bronx, a tough, run-down area of New York City, and Palo Alto, a more upscale neighborhood in California. In time (within minutes in the Bronx; days later in Palo Alto), each car sustained further damage, including broken windows, flat tires, torn upholstery, and body damage, each being stripped for its parts. At this point of the telling, I made mention of the abandoned vehicle on the school lot and the graffiti on the building.

Researchers Wilson and Kelling conducted further study and determined that, if a broken window in a building is not fixed soon enough, other windows in the same structure will end up being destroyed by vandals. This is because the message being transmitted is that nobody cares about the window, the building, or the area. Soon, just as additional vandalism was done to the cars, other buildings sustained additional broken windows, and before anyone realized it, litter and graffiti became commonplace, and petty crimes began occurring, ultimately leading to more serious criminal behavior. The researchers consulted with the New York City mayor and police commissioner. The idea was to extend the theory to policing. The police would be more visible in the community. They would begin implementing policies that addressed crimes that negatively affected the citizens' quality of life. Officers were directed to be more conscious of strictly enforcing laws against subway fare evasion, public drinking, public urination, and graffiti. A follow-up crime study revealed that, "'broken windows policing' was significantly and consistently linked to declines in violent crime. Over 60,000 violent crimes were prevented from 1989 to 1998 because of 'broken windows policing,'" and the decline in crime continued for another ten years.[3]

I informed the custodial staff that we, together, needed to take care of our school building and grounds, keeping those two thoughts (making your bed and "broken windows") in mind as a frame of reference. Taken further, I explained that if we in our own lives avoided paying attention to the small fixes, problems would likely multiply; paying attention to the details transmitted to others the value of something or someone.

I took the liberty of applying the concept of "broken windows" to the school building and grounds, as well as to those interactions among staff and student body, a kind of *cura personalis*, or "care of the whole person," referring to the Ignatian Jesuit concept of individual attention to the needs of others. Teaching, in and of itself, should well be about caring for the whole individual. Through our failure to convey care and/or to correct a wrong at our school, I explained that we risked letting things like deterioration, damage, incivility, abuse, and bullying to spread quickly. If we wanted to avoid further problems, we needed to care of the broken windows in this building, in our lives, and in the lives of others, and when appropriate or possible, address or facilitate the building's repair or pay attention to an individual without hesitation.

The group seemed focused and interested, including the school system supervisor. No, they hadn't thought of such things before, but they each listened attentively, affirmed their understanding, and generally seemed to appreciate the concepts, appearing to give them a more meaningful perspective on their jobs and, with any luck, in their individual lives outside the workplace. I would later share these thoughts and perspectives with the entire faculty and student body.

We continued with the discussion of their job descriptions, including the expectation that they would take the initiative to make any necessary minor building or maintenance repairs. I asked them to take ownership of their livelihood and their role at this school site, find their passion, and commit to doing a terrific job daily; in doing so, they would find they could count on my support. I stated that if anyone did not feel the same as I about the important role that they played in presenting daily a first-rate facility, they were to speak up, and I would work with those individuals and their county supervisor to have him or her placed elsewhere; otherwise, the game was afoot! Not a hand went up; each seemed excited, later stating they felt a new sense of vigor about their role and the expectations that were now in place. I felt the morning thus far had been a meaningful step forward for the school and the community. That afternoon I would get on the phone to take initial steps to have the abandoned vehicle towed from the property, to contact the appropriate agency for removal of the homeless encampment, and to obtain a halyard and a nice-sized Old Glory for the flagpole outside the front of the school.

I returned to my office and observed several folks using a conference room. When I asked my secretary the nature of the meeting, she informed me that several school staff members were meeting with a school district psychologist who was helping them "heal" from the stormy school year they had experienced with the previous administration. I likely grimaced, then knocked on the door, introduced myself to those who had yet to meet me, and asked if they'd mind if I spoke to the psychologist, whom I'd known for several years. I got her take on the meeting and the issues, thanked her for her time, and advised her that she could leave, because we would be dealing with everything in-house from here on out. She was taken aback, then said she'd need to call the superintendent since she was there on his directive. I told her she could use my phone, and after speaking with him for a few seconds, I handed her the receiver; in less than a minute, she wished me well and promptly left the building. I reentered the conference room and spoke with the staff for several minutes, explaining why I had ended the meeting and advising that there would be no similar follow-up meetings throughout the year. I believed such meetings catered to "victimhood" and prolonged the previous years' angst by revisiting their ill feelings. I advised them that we were embarking on a new academic year with a different person at the helm, a seasoned school administrator who, with a new assistant principal about to come on board, would lead the effort to turn things around for the better. Exciting things were about to occur, I informed them, and together, the staff and I would work through any unresolved issues. I designated the specific department team leaders present to gather ideas from the committee and, as the school year got underway, from other staff members, requesting that they note any specific concerns or issues they would like to see addressed or handled differently. I told them I intended to meet regularly with these team leaders and work through every one of their concerns, as we would regularly discuss additional school and curriculum topics. They appeared quite taken by surprise, but my sense was that the majority welcomed the positive change and were cautiously optimistic. Almost immediately, some of the staff expressed excitement for the upcoming school year. I advised them that if anyone thought they would individually benefit from sharing any additional thoughts—personal or professional—with a school system psychologist, they were free to do so. I informed them that I looked forward to welcoming them back in the weeks ahead.

The remaining days before the start of the school year were filled with interviews of prospective staff, readying the building for the return of all staff and, a week thereafter, our student body. Every so often, a teacher or other staff member would make his or her way into the school to check a mailbox or, out of curiosity, to sneak a peek at the new principal, and each time I made it a point to take a couple minutes or so to chat it up with the individual. I liked doing so and found it beneficial to meet individuals with whom I would be working over the next year and beyond; I was able to glean interesting and insightful viewpoints about the school, the students, their colleagues, and the community. In one conversation, several staff members remarked that every year a number of students, called "hallers," seemed to linger in the hallways, often yelling to friends sitting in classrooms. They said the issue had been repeatedly brought before the previous administration, but there was little, if any, effort made to take care of what they described as a "menacing" problem that disrupted instruction daily. I kept that in the back of my mind.

The day was beautiful, and I decided I would ask the custodians to grab their brooms—along with an extra one for me—and meet me in front of the main office in an hour, if their schedules allowed. We met, and I asked them to grab a large trash can and join me at the far end of the parking lot. Together, we were going to sweep the area, making sure to remove any trash, including any syringes, condoms, and all other unsightly debris. We made a line across the width of the lot and began sweeping, picking up trash, and chatting about a host of topics for an hour. They seemed to get a kick out of my joining them in the activity.

I later contacted grade-level and subject team leaders who were in town to inquire about their interest in meeting with me before the academic year got underway. I considered them part of the leadership structure of the school, and I wanted to meet and confer with them on school issues in general, including the academic and fine arts curricula, general student deportment, and any building issues—physical or otherwise——needing attention. It would also be an opportunity for me to size up the caliber of people I had inherited in those positions. Each was surprised to hear from me and enthusiastic that the principal should call them at home and want to meet. It would turn out that I would find the meeting valuable; after all, I became that much more familiar with the middle school curriculum, the school schedule, its related arts component, and the various issues germane to grade levels and individual subject areas. It was clear to me that the previous overall atmosphere had been stifling. The teachers voiced their frustration with low test scores and felt they were spinning their wheels in their efforts to teach, because of the negative atmosphere, poor morale, racial strife, and, in their words, an "incompetent administration" that was repeatedly dismissive of their concerns, whether about the academic program or the deplorable student behavior. The issue of race, they said, had more to do with the administration refusing, in their opinion, to address teacher incompetence and poor student behavior in a meaningful fashion. The team, a diverse mix of race and gender, all agreed it was problematic. They went on to clarify that the lack of holding the total staff to a high-quality teaching standard made it even more difficult for each subject area or grade-level team. They again shared their exasperation with what they said was total and complete student disrespectful behavior, fighting, and stealing (from student peers and teaching staff), which caused ongoing stress, and they asserted that these issues were not addressed by school and central office administrators due to an attempt, they believed, to lower suspension statistics.

I listened intently, because I knew this to be the case in many other schools, both locally and nationally. Whether or not such was accurate here, I did not know; it was their impression, and I would weigh it accordingly. They lamented that they could no longer count on several parents for classroom assistance; most of the parents with whom the staff had bonded had decided not to volunteer, saying that such a negative atmosphere was not worth their effort and time. They referenced the recent countywide school climate surveys, which they indicated placed the school "dead last" (their words) in the district. Such surveys allowed staff, students, and parents to evaluate the overall educational environment, from the school schedule and whether teachers felt they had adequate time for preparation, planning, and collaboration, to whether staff generally felt safe, felt valued, and believed they had an opportunity to be heard. The surveys asked whether students were well behaved, cared about learning, and felt respected by peers and adults. They asked whether parents respected the staff or felt welcome at the school, whether school administrators communicated effectively and involved the staff in decision-making, and whether the school, in their opinion, was a good place to work or to learn. These kinds of surveys are designed to provide a representative picture of the school, and they serve to inform actions to improve in specific areas that revealed concerns. While the team leaders were clearly a dispirited lot, I found them talented, committed, prepared, and ready to start the new school year.

These kinds of meetings clarified that, while the school clearly had a host of problem areas, it also boasted some very fine individuals, who would be a pleasure to have on staff in any school. I was looking forward to working with them; in fact, I was heartened, and I knew that many of us would be working closely to improve their teaching experience and the learning opportunities for our students.

These conversations with colleagues reinforced my view of the importance character would play as the heart and soul of the school. Decisions and polices would be made from the standpoint of how they would advance teacher performance, student achievement, and parent involvement. The student body would become accustomed to the concepts of respect, effort, pride, courage, persistence, compassion, cooperation, a positive attitude, determination, and teamwork. I imagined that this might be difficult to fathom by many in the community, given the challenging, failing nature of things and the dispiriting low morale of staff and parents whom I had encountered on my arrival. Nonetheless, I was personally driven and genuinely felt that we could—together—bring about a renaissance that would result in instructional excellence, improved student performance, and parent satisfaction, a meaningful sense of pride in their—now our—school. I envisioned infusing the paramount importance of character-building into the daily schedule of the school, and I would have to look at how best to accomplish this focus.

My feeling at the time was that, under my watch, this school community was going to begin producing higher caliber students. It followed that such a goal would only happen in an atmosphere conducive to top-shelf teaching and learning, which meant I needed to improve vastly the daily school environment. Only then, I reasoned, would such a change in atmosphere foster improved teaching, active parental involvement, engaged students exhibiting appropriate behavior, and higher-quality overall student achievement.

The community needed to see the confidence, support, and leadership on the part of the principal. I've got a fairly positive attitude by nature, and I generally make it a point to reinforce values and beliefs daily in all of my interactions. The idea here was to motivate and inspire personal and professional excellence, building character in the process. I would give staff, students, and parents—and in the near future, the surrounding business community—reason to get energized and to increase their individual and collective productivity, which would serve to propel our school and community forward.

Parents should feel a part of the school that is serving their youngsters. I wanted some parent volunteers to help with putting informational packets together for staff and students that would be disseminated at the start of the school year. I ascertained from my secretary and staff the names of potential active parent players within the community, and I randomly called those parents whose letters were contained in the "horror file."

I also wanted to get the message out that I was interested in holding an "Evening Tea with the Principal" prior to the opening of the new school year, and I thought a number of parents might get the word out. The idea was to have a parent or parents host me in their home, providing an early opportunity for me to meet community members and students, offer some information about me and my experience, talk about the school, and inform folks of my plans for the school's future. I figured such an idea would be welcome—at least I hoped it would be—after the past few unpleasant years. If successful, it would be something I would consider holding monthly. My first handful of telephone calls netted a family interested in hosting such a meeting—the parents of two students at the school. They were excited about the change in school leadership, and they offered their home—it turned out to be their front yard—for the first evening get-together. We sat outside their home, and a number of neighbors stopped by for light food, refreshments, and their first opportunity to meet the new school principal. People were cordial, interested, and excited about the promising new school year. While some of the negative aspects of the past were discussed, the evening was mostly about allowing parents and families the opportunity to meet me, to gain an understanding of my experience, my educational philosophy, my expectations, and my plans for the new academic year. As the evening went on, I could feel a palpable sense of excitement on the part of those in attendance, and it turned out to be quite successful. I decided that I would do something similar throughout the school year. The next get-together would be held in nearby federal Section 8 subsidized public housing apartments and townhome areas that would present the opportunity for me to meet additional parents of color and varied economic means.

Each day forward grew a bit busier, with folks in and out of the building, mostly parents new to the area, wanting to register their youngsters for the upcoming academic year. I do recall one day, however, when three sets of parents—black, interracial, and white—came into the main office. They were obtaining their children's records from the registrar's office so they could enroll their children in a private school. They were part of a school system–wide redistricting plan, which saw twenty-seven families from a relatively close, well-to-do neighborhood being "forced," as one parent put it, to attend Harper's Choice, if they were going to remain in public school. The parents were pleasant, almost apologetic, clarifying that it had nothing to do with me, but they were not taking the chance on my school, given the population and the school's many problems, which were well known. I thanked them for taking the time to stop by and see me, and I told them that, given the school's history, I totally understood their concerns. However, I informed them, with a smile, that I believed we were going to see a welcomed productive academic year. I wished them well and directed them to the school registrar's office. A year or so later, one of those sets of parents would return to Harper's Choice, and I recall welcoming them back wholeheartedly. They had nice kids who wound up attending our school for a year or so before moving on to high school.

That afternoon presented a clear, sunny, and vibrant azure sky, and I decided to jump out of the building for a few minutes to catch lunch. I walked over to a fast-food place five minutes from the building, and as I sat there enjoying my meal, I observed a host of rowdy youngsters, about twelve to fifteen of them. As one walked by, I asked where he was attending school. He furrowed his brow and replied, "What?" I asked him again, and he just said, "Why? Looking at him with my own eyebrows raised, I said, "Because I'm askin'." "Harper's Choice," was his answer. "Anybody else here attend Harper's Choice?" I asked. He pointed to a group of young people about his age. I looked over at them and said, "Guys, come here for a minute." When they walked over and learned who I was, it caused some commotion. Then I asked if anyone was hungry, and I gave them a few dollars to purchase some apple tarts, after which I told them to step over to a grassy area, because I wanted to talk to them about the school.

We sat together on the grass, ate, and chatted about the school and my experience; they were interested in hearing about each school where I had worked. They were candid about their Harper's Choice experience, saying, "That school's a trip, man." They spoke of teachers and administrators they disliked or thought were "okay," a couple saying that they—the kids—ran the school. I looked surprised and said, "Really? Well, that's about to change, big-time." Some seemed to get a kick out of that retort and laughed, while others weren't amused. Nonetheless, I could see that, while the school and surrounding community had been challenged with a host of antisocial and criminal behavior, there were kids who were still just kids, each trying to make his or her way through adolescence in a challenging neighborhood.

Several minutes later I stood and told them I was heading back to the school and that I looked forward to seeing them the following week. A few thanked me for the apple tart, and as I started walking away, I said to one of the boys, "Where's my change?" He walked toward me, saying, "Oh yea, I was gonna give it to you." "No, you weren't," I replied, "but it's the right thing to do, yes?" He said, "Yea," and I told him to keep it and to get something later with it. He produced a kind of half-grimace, half-smile, thanking me as he ran back to his buds.

Toward the end of the day, a parent and her son walked into the school building, asking to see me. She was upset and told me that her son had been repeatedly bullied the previous few years, both in and out of school, including, at times, on the school bus. The new school year was approaching, and she had heard that there was a change in principals, so she wanted to bring her concerns directly to me. She stated that she had found no assistance at the school or at the central school district office, that she had spoken directly with school administrators, teachers, and counselors, but that she'd seen little to no difference as the days turned into weeks, the weeks into months.

The boy, a meek, articulate, nice-looking kid, said that the bullying started in elementary school and continued at Harper's Choice. He would stay after school sometimes to get help with a school subject, but doing so always stressed him out, he said. There was no after-school bus, so when he'd walk home and see the bullies nearby, he would climb a tree on a trail next to the school that led to and from his neighborhood. There he stayed until the bullies passed by, when he'd then drop his bookbag to the ground, jump down, and make his way home.

I sat there looking at both of them. The mother seemed to be a caring and humble individual, and I could understand how stressful and emotionally upsetting such a dilemma would be for any family. Imagine a youngster having to go through such a routine just to get through his day. In many communities throughout the country, parents work hard to take care of their children; they pay their taxes and expect their children to receive a safe and meaningful education at the local public school. It is appalling that many parents cannot trust their local public school to keep their children safe, much less feel welcomed in the classroom. The fact that so many parents must go to such great lengths to obtain assistance from the school and school district officials, yet receive none, is heartrending, maddening, and inexcusable.

I listened attentively to both the mom and her youngster, shaking my head that life for them and, no doubt, for countless others throughout the country, was often a sad heartache, one that I determined I would ameliorate, if not eradicate on my watch. I asked for the names of the students—male and female, it turned out—who had hurt him and others both emotionally and physically, wondering in the back of my mind if I might have just eaten lunch with any of them. I advised the mom and her son that the school staff and I would be watchful of such poor behavior. I promised the boy that I would deal with the matter—and do so without the bullies or their families knowing where I got the information. I informed the mom that I typically dealt straight-up with such miscreant students and their parents, and when I felt it was warranted, I was quick to include the police department.

I was thinking of the various incidents over my career as a school administrator, when I would address such matters—one case involving an area high school student who had bullied a peer since elementary school. When the problem was brought to my attention, I pulled the miscreant in, stating that I thought better of him, but if he chose to continue, it would warrant his receiving school disciplinary sanctions, including a parent conference, possible suspension from school, removal from the football team, and potential legal problems, including police involvement. I sat him down in my office, called in the other student, and conferred with the two of them together in the effort to find a resolution. Such action was generally enough to avoid any future problems, but not always. There were any number of times over the years when such warnings fell on deaf ears, and I wound up having to take further action, whether it was suspending ten students from a school soccer team; suspending twelve students at a homecoming dance at a "premier" high school, where too many parents thought their kids could do no wrong; or assisting a family with filing for police action against an uncivilized female student, who seemingly enjoyed threatening and bullying any peers whom she deemed inferior. No matter how busy school officials are in the running of a community's school, the issues surrounding disrespectful, disruptive, and threatening behavior must always take priority and be dealt with immediately and substantively. The reader might think that such an important issue is always taken seriously by school staff; you would be wrong. It is clear that the issue of disrespectful behavior, including student bullying, throughout the country is routinely ignored by school officials, or if dealt with at all, often handled in a haphazard fashion, causing student victims and their families unnecessary emotional stress and heartache. More on this issue in a later chapter.

On that particular afternoon, I told the youngster's mom that I would contact her with an update and that I would make a note on my calendar to speak with her son throughout the school year. I advised her that, while dealing with such kids and their families is never a sure thing, no matter the number of issues I had on my plate at any single time, I would be relentless and would go as far as needed to ensure that such nonsense was dealt with meaningfully. The boy's mother took my hand and thanked me sincerely. I got up and thanked them both for coming in to see me, clarifying that I hoped and expected that he would soon feel safe at school. I knew they had walked to the school building that afternoon, and so I asked if they'd mind if I walked part of the way home with them. I wanted to be familiar with the boy's route home, including the location of the tree he often used as a hiding place; it would become a mental picture that would stay with me, reminding me of the challenges some of us face in our lives. The walk would also give me an opportunity to become that much more familiar with the school's immediate surroundings.

The teaching staff would return soon, all interviews and hires were completed, parent volunteers were in and out of the building, helping prepare information packets for staff and students, the lawn was cut, and the building itself was looking far better.

School district grounds staff arrived later that afternoon and we walked about the campus discussing possibilities. We decided that cherry trees on both sides of a walkway from the parking lot to the building would look terrific. They would dig, loosen the dirt, and spread mulch around the front school entrance, planting some small shrubs and perennials. They would do the same around the flagpole. I was pleased that they could start in a couple days. That very afternoon, county maintenance staff arrived to install a new halyard on our flagpole, as well as a finial, completing a separate earlier request that I made. Additionally, they attached and raised a beautiful, larger-than-usual American flag, which everyone thought was spectacular. I would look at that flag on more than one occasion and proudly reflect to myself that this school was well on its way to getting back in the game.

I spoke with staff who were in the building in order to obtain the names of eight to ten students—good, average, and those known for trouble—telling them also to include the name of the "head of the snake," the leading troublemaker. I would call their homes, talk to their parents, and schedule a kind of get-acquainted meeting. The meeting would include a light lunch and would give the kids and me an early opportunity to meet one another and to chat about the school. I wondered if any of them might be among those I'd shared dessert with earlier at the area fast food restaurant. We met several days later, and while the kids were a bit skittish initially, we wound up having a good conversation, they shared some ideas, and I incorporated their ideas and feelings about various issues into future programs. They went away feeling good about having met with the "new guy on the block." In addition, I believe the ringleaders of troublemakers realized quickly that this would be a different sort of school year, and I suspect that he and she shared their feelings with friends. All in all, the kids and their parents seemed to appreciate the reach out from the principal.

Our newly appointed assistant principal was able to arrange her schedule to report earlier than expected. I was happy to meet her, and I thought that, as a black female, she was right for our diverse, multicultural staff and student population. We sat down and spoke at length, and there was plenty about the job that allowed her to hit the ground running. As time would go on, we would learn more about each other, our backgrounds, our history, our education philosophies, and our views on school administration. We enjoyed each other, and it turned out to be a pleasurable, worthwhile experience for each of us.

In the previous chapter, I made reference to the importance of interviewing and hiring the most qualified teaching candidates to fill vacancies. I occasionally will refer to the Latin phrase in *loco parentis*, meaning "in the place of the parent." It's important to understand the doctrine that cites the legal responsibility of a person or organization—in this case, schools and educators—to take on some of the functions and responsibilities of a parent. Parents want the best for their youngsters; as educators, we want—or we *should* want—the very best for their youngsters, too. Such makes it vitally important that school systems exercise due diligence in vetting and hiring competent and responsible employees, including those who, while serving our school communities, get little mention: substitute teachers. Among the responsibilities that fall under the assistant principal's purview is that of overseeing the various substitute teachers working at Harper's Choice on any given day.

Just as we want to ensure that our teachers are first-rate, we want to do our level best to hire, as needed, quality substitute teachers and temporary workers for secretaries and other non-certificated staff. I will point out that it was equally important over the years to hire first-rate secretaries, several of whom were more like executive assistants. They were smart, organized, good communicators with the public and staff, on top of technologies and software, and tireless supporters of their principal; I cared for and respected each of them. They were totally supportive of the staff, and they worked diligently to ensure that teacher job requests were handled efficiently and expeditiously. I had conferred with HCMS secretaries about standard operating procedures and protocols, confirming that the public always be greeted with a warm and welcoming smile. Our administrative, teaching, guidance, and registrar areas began operating at an entirely different high-performance level since I took the helm, and the remarkable difference was due entirely to the diligence, warmth, and professionalism that each individual secretary brought to her position.

Hiring new or additional staff meant that the school had to be safe, warm, inviting, and supportive. I was aware that quality substitute teachers who were familiar with Harper's Choice Middle had stopped accepting positions at the school over the last couple years. Those who still worked at the school were not particularly good, and, as I came to understand, they caused yet additional concerns for the staff and community.

The issue of hiring substitutes for one's staff is generally overlooked by many administrators, who likely do not know those serving in those positions, much less anything about the quality of the individuals working in place of one or more of their professional teachers on any given day—but that's a mistake. It's particularly important to be able to rely on competent substitutes, who are assigned by school district headquarters or a school administrator. Substitute teachers hold an important position when the regular professional teacher cannot be in their classroom. They typically follow a detailed lesson plan provided by absent staff members. They perform the instructional and classroom management duties associated with the position, including taking attendance, assisting as best as possible in clarifying the lesson directions, carrying out in as meaningful a fashion as possible the day's instructional lessons, and explaining homework assignments.

I worked closely with and communicated regularly over the years with my assistant principals regarding the quality of substitute staff working in the building on any given day. We were in agreement that we needed to attract top-shelf substitute teaching staff. We would clarify the importance of our on-staff professional teachers leaving solid lesson plans, we would monitor the substitute teachers' performance, and we would ensure they received any support needed in order to enjoy a successful, professional Harper's Choice experience. The individuals serving in this capacity were expected to take their job seriously, understand that they fulfilled an important role, and believe that they, too, could well make a positive difference in the lives of our students.

As the academic year commenced, we would have the good fortune of developing a cadre of responsible, competent individuals who would substitute when needed, among whom was a former professional teacher who was gracious; had terrific interpersonal skills; and was accountable, confident, and good-natured with the students. Substitute teachers can become a very important part of a school's community, and in our case, years later, I would present this particular substitute with a school staff shirt, embroidered with her name and position as "substitute teacher." The assistant principal, as well as those serving in that position in successive years, made it their mission to ensure that our community's youngsters received quality instruction, even when their regular teacher was absent for the day.

When I attended the first PTA meeting of the year, I was delighted to learn that a fine gentleman had volunteered to serve as the year's president. I clarified my understanding of the school's regrettable overall poor condition with regard to academic performance, teaching quality, student behavior, administration performance, school communication with parents, and the physical plant and grounds. I made clear that I understood the concerns they had about their school. I provided a background of my experience and educational philosophy. I also spoke about the importance of a focus on quality teaching, student academic and behavioral performance, and active parent involvement. We developed mutual respect for one other, and each of the parents appeared fully supportive of the new direction we were going as a school community. I maintained a close connection with the school PTA, the board that reflected new members annually, for the years I served as principal.

I placed a telephone call to the school system security coordinator, a recently added position for which I had advocated over several years. His job, among other duties, was to interview, hire, and oversee various security staff assigned to high schools, as well as after-school events and activities. I valued his years of professional police experience, and I requested that we meet at the school and generally review the building, the grounds, and chat up issues of "school safety and security." I asked him to review ahead of time any school system documentation on this particular school's student behavior statistics, although he was generally aware and certainly knew of the community criminal behavior because of his previous experience as a county police officer; in fact, he was very familiar with the school's atmosphere and community.

We met, discussed my recent assignment to the school community, and toured the building and grounds. I wanted his professional perspective on how I might tighten up overall security, as well as obtain his opinion on several ideas I'd been considering in anticipation of our meeting.

Acting in *loco parentis*, every school official needs to be prudent in doing everything to ensure the safety of students and staff; such is every school official's first responsibility. It would be hard to believe so, given what we know goes on daily in schools across America. To the greatest extent possible, I wanted to be on top of this issue, if I expected to turn around this school community.

I wanted to limit the entry points to the school to one, and only one main door, perhaps with some kind of door-access control system. This idea would soon follow in all schools throughout the county, and it is fairly standard throughout the country today. I wanted a closed-circuit television monitoring system with cameras placed about the interior and exterior of the building. If that wasn't within the budget, I wanted ideas on any available grant opportunities with foundations, or perhaps through the state or federal government, that I might pursue to obtain such a camera system. I also made the case for a school resource officer position (an actual county police officer) to be posted at this school site, even part-time, even though at the time only high schools had these positions. Those were my initial "wants," and I felt they were reasonable, given the school's recent history and challenging demographics.

The security coordinator was attentive and understood clearly the depth of the concerns and challenges in this community. Soon after our discussion, he assisted me in obtaining grant information to participate in a program through the U.S. Department of Justice. I took the time to write and apply for the grant, but we were not selected; however, there would come another opportunity, I was certain, and we would apply again and yet again if necessary.

5

Teachers Return for the New School Year

On the day when all teachers and staff returned to the school, there was enormous excitement and some trepidation, I'm sure. As many entered the building, walking from the parking lot to the entrance, they remarked on how lovely the campus looked. The lawn and front entrance looked terrific—the grass was cut, the weeds were tended to, grass seed and straw could be seen in some areas, cherry trees lined the walkway from the parking lot, and the front of the building and flagpole areas were mulched, containing newly planted bushes and flowers. And, of course, we now had a beautiful American flag that waved proudly, welcoming everyone back. Inside, the front entrance windows were clean, as were the floors.

The administrative team provided for the staff breakfast and refreshments in the school cafeteria—a very clean and orderly looking cafeteria—where I would address staff within an hour of their arrival. I planned to address everyone that morning, and I would take additional opportunities throughout that week—in the early mornings and on Friday afternoon—generally to speak with teaching staff only regarding a host of other topics, including the school district code of student conduct, managing student misbehavior, parent communication, various school system headquarters memos, board of education policy clarifications, and general housekeeping points.

The first week back for staff was well-planned, with various department and grade-level meetings and time provided each day for teachers and staff to prepare their individual classrooms and instructional areas, as well as organize and continue to plan this year's curriculum instruction; after all, showtime was next week—opening day for students.

At the start of the day, I used the public address system to request that all staff join us in the cafeteria. This would include teachers, teaching assistants, secretaries, kitchen staff, and custodial workers. The condition of an organization—whether positive or negative—affects everyone, regardless of one's position, and bringing the entire staff together affirms that each individual matters to the team. I wanted every school employee to hear my welcome and initial thoughts.

I welcomed everyone and then introduced the assistant principal, as well as that year's PTA president; both the assistant principal and PTA president would later welcome everyone and say a few words.

I provided some background about my professional teaching and administrative experience for those who did not yet know anything about me. I also shared with everyone the state education report I had recently received, which showed that the school had taken yet another drop in student academic performance the previous school year, a topic we would discuss more at length during that week. More important to me was the need to address the elephant in the room—the fact that people, generally, were aware of the trying school conditions over the last few years, issues that understandably would wear down faculty and staff, student body, parents, school district personnel, local board of education members, and the wider school community. I made reference to a sampling of concerns expressed by the school's constituencies, adding that there were many schools and school systems throughout the country that regularly faced such challenges. I viewed our opportunity at that moment as a rebirth—a kind of renaissance—and I was excited about the possibilities of Harper's Choice one day, sooner than later, being recognized for its high performance. I was able to stand there and say that because, however short a time span it had been at that point, my experience, my meetings, and my conversations held already with students, staff, team leaders, parents, and others had made it clear that we, together, could well turn this school around, and I clarified, succinctly, that we would. Given the school's poor performance record at that time, I recall hoping that they felt the principal standing before them was someone they felt was steady, measured, and reliable, because I was sincere, I understood the gravity of the situation, and I was determined to turn things around.

I recall entertaining a number of thoughts in my head at that time. I recognized that in any organization, there is a prevailing culture, and changing the culture can be and frequently is a very big deal. Everyone must get used to a different person in charge, a different style of leadership, as well as a change in how things were done. To change the culture required that more desirable qualities would replace the existing unhealthy elements.[1] That would be an understatement in our case, because this was something on an entirely different level. It was clear that I had inherited a poor, if not toxic culture; that's not a complaint, just a fact, and I felt duty-bound to lead the charge in an effort to right the course. After all, the majority of those affected were looking for change, and their interests and the education of hundreds—and in the several years of one's tenure, perhaps thousands—of students lay in the balance.

I reasoned that some staff would be flexible and go with the flow; others would find it to be a challenge. Others still might see it as inordinately difficult or against their wishes and flat-out resist change. I would soon come to know those who were excited and firmly on board. I would also identify others who were set in their ways and were not about to change how they comported themselves, and I would learn just how ingrained—how dug in—some of them were.

Notwithstanding the intransigence on the part of a few staff members, I was steadfast, believing that those individuals would find it within themselves to make needed adjustments, or they would find themselves out of a job at this school. I felt that the personal investment made on the part of so many other staff, students, and parents was far too important to continue allowing mediocre-to-incompetent staff remain in the school, negatively affecting student learning and our school improvement efforts. This would be a heavy lift. As the school year got underway, I would realize just how heavy it genuinely was.

I was in the midst of talking to them about teaching as a profession, when a hand raised. It was a social studies teacher asking if there would be a faculty dress code. I said, rather matter-of-factly, that if we considered ourselves professional, and if we expected to be treated like professionals, we should look, act, and dress like professionals, and that I would expect every staff member to dress accordingly. I stated that a so-called Casual Friday was fine, but even then, we would still dress appropriately.

I advised the staff that I believed they would find me approachable and learn that I valued differing points of view, that I don't make decisions based on how it might be perceived, whether it be by school system headquarters, board of education staff, politicos, or others. I shared that I believed any decision should be thoughtful—not politically correct, but based on discussions, feedback, relevant data, and perspectives—and made in the best interest of our school—our students, our staff, our curricular program, our parents, and our community. I advised them of my meeting and discussions with team leaders and that we would work on any unresolved issues from the past, as we commenced to embark on a different journey. This was a new academic year, after all, and I suggested that it would be healthy to give one another the benefit of the doubt.

Many of the staff that morning, along with scores throughout the community, lamented the myriad issues, problems, and challenges that had made teaching at this school so difficult every day of an academic year. They understandably wanted none of that nonsense in the upcoming year. I reasoned that we were not going to tackle and solve every flaw in how the school was run or not run; no organization had the capacity for dealing with the multitude of issues voiced by so many of the school's constituency. I believed, however, that my experience, philosophy, goals, and plan of action would correct the vast majority of their concerns and provide a far more fulfilling academic school year for everyone. I stated that our country's sixteenth president, Abraham Lincoln, was often credited as having said, "The philosophy of the school room in one generation will be the philosophy of government in the next." To a great extent, this was true, I advised them, so together we needed to renew our efforts and provide our students, their parents, and this community a top-shelf instructional program, because they—our students—were among this community's, and perhaps our country's, future leaders. Borrowing from a line (modified) often attributed to Gandhi, I said that we—individually and collectively—needed to *be the change* that each of us, I was certain, wanted to see happen in our school, and that our main focus would be on the children and producing an educated and well-behaved citizenry, including an emphasis on ensuring quality academic instruction in reading, writing, mathematics, as well as in each of our related arts course offerings. They would come to understand that our mission would be to educate the whole child, and that such a mindset would emphasize daily the importance of what we were there to do and how we were to do it, that future generations stood to be the direct beneficiaries of our efforts.

I shared with them the "broken windows" theory, just as I had done with the custodial and maintenance staff earlier. It was a practice that I found successful throughout my career, resulting in staff and students over the years who were more confident, self-assured, emotionally balanced, and generally more successful, both as professional staff and as successful students who found their share of achievement in and out of the classroom. Regarding the faculty and teaching staff, my expectation would be that each would review his or her role as professionals. Much like "broken windows," we would from now on ensure that we were cognizant of measures or steps taken to enhance staff and student "quality of life" in this building and on school campus grounds throughout the day. Professional staff at all times would act professionally, recognizing and addressing colleagues and students each day; exhibiting courtesy and caring toward one another; making connections with students and their families; and ensuring that students exhibited good manners and followed school rules and regulations, used appropriate language, and treated one another with respect. I advised them that I would regularly clarify and reinforce expected appropriate behaviors to our student body; likewise, teaching staff were expected to do the same inside and outside of their classrooms, and they would be expected to stop a student and correct the youngster(s) immediately, directing to a school administrator any student they felt needed additional emphasis.

Failure to expect and reinforce these basic quality-of-life expectations likewise sends the message that such is of no importance, that nobody really cares about such things in school. Similar to what was evidenced in the research, just as general quality-of-life behaviors and manners are perceived as unimportant or not really expected, ill behavior becomes more pronounced, where disrespectful, disruptive, and frequently violent behavior becomes routine, leading to wholesale deterioration of the classroom and the entire school community. The bottom line is that when you routinely reinforce basic manners and expect respectful behavior in schools, you enhance the quality of life for everyone throughout the school community.

In fact, we would find that the more we required and reinforced good manners, courtesy, and respectful behaviors, the more we began to observe a growing sense of self-respect among our students, which promoted wider respect for student peers, as well as a more professional and gracious demeanor among the staff.

As I related earlier to the custodial staff, I shared with teaching staff my view of "making one's bed" first thing in the morning, clarifying my personal view on living with a purpose. Whether one has a goal to be accomplished for a particular day, year, or during one's lifetime, I generally find being purposeful a useful and gratifying way to go about one's life. Sharing insights into one's personal worldview clarifies for others the kind of individual you are and how you are likely to conduct yourself in a leadership position, no matter the entity—be it an organization, sports team, corporation, foundation, task force, or, in this case, as this school community's principal. My expectation was that each of us would take ownership of our individual job responsibilities, paying attention to and seeing that action was taken to repair or replace affirmatively any "broken windows" we encountered, whether part of our building and grounds or part of our own individual lives or the lives of others. Such caring—*cura personalis*—and attention smacks of character, of principled compassion; it would commence that day, I informed them, and it would become a significant part of our school's culture.

When addressing a group, I found it useful to provide information in different formats. Some people are given to being visual learners, so I sometimes made use of a PowerPoint slide to enhance the group's understanding of an issue or a point I was making. One such slide highlighted the education goals of the federal government outlined in the No Child Left Behind Act, followed by our state's Bridge to Excellence Master Plan, and then our school district's Comprehensive Plan for Accelerated School Improvement, and finally, our specific school's goals for the upcoming academic year. It clarified the role that individual staff members play in American education, and it allowed them at the time to see how their professional teaching efforts linked and fit in with the wider goals set at the national, state, and county levels.Given the problems, challenges, and failures that had blanketed the school and community, I opted not to spend time collaborating with a committee on the direction and goals of the impending academic year. It had always been my view that two specific areas are pivotal to any school's success: acceptable student deportment and productive academic performance. As of the end of the previous school year, both were in the dumpster at this school; that would change. The goals we would set for the year would mirror those presented by the newly hired superintendent at the time, goals similar to those cited by many school systems.[2] The difference now— a crucial distinction—would be the environment in which such goals are expected to be achieved. There would need to be an appropriate teaching-learning culture, an atmosphere conducive to teaching and learning. Such is key yet is absent from many failing schools throughout America. Our school's goals would be specific and substantive. Goals may be appropriate enough, but they must be seen as meaningful and achievable, and many would argue that schools today, in the main, do not at all operate with a meaningful focus on academic achievement in an environment conducive to teaching and learning. Many educrats and school officials talk the talk, mouthing ideas and goals that are seemingly appropriate enough; we would walk the talk, and with good fortune, we would do so with character, passion, and teamwork.

A not-so-minor contrast that day was the fact that I was at the helm of this particular school; I knew what propelled teaching and learning; and I was not about to place the information I shared with my staff on a shelf or in a file cabinet, never to be referred to again. It was important that all saw upfront that meaningful thought had gone into a substantive plan that would guide our teaching and learning efforts for this academic year. The following two goals became our focus and priority:

Goal 1: Academic Excellence

We as a faculty and a staff would commit that each child would meet rigorous performance standards. That meant that all diploma-bound students would perform on or above grade level in all measured content/subject areas.

Goal 2: An Appropriate Teaching-Learning Culture

All Harper's Choice Middle School students, staff, and parents would enjoy an appropriate school culture and climate, resulting in a safe, nurturing, and academically stimulating teaching and learning environment that would value diversity and commonality.

I took a few minutes to clarify my position regarding the use of the word *diversity*—a term very much in vogue with the school system and our current politics. I informed everyone that I felt all of us were fortunate to work in such a diverse community, in a majority-minority school. I also told them that I believed the word *diversity* had been bastardized over the years, and that I personally cherished our nation's thirteen-letter motto: *e pluribus unum*, Latin for, "Out of many, one." By that definition, all Americans are included, valued, and respected. That was my view, I informed them—that no matter our color, religion, gender, or socioeconomic status, I saw us as family, the Harper's Choice family. Some parts of our society seem to revel in criticizing the nation, engaging in identity politics and emphasizing our differences, when I believe we'd all be better off noting and highlighting our similarities, all of the ways in which we are alike as Americans. On that day, I asked our teachers and staff to consider that interpretation—the meaning and sentiment behind the Latin motto—and ask themselves if they understood and agreed with it. They didn't necessarily have to say anything at the time, but I would be interested in their opinions as the school year got underway.

I always thought the business maxim, "What gets measured gets done," made sense, because it kept people attentive and on top of their game, using the gleaned information to make decisions that would improve *results*, our focus from here on out, every academic year. No successful institution or corporation anywhere pursues a strategic direction without establishing benchmarks and continually measuring their progress. We would be no different. We would measure student performance, not as an end in itself, but as part of an ongoing process of ensuring that we were getting things done successfully.

I advised the staff that I would soon structure and convene monthly meetings with a School Improvement Team, consisting of the assistant principal, grade-level and team leaders, parents, members of the business community, students, and other staff. Together we would outline further our goals and refine a plan that would spell out our path to success. While some schools might well have such committees, many operate in a vacuum. They might meet, they might set what they think are goals, and they might even proceed to submit the paperwork to central office school district headquarters, to share with an interested public, or to submit among other documents in an attempt to win an award. However, when the school or school system is devoid of meaningful leadership and a substantive recognition of the important role that character plays in the daily operation of a school, it results in mediocre to unsatisfactory performance. It makes not a whit of difference that you've put a plan on paper if you're not moving daily from words on paper to walking it out, from talk to action. Instead, what you've got is confusion, a dispirited faculty and staff, failing students, and frustrated parents; you do not have a vibrant, academically successful school community.

No, we would have a written Plan of Action for each of our two goals, arguably a bit ambitious, given the academic and behavioral condition of the school community in the previous few years. I imagine some staff members wondered how we would begin to accomplish such a mission; this organized plan added clarification to the details in my presentation and the direction we were heading in the coming year. The top of each plan had an "At a Glance" view of a Summary of Disaggregated Data and Student Performance Indicators germane to each goal. "Goal 1—Focus on Instruction" cited the percentage of each demographic group we served, as well as how each had performed on local, state, and national assessments. "Goal 2—School Culture/Student Behavior" provided data indicating total numbers of various categories of ill behavior (suspension data, discipline referrals, and types of offenses—disrespect, disruption, fighting, bullying, threats, etc.), as well as student performance indicators citing grade-point averages for disruptive youth and student support plan data.

The second aspect of the plan of action for each goal outlined specific objectives, strategies or activities, milestones, and an assessment or evaluation. Any and all targets, goals, and objectives would be written in accordance with the SMART criteria[3] often associated with business management, including the work of Peter Drucker and his "Management by Objectives" concept.[4] Each would be specific, measurable, achievable/assignable, realistic/results-oriented, and time-related. Written out in this fashion, our stakeholders—faculty and staff, students, parents, and the community—found our plan clear enough to understand, and they knew specifically when a target or goal had been reached. Following the above criteria, each of our two main goals—our focus on instruction and an ideal teaching-learning culture, requiring excellent student behavior—had targets that cited specific areas of improvement. Each target, again, was specific; each was measurable—quantified, or at least suggesting an indicator of progress; each was achievable—we assigned a name or group responsible for achieving the target; each target was results-oriented—we identified the minimum percentage of students we expected to achieve the results; and each specified a time by which a specific target would be achieved. Most importantly, our plan revolved around specifically answering pivotal questions that we asked ourselves, or a variant of them, which guided us on our way to academic and behavioral excellence:

- What is it we want all HCMS students to learn?
- How will we provide it?
- How will we know if they have learned it?
- How will we respond if they don't?

Teachers were not just going to be given a school district county curriculum guide, which was—and often still is—standard fare throughout the country. No, in the spirit of meaningful accountability, we took ownership and asked ourselves each of the above questions, and we did so in a totally different environment, one conducive to meaningful teaching and learning. Together, we answered those questions in collegial conversations by way of our School Improvement Team, which enhanced our chances of achieving the two goals outlined that morning.

Additionally, three values served as a foundation for accomplishing these objectives and answering these questions, and the values were cited in the school system plan to improve student achievement, and they were each in play daily throughout the academic year. You will see these values occasionally cited in education literature, but all too frequently these principles are ignored in many K-12 school settings. Nonetheless, I believed their incorporation into our school's mission to be important factors in our total program of instruction, and each of these values figured prominently in our particular school's transformation and eventual academic success.

A Focus on Instruction

Top-shelf instruction would be the first underlying value that would support the renewed teaching and learning at this school. From that day forward, Harper's Choice was going to be known as a hallmark of meaningful, substantive teaching and learning. We committed upfront that each of our youngsters would meet or exceed the State Department of Education's standards, meaning that *all* diploma-bound students would perform on or above their grade level in each measured subject area.

I was well-aware of parents' concerns with "inconsistent teaching practices," and I wanted to touch on this concern upfront with all staff. After all, education is only as good as the teacher in the classroom. I talked about why it is that many Americans choose to go into the teaching profession, why they elect to work in our public schools, and the fact that good teachers develop a passion for a particular subject area and want to share their interest, that passion, with youngsters, and in so doing, they make a difference in youngsters' lives. I asked each of them to think about why they had chosen to enter the teaching profession. I then asked them to reflect for a moment on whether they went into the classroom each day prepared and with the intention of reaching every child, believing that their students— *all* of their students—would be successful and understand clearly their content area class session objectives.

I presented a list of teacher attitudes, behaviors, and values I felt would enhance student (and teacher) success. The idea was to ask the teaching staff to "own" the success or failure of each of the students assigned to them. I cited each attitude, each behavior, on the list (see below), and I then asked if together these behaviors were something they could commit to daily. When they responded in the affirmative, I emphasized each listed attitude again and informed them that I felt these attitudes, these behaviors, were where the rubber met the road, because it was directly *on them* to make these behaviors happen each and every day. In fact, I would look for direct evidence of these behaviors in the various teacher classroom instructional observations that I would be conducting soon, instructional observations that would figure prominently in their end-of-year evaluations.

I asked if there were any questions or concerns about what I was asking them to do. I reaffirmed that I was quite fine in discussing the matter with them, and if they wanted me to expand on any one of the items, I would be happy to do so. One team leader voiced heartfelt support for the idea; others said they thought it was appropriate. I found it terrific that the staff was all-in, and I began to believe that we would—together—begin to change the culture at this school.

I felt at that moment that their commitment was huge. They were teachers committed to making it clear to all students what they were expected to accomplish in each subject; teachers committed to teaching those specific outcomes and to helping those students who were struggling; and finally, teachers who would actively monitor student progress and adjust their teaching strategy accordingly—again, *this was huge!* Each staff member received a copy of this personal/professional commitment.

HCMS Attitudes, Behaviors, and Values
Supporting Student Achievement

- We will identify the specific outcomes that students are to achieve on a course-by-course basis.
- We will teach to the agreed-upon outcomes and accept our responsibility to help each student achieve those outcomes.
- We will monitor each student's attainment of these outcomes on an ongoing basis and adjust our instructional strategies accordingly.

The above values enhanced our efforts to ensure that all students met or exceeded rigorous standards for student achievement.

A Focus on Continuous Improvement

This second underlying value was pivotal to our instructional success. The idea of assessing, analyzing, adjusting, and trying again is the trademark of continuous improvement. This value, too, was critical to our success in every area of academic instruction, student deportment, and overall school climate. In every endeavor, there was this belief that we could, should, and would, indeed, continuously improve our output.[5]

The historical backdrop of continuous improvement in management and systems thinking since the 1930s had played no prominent role *per se* in what I was trying to accomplish. I'm grateful that its history had brought such an idea to fruition, and I always enjoyed a good read on various business management models, but its history and how continuous improvement was used in business thinking was not something I wittingly thought about or felt was necessary to preach to the faculty. My wife Elaine and I had decided years earlier that she would start a small business out of our home, and it became a very successful business for many years. In that regard, we always looked for ways to improve our service to her customers. At the same time, I was a full-time public school principal; assessing, analyzing, examining the data, making needed adjustments, and going about my efforts with renewed vigor was something I lived and breathed. These values, including continuous improvement, boosted staff engagement and cultivated a teaching staff that felt a sense of genuine pride and accomplishment, which led to a meaningful sense of belonging.

A Focus on Connections/Partnerships

The idea of establishing connections with students and their families, developing professional interpersonal relationships among the staff, and forming partnerships within the community was an important third value. I cannot emphasize enough the value of school-family-community partnerships. Many educators have cited their dismay regarding perceived student apathy, poor student attitudes, and overall student disrespect. Teachers' attempts to connect with students can make a huge difference in their attitude, motivation, and how successful they will be in the classroom. More on this later in the book. However, the idea of formally and actively cultivating scores of business partnerships was foreign to this school community. Time and again, the effort showed just how important our partnerships proved to be in our success. We developed well over two dozen partnerships with a host of community businesses, retail establishments, the police department, the parks and recreation department, various foundations, the library system, and other corporations in our community. There would come a time when Harper's Choice boasted more meaningful business-school partnerships than any other school—elementary, middle, or high school—in the entire district. The influence these entities had on our students, the teachers, and our families was invaluable, and it enhanced our school's overall academic achievement.

We would go on to accomplish great things at Harper's Choice, in no small measure because of our unending emphasis on those values encompassing a focus on instruction, a focus on continuous improvement, and a focus on making connections and establishing partnerships.

I informed the staff of the beneficial value I thought a kind of lodestar would be, something to guide us as we worked together in pursuit of our yearly goals. What would that be? I explained my view that the soul of this school, from here on out, would revolve around what the Greeks called *ethos*...character. The entirety of the school community would benefit from emphasizing the importance of dignity, integrity, courage, honesty, perseverance, compassion, resilience, and citizenship, among other such traits. Character would serve as the anchor to which we would tie our school's future fortunes. We later incorporated the teaching of time-tested character traits within the students' daily schedule, coordinated by the teachers. These character traits were taught to our students and served as a framework for how students were expected to behave and how staff would be expected to carry themselves daily.

I asked the staff to think about those character traits that, when practiced throughout our daily teaching and interaction with one another and our students, would increase our personal accountability and commitment, cultivate a sense of passion for teaching and learning, enhance our connections with one another and our students, and simultaneously elevate the school community. As outlined in the earlier chapter on character, among the useful sources we used was former U.S. Education Secretary William Bennett's *Book of Virtues*. We were no longer going to be known for the problems, failures, and chaos that so defined the school previously; we would, instead, feel a palpable sense of pride at being called "The Choice," and I thought to myself that one day we would be just that—a school where teachers would choose and prefer to be, a place where parents wanted to send their youngsters to get an education. I emphasized that they should not at all confuse character with the "self-esteem" nonsense that is so prevalent in American education today. I have shaken my head at how "self-esteem" has been addressed over the years by well-meaning but naïve educators and school administrators. I provided examples of ridiculous practices followed by school officials, among which was the time a principal contacted a student at home on suspension and requested that the pupil return to school—in the middle of his suspension, mind you—to receive his "Student of the Month" award, because he had received fewer discipline referrals the previous month. It seemingly was no matter that the principal and staff ignored a host of other students, some of whom came from difficult backgrounds, who worked beyond expectations to achieve credible academic performance, but were simply ignored. When addressing the inanity of what he and several staff members—those who were assisting with the program—were doing, he responded offhandedly, "Oh, Steve, you're all about that 'character and standards' thing," as though such was not important, not relevant.

These mind-numbing practices are followed regularly in many schools, a number of which will tout—whether or not it is accurate— "nurturing environments," an "appreciation of diversity," and "lifelong learning," but they miss the boat on putting in the hard work that would otherwise create a genuine teaching-learning environment allowing such to be cultivated and to blossom.

No, our students would be different. They would be a major beneficiary of this emphasis on character, as would our faculty; students would learn what it meant to understand, to appreciate, and to extend kindness to others. They would learn the importance of trustworthiness and self-discipline, the value of hard work, and the importance of being honest—to themselves and to others. In turn, we would find our youngsters would soon understand and feel a genuine sense of self-concept—real, substantive self-esteem, which would enhance their efforts to become successful students, and beyond that, better, stronger, more productive, and proud citizens of American society.

Given the school's sour climate over the past years, you can imagine the number of skeptics in the audience that morning, wondering how on earth anyone could find himself standing in front of this group and believing for a moment that such would ever fly in this school community, one so penetrated with problems that it seemed to cripple, at times, any sense of the school's mission, most notably, instruction and learning. No, it would be anything but a cakewalk, but I was determined. I had been asked to consider taking the principalship of this specific school, with all its challenges, and I had accepted the challenge. At this point, as I indicated earlier, it had become a matter of duty. We were going to take ownership of our individual roles, and together, we would weather the storms. I knew it was likely that not every member of the school's constituency would be on board, Nonetheless, I was prepared for the long haul. We needed to believe in our purpose and remain steadfast; with character at the core of our worksite, success, I promised them, would eventually prevail.

Since my arrival, I had been mulling over something more meaningful than a standard motto behind which the faculty and school community could rally, something almost spiritual that would serve to inspire and motivate our staff, students, parents, and the wider business community to believe in our goal of becoming a successful, first-rate public school. Spiritual was not far from the mark, as I was well-aware it would take this side of a miracle even to begin turning around what some had called a hellhole of a school.

What I had in mind was an idea that focused on three specific pillars I had always believed led to a successful teaching and learning experience for any educational institution. I included it in the "Welcome Back" letter to staff that I had sent out a couple weeks earlier. It would highlight the importance of qualified, if not gifted teachers, those who had a passion for their content area and loved being around youngsters. It would underscore what I believed was essential for a child's success, which began and ended with his mom and dad's or guardian's involvement—active involvement—in his education. The third pillar was particularly critical to a youngster's educational success—each student would need to exhibit both behavioral and academic excellence, and one could not occur without the other. It was not enough to be smart; you had to behave, which meant showing good judgment, making good choices, and respecting and caring about others. The salient key that would enhance our chances of profound success would be that we stopped making excuses for other individuals' poor decisions, their failures, their living or social conditions. No matter one's station in life, of paramount importance was the recognition that we can do, we can perform, and we can achieve; yes, at times it's a real leg up to have a bit of guidance, support, and resources afforded to you, but more importantly, it takes pure grit and a personal resolve to improve one's condition or that of another. The following motto—which, for many, became more of a mantra—is the one I offered for their consideration and one that everyone unanimously approved. It became ubiquitous throughout the school community: Soon it could be found on schoolwide banners in the hallways and outside the building, on school letterhead, on the school-parent newsletter, and on virtually all correspondence, as a reminder of our focus on the quintessential elements for a top-shelf education:

High Quality Teaching + Parental Involvement +
Student Academic and Behavioral Excellence
First Step: NO EXCUSES

I have stated over the years that there are successful public schools that dot the American landscape, but they operate differently from those in the main. Just as there are characteristics shared by successful corporations, so, too, are there identified character traits that are shared by those schools in which the students achieve. I have been a longtime advocate of the so-called Effective Schools Movement, a product of the thinking and research of Harvard researchers Ron Edmonds, Larry Lezotte et al.[6] The guiding principles of the movement always tied in nicely with my belief that all children can learn, that all schools can be meaningfully productive, and that every school throughout the country ought to be held accountable for providing substantive learning for all of its students. This is among the reasons I was a proponent of the 2001 No Child Left Behind Act, President George W. Bush's education reform and accountability bill, the most sweeping education reform legislation since 1965, when President Lyndon B. Johnson passed the original Elementary and Secondary Education Act.

The following correlates characterize effective schools:

Instructional Leadership

The principal acts as the instructional leader, who effectively communicates the mission of the school to staff, parents, and students, and who understands and applies the characteristics of instructional effectiveness in the management of the instructional program at the school.

Clear and Focused School Mission

There is a clearly articulated mission for the school through which the staff shares an understanding of and a commitment to the instructional goals, priorities, assessment procedures, and accountability.

Safe and Orderly Environment

There is an orderly, purposeful atmosphere, free from the threat of physical harm for both students and staff. However, the atmosphere is not oppressive and is conducive to teaching and learning.

High Expectations for Success

The school displays a climate of expectations in which the staff believes and demonstrates that students can attain mastery of basic skills and that they (the staff) have the capability to help students achieve such mastery.

Opportunity to Learn and Time on Task

Teachers allocate a significant amount of classroom time to instruction in basic skills areas. For a high percentage of that allocated time, students are engaged in planned learning activities directly related to the identified objectives.

Frequent Monitoring of Student Progress

Feedback on student academic progress is frequently obtained. Multiple assessment methods, such as teacher-made tests, samples of students' work, mastery skills checklists, criterion-referenced tests, and norm-referenced tests, are used. The results of testing are used to improve individual student performance and to improve the instructional program.

Positive Home-School Relations

Parents understand and support the school's basic mission and are given the opportunity to play an important role in helping the school achieve its mission.

The philosophy espoused that morning—the broken windows theory, our school year objectives, the school improvement plan and guided questions that would shepherd us in achieving them, the pivotal values that undergird their success, the *HCMS Attitudes, Behaviors, and Values Supporting Student Achievement*, the role that character would play in our school, and our No Excuses motto—together would dovetail nicely with those Effective School Correlates that would enhance our efforts to succeed. Every staff member—both in and out of the classroom—was understanding fast that this would be a demonstrably different school year.

For years, I've had an interest in and have believed in the efficacy of Total Quality Management practices popularized in business management. When I was teaching English, and later, as I developed an interest in and became a school administrator, the idea of continually improving one's performance proved of value. My hope—my challenge—was that others would see and feel the genuine passion and drive I had to effect a complete change in the culture of the school that would see everyone enjoy more gratifying academic school years ahead. The challenges were huge, and my more immediate goal was to focus on the current school year, taking the substantive steps needed to create meaningful change for the better for each succeeding year.

Later in the week, I took the opportunity again to speak to the teaching staff. I congratulated many on their classrooms, which, when organized and tastefully presented with posters, classroom expectations, samples of student work, and bright colors, interesting fun facts, and other subject-relevant items, "beckoned" the students, I believed, to share in the fun of learning. Yes, students must attend class on time, but we can also do our best to "invite" them into each specific instructional area, giving them that much more reason to be there on time daily, ready and eager to learn.

The teachers appeared excited to be back. Many of them seemed enthused with the change in the administration, and they looked happy to see one another after a previously tense school year and summer break. Even veteran staff were enthused about preparing their classrooms for what they believed—hoped—would be a much improved, satisfying academic year.

This morning's presentation to them would be a natural follow-up to my initial welcome, their introduction to our new objectives, and the underlying philosophy behind everything we would do this year. Specifically, that morning, I wanted to address student behavior and how the staff would be expected to handle various disciplinary issues. I advised them that I planned to discuss the topic, among other items, with the student body, when I addressed each grade level over the course of the first few days of the opening school year.

Among the major two goals of the academic year presented at the beginning of the week was the much-talked-about issue of an "appropriate school learning culture," one that, in my view, by its very definition, was a safe, nurturing, and academically stimulating teaching and learning environment. Devoid of an appropriate school learning culture, I maintained, there would be no teaching, and there would be no learning. This school had struggled greatly with student ill behavior and was yet another example of schools throughout the country where such is standard fare. No more, I informed the staff.

To make a point, I took a few minutes to discuss the laws regarding compulsory attendance, informing the staff that, according to our specific state's laws, every child between the ages of five and sixteen (now seventeen, with a change in Maryland law in 2015–2016) must be enrolled in a state public or private school, unless the youngster was homeschooled.[7] The home was considered a safe place (notwithstanding the fact that many homes, sadly, are not), and since, by law, the government was mandating that children be enrolled in schools, the expectation was that educators would act in *loco parentis*, or "in the place of a parent." As explained earlier, this refers to the legal responsibility of a person or organization to take on some of the responsibilities of a parent. Therefore, because students must be in school, we must ensure that the school setting was safe and secure. Interesting, I found it, that this information was new to the staff; a number had said they simply had never heard of it, nor did they have such an expectation, much less had any legal reference ever been made to them. That was okay with me; now they knew.

Could it be, I thought, that so many school officials and boards of education associated with disruptive, violent school settings throughout the country also are ignorant of this extraordinary responsibility? How is it that scores of schools and school systems neglect to do everything required to ensure that they diligently exercise prudence in ensuring that their schools are safe places for everyone, everyday.......as well as avoid the potential for a sizable class-action lawsuit?

I placed a copy of the county school district's student code of conduct on the screen and reviewed the expected appropriate behaviors, among which it was stated that students would engage in learning activities and take school seriously; take responsibility for their own behavior; be courteous; respect the personal, civil, and property rights of others; attend school regularly, on time, and be prepared to learn; complete all assignments on time; speak appropriately; dress appropriately; exhibit self-control; seek alternatives to verbal or physical conflicts; cooperate with others; and behave ethically. Each expected appropriate behavior contained examples. Yet most of the staff members were generally unaware of such a list. Further, they respectfully stated that not a single expected behavior listed had been reinforced at the school, with one teacher saying, "I don't know, boss; None of that is generally seen at this school. I'm sorry, things have been just crazy." Several staff members who had experience in other schools—within the county, as well as outside the county and the state—chimed in that they were not aware of such behaviors being reviewed, much less ever being reinforced at their previous schools. Indeed, they added that teacher unions were utterly ineffective in providing assistance when teachers were confronted with horrendous student behavior and equally feckless school administrators, adding that they simply felt abandoned—a view I found appalling but not surprising, really.

School-based administrators from time to time openly expressed that they never felt that the list of expected behaviors ever received appropriate recognition by school headquarters administration or board of education members during districtwide training and informational seminars or in disciplinary matters that were appealed to school district headquarters. It was a handout that had been routinely given to administrators at countywide meetings, but it never made it as an agenda item, and it was never discussed. To many administrators, this was just another document that remained in a file or was placed on a shelf. I always felt that this was too bad, because it is imperative that school systems and boards of education understand just how important these behaviors are to successful teaching and learning. They should clarify their support to school-based administrators who, in turn, should support teaching staff in seeing that respectful behavior is standard fare in classrooms throughout the country. It is worth noting, as well, that many students in schools throughout the country exhibit exemplary behavior; they, too, along with their parents, express dismay at the deplorable manner in which so many peers and adults conduct themselves on school campuses, making teaching and learning so difficult, so very challenging.

Nonetheless, I said that while I appreciated their comments and perspectives, the behaviors outlined, in fact, would be expected at this school site from day one, starting the following week. They needed to know how pivotal I thought these behaviors were to our success; equally important was that we had a process in place to manage the expected behaviors. They were not to think I was confronting this "behavior" issue for the first time. Still very fresh in the minds of everyone in the country was the horrific occurrence in Littleton, Colorado, where two teens had gone on a shooting spree that killed thirteen people and wounded some twenty others, before they had turned the guns on themselves. (I would later have the opportunity to talk to Columbine High School staff members and students while vacationing with my wife in Colorado.) I briefly read aloud various paragraphs from an op-ed that I had written, which had appeared in some three hundred newspapers nationally—this one from a June 1999 issue of the *Cincinnati Enquirer*:

> "The enormity of the tragic violence to visit Littleton, Colorado, can now be added to a list of those cities throughout the country to experience the horror of school violence. Far more pervasive than the violent statistics, however, is the disrespectful, disruptive behavior that is cultivated by

school officials on a daily basis throughout schools, ill behavior that is equally tolerated in too many homes.

"The most pivotal reason for this country's lackluster educational performance continues to revolve around the lack of civility that is all too evident in our schools and communities. We can no longer assert the need to set rigorous standards and then ignore the very reason this is unachievable. The number of classroom disruptions, including threats and injuries to teachers and students, grows exponentially; further, the acceptance or acquiescence to ill behavior has a negative cumulative effect on the school community that lays the groundwork for still further escalating incivility and violence.

"The salutary effect of behavior and discipline policies and statutes is contingent on the degree to which school officials employ them consistently. Unfortunately, they do not. The lack of consistency is often due to feckless school officials too concerned with image, who dread criticism of suspension rates, or who lack the intestinal fortitude to deal directly with ill behavior. It does not occur to them that a more proactive approach would reduce instructional interference, enhance student achievement on a wider scale, and provide a better service to the citizenry."

While I wasn't particularly looking for a response, the staff applauded, with a number saying audibly, "Thank you, Mr. Wallis." They were appreciative, and I believe they felt validated. I was hopeful we were off to a different, if not, a far more productive and enjoyable school year.

Since opening day for students would be the following week, I wanted to clarify some items. I advised them that no student should leave a classroom without having signed out and signed in on their return, so the school had a record of specific students who were away from classes at any one time. There would be none of the nonsense practiced in too many schools, that saw students leaving the classroom after a raise of the hand, if even that is done, allegedly to use a bathroom. This was new to staff and generally not practiced in schools; nonetheless, in the interest of safety and security, it is an important routine to know exactly when and why a student is away from one's supervision. It would prove to be a most helpful routine when various issues over the course of the school year presented themselves and there was a need to verify or confirm a particular student's location at a specific time during the school day.

I clarified how we, as a school, would handle student discipline, since this was a major concern on the part of the school's constituencies, an issue noted, as well, in the school system climate survey. There would be none of the haphazard, inconsistent handling of these matters that had so concerned teachers and other employees in the past. Our character infusion would figure prominently in our discipline program, not totally unlike a future discipline program that the school system would later implement, called Positive Behavioral and Intervention Supports (PBIS), because all along we were teaching kids good behavior, good personal self-conduct, good habits for success. I assured them that we, as an administrative team, would include this topic in our meetings the following week with the student body, meetings I had asked the PTA representative to feel free to attend, as more and more I wanted the community to feel a part of the school, that we were all in this together.

Unless the student transgression was egregious (and I gave several examples), the teacher would be expected to handle any disciplinary matters as they felt appropriate. Generally speaking, however, before a student was referred to an administrator, teachers were to have already contacted the parent(s). My view is that it is important that parents receive contact early on so they can communicate directly with the teacher and be given the opportunity to intervene and get their youngster back on track. Such contact also provides a chance for the teacher and parent to connect and communicate on the child's behalf.

Staff in many schools are regularly directed to take care of all discipline matters. "Keep it out of the front office," they are told, because administrators are already "too busy." Teachers in these schools find that they regularly must stop their instruction and deal with repeated student disrespectful or disruptive behavior, with no support from the school administration. No more, I informed them. If the teacher and parent together are unable to effect a positive change, the assistant principal and I would handle subsequent student discipline matters—and that was the way it remained for the entire time I led that school. I can say that the policy elicited stares that morning; some of the staff were quite surprised, perhaps incredulous; others were outwardly gratified at the prospect of a more civilized school setting.

I paused for a moment and again cited our two major goals—academic excellence and an appropriate teaching-learning culture—emphasizing again that they went hand in hand, that we would have no Goal 1 without having this specific Goal 2. I asked, rhetorically, why that would be, then proceeded to inform staff that every teacher, every educator, in this school, henceforth, needed to see their individual classrooms as sacrosanct, near-sacred environments for teaching and student excellence and conduct themselves accordingly. Anyone who intentionally created a disturbance in the class that directly interfered with a teacher's instruction—which, of course, negatively impacted other students' ability to learn—would be considered disruptive...period.

I informed them that I expected them to differentiate what might be minor infractions and ignored, from any behavior that might be defined as going beyond rudeness, where the teacher must stop instruction to attend to a student(s) behavior. Goal 2 was important because disruptive behavior in class can—and regularly does—have obvious negative effects on teaching, learning, and the entire school community. Such has been all too clear for many educators for decades, and it was no different in this school community.

Negative Effects on Teaching

Disruptive students interfere with the teacher's ability to teach effectively. The behavior requires large amounts of the teacher's time and attention. The teacher must stop the lesson or the discussion to address the behavior, and this takes away from the valuable time needed to instruct the rest of the class. If the disruptive behavior is threatening, it may challenge the teacher's authority, and thus it can create tension in the classroom, which pushes learning into the background. Disruptive behavior by one student also encourages other students to do the same, which compromises the teacher's authority and ability to control the group.

Issues for Students

The learning process for other students is affected when one or more students behave in a disruptive manner. Constant interruptions can interfere with focus. Students are forced to wait while the behavior is addressed, or they are sidetracked by the disruptive student's attempts to be noticed. This can result in lower grades and behavioral issues with other students, as well as with the student who is causing the interruption. Peers tend to have a significant influence over each other, and if one student is disruptive, it may encourage similar behavior in other classmates who might not have had trouble otherwise.

Negative Impact on the School

Often, schools must focus time and resources that could be used elsewhere on trying to stop disruptive behavior in students. This takes away from the educational mandate of most schools, which is usually to provide a safe, effective learning environment for all students. Teachers are often not equipped to deal with some types of extreme disruptive behaviors, and as a result, the student is either sent out of class or the school must enlist the aid of outside professionals to try to intervene. This takes resources and funding that could be better used to improve the educational environment for all students instead of just one.[8]

I clarified the fact that misbehavior in class, in fact, negatively affects teaching, taking time away from instruction, which then impacts learning for the remaining well-behaved, responsible children in the classroom. While this, too, has been clear to many a classroom teacher and parent for decades, it was later borne out by way of empirical research demonstrating that inappropriate behavior in school, in fact, adversely affects learning opportunities for other children in the classroom. A nationally representative survey by Public Agenda found that 85 percent of teachers and 73 percent of parents agreed that the "school experience of most students suffers at the expense of a few chronic offenders."

Research results cited in EducationNext explain the domino effect that poor classroom behavior has on the entire class. Children from troubled families, as measured by family domestic violence, performed considerably worse on standardized reading and mathematics tests and were much more likely to commit disciplinary infractions and be suspended than other students. It was also found that an increase in the number of children from troubled families reduced peer student math and reading test scores and increased peer disciplinary infractions and suspensions. The effects on academic achievement were greatest for students from higher income families, while the effects on behavior were more pronounced in students who were less well-off. The results of the analysis provided evidence that, in many cases, a single disruptive student could indeed influence the academic progress made by an entire classroom of students. Specifically, troubled students had a statistically significant negative effect on their peers' reading and math test scores. Adding one troubled student to a classroom of twenty students resulted in a decrease in student reading and math test scores of more than two-thirds of a percentile point (2 to 3 percent of a standard deviation). The addition of a troubled peer also significantly increased the misbehavior of other students in the classroom, in effect causing them to commit 0.09 more infractions than they otherwise would, a 16 percent increase. These are effects that could accumulate over time if the same students were repeatedly exposed to troubled peers.[9]

As mentioned, these average effects mask a few interesting differences across student groups. Again, it was found that troubled peers had a large and statistically significant negative effect on higher income children's math and reading achievement, but only a small and statistically insignificant effect on the achievement of low-income children. However, the opposite pattern was found for disciplinary outcomes. The presence of troubled peers significantly increased the misbehavior of low-income children, but it did not increase the disciplinary problems of higher-income children (see Figure 2).[10]

Income Matters (Figure 2)

*The presence of troubled peers in school lowered achieve-
ment and increased behavioral problems among students
as a whole. For students from low-income families, these
effects were concentrated on behavior rather than on
achievement, while the opposite was true for children
from higher-income families.*

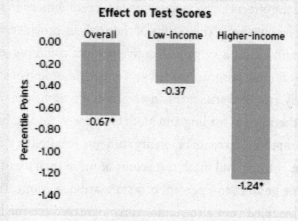

Effect on Test Scores

Effect on Disciplinary Infractions

Note: The bars in both charts represent the causal effect of adding one
troubled student to a classroom of 20 students. * indicates that the
effect is statistically significant at the 5 percent level or greater.
SOURCE: Authors' calculations

Figure 2

Understanding the real effect of student disruption on the entire school community dramatically underscores why this issue is so germane to school, teaching, and student academic improvement throughout the country.

Staff were informed that the handling of those subsequent student discipline referrals by the school administration would follow a graduated process put in place to deal individually with each referral in a comprehensive fashion that included a conference and parent contact. The offending student might be given a written assignment that allowed the student to reflect on his or her behavior and how such behavior was counter to our prominent schoolwide established goals. The offender could always count on completing a written apology to the teacher—a healthy idea, no matter how sincere or insincere on the part of the student, as it allowed the student to think about what he or she had done; to reflect on one's misbehavior and to express remorse is a humbling, useful character-building activity for anyone. Offending students might also be assigned lunch detention or after-school detention, depending on the infraction. These youngsters could receive a lengthier detention in the way of a Friday Twilight School (3:00 to 6:00 p.m.) or a Saturday School (8:00 a.m. to 12 noon). Misbehaving youngsters may be provided a mediation, when warranted, between or among students. A conference with the teacher and administrator may be required, and where appropriate, may involve a school guidance counselor, pupil personnel worker (PPW-- our link between the school and home, a school system staff worker familiar with outside agencies and community service providers that might assist homes), pupil psychologist, or in-school alternative education coordinator. Unless the offense was egregious enough to warrant an out-of-school suspension or a referral to school system headquarters, you could bet that any misbehaving youngster (and often his or her parent/guardian) was afforded the services of some very fine professionals and given multiple chances to turn the behavior around before being suspended or referred for school system alternative education placement.

Throughout the years I was in the profession, we would make use of older student peers to assist the younger disruptive student in attitude adjustment, another intervention among options in the attempt to keep youngsters in schools and help them to make better decisions. We established meaningful, substantive, comprehensive protocols absent previously and all too often lacking in many schools today.

I informed the staff of my view that a good portion of public education is about connections and partnerships, one of the set of values (along with the focus on instruction and continuous improvement) that I referenced in our initial welcome back meeting a few days earlier. There are numerous avenues for creating formal and informal partnerships, both at the administrative and teaching levels. On that particular morning, I was focusing on teachers specifically making connections with their students. I stated that when I interviewed our newer teachers, they recall that I wanted to know how much they knew about their subject area, as well as the extent to which they had a passion for teaching that subject to youngsters. That was important, of course; so was their ability to connect with students. Among the comments that teachers and staff who've worked with me over the years might say that they have heard me emphasize on more than one occasion is that "Students don't care how much you know until they know how much you care." Being the one in any classroom with a college degree(s) does not guarantee you respect; kindness and compassion to others, as well as commanding and giving respect will see the cherubs under your charge very much wanting to show you that they care.

Years ago, as a high school English teacher, I came across a brief sketch that I believed was poignant and insightful. For years, I thought it was anonymous and later learned it was penned by a former teacher in 1937. I framed it and hung it in my classroom. It followed me for over thirty years, hanging on my office wall in every school community where I served to the very day I retired as school principal. It always reminded me that the relationships we build with our students is well-nigh the single most important factor in our effectiveness as educators:

> I have taught high school for ten years. During that time, I have given assignments, among others, to a murderer, an evangelist, a pugilist, a thief, and an imbecile.
>
> The murderer was a quiet little boy who sat on the front seat and regarded me with pale blue eyes; the evangelist, easily the most popular boy in school, had the lead in the junior play; the pugilist lounged by the window and let loose at intervals a raucous laugh that startled even the geraniums; the thief was a gay-hearted Lothario with a song on his lips; and the imbecile, a soft-eyed little animal seeking the shadows.
>
> The murderer awaits death in the state penitentiary; the evangelist has lain a year now in the village churchyard; the pugilist lost an eye in a brawl in Hong Kong; the thief, by standing on tiptoe, can see the windows of my room from the county jail; and the once gentle-eyed little moron beats his head against a padded wall in the state asylum.
>
> All of these pupils once sat in my room, sat and looked at me gravely across worn brown desks.

I must have been a great help to those pupils—I taught them the rhyming scheme of the Elizabethan sonnet and how to diagram a complex sentence.[11]

There is simply no downside to connecting with students. It's not about making friends with students, which I believe is naïve, immature, and wrongheaded; youngsters generally have more than enough friends at school. What students need is a role model, someone who knows his or her subject well, has a passion for it, and tries to communicate and connect with students on a daily basis. You enhance your chances greatly to cultivate a meaningful, enriching teaching-learning environment when you establish meaningful connections with students. The more actively engaged students are in your classroom, the more intellectual stimulation and growth they will derive, as the majority of students are serious enough and want to learn. Those who are immature, are not as well raised as their peers, or generally have a proclivity to act out are less likely to do so, less inclined to be a disrupter to teaching and learning, when they feel the teacher "gets" them or otherwise shows daily that they, too, matter. My hope, I advised them, was that all staff members, both in and out of the classroom, would see the beauty in each individual student under their charge just as vigorously as they would reject inappropriate, disrespectful, or disruptive behavior.

I mentioned the idea of being a role model, and on that note, I asked that they be conscious of my earlier mention of "broken windows" and watch how they spoke, how they acted, and how they carried themselves. I wanted us to reinforce those characteristics in our students, as well. This was *our school*, where we worked every day, every week. I asked them to care about how our building looked, and I reminded them that I hoped they would care about those who occupied this building daily. They were to use appropriate English when speaking, being cognizant of correct usage, and to remind students as they heard them make mistakes. As they heard students use bad language, they were to remind students that "they are better than that." Vulgarity is highly inappropriate and hastens the coarsening of our culture to ignore—and thereby accept—the incorrect, offensive language that too often passes for communication today. I advised them that if they saw trash on the floor, it was appropriate to pick it up; if they noticed an item on the floor suitable to be touched and near a student, they should ask the youngster to pick it up and dispose of it. Yes, we had custodial staff who would routinely "run" the floors (or they would—and did—starting that year) throughout the day, but it was a courtesy that we could extend as thoughtful and caring staff members and students. The more students saw how their teachers and other adults carried themselves, the more they might understand what it was that made for good behavior, and they just might begin to think about how they treated one another.

We've all seen it throughout the profession, individual teachers and other staff members over the years whose ability to connect with students impacted those youngsters' trajectory of academic achievement and their social well-being. I would argue that teachers also gain immeasurably when, over their tenure, they can state that they genuinely cared for and were able to connect with and reach so many of our youth.

Staff members were advised to connect with students and provide them a reason to arrive early and ready for class daily. Students would feel invited, warm, safe, and part of the learning process. They might be bright, or they might be among those who struggled for their grades; no matter, having a good relationship with teachers is often critical for a youngster's academic success, and as professional teachers, the staff must assume that it starts with them. I advised them to make it happen...to make the attempt, and never stop trying.

The end of the week saw me meet with the faculty once more before opening day the following week. We assembled just after lunch for a few minutes, and it gave me the opportunity to clarify additional school system or board of education policies. The teachers appeared organized and ready to meet with students in their homerooms, a time set aside before the academic day to clarify their daily class schedules and assign individual student school lockers. Teachers would also distribute specific documents that students would need to take home for their parents' signature.

There are any number of times during the day when individuals on school grounds may or may not have business being on school property. Appropriate monitoring and supervision should be a given at all times. Whether in the morning, when you have hundreds of school-age youngsters walking up to the building and/or alighting from school buses, during the day as students make their way to various classes, or at the end of the day, when students are exiting the building to head for home, it is important that there be an adult presence with staff interacting with one another and with students. The assistant principal shared with all staff a list of various duty stations, with assigned names of staff members, so that appropriate supervision was in place throughout the interior and exterior of the building. Such is all too often ignored in schools, an unnecessary and foolish disregard for the safety and security of both children and adults on campus.

Finally, before staff returned to work on their classroom prep, I presented each staff member with a list of instructional leadership standards that this principal and assistant principal—the administrative team—would commit to and to which they could hold us accountable. Just as they committed to specific behaviors that would enhance student instructional success, I made a commitment to them, to the school community, that we as an administrative team would demonstrate, and to which we expected to be held account-able, specific standards of instructional leadership. It read as follows:

Principal's Commitment to the HCMS Community

As we continue to forge ahead in advancing student achievement, know that this administrative team is committed to the following standards (NAESP 2001) of instructional leadership:

- Lead HCMS in a way that places student learning and adult learning at the center
- Set high standards for the academic and social development of all students and the performance of adults
- Demand content and instruction that ensures student achievement of agreed-upon academic standards
- Create a culture of continuous learning for adults tied to student learning and our other school goals for the coming years, using multiple sources of data as diagnostic tools to assess, identify, and apply instructional improvement
- Actively engage the community to create shared responsibility for student and school success

I informed the staff that I would ask that they complete—anonymously—a midyear and end-of-year evaluation of my performance and adherence to these standards.

We ended the meeting with ice cream for the faculty and staff, a chance to mingle and chat with one another, after which they returned to prepare their classrooms, some asking if they might stay past the end of the workday so they could continue with their classroom and curriculum preparation.

6

Opening Week for Students

The first day of the school year is always exciting, if not frenetic. Given this school's condition and recent history, I was not alone in looking forward to greeting our students, while at the same time feeling a bit of disquiet and angst. Any misgivings, however, were outweighed by our solid preparation, organization, and a comfort level I had with my educational philosophy and what I believed constituted a successful school. We were ready to accept the hundreds of students, as well as those parents and youngsters new to the school community and interested in registering their children for the academic school year.

We had staff on duty outside the building and throughout the interior. I was out front of the building, greeting students and parents, and generally observing and surveying the area to look at the logistics of accepting several hundred youngsters walking to school or stepping off a number of school buses that were arriving. Faculty and staff were greeting and chatting with students. I had asked key staff members prior to the opening first week to position themselves in the hallways, and as the late bell rang for each class, assist in ensuring that the hallways and bathrooms—all day, every day of the week—were clear before they proceeded to other activities. If they identified any student known in previous years as a "haller," they were asked to bring that particular student to me immediately, at which time I would have a "chat" with that youngster.

Just off the far parking lot, I could see a couple or so Citizens on Patrol members, the volunteer folks who were monitoring the various paths to the school. It was not yet time for students to enter the building, and the voices were loud with excitement, gathering about the front entranceway with youngsters talking about their summer activities, trying to determine whether friends were in the same classes, and making positive comments about the new landscaping, the beautiful crepe myrtle and cherry trees, and our American flag atop our flagpole.

The tone indicating the start of Homeroom had not yet sounded, when a scuffle and a couple incidents saw students—and a parent—being directed to the school's main office. I directed one injured student to the nurse, asking a secretary to contact the youngster's parent; the youngster with whom he had been fighting was placed in another office. I escorted the other youngster and his parent to my office. The assistant principal walked in with yet another student, well known to the staff, who was caught stealing a staff member's purse, and with it sixty dollars.

As the tone rang, indicating that the school building could be entered, students were directed to their appropriate homeroom (sometimes called advisory) classrooms, described earlier as a teacher's classroom in which attendance is taken, general announcements for the day are made, various forms are distributed to and collected from students, and student locker assignments were to be made. Students who were not certain where they belonged were directed to another area, where they could receive a copy of their schedule. Parents and families new to the community and wishing to register their children for the school year were directed to the school registrar.

I was approached by staff (both black and white) regarding disparaging remarks that had been made in the faculty lounge just moments earlier by a prominent black community member who was serving that day as a substitute teacher; she had been subbing at the school for years. I asked one of the office secretaries to page her to the main office so I could discuss the issue and get her take on the matter. She confirmed that she had, indeed, made the racially charged and insensitive remark, one that she said she had also placed in writing weeks earlier to the local board of education. Then she stated that if there was nothing else, she had students in a classroom waiting for her. I surmised quickly that she was a bitter, dismissive hump, and in my view, a negative influence around her peers and our school-age youngsters. As busy as we were at that moment, I had neither the time nor the inclination to entertain what appeared to me to be her ingrained, years-old, narrowminded, and destructive views about race and life in America; I knew at that moment she would be leaving the building and the grounds. She would have to observe from the outside the advances that could be made among people of every color and ethnicity who understand the importance of character, of goodness, of checking and examining one's biases, and, in this case, of focusing on avenues that advance teacher and student success without politics or personal animus.

I asked her to hold up a moment and allow me to page the assistant principal, whose responsibility was to acquire substitutes for any given day. As the AP arrived, I informed her that we would need to obtain another substitute teacher for the classes that had been assigned to this particular substitute standing next to me. I immediately and matter-of-factly informed that morning's sub that she was being dismissed—fired, as it were—that she was never again to step foot in this building. I then directed the AP to escort her out of the building. I still recall the expression on the AP's face when the sub began raising her voice, saying she would not leave. I calmly informed her that such was her decision, but if she did not leave immediately, she would soon leave with a county police escort. She left, and I asked the AP, along with my secretary, to ensure that the classes were covered with volunteer teaching staff giving up a portion of their planning periods, until a new emergency substitute teacher arrived. Staff members throughout the day thanked me, saying that the woman had been a thorn in their sides for years, routinely creating mischief and sowing seeds of racial disharmony. She would be the first of several folks over the years whom I would have removed from Harper's Choice.

Not a half hour later did I receive a call from the same school system director who'd hung up on me earlier in the summer. She was upset with my decision, telling me that the individual I'd just fired had been a "pillar" in the community for years and was a fine substitute teacher. I expressed my disappointment to hear her take on the individual, that it was abundantly clear to me that the lady was a "poison." I shared further that I intended to address the matter with school system human resources, because I thought it inappropriate for her to work in any school anywhere in the county. Not surprisingly, the director hung the phone up on me again.

It struck me that the behavior of the individual on the other end of the telephone was indicative of why schools and school districts were often so unsuccessful, causing so many teaching staff to leave the profession and so many parents to withdraw their youngsters from public schools annually. Among the challenging aspects of a long career in public education was the repeated incompetency exhibited by the many unserious people in decision-making positions, from superintendents and education board members to directors and principals, people who regularly made unwise decisions and nauseatingly tolerated abysmally poor behavior from students and the equally unprofessional and incompetent performance of teaching staff within the profession, and who generally made life difficult for the many well-behaved students and solidly professional and caring staff in and out of the classroom.

I stopped by my office to advise the parent and youngster that I would need a few more minutes to use the public address system and welcome students to the new academic year. Once on the PA, I asked everyone to stand as I recited the Pledge of Allegiance. I then made several introductory announcements and advised everyone that the school administration would plan to meet with each grade level the first week of school. I shared that I hoped they enjoyed their first day of school, and that I was looking forward to everyone enjoying a successful academic year.

I returned to my office to address the issues involving the parent and his son, and the father's inappropriate deportment, as described by a guidance counselor. The bottom line was that the parent apologized. Both were directed to leave the school and grounds for the day; the father could return the following day to register his son.

I met with the volunteers who manned the trails leading to the school to discuss the issue of young high-school-age males loitering, harassing, and attempting to sell their dope to students walking to their respective schools—elementary, middle, and high school.

I then called the police to discuss the issue and met an officer assigned to the community, someone who would become a longtime professional associate and friend. He worked our area and welcomed the fact that the new school principal was willing to work meaningfully with the department to deal with the destructive behavioral issues that plagued the community. He was a black male, a positive role model who knew our kids and families, and he eventually mentored many of our students. He and other officers over the years lamented that so many schools, in their view, were ill-run, with administrators, on the one hand, portraying a positive view of the importance of a working relationship with the police, while in reality tolerating repeated student bad behavior, sometimes criminal offenses, that were frequently kept hidden from the police; moreover, the officers contended that, in some cases, the police were frequently made to feel unwelcome on school grounds. I held an opposing view. I always felt it was a useful and good thing to partner with various members of the community, including our first responders, and they had an open invitation to come to the school, chat with the staff, and eat with the students in our cafeteria. The local fire department would occasionally conduct area checks, confirming the location of fire hydrants and standpipe connections (vertical piping in multistory buildings to which fire hoses can be connected), reviewing and confirming addresses and street names, taking note of any temporary construction that might prevent access, and the like throughout their first-due area; they, too, were invited to stop by occasionally to check out the building or chat it up with kids during the lunch hour. They, the staff, or parents might be seen conducting business with me in the cafeteria during lunchtime, where throughout the school year, for some nine years, I usually could be found sitting and eating with students, during the sixth-, seventh-, or eighth-grade lunch hour on alternating days. I frequently chose to sit with students who appeared to be sitting by themselves, striking up a conversation as we ate. Other students would lean toward me from another table to engage in conversation; when I would feign like I couldn't understand them, they would wind up moving to our table and eating with me and the student who had previously been sitting alone. I would later tell the sometimes-more-popular students that it wouldn't hurt for them to acknowledge students who were sitting by themselves in the cafeteria, maybe even inviting them to his or her table. Almost all students would reply, "Alright, cool, Mr. Wallis." As the school years progressed, it became not at all uncommon occasionally to see a police officer or firefighter whom the students knew sitting, eating, and chatting with them during their lunch periods.

Another word on police-school relations: The police take a fair amount of undue criticism, and I don't doubt there are times when criticism can be shared both ways. When working with the police, a school principal should want someone who cares about youngsters, is good at his or her job, understands the workings of a public school, and genuinely wants to work in concert with school administration and staff for everyone's welfare. Having served in a number of busy demographic school communities for many years, I never observed or had reported to me that an officer had abused his or her authority. When an officer is alleged to have been more abrupt or tough with anyone, it is generally because the individual has run afoul of the law and has acted in a way that warranted the officer's action. Like any profession, there will be those who abuse their authority and ignore protocols. My experience and the research I have read over the years indicate that such is rare; I certainly hope so. The police can be and generally are valuable, reliable partners with school administrators, working in collaboration with the school and community in maintaining a safe and secure school campus, as well as helping to provide knowledge, experience, and a caring connection with students, teaching staff, and parents in communities throughout the country.

At the end of the first day, I strolled over to the parking lot area where the trails to various neighborhood areas began and where my senior monitors were present. I respectfully informed those who were up to no good that they were *persona non grata* and they were not to hang about the school grounds any longer. I suspected some of them were high school students, so I called the nearby high school administration, requesting they make a schoolwide announcement that students were to steer clear of Harper's Choice Middle or risk being charged with trespassing. There were the customary hardheads, but our persistence in supervising the areas, the continuing daily appearance of the volunteer adults along the paths, as well as the steady appearance of officers, eventually cleared the areas that for quite some time had seen youngsters and other community folks hassled, followed, and at times assaulted or robbed of their possessions.

I thought about the hundreds of students gathered out front of the school building on the morning of opening day—walkers, bus students, and those cherubs dropped off by their parents. Such had been the scene for years—no different from almost all other schools—but I didn't like it. I preferred to see a more orderly way of supervising so many members of our student body. In the late afternoon, I called the bus contractors, the owners of those buses carrying HCMS students to and from school, to inquire how tight the morning pickup schedules were and whether they would be willing to keep their youngsters on the buses upon morning arrival until the tone sounded indicating everyone could enter the school. Most were amenable to the idea, but I recall a robust conversation with two or three of them who were not initially onboard with the idea. However, given that I knew the drivers had enough time available each morning to make their next school pickups—and I was adamant about the concern for the overall safety of students and staff—they eventually agreed. It made all the difference in the many mornings of those remaining years for me to be able comfortably to observe, to assist, and generally to supervise the many youngsters who arrived each day for school.

As the week continued, I took the opportunity to call together and speak directly with students, each grade level separately escorted to the cafeteria by their respective teachers. The school had gone through considerable turmoil, and a meeting with the administrative team was an appropriate avenue for students to meet the school's new principal and assistant principal up front and close. I took a quick minute or so to introduce myself and mention my family, my experience, and my interests. I welcomed the sixth-graders and clarified some differences between their former elementary schools and life now as middle school students. The seventh- and eighth-graders had a different experience than their younger classmates, because they had witnessed and experienced a previous, less-than-wholesome educational experience at Harper's Choice Middle, which, I was certain, at times had seemed chaotic. That was confirmed when I asked for their opinions of the school and their experience. I informed them that those days, those negative previous experiences, were now behind us, and I assured them the school would operate differently—that I wanted every youngster to feel safe, welcomed, and successful at Harper's Choice; they mattered, each and every one of them, I told them. I also informed them that I expected students to be on time to every class; no one was to be seen in the school hallway without his or her agenda book pass, an organizational note-keeping book we provided to each student.

I then introduced the word *character* to them, and after inviting them to tell me what they knew about the word, I clarified that the soul of the school, the most important aspect of Harper's Choice Middle School from that moment forward, was all about *character*. How we spoke, how we carried ourselves, and any major decisions the principal and staff made, would be based on character traits like respect, courage, perseverance, compassion, dignity, honesty, and hard work. Harper's Choice would be about teamwork, a positive attitude, and high morale among students and staff, because from there on out, I reminded them, everyone counted, everyone mattered. I would provide strong leadership, and we would correct those issues they had mentioned moments earlier—the disrespectful behavior, fighting, bullying, cursing, running in the hallways, butting in line, and stealing. I affirmed to them that we would correct every bit of that nonsense. All of us would learn to adapt to a new environment, a healthy place that valued every individual, as well as hard work, honesty, fair play, self-discipline, responsibility, and caring for others. I reminded them that I would need their individual and collective assistance so the entire school community would benefit. In the grade-level audiences, I saw the familiar faces of the youngsters I'd recently met and eaten lunch with at the nearby fast-food restaurant.

I informed students to step to the plate and get involved in performing well at Harper's Choice, emphasizing that this was the time to begin focusing on their own academic and behavioral performance that would lead to success throughout their school years. I advised them to "Avoid the Urge to Be Average," reminding them that "If you believe it, you will achieve it." The fact is, we had some terrific students attending Harper's Choice, and on more than a few occasions over the years, I would take a moment to thank their parents for doing such a wonderful job in raising these youngsters.

I then made mention of a years-ago student questionnaire that some of them might recall completing when they were attending elementary school.[1] It was part of a research project that the school system had conducted, administered to over twenty thousand students—low-, average-, and high-achieving youngsters, elementary grades through high school, throughout the entire school district. The various responses came from the perspective of the students. Whether they were commenting on their school, their academic performance level, or how engaged their parents were in their schooling, the report contained the students' individual perspectives about how they saw themselves as students. I found it interesting, if not insightful, and I had made some notes at the time. I would, over the years, share the youngsters' perspectives and research conclusions with staff, students, and parents at the high school level. Some of the findings were not surprising, but I found them reaffirming. I informed the youngsters that, for example, students who valued learning, who had high expectations, who were committed, and who worked hard at acquiring knowledge generally earned A/B grades and did well on standardized tests, *regardless of their race or economic situation.*[2] I repeated this fact to them; they were paying attention, and I wanted them to absorb these findings. Everyone in the school was capable of learning and excelling at Harper's Choice Middle; it did not matter what a student looked like or where they lived—everyone could achieve here, and that was my expectation from there on out.

The youngsters were advised that student success required them to accept responsibility for their own learning by demonstrating academic value, expectation, and commitment behaviors. The three went together. Saying that you value education and have high academic expectations but doing little to make it happen will not result in the attainment of your desired or expected outcomes. Students must follow through with the academic behaviors that support their belief statements. We discussed so-called commitment behaviors, and they made a commitment that day that all students would arrive to school on time, be respectful, complete their homework, ask teachers for any help they needed, and at all times, value their fortune in attending what would become one of the finest schools in the nation, because I counted on them to help me make that happen.

The content and ideas I shared in my meetings with them would also be elaborated upon further by their teachers in a different block of time, several minutes, for each grade level that we incorporated into their daily schedule, called Academic Enrichment, or AE. We would use this time to complement our instructional program. As an example, I would soon designate a first-rate teacher to coordinate and lead the effort to design *character* lesson plans for all teachers to present during their grade-level AE periods, which would see students learn individual character traits. We would incorporate a "Gotcha" reward program, periodically citing individual students who were candidly "caught" demonstrating a specific character trait. Their picture would be taken with the school principal and placed on a school corridor bulletin board citing various character traits; they'd also receive a school-monogrammed T-shirt, lanyard, or sweatshirt.

The grade-level meetings also saw me introducing our new school motto, citing high-quality teaching, active parental involvement, and student behavior/academic excellence; importantly, I told them, we would entertain *no excuses* for anything less than what we cited in our motto. Students also learned that, starting that school year, they would have to sign out and back in when they requested to be excused from a classroom to use the restroom; any time they were out of class, they were to have their student agenda book or a readily identified classroom pass with their teacher's name on it. I shared the student code of conduct and clarified that a school of character expected to see good conduct on the part of its students. I spent several minutes discussing the issue of bullying (on which I elaborate further in the book) and the fact that there would be zero tolerance for such behavior.

Just as I had with school staff, I shared with the students the importance of making one's bed in the morning. I wanted to introduce the kids to the idea of waking up each day with purpose and a healthy routine that would build self-discipline. I advised them that some families might require it as part of receiving one's allowance, that making their bed first thing already saw them achieving an accomplishment, allowing them to go on to their next assignment, all the while building a habit for accomplishing tasks, including those associated with school and academic success. I introduced the broken windows theory and clarified that they would be expected to display quality-of-life, successful school behaviors— committing themselves to behavior and academic success, practicing self-discipline, respecting one another, attending class daily, arriving to class on time, raising their hand in class, walking—never running—in school corridors, keeping a respectful tone of voice, and caring and helping one another. These are the kinds of smaller, basic, but all-important everyday behaviors that would see students avoiding the larger ill behaviors that had once scarred our school community. Practicing such self-discipline would see all students enjoying that much more personal success, behaviorally and academically. The idea, again, was to clarify to the youngsters that we were all in this together, that each of us needed to care about others, demonstrating *cura personalis*, or "care for the whole person," and to extend a helping hand to fix any "broken windows" in the lives of our friends and classmates.

The importance of staff connecting with students cannot be overemphasized. Among the benefits is the fact that students are often our quickest, strongest sources of information that something is awry with an individual or clique of students, including bullying or other matters that might be occurring on school grounds, in the community, or online. I wanted students to know how important it was for them to contact a school staff member immediately—in private, if preferred—should they become aware of or concerned about the emotional state or behavior of any student or group.

I went on to explain and clarify various district-wide and HCMS-specific rules and regulations, as well as how discipline would be handled. I ended with a discussion of values: the standards or characteristics deemed important that all of us—both children and adults—should exhibit daily, in and out of school. These included that family is of fundamental importance, that honesty is always the best policy, that trust has to be earned, and that they needed to begin believing in themselves; these values would go hand in hand with our emphasis on character. They would hear me often say to them, as cited earlier, "If you believe it, you will achieve it." At times they would find accomplishing something particularly challenging; at those times, I informed them, they would need to work harder and continue to believe that they would achieve their goals. The idea of "not ringing the bell" would soon make its way around the neighborhood (see the next chapter for clarification). Further, I advised students that our emphasis on *character* and practicing positive core values every day would reinforce healthy guiding principles that would make each of us the best that we could be in life.

The students were generally attentive and appeared to understand the overall message their school principal was conveying. I referred to the American flag, specifically our new beautiful American flag, sharing that it was more than threads or cloth or material, that it symbolized the very fabric of our country. It stood for the many Americans who came from all walks of life, and especially those who gave their lives for our freedom and our nation. I wanted them to realize the special significance of the new flag in front of the school. I would ask specific individual students from time to time to assist school staff, usually the custodian, in raising the flag in the morning. They were kids, after all, and I was certain some students weren't totally on board, but the vast majority appeared genuinely interested, were respectful, and understood that our new flag stood for something really special. I would go on throughout the years, in my daily morning and afternoon end-of-day announcements, to make reference to issues of importance that might not otherwise be explained to our youngsters in or out of school, including clarifying the significance of various national holidays—on Veterans Day, for example, being sure to mention the names of any staff, who served our country. Always at the end of the school day on Fridays throughout my tenure I would remind students to do their chores, to express their love to a family member, and to return the following Monday with a positive, can-do attitude, always prepared to give their best effort to succeed.

The idea was to make the school community more familial, to recognize the goodness of our country, to promote a shared American identity that has seemingly been lost in education today, to be appreciative and thankful for what we have in life, and to emphasize that we are all family. This approach, rooted in sincerity, worked well throughout all the years I spent in that community, and it all started with those initial meetings with students so many years earlier, continuing for the near-ten years I was their principal. The connections we would make—and the emphasis on family, hard work, courage, self-respect, perseverance, compassion, respect for others, responsibility, self-discipline, the fact that nothing replaces hard work—were, much as it might be hard to believe, new to many, if not to the vast majority of these youngsters, and they generally very much liked the idea of living and learning in such an environment. It was up to me as their school principal—up to us as a community—to ensure that we lived by our motto daily. Only then would we be able to cultivate substantively a culture for teaching and learning that would lead the student body and their teachers down the path to academic excellence—and we would go on to do just that.

We were just a few days into the new academic year when the manager of an area supermarket came to the school asking to speak with me. He was frustrated with the continuing bad behavior, loitering, and stealing by students, as well as the belligerent, threatening behavior of their parents at the store adjacent to the school—this was a large, well-known supermarket chain. He said he had tried over the last few years to elicit the help of police and school administrators at this school and other school sites in the area, but to no avail. He had recently met with the supermarket corporate regional director, who advised they were considering closing the store. It had opened years earlier after another major store was shuttered because of similar concerns. I asked him if the police substation in the shopping center had provided any assistance, and he responded that it was often empty, and his pleas had been met with indifference. I suppose I furrowed my brow, when I told him I would walk with him back to the shopping center as we discussed the matter further. As we entered the supermarket, I noted a police cruiser nearby. I told him I would stop at the police substation and return with an officer shortly.

It turned out there was an officer present in the substation, and I introduced myself, explaining the problems the store manager shared with me. I asked if he had a few minutes that would allow him to join me in the store to discuss how we might tackle the ongoing problem, but he advised me he was busy at the moment. I then asked if he'd mind contacting his duty officer—usually an officer holding rank that is seen as one's supervisor for a particular shift—regarding the issue. The duty officer turned out to be a lieutenant with whom I had worked years earlier, when I was a high school administrator. We exchanged pleasantries, and I shared with him the challenges that the store manager was confronting on a daily basis, that the manager had requested an assist from me. I shared that I requested that the substation officer accompany me to the store so we might review the matter, but the officer stated that he was busy and wouldn't have time to lend an assist, when the lieutenant asked to speak to the officer. Seconds later the officer hung up the phone and said, "Mr. Wallis, I apologize. I'm yours." I thanked him and said, "Let's do this." We walked over and entered the store to discuss next steps with the manager. When we looked at the bank of cameras in the store, we noticed some that were not operating effectively. I asked the manager to review and ensure that the system was working well, then asked that he print out photographs of those involved in stealing or loitering, youngsters he thought attended our school, as well as share with the elementary and high schools the photographs of students he thought might attend those schools. I told him I would contact and discuss the problem with the area school administrators. The officer was not certain that he had a standard "no trespass" letter that the manager might use, so I offered to draft such a letter for the manager that he could issue to the miscreants. The store would also share with the police the photographs and, if known, the identities of those adults who were stealing or verbally threatening store employees. The officer affirmed that he and his department would respond to the store manager's calls for assistance, attempt to identify any scofflaws, and file appropriate charges accordingly.

I contacted the state's attorney's office to discuss student criminal behavior on the way to and from school, including bullying, stealing from commercial establishments, loitering, and physical assault. I inquired if they would support my argument that students on the way to and from school could well be held accountable to me, should they elect to involve themselves in such behavior. I received the state's attorney's enthusiastic support, and I then shared this information with the entire student body and parents via the school newsletter that I was in the process of revamping and writing. Students were reminded that they were attending a school of character, a new and improved Harper's Choice Middle School, with the expectation that they would carry themselves responsibly and respectfully on and off school grounds. Henceforth, no student was to enter the supermarket without being accompanied by a parent or responsible adult, and anyone ignoring this warning risked being charged by the county police and would have to be picked up by a parent or guardian at the district police station. Further, the school would also take appropriate follow-up disciplinary action. I explained this new policy, as well, in the parent newsletter sent throughout the community. Parents had been disillusioned with the school for several years, but this was seen as a positive and caring "wake-up call," as one parent noted to me. It was welcomed by the vast majority of the school's constituency. The few folks who objected—black/white, rich/poor—were those whose kids were known problems for the school and the community at large. I advised those parents that, while I respected their right to voice their displeasure, I still expected their youngsters to comply, and I would expect and appreciate their support. Once the first two or three arrests were made, and parents were inconvenienced by having to take time from work or home to retrieve their kids from the county's southern district police station, they complained about it, but the thievery and the loitering soon all but disappeared; the store manager could not have been happier. He could not thank me enough, saying things like, "You're like that guy from New Jersey" (referring to Joe Clark, the bat-wielding school principal from Patterson High School, a problem-plagued New Jersey school that the principal had tried to turn around years earlier). While I appreciated his sentiments, I hoped most folks saw me as taking a caring, inclusive, and comprehensive approach...and one that was a bit more subtle, I dare say, than Mr. Clark's, although I am not at all a critic of the gentleman—I'm certain he had the best of intentions and made his school much safer for most of his students because of his actions. Weeks later, the store would return the favor with a terrific gesture.

On a separate note, the school restrooms had always been a problem area in our school—as it is for many schools in general. They are frequently vandalized or defaced with graffiti. On my arrival to the school, I was able to get some immediate attention paid to these areas, including new hardware, repaired toilet seats, and fresh coats of paint. At the start of the academic year, I asked custodians from the outset to add a particular routine to their daily schedule. Every hour, on the hour, they were to check the bathrooms, noting on a clipboard whether they were clean or vandalized. On the occasion they noticed vandalism, we could ask the staff to identify any students who had been released from the classroom for whatever reason, including bathroom use, and attempt to identify those responsible.

I look back with amusement at a tactic we used to try to maintain cleaner female bathrooms, as well. During the school year, individual females would enter a bathroom between classes and use lipstick to write on bathroom mirrors, frequently blotting their lips and kissing the mirrors. I asked a female custodian to enter one of these bathrooms with a cleaning rag and squeegee at a time she knew there were several girls present. She was to greet the youngsters and act as though she routinely dipped her cleaning rag in toilet water before she squeegeed the mirrors clean, and then proceed to walk out. I told her to give it a week or so and give me an update. At that time, she smiled and reported that restroom mirrors thereafter had not only remained clean, but she noted that the bathroom stalls also had fewer, if any, instances of graffiti. Problem solved.

7

Game On!

We were into the academic year, the days were busy with a host of issues, and I was mindful of the need to satisfy the school's considerable debt. For years, I had known central office headquarters folks, some of whom with children who attended high schools where I had been assigned, and they were kind enough to convey their respect for my work. I capitalized on those connections to ask, from time to time, how I might obtain funding for various ideas, and frequently they knew how to tap into a particular funding source, always ethical, always above board, but not necessarily known to other administrators. Money was already tight, and we owed several thousand dollars to the state governor's office for the previous year's mismanaged after-school funding grant, which I alluded to earlier. The state had made it clear that the money would need to be returned, and their view was that it was not their problem that the issue had not occurred on my watch; they still expected repayment. I understood, and some school system contacts did lend an appreciative hand; the remaining funds were derived via steady PTA–school administration combined fund-raising efforts.

At this juncture, there were several organizational elements in play, such as a school improvement plan, schoolwide goals, an established focused direction, and meaningful committees to look at teaching, learning, and student behavior. These elements had previously been shoddy, ineffective, or virtually absent, which had negatively impacted the school's instructional program and the emotional-social component of our students. Although we felt good about our new focus, our direction, our priorities, the connections we were making, the accountability, and the effective instructional components that were in place, we were nonetheless awash in daily time-consuming issues surrounding student ill behavior.

Looking back, I shake my head at the level of poor conduct and disorder exhibited daily in this school and community. Throughout the country, there continues to be an acceptance by the public of poor deportment, often viewing it as normal and simply to be tolerated. Such was certainly the case in this community among the teaching staff, school system officials, and many parents. I was reminded of the term "defining deviancy down," coined in 1993 by former New York senator Patrick Moynihan in a piece on the subject that appeared in the *American Spectator*. His thesis was that, as a society, America had been "redefining deviancy" so as to exempt conduct previously stigmatized, while simultaneously and quietly raising the "normal" level for behavior that was considered abnormal by earlier standards.[1] He was right, in my view, and I think in the view of many Americans today.

We have, in fact, redefined deviancy and general poor conduct, accepting poor personal behavior today that would have been found completely unacceptable years ago, the idea being "that each generation is more tolerant than the one that preceded it of behaviors considered outside the norm."[2] Society's progressively lowering its standard of what is regarded as acceptable behavior has been pervasive throughout America and no less observed all too frequently in our schools, and—I will add—to our own peril. I have made the observation for a number of years that among the majority of hardworking, respectful, responsible, and successful students who came through my high school English classes or with whom I came in contact in my years as an administrator and principal, there were far too many other students of every race and socioeconomic level, who were among a generation seemingly raising themselves, almost feral in the manner in which they carried themselves, wholly unhealthy, I always thought, for American society. Robert Woodson Sr. is a former civil rights activist and founder of The Woodson Center, an organization that helps residents of low-income neighborhoods wrestle with and address the sundry problems plaguing such communities throughout the United States. He references an American society "moral break-away that has become a virtual spiritual free-fall for a generation without a foundation of guiding principles."[3]

I was aghast at the number of school and school district officials who, over some thirty-five years, routinely thought such misconduct was simply part of schooling, and that to deal with such behavior in any manner, no matter how appropriate or logical, was inappropriate if it upset the parents of ill-behaved children or the misbehaving students themselves. Imagine—they thought it was not fair to those very families causing the disruption! They and their ilk across the nation were, and are, not just wrong; they smugly propound the very opposite of what has always been, and is today, true: They seemingly do not get that teaching and learning must be inviolate, and that those students—and their parents/guardians—who routinely hold complete disregard for respectful behavior, civility, and the dignity of others cannot be allowed to continue that kind of deportment in our schools. Rarely, if ever, do such benighted school officials or school board members—locally or nationally—ever express a concern for the rights of the majority of the well-behaved students and their hardworking teaching staff.

I share this perspective on the importance of a school's appropriate teaching-learning environment, because the principal's first priority is, in fact, to provide a safe and secure schoolhouse for the community's youngsters and professional staff. The reader would be forgiven for feeling that such is hard to believe, given the failing and disruptive condition of so many of our country's K-12 schools. Nonetheless, recognizing that responsibility, as much as any other idea or intervention outlined in the following pages, was responsible for our school's turnaround and academic success. Clearly, that priority is not shared throughout the country, as teachers who leave the profession cite "meagre administrative support" (read school and district administrators, including school board members and policy makers) among the reasons for their dissatisfaction, according to Preeti Varathan, writing in a June 2018 article appearing in the global digital-only news publication Quartz. Overall, around 8 percent of teachers leave the profession every year, according to the Learning Policy Institute, citing Department of Education data.[4] Think about that statistic: Over the years, with the passing of each academic year, *over one thousand teachers a day leave the teaching profession*, citing among reasons for leaving "student discipline challenges" and "lack of support."[5] Former teachers with whom I've spoken over the years cite a now-familiar refrain they claim to have written on school system human resources exit surveys, saying succinctly, "I didn't like how I was treated." Picture me shaking my head, when thinking about the circumstances that cause educators to suffer embarrassment, or to feel a loss of dignity, such that it results in a decision to quit their job—likely a job to which they always aspired, about which they always dreamed—and knowing that such circumstances could well have been avoided with respected strong leadership and sensible school expectations. It is an unfortunate commentary that so many Americans have come to accept from our schools the poor behavior and equally inferior academic performance that has become standard fare in neighborhoods, cities, and communities across our great country. It makes what the students, staff, and parents accomplished at Harper's Choice all the more exceptional, as we were able to take what was handed to us in the way of ill behavior and failing academic performance and create a first-rate, student-engaged, teacher-respected, parent-proud, and community-appreciated academically strong school setting.

In the same June 2018 *Quartz* article, the author also wrote that teacher turnover can be particularly destabilizing in education.[6] He cites the Learning Policy Institute's report on the toll that teacher turnover takes: "In particular, when turnover contributes to teacher shortages, schools often respond by hiring inexperienced or unqualified teachers, increasing class sizes, or cutting class offerings, all of which impact student learning. Research is clear that both teacher inexperience and rates of turnover negatively affect a student's education, which means that students in schools with high turnover and few experienced teachers are at a decidedly educational disadvantage."[7] A research abstract on this topic, again by the Learning Policy Institute, states that each year, schools nationwide must hire tens of thousands of teachers as a result of beginning and mid-career teachers leaving the profession. It goes on to state the following:

Without changes in current policies, U.S. teacher shortages are projected to grow in the coming years. Teacher turnover is an important source of these shortages.

About 8% of teachers leave the profession each year, two-thirds of them for reasons other than retirement.

Another 8% shift to different schools each year. In addition to aggravating teacher shortages, high turnover rates lower student achievement and are costly to schools.

The research abstract makes this conclusion:

With high turnover rates driving teacher shortages and undermining student learning, policymakers should pursue strategies that can improve teacher retention in all schools, but especially in those where turnover rates are most extreme—namely, schools serving students of color and students in poverty.

By addressing the key factors that drive teachers from their schools, tailored policy interventions can, over time, stabilize and improve the teacher workforce and better serve all students.[8]

Teachers leave the profession in droves; newspapers, periodicals, and newscasts on any given day cite the shoddiness, if not, outright chaos that passes for education in scores of our schools. We know that the reason teachers leave revolves around job dissatisfaction—meaning meager, if any, administrative support and working conditions. A better compensation package is an idea suggested as a way to stem the tide of teachers leaving the profession, and while that might well be a deserving consideration, the teacher turnover crisis is far and away more than about the money. Yet the conclusion of researchers is that "policymakers should pursue strategies that can improve teacher retention in all schools." How 'bout this for a strategy: instill character education in schools and take substantive measures to rid all schools of disrespectful, disruptive, violent behavior; hire outstanding principals and teaching staff; ensure that principals are given appropriate latitude to perform their jobs, including supporting teaching staff; ensure that schools are staffed according to school-specific and community-specific needs (meaning that schools with a busy demographic, including poverty, criminal behavior, disparity of family income—like HCMS—receive a higher grade of staffing in the way of additional teachers for smaller class sizes, more guidance staff, school psychologists) to deal with the various social-emotional issues of students that are far and beyond that which one might encounter in a school located in a more stable community. Replace ineffective principals who cannot promote a positive change in a school's climate, that would otherwise result in increased student academic performance, teaching excellence, and parent satisfaction.

You can well see that a poor school climate can have dreadful ramifications. And you should have a good idea by now of how important I believe it is for schools to operate in a calm, respectful, and professional manner, if top-shelf teaching, academic learning, and student achievement are to occur. Just as a poor school climate will accelerate the degree to which teaching staff will transfer or leave the profession, so, too, will a positive school climate see teaching staff wanting to come to work each morning feeling valued and students who feel that their school is safe, clean, and caring. High expectations for success are far more apt to cause students to put forth the effort to achieve academically. It is true—we watched it occur at "The Choice."

So, there we were, all of us, that first year when I took the helm of Harper's Choice Middle School, right in the middle of a less-than-savory school climate, I decided that we would tackle the ill behavior head-on, up-front and close, if anything remotely resembling academic achievement was going to come to fruition. How would that be done? For starters, no matter how busy or involved I was with a particular issue, dealing with a student behavior issue and returning order immediately to one's classroom instruction was of paramount importance, throughout the school day, every day, every month, every academic year. Such had been my personal belief, my viewpoint at the high school level for years, and it would continue at this school site. My philosophy—*our* philosophy—was that teaching and learning were sacrosanct, and both the assistant principal and I would readily stop what we were doing at any given time to ensure that meaningful instruction would continue. I knew that if we maintained our steady, determined, almost maniacal focus on this issue, we would see a diminution of disrespectful and disruptive student issues. And, in fact, we would eventually experience just that—but not at all soon enough. So, we steadfastly continued the good fight, dealing—more than a few times confrontationally—with students, staff, and parents literally day in, day out, all the while forging full speed ahead with elevating the instructional program; establishing business-school partnerships; and developing cogent, meaningful professional staff development programs.

Each segment of the school community (faculty, staff, students, and parents) felt that previous disciplinary issues, if they had been dealt with at all, were dealt with inconsistently and haphazardly. We instituted a graduated response to disciplinary referrals. Individual student issues would be dealt with in an inclusive, graduated, and comprehensive manner; parent-home communication was an important factor. As the reader will recall, it was expected that after routine intervention by the instructor, including parent contact, any subsequent referrals would be handled by an administrator. It could be that administrative intervention was enough to turn the student around. We made wide use of student mediation to bridge communication and repair ill feelings among students, and at times, their teachers. A general classroom referral always included a student-written apology to the teacher and a parent telephone contact and/or follow-up document sent to the home. A student might be assigned after-school detention, but no matter the disciplinary assignment, each cherub, again, always had to complete a well-written apology to the staff member. Years earlier, at the high school level, I was among those administrators who developed a "Saturday School," similar to that portrayed later in the motion picture *The Breakfast Club*, whereby misbehaving students would report to one of the schools on a Saturday morning, from 8 a.m. until noon for having misbehaved earlier in the week. The program had not reached the middle school level at the time, likely for budget reasons, but I felt such was sorely needed at HCMS, so I used some creative financing within my purview to start the program. I hired a staff member who was looking to make extra money, someone who had a non-indulgent bearing but who was very much able to connect with students. In my version of the program, students would remain silent throughout the detention, unless speaking with school staff. They would need to complete a writing assignment about why they were in detention, how their behavior had gone against our focus on character, how it impacted the teacher's instruction and the student's and other students' learning, as well as cite thoughtful steps the youngster would take to avoid being referred to the main office again for disciplinary reasons. The staff member would review their work, correct grammar usage and spelling errors, and return it to the student for a rewrite before it was accepted. Those students, however, who couldn't meet these expectations, had their parents called to retrieve them, and they would be reassigned to fulfill the next two Saturday School assignments.

The students who refused to attend the Saturday School assignment would see their parents notified, and the disciplinary measure would be doubled. If they chose again not to attend, they were suspended from school, and a conference with a parent would be required before they returned. In many schools, disrespectful, disruptive behavior is met with impunity; the student is simply returned to class, and a parent or guardian may or may not be notified, which is how schools become chaotic. The general public will not be informed of this fact, of course; after all, there are school system policies in place for such disruption. However, those who teach know full well that in reality disruptive behavior is nauseatingly tolerated by school and school system administrators, and that policies are rarely, if ever, followed. Not at Harper's Choice, where character was now the heart of the building and instructional program. The suspension that the misbehaving student incurred was for the insubordination, the choice not to attend the Saturday assignment; the double Saturday school assignment still had to be fulfilled by the student upon his or her return to school.

The Saturday morning program was effective, but it wasn't enough, so we put in place a Friday afternoon "twilight school" for those "cherubs" who still couldn't behave themselves. They would remain after the normal school day until 6 pm. The funding I secured allowed me to pay yet another staff member to provide supervision. Our students who "qualified" for this assignment detested it; I liked it. Students assigned to the program would meet at the end of the school day in a specific area of the building adjacent to the school's main office; I wanted them to observe their friends heading out the doors, catching school buses or walking home for the weekend; twilight school students would be escorted by the supervising staff member, where the same requirements as Saturday School would be in place.

Those students whose behavior was viewed as more serious were subject to more stringent disciplinary measures, which would include in-school or out-of-school suspension.

There are those who clamor about the use of suspension at all, and I respectfully disagree with their viewpoint. The in-school suspension (ISS) option was slated for students whose immaturity and repeated poor judgment recklessly interrupted instruction or caused the student to act out disrespectfully but not in a way that I would call major. These students were assigned to this classroom area for the entire day, where they remained quiet, including during their lunchtime, sometimes for two to three days. The supervising staff member would obtain student classwork and homework assignments that would have to be completed. Students would complete a writing assignment examining their behavior, as well as complete written apologies to their teacher(s). The school guidance counselor and school psychologist would receive notifications, one of whom would take a few minutes to touch base with the child, including a discussion on how he/she might develop better social skills or strategies for more appropriate behavior. These students generally appeared embarrassed, sometimes mortified that they had incurred such a consequence, and they usually made better decisions in the future to avoid being reassigned to ISS.

Out-of-school suspension (OSS) was typically temporary—but it could be lengthy, depending on the severity of the offense—and it involved complete exclusion from school and related activities. It was usually meted out for what was considered complete and utter disdain for the dignity of staff, reprehensible actions committed by the student(s), or dangerous behavior that posed a threat to the offending student(s) or to others. Depending on the reason for and the length of the suspension, I would extend an offer to parents interested in shortening the term of suspension, just as I had done at the high school level. I would offer to take a day off a youngster's suspension if the parent gave a day's time, attending school classes with their misbehaving child, including sharing lunch with their child at a separate table in the cafeteria. Several parents accepted this offer over the years—none of them happy about it—but I wasn't particularly happy with them or their child's misbehavior either. I was willing to give them the opportunity to come to the school, meet their youngster's teachers, and participate in the classes. It usually gave them a clearer perspective on the effort teachers extend in preparing solid instruction daily for the community's youngsters, and they sometimes expressed their appreciation to the staff. Their youngsters, by the way, hated the idea of attending school with their mom, dad, or guardian, and their behavior and decision-making generally improved from that point forward.

Considering that many students were given to striking other students physically, I took a zero tolerance position on anyone physically assaulting another. I clarified to the student body that parents did not send their youngsters to school to suffer mental anguish or bodily harm and transgressors could well expect to be disciplined accordingly. There were at least two instances when I allowed eighth-graders to be charged by the county police and escorted from the school in handcuffs for wantonly beating another youngster. Such nonsense behavior was going to end—and it did at Harper's Choice!

As mentioned earlier, I reminded teaching staff to pay attention to the school's culture, including student use of vulgar language that many staff in schools regularly avoided correcting. I was also aware of the widespread bullying taking place throughout the school community—yet another issue that was best dealt with by meeting it head-on, in my view, owning the problem and eradicating it. I brought the issue directly to the faculty, students, and parents.

I addressed these topics at a faculty-wide meeting so that teaching staff would understand how important it was to their principal, that such issues of ill student behavior warrant being discussed with them at the meeting. I also brought it to the attention of the school over the public address system, and I followed up by speaking in the cafeteria to students at each of their lunch shifts, after they had been served and while they were eating. I clarified the student code of conduct and reemphasized our disciplinary procedures. I advised them that they needed to learn to stand up and look out for each other, all the way through high school and beyond.

I took the time to speak with each of the school bus drivers assigned to transport the students to and from school daily; I emphasized the importance that these professional drivers be alert to bullying behavior and put a stop to it immediately, notifying a school administrator of any particularly noteworthy incidents. I also addressed the issue with our custodial and cafeteria staff, clarifying that they were to admonish the offending student immediately, alerting an administrator as appropriate.

On this issue, I addressed the school's PTA, a number of whom also had children attending the elementary and high schools. I informed them that, as their kids matriculated through school, they would be well advised never to allow a staff or administrator to brush aside the need to take an instance of bullying seriously. The audience—including, I observed, parents of offending boys and girls—could expect to see police involvement with any such incident at this school. They were advised further that bullying must be dealt with in a "take no prisoners" approach. I advised them that, as they and their children progressed through the school system, and they found no help or relief from a teacher or school administrator on this topic, including the school principal, they should take the issue directly to the school district headquarters. Every school has some headquarters director or assistant superintendent who can look into the matter. If needed, parents should take the issue to the superintendent and the board of education. Don't give up; contact the newspaper, and if needed, the police, requesting that an officer be dispatched to take a report. There is no one more dear, more important than their children, I informed them. They needed to fight for their kids, and in the process, they would set the example and be the kind of role model that exemplified how important it was in life to stand on principle and affirmatively take care of issues important to them.

Bullying behavior is particularly egregious because it is an age-old social phenomenon with which everyone has some familiarity. I explained to the staff that bullying of any kind, whether verbal (name-calling, sexually suggestive language, offensive remarks), physical (hitting, kicking, punching), relational/social (excluding someone from a group setting, be it a cafeteria table or a recess activity), or electronic (telephone calls, cameras, email, social media) was not to be tolerated, and it warranted an adult staff member's intervention immediately. Anyone on our staff not familiar with bullying needed to get up to speed fast, because I would entertain no excuses for not stepping in and addressing the issue. A child being bullied—anyone being bullied—exacts an emotional, stressful toll on that individual; it is painful to one's psyche and one's ability to perform well in or out of school. Bullying behaviors go on unabated frequently because adults lack the intestinal fortitude to intervene immediately. Such detestable behavior is then allowed to take root and cultivate in any setting where people allow it, when adults choose not to do anything about it. I was well aware that this was an issue at Harper's Choice, and just as I would not entertain such nonsense at the high school level, neither would it be allowed here. Too many staff and school administrators in too many school settings do not readily pick up that a particular comment or an activity is a form of bullying. When the adults know or should know better, the impression is that they are too willing to kick the issue into the long grass. Perhaps an adult will offer the hackneyed cliché that "boys will be boys" or "girls will be girls," saying that an action of bullying was just "a joke," or "just horseplay that went too far." Each such response from a grown adult should be met with disdain, if not outrage; those individuals have no place working with youngsters, and certainly not at this school. It was clear that we would no longer entertain professional employees who brushed off dealing with an issue because they were passive, dismissive, cowardly, or just didn't like dealing with confrontation. That was not who we were, I explained, and from then on not for a minute would we brook any such behavior. The point was clear to staff and the student body: Bullying behavior occurred in schools and communities because the culture allowed it, because those who bullied others were not at all held accountable. Not here, not ever; our school was for teaching and learning, so that youngsters could grow into responsible, caring young adults.

My commitment was that students, staff, parents, and community members would always feel safe and welcomed at our school. Teachers, staff, guidance counselors, and the school psychologist were advised that if they felt something should be brought to my attention, they were to do so directly. I needed to know immediately if bullying was ever an issue. We were, from then on, a safe, supportive, and positive school environment, and they knew well that I was capable of taking the legal route to ensure that all kids felt safe and welcomed at HCMS.

We would use our Academic Enrichment time, or AE period, to present follow-up activities on bullying. The idea was to equip our kids with the social and emotional skills that in the future might prevent bullying behaviors or at least allow them to identify it and take a position to denounce it as wrong. I mentioned earlier that I often ate lunch with students in the school cafeteria, each day with a different grade level. I would frequently ask any students who were eating by themselves if they would mind if I sat at the same table. I would make conversation with him or her, as well as other students within close proximity, to try to make the lone student feel a part of the group conversation. As cited earlier, I reminded students in separate conversations about bullying, that it would be a good idea to consider asking someone sitting alone to join their lunch group, at least giving them the option. I asked them to consider partnering up with a student who wasn't always asked to be part of a team. And I told them to always make it a point to address another student, maybe saying hello or just being plain nice to a lonely individual. No youngster should feel socially isolated from his or her peers. Time would show that we, indeed, achieved a far better, more enriching school environment through these practices; each year we worked hard, and the poor language and bullying behavior all but disappeared at Harper's Choice Middle, as more and more students understood how enriching their lives could be by understanding and making connections with others.

I made it a point to confer with individual students whose behaviors I noticed in the hallway or were brought to my attention by another. This included those students who had bullied the youngster who had visited me with his mom earlier in the summer. Student and parent knew well that I would take any measure I felt was needed to curb such uncivilized behavior. I should mention that the former bullying victim, sooner rather than later, began to look more comfortable at school and would occasionally give me a thumbs-up indicating that everything was fine. He was smiling, engaged socially with peers and staff, and performing well academically. I smiled every time I would see him about the school, looking happy, comfortable in his skin, and confident.

My assistant principal later moved on to a central office curricular position and was replaced by another female, a former high school English teacher, a hard worker who was bright and capable and who immediately connected with students, staff, and parents.

Given the nature of a busy demographic school, I lobbied each year for additional administrative assistance, and after a few years, I was able to bring on an administrative intern, one of my successful science teachers and a team leader, who was working on her graduate degree in school administration. She was black, bright, and thoughtful—and she shared my sensible and sensitive but no-nonsense philosophy of student, professional staff, and parent conduct that we believed would enhance our efforts to improve instruction and student achievement. The three of us made up the administrative team, and she was included in all of our deliberations. She supported and assisted with supervisory duties and the handling of student discipline. She was on top of her professional development and able to discuss concerns of mutual interest with staff and parents, she attended any extracurricular activities during the day or evening, she assisted us in promoting quality instruction, and she worked well in guiding and supporting all of our students.

> *On a side note:* This school system, like many school districts, often hired solely based on an applicant's race or gender, even if it meant overlooking a more qualified individual, although they would never admit it—a mistake, in my view. My decision to select specific staff to work at HCMS, including assistant administrators, was based on merit, need, and the quality of the individual, and each one I hired proved to be a successful and respected addition to the Harper's Choice school community.

I wanted an active drama production program, and the same teacher who volunteered to coordinate the character education modules offered to oversee our drama club. I requested that the music department get actively involved in competitions, and they did so, demonstrating some genuine talent in their performances. At this point in my career, my wife and I had grown married children who were starting their own families, and I had time to spend at the school building on weekends. I would go in and do my share of reading, research, and preparation for the following week. It was part of "owning" my position, and no one was more prepared than I. On one particular weekend, as I arrived, I observed two kids sitting alongside a curb adjacent to the building. I asked what they were doing and, of course, they replied, "Nuttin'." I kept a football atop my office credenza, and I asked if they'd be interested in tossing the pigskin around for a bit. They were a bit taken aback, but they said, "Okay." I entered the building to retrieve the ball, then went back out and threw it to them, asking if we could find a few more for a pick-up game. With that, we were off to the adjacent homes and federal Section 8 subsidized housing areas, as they knocked on door after door, yelling, "Hey, Tarkese, Shiquanda, Latonya, Donnell, Kendall," and a host of other names, "come outside, we're gonna play football with Mr. Wallis!" That chance happening that morning led to several successive years of playing touch— more often tackle—football on the school grounds each Saturday or Sunday morning. The kids knew that if anyone "dissed" an adult (teacher, staff member, or parent volunteer), he or she would be prohibited from playing with the principal's team that weekend (along with any administrative consequence received for the ill behavior). My point was to find avenues that would tie more of our students to a social group, give them an identity that would provide a sense of focus, and keep them actively involved in school. Students who saw my car in the parking lot on any given weekend would come up and tap on my office window. Those initial two youngsters eventually grew to a group of, on average, eight to thirteen kids every weekend who played football with me for nine years. Prior to a game, I started a routine that had them doing exercises with me, including push-ups, stretches, crunches, and back presses. Again, this was combination touch-tackle football, and the players were boys *and* girls, some of whom were faster than the boys. A passing adult community member would occasionally observe us and, I'm certain, wonder what was happening, as I would fairly aggressively grab a player carrying the football and spin him around to the ground, one time separating a youngster's shoulder. I felt horrible about it and drove the child home. The mom said, "Mr. Wallis, don't you worry about it. He'll be alright." The boy then asked me if we'd be playing again the following week—great stuff! The "cherubs" (as I would often refer to many of the students) derived great pleasure out of tackling the principal, and often I would find myself at the bottom of a pile five or six kids high. The community high school coach, with whom I had worked years earlier, heard what we were doing and stopped over one Saturday, wearing a big smile. It turned out some of the youngsters would later play for him, and some went on to play college ball, with one later playing in the NFL; one of the female youngsters would later go on to play college basketball at a university in the Northeast.

Following the game, I would offer to buy them lunch at the neighborhood McDonald's, but only if they first ran through the neighborhood with me. I wanted them at their age to begin developing an appreciation of the benefits derived from regular physical exercise. The two to three kids who had initially declined to run thought twice about it, then decided to join us after all, as they wanted in on the free lunch. Picture this white Irish guy running through the neighborhood with eight to twelve kids, mostly of color, chasing him; it was a scene. We would then grab lunch, while I spent considerable time introducing them to or reminding them of etiquette, courtesy, and manners. They learned to say, "Excuse me," "Thank you," "Yes, ma'am," and "Yes, sir." We had many conversations—sometimes serious—either after a game as we were lying on the grass resting before our run, or as we were lunching together. A couple conversations come to mind: One revolved around the military, the fact that students had family members and friends serving, and they asked about my service in the U.S. Army. One youngster stated he was going to be a Navy SEAL one day, and I told him that would be a remarkable achievement, as most do not make it, and if he was serious, he had to start applying himself to his school studies and put more effort into his exercise routine. Perhaps one day he would find himself among those who qualify, then he would graduate from BUD/S— Basic Underwater Demolition/SEAL training. I informed them that among the famous aspects of SEAL training is the "Bell," referring to a ship's brass bell that looms over the training ground. SEAL training is intended to test a person's mental and physical limits; fewer than 20 percent complete the training, which means 80 percent or more failed, I told them. The youngsters were attentive. I stated that when exhausted SEAL candidates—solid human beings, patriots all—reached their breaking point, they would ring the bell three times. The sound echoed through the training grounds, indicating that another candidate had "volunteered out." Others gained insight and strength, reached within themselves, and with enough grit, determined that they would graduate from SEAL training. I told them that when they were having a tough time attending school regularly or when they were not working as hard as they knew they could in their classes, or when they thought they might lash out at someone, they should think again and find the determination to make a better decision. In other words: Don't give up on yourself, don't lose your cool, and don't quit—don't ring the bell.

As the school year would progress, I occasionally would ask a student how he was doing in classes; one morning in a crowded hallway, one student, "TJ," shouted back with a big smile, "I ain't ringin' no bell, Mr. Wallis, if that's what you're asking." I smiled back, shook my head, and reminded him to avoid saying "ain't" and use of a double negative, thinking maybe that would be another good lesson to share one weekend while we were eating lunch.

On another occasion we were eating, when both girls and boys asked, "Mr. Wallis, what do you have to do to be successful, to make money?"

"This is a great time in your life to ask that question," I began by telling them. "As you continue to grow up, it's good to reflect from time to time and confirm that you're doing the right things to put yourself on the road to success. Successful people have a sense of pride; they are doers. Many begin their day by making their bed and getting themselves organized, and they know what it is that they want to accomplish. They respect themselves and take personal responsibility, and they respect their elders and others; they develop a curiosity about things, just as you are showing now by asking that question. You should remember that showing character is of utmost importance—being honest, working hard, showing compassion for others, and developing self-discipline and self-reliance, that is to say, learning to be independent and doing things on your own efforts. These characteristics will put you on the road to success." Sometimes the discussion would go on for a few minutes, and those who were within close proximity would listen intently. I often advised them that "there is a kind of success track you want to think about, as well, and keep in mind, a sequence of things you want to start thinking about right now."[9] Essentially, they needed to do well in school, academically and behaviorally; they needed to graduate from high school; they needed to get a job (or attend college, trade school, or technical school, or join the military); if they chose to marry, they should do so only after the age of twenty-one; and only then have children, should they choose to become parents—and they needed to do things in that order. If they knocked any of those out of sequence, they were likely heading for poverty. I told them I knew they were better than that, and if they kept that sequence in order, they would go on to do well, they would be successful, and yes, they would "make money."

Lunch was my treat for a few weeks, until the owner of the eatery, a black female who owned another one or two restaurants, approached me, saying, "Mr. Wallis, I've watched you and these kids for weeks now, and I love what you're doin'. I wanna be among your school-business partners that I heard you talking about recently." She was terrific; it proved to be a wonderful partnership with the school, and for the years that I was their principal, the kids and I received a free meal each weekend at the "Golden Arches"!

8

A Focus on
Instruction

Public schooling has taken a shellacking over the years, and for good reason. Successful public schools dot the American landscape, but such schools operate differently from those in the main. It is generally acknowledged throughout the country that a diploma does not necessarily denote that a youngster knows or has mastered anything, as much as it indicates that one has completed a minimum number of credits (though not always, as the reader has learned). It doesn't have to be that way. We can change this, but it will require what we used to call a paradigm shift. Plato once said that "Education is teaching our children to desire the right things." This should start in the home. Parents should also be able to trust that their community school—elementary, middle, high—will be safe, warm, inviting venues that reinforce traditional family values and a sense of patriotism, a sense of identity and mutual respect. We know that a top-shelf education revolves around instructional excellence, and the classroom teacher is the linchpin in producing quality student academic achievement performance.

Opinion polls also indicate that having better teachers is widely seen as a favored solution to public school academic problems. According to the American Council on Education, the quality of the classroom teacher is key to improved student performance, regardless of school condition, affluence of the child, nature of the community, or any other element.[1] Looking at where the school was at the time, the atmosphere and conditions that existed at that point, and the goals and direction I had in mind, I was well aware that we had so very much to do. I was hell-bent on cultivating the kind of quality in a teaching staff that would move students to want to be the best they could be in each of their classes. That takes a smart, caring, respected staff—both in and out of the classroom—that can connect with students, all of our students. I thought at the time that determination, perseverance, and fortune would one day see more than our share of students seeing reason "to desire the right things," making better decisions about learning, friendships, family, and life. I am of the mind that every child can learn, and I wanted every staff member to share that belief; our singular focus would be on teaching the kids—and teaching them well. That was our mission, nothing else to interfere. Yes, where I or we could, within reason, positively impact issues related to poverty, low education within the community, criminal behavior, poor parenting (no matter one's socio-economic status), and other blights that affected a youngster's schooling, I was all in, but our primary focus would be on teaching these cherubs, which would require a school culture conducive to quality teaching and student academic achievement. Read on to learn how that came to be.

During the time that I was principal of Harper's Choice Middle, hardworking, conscientious professionals, both in and out of the classroom, gave a new and improved connotation to school accountability, and for the purposes of this chapter, instructional excellence. It was my job to see that the entire staff accepted responsibility for successful student academic performance, and it's appropriate and important to own one's responsibility.

I immersed myself in learning about this school community, and I vowed that Harper's Choice would be known as a hallmark of meaningful, substantive teaching and learning. We committed upfront that each of our youngsters would meet or exceed our state's department of education standards, meaning all diploma-bound students would perform on or above grade level in each measured subject area. I had met and watched some terrific teachers since arriving at Harper's Choice, and I would have been proud to have them work with me anywhere. I conferred at length with these teachers, a number of whom struck me as having a solid grasp of pedagogy and content. I surmised they were very likely good at crafting lesson plans that, given our multicultural community, would adapt to various learning styles and reading levels. They were teachers who would work in concert with me to get results, meaning improved student performance. I felt that out of respect for them, I needed to transform the existing culture of low expectations and inconsistent-to-shoddy teaching practices, as outlined earlier by parents, staff, and school system headquarters staff. A number of the school's respected staff had already indicated to me their disappointment with what passed as teaching on the part of some of their colleagues, poor teaching practices they also observed in other schools where they had taught. I vowed that we would change the dynamic and create an environment in which higher standards of instructional and behavioral excellence would be the norm, with the belief that *all children can learn.*

I would exhort teaching staff to believe that they, individually—and certainly all of us collectively—could raise student achievement for every student, despite any negative conditions outside the school for so many of our cherubs. Given the trying circumstances surrounding this school and community, I quite understood that observers might have thought such an idea quixotic, but I'd always had a good sense of self, and I was thoughtful, measured and determined. The challenges would be met; after all, an entire community was now hopeful and depending on our success. It was a plus that I also felt a good vibe about some of the teaching staff whom I had recently met, and so from my standpoint, it was full speed ahead. I was prepared to redefine teaching excellence as first-rate instructional performance that would become the norm in every classroom. I would define, with clarity, what solid instruction looked like, and we would entertain "no excuses."

Having served in the military, I was intrigued with the unusual success that schools enjoyed on America's military bases. I recall poring through the results of the 1998 National Assessment of Educational Progress (and later its 2011 statistics), finding that eighth-graders in these schools outperformed most all the states; they tied for fourth in reading at the time. According to a follow-up piece in the *Wall Street Journal* by Dan Gordon, it wasn't just the test scores that made these schools special. Some 80 percent of graduates of these military base schools attend college—the national rate was 67 percent at the time (currently 69.1 percent)—even though many of these students typically switched from one school to another during their school years, always meeting new teachers and friends in the process. Poverty? Interesting that half the students qualified for free/reduced lunch in the federal school-lunch program (an accepted measure of poverty) because their parents were in the bottom of pay rank; two out of five are black/Hispanic, but they achieve at or above proficiency at rates far exceeding those in the civilian world. No surprise that parent satisfaction is so high that the department has had to crack down on those trying to sneak their children back into the system after leaving the military or moving off base.

There are several reasons for the success of the Pentagon's schools. Some are pedagogical. Interim director of Pentagon Schools Ray Tolleson states that "the schools are effective because we spend extra time and effort training teachers and trying to involve parents in school life. Military authorities grant service members release time—typically an hour a week or a half-day a month—to volunteer in the schools. At Fort Knox, every school also is adopted by an Army unit, which may do anything from mentoring to proctoring." Other reasons revolve around the presence of parents, particularly fathers, who are both self-disciplined and accepting of military discipline; parents who believe their own efforts—not race, special concessions, or breaks—are the chief determinant of their success. The military, for all its shortcomings, was and is thought to be fairer than the civilian world, believing that requirements for advancement are clear, attainable, and usually fairly administered. Perhaps people who believe they can achieve based on their own efforts tend to raise children who share that belief.[2] Former *Washington Post* writer William Raspberry commented that "too many children in civilian world harbor a defeatist view that life is unfair, that breaks are haphazardly distributed, and that race is a barrier to success." I was always mindful of these Pentagon school findings and would share them over the years with high school colleagues. Some of these ideas would take shape in one form or another at Harper's Choice.

I was poring over information about HCMS and noted that a number of youngsters had chronic absences from school. I felt that there was much in the way of instruction that we could offer. However, it required that students be in those seats daily, and it was apparent that we would need to address student chronic absenteeism among several of our cherubs.

Research shows that missing 10 percent of school—about two days per month—can negatively affect test scores, reduce academic growth, and increase the chances a student will drop out.[3] It is also true that education can only fulfill its promise as the great equalizer—a force that can overcome differences in privilege and background—when we work to ensure that students are in school every day to receive the supports they need to learn and thrive.[4]

The issue of chronic absenteeism is a concern throughout the country, and in many schools, if it's dealt with at all, it can be rather haphazard. We put a graduated intervention process in place that saw guidance counselors and additional school-based staff confer with the child and family. This was followed by a letter to the parent, in which we explained the negative effect of absences on their youngster's academic progress. In fact, we sent similar letters to the families of students who were chronically late to school, citing the number of tardies and clarifying student expected arrival time. Such attendance "nudge" letters have been effective in areas throughout the country, in some cases resulting in an 11 to 15 percent reduction in absenteeism.[5] If the problem continued, we would ask the school headquarters staff, in the form of a pupil personnel worker, to confer with the youngster and make a home visit, clarifying the legal ramifications for the parent should the absences continue, ultimately having to go to court, which occurred on occasion over the years I was in the profession. Interesting research suggests that parents underestimate their children's absences by an average of 50 percent, believing their children's attendance is as good as or better than that of their classmates, thinking that missing a few days of school every month is okay, and believing that excused absences do not affect student learning.[6] The bottom line was that we needed our kids present in school if we were going to have a chance at improving overall student academic performance.

As cited earlier, among the correlates of effective, successful schools is the issue of providing an opportunity to learn and time on task. Research indicates that we increase our chances for overall student academic achievement when we allot a significant amount of class time to instruction in the essential skills, where students are actively engaged in teacher-directed, planned, and organized learning activities. You may recall that I arrived at Harper's Choice later in the summer than I would have preferred, amidst a disorganized, chaotic, and dispirited school environment. Much needed to be done, and while course scheduling is important, that issue at the time took a back seat for the immediate present. However, I did have experience with scheduling, and I had done a fair amount of research on the topic over the years. I called and spoke to a few instructional team leaders, discussed some options, and decided we would go with an "A/B," or alternating day block, schedule, where students would take ninety-minute classes that met every other day. It turned out well, and we remained with that schedule. Staying for the moment on the topic of the school schedule, the reader will recall that we also incorporated within our daily school schedule a thirty-minute block of time called Academic Enrichment to provide extra enrichment for students. While this time allowed for specific students to meet with their band, orchestra, and chorus music teachers, each grade level would have this block of time to develop activities to support our school goals surrounding academic and behavioral excellence, instructional packets for which were supplied to our music program participants, absent students, and their families. It was during this time of day when we provided lesson plans on what we called *Building Cougar Character* (named after our school mascot) and the *7 Habits of Highly Effective Teens*,[7] both wonderful additions to our total school program that made a wholesome, worthwhile, and positive difference in the lives of our students, staff, and parents.

The county school system had in place a "Framework for Excellence in Teaching and Learning," which was used as the basis for teaching evaluations. It stemmed from the work of former economist, K-12 and college teacher, and educational consultant Charlotte Danielson, who spent years analyzing the performance of distinguished, proficient, and underperforming teachers. Her Framework for Teaching[8] cites a rubric on teaching that included, at the time, five specific aspects, or domains, of a teacher's responsibilities. The framework is supported by empirical studies and is meant to enhance improved student learning. I thought it dovetailed nicely with my educational philosophy; our newly adopted HCMS *Attitudes, Behaviors, and Values Supporting Student Achievement*; the Effective School Correlates, our school goals, and the multiple positive changes in student academic and behavioral *performance* that we committed to making as a staff.

The framework was comprehensive and cited specific domains that identify teachers' responsibilities to improve student learning: *Domain 1: Interpersonal Skills* included relating effectively with students; developing collaborative relationships with administrative, teaching, and support staff; and fostering positive relationships with families and community members. *Domain 2: Planning and Preparation* would see the teacher demonstrating knowledge of content and instructional practices, demonstrating knowledge of students, selecting appropriate instructional goals, demonstrating knowledge of resources, designing coherent instruction, and assessing student learning effectively. *Domain 3: The Classroom Environment* cites how the teacher establishes a culture for learning, manages classroom procedures effectively, manages student behavior effectively, and organizes physical space appropriately. *Domain 4: Delivery of Instruction* looks at how the teacher communicates clearly and accurately, uses questioning and discussion techniques effectively, engages students in the learning, provides effective feedback to students, and demonstrates flexibility and responsiveness. *Domain 5: Professional Responsibilities* references how the teacher reflects on teaching, maintains accurate records, communicates with families, shows professionalism; and grows and develops professionally.

I cannot emphasize enough the central importance of a quality, first-rate staff, whether you run a company, institution, foundation, corporation, or in this case, a community's school. The idea was to recognize the staff as the professionals I believed they were, until individuals proved otherwise. I wanted them to feel they had the pedagogical tools, the autonomy, and the outright faith and support of their instructional leader, their principal. It fell within my purview to ensure, as best as possible, a quality instructor for every student, because the classroom is where all the effectiveness is tested, where the "rubber meets the road."

Imagine a student being fortunate enough to have a teacher who regularly practices our newly established *HCMS Attitudes, Behaviors, and Values Supporting Student Achievement* and actively demonstrates daily in every class the excellence captured in Danielson's Framework for Teaching. Oh, were that the kind of outstanding teaching performance exhibited in every schoolhouse throughout America! It was, indeed, the kind of teaching-learning excellence that I planned and hoped to achieve in every classroom in our school.

The administrative team would conduct formal "announced" and "unannounced" classroom instructional observations that would allow us to evaluate teacher instructional and classroom performance regularly throughout the academic year. The above framework would also, as I mentioned earlier, serve as the basis of each teaching professional's annual performance evaluation. I asked (read, directed) staff to have a written lesson plan at the ready for each and every class lesson daily, throughout the academic year. It didn't have to be elaborate, but I did require an organized game plan for every class session. Such plans typically included an objective/purpose, anticipatory set or "hook," modeling/modeled practice, a check for understanding, a guided practice, independent practice, and closure, straight out of the years-old lesson plan model, developed originally by former UCLA professor and education author Madeline Hunter. It was a document typically given to me at the start of a teacher's formal instructional observation that I could peruse while I was observing and writing up that particular class lesson. I would attach the lesson plan with the instructional observation form, which I would share with the teacher during our post-observation conference usually later that afternoon or the following day.

My view is that the professional teacher is organized and operates from a well-thought-out plan. I knew from conversations with staff that lesson plans had not been required previously. That would not work here anymore. I was well-aware there were those who had years of experience, and I surmised that a few of the staff thought it fine to use their intuition and experience rather than a plan. Nonetheless, I didn't think it was an unreasonable expectation, and I asked those few staff members to "humor me" and incorporate written plans with their daily instruction.

School principals should know the degree to which every classroom is exhibiting and producing first-rate teaching and the accompanying student academic performance. It's their job, and they should be on top of those staff who are producing stellar performances, as well as those who need to amp up their game. Good principals are highly visible; they are in the hallways, they are in and out of classrooms, they attend extracurricular activities, they recognize the importance of being approachable and showing interest in their staff, students, and their families. Among the responsibilities of the job is that of formally observing classroom instruction. The following was typical of the classroom instructional write ups I would complete for teachers:

NAME OF DISTRICT PUBLIC SCHOOL SYSTEM
NAME OF SCHOOL

Traditional Observation Form

Teacher:_____ Date:_____
Observer: Stephen Wallis Announced / Unannounced
Subject: Social Studies   Grade: 7
Time: 8:28-9:35   # of Students Present: 29   Tenured/Non-Tenured

_____

Description (attach other data as appropriate):

8:28   As administrator enters the classroom, the social studies teacher is at the front of the class addressing students working on their "Skills Check" on longitude and latitude. A special education instructor also works with the class. Additionally, a student assistant works with her ALS student, and a PDS teacher intern observes the instructional lesson.

The day's instructional objectives are cited on the chalkboard; additionally, a written lesson plan is presented to this observer. The plan cites the objective, materials, procedures, and evaluation of the lesson.

Both instructors distribute worksheets to students. One sheet is a blank map of Europe; the other is a homework schedule sheet entitled "Europe—History and Geography."

8:40   A show of hands indicates that some students are still working on their map skills warmup.

(The classroom walls, bulletin boards, and chalkboard depict various posters, a world map, and student projects that reflect the world of social studies taught daily.)

The teacher directs students to put pencils down and look at their homework schedule. She introduces the geographic regions of Europe. She asks students to cite a country recently in the news. A short discussion takes place on the United Kingdom, the recent death of the Queen Mum, and the monarchy as a form of government. Students are reminded that they are to have no zeroes, i.e., all work is to be completed. The entire homework schedule is reviewed.

8:48   The special education instructor takes several students from the class so she can work with them separately at their skill levels. Both teachers ensure that specific accommodations are made to enhance the success of all students.

9:01   The teacher uses a transparency and overhead projector to review with her students those countries that make up Western Europe. She calls upon individual students to cite each country aloud. Students are directed to write down the names of the countries and the corresponding number on the transparency.

9:08   Students are directed to partner with another peer to drill each other. The instructor states that students may want to use "memory devices" to help them remember some of the names (e.g., "I remember Not So Fast" for Norway, Sweden, and Finland). Following this exercise, individual students are called upon to stand and cite the specific countries studied. They do so. Other countries are introduced, and she explains how some of them came to be as a result of the breakup of the former Union of Soviet Socialist Republics.

9:20   The teacher and students continue to review additional countries on the continent. Again, they are asked to partner and drill each other. Those who haven't had a chance to answer yet are called upon. She continues to use appropriate positive reinforcement to student responses.

9:27   As the class completes a good portion of the map, the teacher asks for volunteers to stand and cite all the countries and their locations. Two do so and are rewarded with "bonus" points (instead of candy, "argh!"). As the class session ends and students begin to leave, they are asked first to inform the teacher of a specific country they know they will need to study.

Observer's initials_____   Teacher's initials_____

Analysis and Recommendations (based on the domains below):

1. INTERPERSONAL SKILLS   2. PLANNING AND PREPARATION
3. CLASSROOM ENVIRONMENT   4. DELIVERY OF INSTRUCTION
5. PROFESSIONAL RESPONSIBILITIES

Ms. _____:

Thank you for the opportunity to observe this morning's social studies lesson. It was a fine lesson—lots of organization, time on task, and solid communication with students. Your interactions, communication skills, and knowledge of your students allow you to relate quite effectively with them. The respect and rapport you have developed allow for collaborative relationships with colleagues and foster positive relationships with students and their families.

Planning and preparation are a strong suit with you, and they clearly enhance your daily instruction. Your instructional units and daily lesson plans follow the Essential Curriculum, from which you select appropriate instructional goals. Such planning gives you the opportunity to design coherent instruction. You demonstrate knowledge of content and instructional practices, and you ensure that you incorporate varied approaches to learning. Particularly noteworthy is how well you and your co-teacher, _____, work on a daily basis to service the needs of all of your students. You continue to demonstrate knowledge of resources for teaching and student support. The criteria and standards you employ are aligned with instructional goals and allow you to assess student learning effectively.

Your interaction with students and expectations for their learning and achievement have established a culture for learning and success. Transitions from one activity to another are managed well, and behavior is monitored effectively.

Directions and procedures are communicated clearly and accurately, and you elicited responses from a wide array of students. The idea, of course, is to involve actively everyone in the morning's instruction, and you do that well. Students were engaged throughout the lesson, and the feedback you give students is immediate and meaningful. You continue to demonstrate responsiveness and a flexibility that puts students at ease, providing a continuing kind of "invitation" to participate. This mode of operation serves to enhance their sense of confidence regarding the subject and will increase their chances of success.

You affirm your following procedures for MSDE initial student attendance, and you follow established policy regarding grade and attendance recording. You communicate well with students' families and are your students' most outspoken advocate. This community is fortunate to have you teaching its youngsters.

We are a better school because of people of your caliber. Best wishes for a successful remainder of the academic year.

_____

Observer Signature

_____

Teacher Signature

_____

Date

Those teachers demonstrating substandard teaching performance, who could not—in some cases, would not—effect positive change in their teaching, were documented as unsatisfactory by me and the administrative team. I always ensured throughout the years that the administrative team treated every staff member with dignity. Each teacher in jeopardy of losing his or her job was treated openly and fairly; each written unsatisfactory performance was clearly documented. Every unsatisfactory employee was placed on a so-called action plan, designed with the individual's input to shore up deficiencies and begin to bring about wholesale positive change in their teaching performance. The appropriate content area district headquarters supervisor or facilitator would be notified and asked to assist in conducting follow-up instructional observations. The action plan would cite a specific goal as well as the domain area (interpersonal skills, planning and preparation, classroom environment, delivery of instruction, professional responsibilities) on which strategies for assistance would be focused. It would involve a schedule of meetings with an instructional leader, an administrator, and a subject area supervisor; an observation of a master teacher; a video recording of the unsatisfactory teacher's instruction for self-evaluation; participation in staff development courses/seminars; frequent classroom observations by supervising staff, providing oral and written feedback; as well as periodic goal conferences with an administrator to evaluate progress. Absent genuine performance improvement by the teacher, I would issue another unsatisfactory rating, indicating that minimum standards of professional quality were not in evidence, that the teacher had failed to show improvement regarding stated criteria, and in my professional opinion, had not met the minimum performance expectations established by the school system. The evaluation would be a recommendation to terminate the individual's contract with the school system.

Over the years I was principal, a number of teachers and other teaching staff were removed from their teaching assignments, as well as those serving in positions outside the classroom from school health nurse to secretary. Some chose to transfer to another school site or retire. Often these teacher unsatisfactory ratings could be stressful, if not confrontational, and they involved teacher union representatives, headquarters staff, lawyers, and sometimes cries of racism or unfairness of one sort or another. Unfortunately, for each of these individuals, I was resolute and organized, knew what I was doing, and was confident the process I had in place was wholly fair and professional. I also knew that the individual's teaching peers, the student body, and the parent community deserved the highest level of instructional excellence, which heretofore they had been denied. It was the right action, even though I knew that school district headquarters staff would have preferred not to get involved in the verbal sparring with the union, contentious hearings, sometimes vociferous arguments made by the employee, and the occasional inordinate amount of time spent in those hearings.

Critics throughout the country often cite—justifiably—teacher unions and tenure as frustrating obstacles to firing incompetent teachers. I have observed—and have been so advised on occasion by teacher union representatives over the years—that as long as any teacher is a dues-paying member, the union will fight to protect them, no matter the facts. I would shake my head, stating on more than one occasion that such is not good for kids, their families, or schools. Contrary to what is said and portrayed by the American Federation of Teachers and the National Education Association, they are *not* all about the welfare of students; they are about representing their dues-paying adult members. The position they take on teacher incompetency can be problematic but not completely insurmountable. Unlike the position taken by too many school administrators, I never viewed tenure as lifetime protection. Tenure really mandates—rightly, I believe—that fundamental due process protections be in place and met before a tenured teacher can be fired for cause. If schools have one incompetent teacher, much less a host of substandard teachers in their building, staff who are ineffective, unprofessional, and not at all contributing to raising student performance—academic or otherwise—it's a safe bet you have equally uninspiring, feckless school principals and school district administrators. More often than not, in the nearly forty years I was in the profession, it was an ineffective, deficient school district administration and equally indolent school-based administrators who routinely failed the community's students, parents, and wider business sector by refusing to hold accountable ineffective, unsatisfactory teachers. I personally knew and have spoken on occasion to school principals who matter-of-factly advised that they had never written an unsatisfactory evaluation; directors and an assistant superintendent who pleaded with me to reconsider an unsatisfactory evaluation of a teacher because they lacked the fortitude to deal with the anxiety, heated discussions, and confrontation that sometimes accompanied the hearings at headquarters; and superintendents who cravenly turned a blind eye to documented incompetence and, instead, chose simply to place inept teachers—and equally ineffective, unworthy school-based administrators—at another school location, where they would continue their unacceptably second-rate, substandard performance, vitiating the quality of overall instruction at their new assignment.

In every case, these headquarters staff—all of them—were kept apprised of the evaluation process in place and provided months of documentation that clearly identified incompetent—sometimes clearly unprofessional conduct unbecoming a professional teacher—yet they preferred to avoid doing what they were paid to do, that is, ensuring quality teaching instruction throughout the school system. It was clear that the inability to make the correct, ethical, moral decisions regarding documented cases of staff incompetence was about the lack of character, the absence of moral turpitude on the part of those occupying pivotal decision-making positions at school district headquarters. It was about them, their myopic sense of what they thought was right or wrong, and their unmitigated inability to step to the plate and essentially defend the many students and parents who had been receiving less-than-competent instruction. While paying their fair share of taxes, supporting their school system, and wanting the best for their children, parents in these scenarios were simply pushed aside, and ineffective teachers or school administrators, again, either remained at the school site in which they worked or were simply transferred to another school and allowed to continue their pattern of unsatisfactory performance.

Above and beyond classroom instructional observations, I made walk-through visits in classrooms daily, a takeoff of the old business management style—management by walking around (MBWA)—involving managers walking through the workplace to check with employees, review equipment, and obtain the status of ongoing work. In this case, I would often take any paperwork or correspondence with me and take several minutes to sit in a class or classes, sometimes grabbing an empty classroom chair and sitting in a school corridor. It felt good and appropriate to get out of the office and into the hallways and classrooms at different times of the day throughout the year. It's always a good idea as principal to be visible to staff and students, maybe greeting the occasional pupil with a classroom pass authorizing him or her to be out of class or a staff member walking through the hallway, on each occasion a nice opportunity to chat with folks. I used a two-way radio to stay connected with main office staff; my secretary knew to direct anyone needing to confer with me to wherever I was located, in which case I would grab another empty chair. It was not at all out of the ordinary to enter the building and observe me sitting or standing in the hallway, having a conversation with a staff member or someone from outside the building, perhaps a visitor, parent, police officer, or prospective outside fund-raising representative.

I mentioned that we had put together a School Improvement Team, which would meet monthly to oversee and monitor our major academic year goals and objectives, folks who would provide a comprehensive review of our total instructional program. The team consisted of the administrative team, grade-level and subject team leaders, parents for each grade level, the business community, students, and other staff. We met monthly, we were organized, and we set ground rules (maintaining a definitive start and end time, making sure to take time to listen and understand each person's viewpoint, respecting the roles and responsibilities of team members, assigning follow-up actions, summarizing what we accomplished). The idea was that every committee or any meeting throughout the year would be purposeful and meaningful. We had a process in place to ensure that the minutes of our meetings were shared among the various school community stakeholders. The entire school community needed to know what their school was all about and how we planned to transition to one that was noted for its warmth and safe environment, as well as its exceptional teaching and student academic performance.

I stated earlier that I was a proponent of the maxim "what gets measured gets done," an axiom whose origin is up for debate and a variant of "you can't manage what you can't measure," attributed to Total Quality Management guru W.D. Deming and management consultant Peter Drucker. Regardless of its origin, keeping track and measuring our progress would keep us focused on achieving what we set out to do. Our Goal 1 focused on academic achievement, namely, that each child, regardless of race, ethnicity, socioeconomic status, or gender would meet rigorous performance standards. Given our school community and its recent history, that goal by any metric was a heavy lift. As cited earlier, the written plan for this goal included at the top of the front page an At-a-Glance view of the relevant summary of disaggregated data, including the number of students in various demographic categories—Free and Reduced Lunch Program, English for Speakers of Other Languages, special education classes, mobility (new entrants and withdrawals), and ethnicity breakdown. It also included state functional test pass rates for each grade level, as well as for each ethnicity, so we could immediately view our current focus, the initiatives in place, and how specific student groups were faring at the time on state English, mathematics, and writing tests. We would also include report card data and local assessments (similar to the state assessments that allowed local jurisdictions to identify instructional areas in need of strengthening prior to taking the statewide assessments).

Following the summary of relevant data, we articulated our actual plan. Specific content/subject area teachers worked with their respective team leaders to cite specific objectives, strategies, milestones/timelines, and an evaluation or outcomes for each subject taught. These written plans and strategies would come before the School Improvement Team, where the subject or content area team leaders would individually expound on how each of their subject-area teaching staff planned to answer the relevant questions: *What do we want for our students?* Each content area clarified measurable yearly student results. *How will we provide it?* Subject area teachers would specify methods, techniques, programs, and interventions they were employing to present their subject area material to their youngsters. Each content area would also identify *milestones or timelines*, specifying the minimum percentage of students expected to achieve results, as well as when they were to be achieved. They would also cite meaningful responses to the last two questions: *How will we know that we've done it well, and how will we respond if we haven't?* The school plan listed various statements that identified the actual results achieved, and/or the interventions that would take place and be used to reach the desired results.

The entire school staff was on board. Our related arts classes—art, music (instrumental, vocal, strings classes), physical education, family & consumer science, technology education—while not subject to state testing, were very much a part of the school's effort to bolster our overall academic standing. To that end, each of these classes worked with English, mathematics, and reading teachers to develop follow-up activities that they might incorporate into their own specific subject area in the effort to support student achievement in those more academic areas. In the area of reading, as an example, we wanted to bolster the skills of our students so they could, with confidence, *read to perform a task*, an area assessed on local and state tests. Each related arts subject provided a lesson using *reading to perform a task*, which the school reading specialist would critique. She would review and make suggestions that related arts teachers would incorporate into their individual subject area lessons. Indeed, the related arts teachers reported that students wound up being able to utilize this strategy with greater success. The focus on improved instruction and learning was a total school effort, and as such, we began to see more of our students meeting academic success each grading quarter of every successive school year. Monthly meetings followed throughout the year, each time seeing subject area team leaders presenting updated information on their subject area, including research-based high-level strategies or best practices being used in classes. They would share data points that indicated student academic strengths and weaknesses, and they would advise of follow-up activities in place to shore up student deficiencies. Support staff in the way of guidance counselors, alternative education staff, and our pupil psychologist were also present and provided suggestions and resource activities to assist these students; they literally noted the names of students so we could put a face with a name and develop an academic support plan tailored for each student—a lot of work throughout an academic year, but it brought a great deal of satisfaction.

Through some creative scheduling, I was able to free up a block of time daily for the Spanish teacher I hired, from Colombia, South America, to work with our growing Spanish-speaking student population. I asked that he coordinate with staff and work with these kids who were new to our school and grappling with English. Some of these students felt unsettled, understandably so, as they experienced a kind of culture shock, when students find themselves in a new country, trying to understand what is happening and what is being said at any given time. The Spanish teacher would contact homes and, on occasion, assist staff with parent conferences. He would help students with their various studies, make them feel comfortable, while simultaneously introducing them to and assisting these students in feeling a sense of calm and comfort around teaching staff, administration, and the student body. At times I would observe him repeating a word in context multiple times before students would understand the meaning, and another several dozen times before he expected them to recall a word or use it in a sentence or conversation. He would sometimes team teach with a colleague or otherwise work with fellow staff members, who would engage in more so-called cooperative learning strategies that would see students involved in group work, some of whom could be seen caring for and working with younger student peers. It was not uncommon to hear some teaching staff saying to their newly arrived students, as they would participate in class, "*¡Que Bueno!*" or "*¡Excelente!*" The idea was to find avenues that might increase academic performance for our total student population, and in due time, many of our Spanish-speaking students were making positive strides in their academic performance.

There had been a host of ineffective, time-wasting committees from years past that I thought it best to jettison, preferring our time be spent on providing first-rate instruction or working on activities that would lead to improved instruction and learning. We held a high regard for professional staff development, and we put together a committee of fine professionals who, together, would play a major role in facilitating and planning our various schoolwide continuous-improvement initiatives, revolving around what we called "Enhancing Instructional Practices and Student Achievement at 'The Choice'." (More on that topic in the next chapter.)

I frequently asked—if not implored—our teaching staff, when thinking about their own instruction, to use the school improvement plan as a touchstone, always asking themselves and then answering our pivotal questions: *What is it I want my students to learn? How will I provide it? How will I know if they have learned it? How will I respond if they haven't?* Given these focus questions, I urged teaching staff to insist that each student's learning be monitored in a timely fashion, and as appropriate, to provide additional time and support for those who needed it.

Emphasis was made on their asking themselves these relevant, important questions to ensure a culture of learning within their classrooms and thereby support the same sense of serious importance of teaching and learning throughout the school. This would require that they ask their students equally meaningful, quality questions and expect reasoned, substantive explanations, getting the youngsters not just to respond but to think. Couple that with frequent assessments to gauge their instruction and student understanding of concepts taught, and we had pretty first-rate classroom experiences happening on a daily basis.

I advised instructional team leaders and their staff to take time and listen to their students. They should ask from time to time how students feel about the subject they are being taught. They should ask if the students would like to share any personal comments about the subject, their teaching style, the amount of work being covered, and how well they felt they were understanding and grasping the concepts. Administering regular formative assessments was a good idea, too, one that would provide immediate feedback on overall class understanding of concepts, allowing the teacher to make any necessary instructional adjustments. Our focus on instruction, high-leverage strategies, the research-based best practices approach, and adjustments to their instruction that were offered were not seen so much as an add-on, as they were opportunities to enhance teachers' instructional delivery and the academic success of their students. Instructional team leaders met with me regularly, as well. I asked that they and their subject area team members regularly review available student data points and monitor the academic and behavioral progress of all students, individually and as student subgroups, ensuring that individual student support plans were in place that would enhance these youngsters' efforts to be successful. Staff would consult with parents and, as appropriate, with guidance counselors and other student support services personnel in the building. Student progress reports would be issued regularly, at a minimum of every four weeks, so students and parents could stay in sync with school efforts.

On that note, I referenced the research survey/questionnaire the county school system had conducted several years earlier that I had discussed previously with the student body.[9] Administered to several thousand elementary through high school low-, average-, and high-achieving youngsters throughout the school system, the tests provided various student responses and conclusions that reaffirmed my beliefs, among which was the following that I cited earlier to our pupils:

> Students who value learning, have high expectations, are committed, and work hard at acquiring knowledge, generally earn A/B grades and do well on standardized tests, *regardless of race or economic status.*

We had a large minority student population, and I emphasized to staff, as I did to students and later to parents, that success revolved around commitment behaviors, and that everyone was capable of making these commitments to success (i.e., attending school daily, being on time, being respectful, completing homework assignments, etc.). The results also revealed that low-achieving students wanted individual help from adults and/or teachers, as well as small-group instruction.

The research project reaffirmed the belief that academic success is dependent on the following:

- Students valuing learning and working at acquiring knowledge
- Parents setting high expectations, communicating those expectations, and seeing to it that they are met
- Teachers providing support and continuously engaging students
- Administrators structuring learning environments so that student commitment behaviors result in learning, good grades, and post–high school success

Only approximately one-third of all students perceive teachers "most of the time" as giving assignments that are challenging. Only approximately one-third of secondary students perceive themselves as receiving attention and praise "most of the time."[10]

I asked that teachers challenge youngsters intellectually in and out of every classroom throughout the school, blending rigor and empathy; students will generally appreciate it and more often than not will rise to the challenge.

I reveal a bit more about the survey results in a later chapter on the achievement gap. The survey and follow-up conversations with students and parents over the years provided some meaningful, relevant perspectives. For example, the report concluded the following:

We cannot overemphasize the importance of student commitment behaviors (including turning homework in on time, finishing homework, and persisting even when schoolwork is difficult, etc.) in the teaching-learning process.

The repertoire of teacher skills must be broadened to include motivation strategies that will engage students who are extrinsically motivated, match the modality and style of instruction to the preference of students.

In education, the four learning modalities are visual, auditory, kinesthetic, and tactile. Learners who are visual, for example, may learn better when things are presented in a way they can see, like charts and graphs. The data cite that low-achieving students prefer individual assistance and may take the form of adult, teacher, or small group interaction. We need to do what is necessary to make students an active part in the teaching-learning process. Unless we engage students, the achievement gap will continue.[11]

Students must commit themselves and need to be reminded of their personal responsibility. Teachers were reminded, again, "Students don't care how much you know until they know how much you care." I advised them to let their students know that they, their teachers, were invested in them, and at this stage, that the teachers wanted them to go into high school fully prepared to perform well, graduate, and go on to college or get a job in the workplace. It's been my experience that students who feel that connection often want to do well. I saw, among my responsibilities when I took the helm of Harper's Choice, that kids needed to feel that connection—and staff needed to feel such a connection, as well. I asked staff to think about the student perspectives shared in the survey, incorporating them, as appropriate, in their instruction. This would include, where appropriate, differentiating or tailoring one's instruction to meet those various modalities (whether visual, auditory, kinesthetic, or tactile) and students' personal preferences, particularly important since we were uniquely fortunate to have so many youngsters from throughout the world—over a dozen different countries at any one time—attending Harper's Choice.

Differentiating instruction is not lightly suggested; it takes extra time, thought, and energy, and sometimes extra resources. After all, it requires that the teacher ensure that his or her students are actively engaged in the teaching-learning process by devising tasks that match the individual student's needs, providing different avenues for understanding. This can be done by flexible grouping (whole class, small group, partnering up students), independent study, tiered assignments in varying complexity, etc. It takes time, energy, and a creative bent, at times, to conjure ways to tailor one's instructional delivery to meet individual needs, and I thoroughly respect those teachers who seemingly are gifted at making this happen regularly in their classrooms.

I also asked that staff balance their use of so-called cooperative learning groups. Cooperative learning, when used appropriately, can be a successful teaching strategy, in which small teams, each with students of different levels of ability, use a variety of learning activities to improve their understanding of a subject, but such requires active supervision on the part of the teacher so that one or two students are not saddled with doing most of the work. While this particular teaching strategy can be useful, it is also important for children to receive direct instruction from their teachers. In fact, studies have shown that below-grade level students, in particular, benefit more from direct instruction, frequently resulting in stronger academic level skills in students.

I reiterated my request that everyone consider obtaining student feedback from time to time throughout the year, in the effort to include motivation strategies that would engage more and more students, to improve in an ongoing fashion their teaching style, to improve their ability to make those human connections, and ultimately to enhance overall instructional efforts that would see an increasing number of our cherubs reach academic excellence. More on this topic, as well, in the chapter dealing with the achievement gap.

As I would meet with parents individually, in small groups, and in our monthly Parent Teacher Association (PTA) meetings throughout the year, as well as in meetings with our various school-business partners throughout the community, I would echo these academic findings, clarifying how important it was that parents stay actively engaged in the education of their youngsters; I clarified just how we incorporated these academic and behavior success correlates into our daily instructional program.

Another factor in the field of education that is among the important characteristics of high academic performance revolves around the issue of motivation. It competes with solving the nation's achievement gap for being viewed as the holy grail in education. Interestingly, it's never been a formal topic of discussion the many years I was at the high school level. It should have been. I specifically wanted the topic of student motivation to be part of my conversation with teaching staff at Harper's Choice Middle. I had hoped it would be discussed at length with students, as teachers periodically elicit feedback or input from youngsters. Motivation, after all, arguably is key to solving our education malaise in America. Surveys reveal a steady decline in student engagement throughout middle and high school, a trend that Gallup deemed the "school engagement cliff."[12] The company's student poll survey found that 74 percent of fifth-graders felt engaged, while the same was true of just 32 percent of high school juniors. This should be concerning, as the findings in the earlier survey that I referenced concluded that student engagement—their involvement, their enthusiasm—was, and remains, most important if students are to be academically successful. The "school engagement cliff" poses a challenge for school leaders, with the starkest engagement differences occurring during the middle school years. There is a thirteen percentage-point difference in engagement between sixth and seventh grade and a nine-point difference between seventh and eighth grade, with engagement declining at each successive grade level as students matriculate through high school.

Gallup research strongly suggests that the longer students stay in school, the less engaged they become, with our educational system sending students and our country's future over the school cliff every year.[13]

I advised staff that when talking with students over the years about motivation and teachers for whom they liked to work hard in the classroom, I would ask the reasons why those teachers struck a chord with their students. They usually cited that these specific teachers "motivated them to push themselves"; "were an inspiration"; "provided a course that was challenging, tough, but fun"; "explained things really well"; "were not boring"; and "helped along the way." It was information that I wanted staff to digest and consider, as they thought about their own teaching and instructional delivery style on a daily basis throughout the academic school year.

On a different note, there is something to be said for getting youngsters on a routine, establishing early on those habits of success. I would frequently share with staff how students failed and how they would succeed. Students often get low grades because they simply aren't certain or do not know what they are responsible for doing or getting accomplished. When I taught high school English years ago, I made it a point to place the daily instructional objectives on the board each day of the week. The objectives of any particular day's lesson were reviewed from the outset of each class, something many students would commit to their notebooks. It's a healthy practice to get into the habit of doing as a teacher, and we did so at HCMS. I advised staff early on to establish daily procedures, clarifying each day's lesson objectives; it made no difference if the subject area was mathematics or physical education, French or family and consumer economics, or social studies and technology education. While learning very much has something to do with what the teachers present to their class, it has everything to do with what the student accomplishes; students get more done if they have a clear idea and know what they're doing and see where they're going.

The reader will recall that teaching staff had committed earlier to the newly adopted *HCMS Attitudes, Behaviors, and Values Supporting Student Achievement*. It seemed appropriate to discuss with faculty the idea of measuring the effect of what we do in the classroom. As a school, by way of our School Improvement Team, we would measure our progress, continually and steadily staying on top of and reviewing our schoolwide improvement plan and its benchmarks, making any needed adjustments throughout the academic year. We were asking and answering our focus questions daily. I clarified to teaching staff the importance of measuring student understanding of concepts, skills, or a learning standard *during* the lesson instruction, using formative assessments that would allow the teacher to evaluate student understanding as the lesson was being presented. The teacher, for example, could make use of pop quizzes; review and analyze student work, including homework; and provide a Think-Pair-Share activity, requiring students to think about a question, pair up with a classmate, and share answers with the teacher. Good teachers know such is good teaching, but they don't always do so; they should reconsider. Each activity described would be a type of formative assessment that would allow instructors to know if students were, in fact, understanding the material being presented. They should identify concepts or skills that youngsters were grappling to understand as the instruction was taking place, as opposed to teaching a lesson and giving what we call a summative assessment at the conclusion of the unit taught. I asked them, "Why wait until the end of a teaching lesson or unit of instruction to ascertain if students understand what was taught?" In my opinion, such was a waste of both teachers' and students' time.

Emphasis was placed on teaching smartly, providing ample formative assessments along the way, making any necessary adjustments to the instruction and thereby enhance instructional and student academic performance. If a teacher found that a good number of kids had not fared well, it would make sense to look at how the instruction was delivered and/or instructional interventions that might be considered to get each student up to speed in that teacher's class. The idea was to build on previous instruction *and* student success. Their commitment to student achievement meant that every instructor would now identify specific outcomes; teach to and accept responsibility to help each student achieve; and monitor student success, adjusting teaching strategies, as appropriate. Ideally, if everyone was sincere on the day I presented these values and teacher behaviors, which they affirmed they would do, then it followed that our students were going *to meet or exceed rigorous standards for student achievement,* our school goal, and among the goals for both the county and state.

We were fast becoming a Professional Learning Community, teaching staff who met regularly, shared expertise and reflective dialogue, established norms and standards, and worked collaboratively to improve our teaching and learning. That was precisely our *modus operandi*. The emphasis on teacher instructional excellence and student academic achievement; the attention given to teaching staff collaboration; our near-monomaniacal focus on results by way of research-based best practices; the critical four questions that we asked ourselves daily; along with our emphasis on continuous improvement and partnerships already were, in my mind, hallmarks of such schools. At the time, it was a concept that was coming into vogue, and the research (to me, commonsense characteristics that we, in fact, were practicing) saw it as the most promising strategy for sustained, substantive school improvement. The idea was to build the capacity of school personnel, recognizing that the path to meaningful change in the classroom lies within and through professional learning communities. The emphasis was on student learning; and I understood that. However, while we often used that very term, I seemed always to add the word "teaching" to it, so it came out that we considered HCMS a Professional Teaching-Learning Community, a meld of two of the most important aspects of education. How so? I had embarked on a mission to change the culture, and in so doing, placed a passionate emphasis on enhanced, research-based teaching and instruction that, I reasoned, would result in improved student learning, beneficial not only to our kids and staff but also to their families and our community. That reasoning turned out to be spot-on.

Among the early leaders of professional learning communities was former Illinois school administrator Richard DuFour, who stated the following in an issue of *Educational Leadership*:

> The professional learning community model flows from the assumption that the core mission of formal education is not simply to ensure that students are taught but to ensure that they learn....

School mission statements that promise "learning for all" have become a cliché. But when a school staff takes the statement and literally—when teachers view it as a pledge to ensure the success of each student rather than as politically correct hyperbole—profound changes begin to take place. The school staff finds itself asking, What school characteristics and practices have been most successful in helping all students achieve at high levels? How could we adopt those characteristics and practices in our own school? What commitments would we have to make to one another to create such a school? What indicators could we monitor to assess our progress?

When the staff has built shared knowledge and found common ground on these questions, the school has a solid foundation for moving forward with its improvement initiative.[14]

The Harper's Choice Middle School professional teaching-learning community was rooted in character, asking ourselves four questions regularly in our instruction: *What is it we want all HCMS students to learn? How will we provide it? How will we know if they have learned it? How will we respond if they don't?*

We had an organized graduated intervention process to answer our fourth question, "How will we respond if they don't?" Each schoolwide intervention in place, regarding each of our two major goals dealing with academic achievement and student behavioral performance, was a collaborative venture based on a thorough review of the literature. The fact is that so many of our students were at below-grade level in reading and mathematics, that it made it inordinately difficult for many kids to understand the material in their other subjects and all but impossible to perform well academically.

There were certainly those times when we felt that we were working as hard and as smart and as fast as we humanly could, and yet for a number of our children, any academic advancement was glacial at best; it was, at times, maddening. It was frustrating to staff; I heard and very much felt their frustration, but we had to remind ourselves that it had to be all the more disappointing for these students, who continued to perform less than expected, sometimes expressing their own individual frustration. Everyone knew that it meant a recommitment to working still harder and smarter in the effort to boost the achievement of these youngsters. Everyone knew the importance of role-modeling the character traits taught to students throughout the year, so we would persevere, continue drilling down on the data, review additional research-based best practices, and employ differing high-leverage strategies with the sole focus of advancing our students' academic performance levels.

We employed strategic use of co-teaching, the practice of having two or more educators in the classroom providing instruction to students. Our model paired a general education teacher with a special education teacher, since a number of classes included students with learning disabilities. Each of our non-Challenge Reading classes had co-teachers at all three grade levels. The teachers had taken professional development training in this area, and together, they employed instructional strategies that enhanced their efforts to reach and to advance the reading performance of their students.

Various intervention practices by staff were in place to assist struggling students, so those youngsters encountering below-grade level performance in all their classes received immediate attention. These strategies allowed us to stay abreast of student academic and behavioral progress in each grade level, among which were our weekly KidTalk meetings and Instructional Intervention Teams (IIT), composed of the assistant principal, guidance counselors, school psychologist, special education teacher, alternative education teacher, health nurse or aide, reading specialist, speech pathologist, and mathematics instructional support teacher, all of whom were solid professionals who graciously expanded their individual roles to look at how best to address students' academic and behavioral needs.

Grade-level teachers would regularly review various data points, from tests, formative assessments, report card grades, attendance, local assessments, state functional testing, and behavior information, to understand how best to assist those students struggling in classes. It might have involved only a teacher conference with the youngster to get the youngster back on track. If more assistance was required, the instructional team leader and another staff member would schedule conferences with the student and parent, offering any ideas that might support the youngster academically, with the intention of improving the youngster's academic progress. There would be no delay in the stopgap measures we provided. Where more of an intervention was required, the youngster's name was referred to our school IIT. They would collaboratively problem-solve with the referring teachers who requested assistance.

One of the team members would volunteer to be the youngster's case manager. Together, the team would develop appropriate interventions, *student support plans* (referenced earlier), ensuring that struggling students received timely academic and social-emotional supports, enhancing school efforts to bring about each youngster's academic success. I asked to receive a copy of the names of students on academic support plans, as well as their report card grades for each grading period in English, mathematics, reading, science, and social studies. In various meetings with staff, students, or parents throughout the year, the list was a ready reference, allowing me to address directly the progress of any of those students. On the subject of student supports, we also compiled Student Support Plans each grading quarter for those students who were new to the school and in need of assistance. This would include, as well, students reading below grade level and having a group support plan; these identified students very close to passing one of the state functional tests.

Try as we might, and as we would continue to do mightily throughout each successive academic year, we would invariably have kids who were likely going to be retained; there would be no so-called social promotion to the next grade level, and there was no thought that we would leave it at that. No, we developed a Retention Program, a well-thought-out student support plan for those cherubs who would not be promoted to the next grade, a program we also put forth to address our at-risk students the following year, an effort that required the shared partnership of and a contract signed by the student, parent, and school principal. Essentially, the students would be assigned a specific homeroom class with other students retained in grade, with a member of the student services staff as their homeroom teacher; this might be a guidance counselor, pupil psychologist, or alternative education staff member. Their students' daily schedules would be modified to reflect how best to address their needs, including a tutorial in mathematics and reading, and any additional academic support as might be needed. We left open the possibility that students meeting the criteria outlined in the contract could move on to the next grade level at the end of the first grading quarter, after which no promotion would be granted. Those students so promoted would receive a binder of notes, activities, and projects from the first marking period subject areas to study and get on top of, as their progress would be followed by staff.

The retained students also were assigned to the same academic enrichment class within their daily schedule and led by their homeroom teacher, the same member of our student support services staff. This would allow for close monitoring of their daily progress, as well as provide support for and instruction by rotating staff members in social skills and developmental assets (support, empowerment, boundaries and expectations, constructive use of time, commitment to learning, positive values, social competencies)[15], organizational and study skills, academic tutoring, and homework assistance. These students would also be placed on our alternative education caseload, and support would be provided as needed in their academic classes.

Ongoing parent involvement would be required through regularly scheduled parent conferences (sometimes having to be done in the evening, and then only if I/the school was offering pizza, which I learned early on was a major incentive to increasing my parent involvement after school hours for our at-risk student population). The progress of these students would be monitored throughout each grading quarter by the school Instructional Intervention Team. This would include reviewing the data, including subject area tests/quizzes, their status on state functional tests, any disciplinary referrals, and report card grades. Documentation of each student's progress was provided to school administrators.

Such organized schoolwide supports became a hallmark of the Harper's Choice Middle School professional teaching-learning community, ensuring that those students encountering difficulties triggered a response that was *timely*—we quickly identified those students needing additional support; *based on intervention* rather than late remediation—staff provided immediate assistance, rather than having to rely on later summer school, retention, or, as cited, remediation; and *directed* rather than suggested—that is, instead of inviting students to seek additional assistance, our strategies in place required the students to devote extra time or receive additional assistance until they mastered the necessary concepts. Their parents were always contacted, and where I had to become involved in the matter, I would explain to the parent and student in my office why such was required, not voluntary, and that they could thank school staff later. Where it was an issue that concerned academic achievement, I do not recall an instance—not a single occurrence—when a parent was not cooperative in seeing that their youngster complied with our efforts to see him or her successful.

One could observe instruction and learning reinforced in some fashion in the way of academic interventions every day of the academic year. Teachers and parents could refer youngsters to get additional assistance in mathematics in an early morning program, five days weekly, before the school day began. The mathematics instructional support teacher, sometimes with an extra participating mathematics teacher, would communicate with the youngsters' classroom teachers as to the skills covered. We had a partnership that saw senior citizens tutoring/mentoring our youngsters in reading. More on that later.

Our mathematics and reading specialists worked in tandem with our ESOL students twice weekly to support mathematics objectives and, given that English was their second language, on mathematics word problems, the reading specialist providing strategies for how to use their reading skills to problem-solve. We offered an extended-day program until 6:00 p.m. called Cougar Time (named for the school mascot), in conjunction with the county parks and recreation and police departments. Led by HCMS participating teaching and support staff, the program provided strategies for both the students and their families designed to improve academic performance and personal growth, while providing youngsters with a safe, nurturing, and enjoyable environment during after-school hours. This program provided benefits far beyond the additional instruction and learning during this time of day. More on this program in the pages ahead.

Students whom we found would benefit from an additional, smaller class size with more individualized instruction were placed in an accelerated mathematics class. We were able to offer one class per grade level, and we purposely kept the number of students in these classes to twelve or fewer. We would pore over data nonstop, and those students scoring Basic on state testing, but 25 points away from proficiency, would find themselves given a "second mathematics class" during the Academic Enrichment portion of the daily schedule, where they would focus on test-taking skills, those skills not related to any subject matter but more related to a student's attitude and approach to taking a test. They would learn about the importance of being prepared, arriving on time, being relaxed for a test, being sure to listen attentively, reading test directions carefully, learning how best to use allotted time and to look for cues, and being certain to answer all questions. These are skills that I, via the school public address system prior to state testing, would regularly remind students to practice over the years at both the middle and high school level.

Specific students, based upon assessment scores and report card grade level designation, would receive instruction in a Soar to Success reading program focused on vocabulary, comprehension, and fluency, where they would focus on reading strategies regarding summarizing, clarifying words, questioning, and predicting. Still other students needed assistance in the areas of decoding (learning letter-sound relationships that allow one to pronounce words correctly) and phonemic awareness (the ability to hear and understand that spoken words and syllables are made up of speech sounds). This intervention, called Spell-Read, allowed for small group and individualized instruction. I was fortunate to have hired two specific instructional assistants who went beyond the scope of their job descriptions to go through the considerable training required for this specific targeted instructional delivery; they were, in effect, these youngsters' teachers. They "owned" the program, and the students under their charge—if they continued to make the right choices as growing literate adults today—likely realize their success is based in no small part on the love, care, and expertise they received when learning to read at HCMS.

We also offered Math Odyssey and First-in Math web-based mathematics programs and a web-based Study Island reading program, not to mention an academic intervention four-week summer program for some one hundred targeted students who were below-grade level and needed time for review and reinforcement of basic skills. The point is that teaching and learning now was at a peak level at Harper's Choice, with the entire staff operating on all cylinders to shore up student academic and behavioral deficiencies that would soon see them encounter more regularly their first share of success in school and beyond.

The school was also a regional site for students with emotional needs, youngsters who required intense services. These students with special needs fell within the purview of IDEA, the federal Individuals with Disabilities Education Act. It is appropriate and sound—and it is prescribed by law—that these unique, special youngsters be educated in the "least restrictive environment," but reason also needs to be exercised. A regular education student, in my view, gains a great deal by working alongside those less gifted in ability, and likewise, special needs youngsters gain much from being able to attend classes with other regular education students. Where outbursts or other disruptive behaviors occurred regularly, a review of the youngster's individual education plan was found to be in order, and the school increased resources to provide more meaningful assistance or determined that another placement, perhaps out of school in another more intensive special education center, was more appropriate. In all these matters, we wanted to be as caring as humanly possible without losing sight of the school's overall mission of providing a quality teaching and learning atmosphere for staff and the student body.

In many communities—both rich and poor—there are those who have their own agendas and may mean well. My particular commitment was that there would be no politics or favoritism interfering with our focus on results—meaning, success for all of our students. Politicos, school advocates, local board of education officials, and community members occasionally would request a tour of our school, but political positions on issues itself were not entertained. I was specifically eradicating any semblance of identity politics and the willful segmenting of a race or group for special attention that is now so regularly observed in school systems. On this subject I would suggest that school districts consider ending the use of race as the metric and begin focusing on specific performance results for all student groups, notwithstanding educrats and various activists likely viewing such as heresy.

Over the years staff, students, and parents have commented on the existence of race-based groups in schooling. Those advocating such groups frequently are viewed as believing their racial focus should be a kind of special interest, where "their" students should be treated differently (they will deny this), should play by different rules (they will refute this), and, in effect, should receive special treatment (they will reject this). Why the existence of such programs? Proponents will argue that they are "leveling the playing field," but that is an accommodation, a benefit that ought well be provided to all students, no matter what they look like, kids who, for whatever reason, need a "leg up."

There are many students of all backgrounds, no matter one's race or socioeconomic level, who have unique challenges or hardships and find themselves academically or socially challenged, irrespective of the color of their skin, their zip code, or the positions in the workplace held by their parents, and they deserve the same level of attention and care that school officials purport is given by way of singular-focused race-based initiatives. Such programs are misguided, unwise, and fundamentally unfair. There is a clear sense of—read actual—separation when only one out of many belongs. In point of fact, the staff and I viewed the student body at our school—each and every student—as *our* students, belonging collectively to our staff, our parents, and our community.

Everyone with a view on our education system and how schools are run generally means well and wants the best for the youngsters, their teaching staff, and the greater community. The current and continuing philosophical bent throughout the country on how best to improve minority achievement has not been particularly successful and does not bode well for our students' futures. It is in that spirit that I would argue we take a different tack and look at student achievement with an eye for better serving our total national student body and provide services more equitably that would enhance efforts to reach *all* youngsters. We did so at "The Choice," with total success.

Years ago, I made such a suggestion to a local school system that provided—in fact, prided itself on offering—such a program, focused on a particular race, which, of course, meant excluding other races within the school district. I recommended that if they insisted on touting such an utterly divisive race-based initiative, they should replace the name of the program with the term "multicultural," a term in vogue at the time and one that, at least, would be inclusive, which is what schooling should be. You could have heard a pin drop in that room of several hundred school district administrators, directors, and assorted staff. Not a single individual raised an objection.

Such seemingly hidebound and parochial race-based programs are, by their very nature, exclusionary and divisive, which is antithetical to the goal of providing an enriching education to all of a community's school-age youngsters. I suggested they jettison the so-called Black Student Achievement Program in favor of a *Multicultural Achievement Program*, whereby the school district(s) could individually "map" out avenues to success for underperforming students, no matter the color of their skin. School districts could then make better use of taxpayer funds by employing those proven, "best practices" across the country to advance the academic performance for children of *all* races. Such a change in school district program offerings would be more in keeping with the spirit and promise of a stronger, more inclusive America.

This very school site where I was at the helm boasted such a race-based organization, and it was brought to my attention by staff—including those of color—that the program was frequently seen as a distraction. They stated that some students felt "targeted" and unwillingly "separated" from their non-black friends.

I recall a similar incident at a high school, in which a black student—a great kid and a fine wrestler—felt he was singled out by that school's race-based program coordinator for declining to participate. He was subsequently asked, "Why are you not proud of your culture?" He asked an administrator for some intervention with the matter. School administration, the parents, and the student met with the sponsor to clarify the inappropriateness of her approach and the manner in which she had conducted herself. She apologized, and the matter was closed, with the parents shaking their heads. The student graduated and went on to do well.

HCMS staff expressed that too often were kids associated with this race-based program seemingly taken out of their academic classes for no substantive reason. Teachers reported being told by the students themselves that, among the reasons they were taken out of class pertained to discussing neighborhood get-togethers, deciding who would run for offices with the student organization, and in one instance, a youngster reported being asked if she thought another staff member (of color, incidentally) was racist against other blacks. It was early on in the year, prior to the opening day of school for students, when I sat down with the program's school sponsor to discuss the organization and obtain her perspective on its effectiveness.

I thought about it and later decided it best that the program not operate during the school day, but that it could remain, for the time being, as part of our after-school club offerings, which did not sit well with the staff member nor with school district headquarters staff values or sensibilities. Not long after our conversation, the sponsor tendered her resignation, and shortly thereafter, the organization's school system headquarters "director" called to tell me she would send me a replacement. I said, "No, thank you. As you know, we're operating the program differently now, and while it will be offered as an after-school club, I prefer to interview the candidate myself and approve the next hire who will be part of our staff, as opposed to someone being 'placed' at the school." I suspect I was viewed as a turncoat, a renegade. Nevertheless, it is entirely appropriate--and wise-- that any staff member assigned to a school have the approval of its principal. As stated earlier, those school principals who routinely rely on school headquarters human resources departments to interview, select, hire, and place teaching staff in their schools gamble that those new individuals to the school are a good fit for their specific community; not a good idea. Know your staff, each and every person working in your school. For the record, no candidate files for the race-based program were sent or referred to me for review for the remaining years that I was the school's principal. Noteworthy is the fact that we were among the few schools, if not the only school, in the district without such a program, and our black kids, as a cohort, still very much went on to improve academically and behaviorally, above and beyond some schools that had such race-based programs. The receiving high school's principal and administrative staff regularly informed me and my staff of how pleased they were to see the turnaround, the academic and extracurricular involvement, and the success that all our kids—including our minority populations—were now enjoying since I had taken the helm of Harper's Choice. Truth be told, none of our success would have occurred without the tireless efforts and expertise of a professional, hardworking staff; supportive parents; and the many students who began to see the promise within themselves and who responded accordingly. It was a total teamwork effort, the results of which were terrific to experience by everyone over those several years when I was privileged to be their principal. More on race and achievement in later chapters.

The excitement; the buy-in on the part of staff, students, and parents; and our palpable initial progress led me to want to establish a professional partnership between Harper's Choice Middle and an area university. The school previously had such a partnership, but that program wound up spinning its wheels because of the school's negative climate, and the school system ended the initiative. I intended to resurrect the idea, but I wanted to do it in a meaningful and professional manner. Staff indicated that the prior school environment was simply too chaotic, though staff affiliated with the program were giving it their best efforts. They cited repeated poor student behavior, inconsistent teaching practices, and perceived indifference on the part of numerous staff, school administration, and community, which made for a troubled experience for visiting teaching interns.

However, this was a far different school in so many ways. We were, in fact, exhibiting all the characteristics of an effective, successful school, and I believed this merited consideration of such a professional school-university partnership. On more than one occasion did I make our case to school system headquarters; they listened and appeared open to the idea. I continued to keep them apprised of our progress, and it was not long before we received the approval to move on such a project again.

In the same vein that a hospital is affiliated with a medical school, in which medical students receive practical training, a Professional Development School (PDS) would enhance our efforts to improve instruction, to provide practical training for teaching interns, to support and encourage ongoing continuous improvement, and to advance student learning through research-based teaching and learning. We would enjoy a collaboratively planned partnership for the academic and clinical preparation of teaching interns and the continuous professional development of both Harper's Choice teachers and university faculty. I appointed a terrific teacher among our staff as our PDS site liaison, working with HCMS and Towson University, just outside Baltimore. Working with teaching interns allowed teachers to stay that much more abreast of education trends and research on effective teaching techniques and student academic achievement. There would be innovative and reflective practice by the participating interns and professional teachers. As a PDS site, faculty and administration could take advantage of coursework and clinical experiences. The experience provided me, as principal, a pool of potential teaching candidates that later would take professional teaching positions at our school. HCMS staff were contacted to share their experiences with schools throughout the state considering such a partnership. As a Professional Development School, we were further elevating the level of instruction at Harper's Choice. It was yet another positive trait that continued to raise our stature as a solid public school competently serving both our community and school district.

"The Choice" would begin a steady climb, making progress each year on state tests, reaching the point where *all* our student groups would, in fact, make AYP, what the state called Annual Yearly Progress on state standards, an achievement not reached by many school communities with "stronger" demographics. We were proud of our students; I was proud of our staff.

I was regularly making an argument with central office headquarters staff that we could use additional staffing, to the point that they'd run in the opposite direction when they spotted me. Among the staffing acquisitions that impacted our instructional focus was that of mathematics instructional support teacher (MIST), a position that would provide direct instructional support to teachers already working hard, a position that would further allow us to rachet up our professional development efforts in this area. She was a seasoned teacher and knew some of our staff. We talked about education philosophy, the incremental advances we felt we were making at Harper's Choice, and our current mathematics program. I felt it was a good fit, and she went on to provide meaningful support to our mathematics team, our youngsters, and their families. She had successful teaching experience herself and did a nice job mentoring our newer staff. She was proficient at data gathering, and she took the initiative to work with scores of our cherubs in need of bolstering their mathematics skills. She was a terrific choice, and I was delighted with her performance.

Remember that I, too, had made a commitment to staff, students, parents, and soon enough, to the wider business community that I would lead HCMS in a manner that prioritized teacher instruction and student learning; set high standards for student academic and social development and adult performance; that I would insist on content and instruction that ensured student achievement; that we would create a culture of continuous learning for students and teaching staff; that we would use multiple sources of data to assess, identify, and apply instructional improvement; and that I would actively engage the community to create a shared responsibility for student and school success. It was a tall order, and I made it a point to review regularly my commitment, examining just how I was adhering to those standards, which I felt became part of my DNA; I lived and breathed HCMS instruction and student performance. I owned it!

You could feel the transformation occurring at our school. We were all about instruction, learning, and finding ways to boost our students' academic and social-emotional components. I had the support and confidence of the superintendent, who gave me the latitude to make the changes I felt were necessary; I had the respect and growing support and confidence from staff and students, the parents, and now the business community. I was not at all concerned with other central office administrators or politicos or anyone I knew who had their own issues or axes to grind or might not have approved of whatever it was that we were doing. Our focus was delivering high-quality instruction, and I was not entertaining any blather that might get in the way of teacher and student success.

Since we were serving a busy demographic community, I emphasized to staff on more than one occasion that, no matter how disconcerting or dramatic the topic or issue at hand (we had our share of family disruptions that spilled over to the school, social service investigations, and police or other law enforcement inquiries) in or outside of the school community, they were to maintain focus on providing high quality instruction; we (the administration and support staff) would work to resolve the issues that might arise, but their priority, daily, was to concentrate on delivering top-shelf teaching to each of their students. As that occurred, we found that a growing percentage of our students began to value learning and to work at acquiring knowledge.

I brought on staff an alternative education teacher, who was returning to the States from Europe, a responsible and effective educator with whom I had worked previously at the high school level. She jumped at the chance to work with me in this school setting, and she did an outstanding job meeting the needs of students with significant behavioral and academic challenges.

I had reviewed the files of a host of students who were repeatedly responsible for interrupting instruction. There were those cherubs whom I thought could remain at HCMS, if they had meaningful one-on-one assistance that I believed a school-based alternative education program could provide. Such a program would—or ideally should—provide academic and behavioral supports and interventions. This teacher worked with outside community agencies, including the police and social services representatives, much like a pupil personnel worker, and she was particularly good with parent outreach. She stayed on top of monitoring the progress of those students assigned to her and her assistant, all the while providing meaningful skill development in conflict resolution and anger management, which many of our youngsters sorely needed. It would turn out that these kids would benefit greatly from the program, as they went off to high school, having tasted success and feeling far more confident than they might have felt otherwise.[16]

There still remained a number of students who exhibited repeated disrespectful, disruptive, sometimes violent behaviors, individuals I knew needed to be out of our school, educated at the school system's countywide alternative education program. I recall at the time being disappointed and, frankly, exasperated with the staff and previous administration that such students had been allowed to remain at the school; these were older, hardened youngsters who regularly stole, fought, cursed staff, and generally were well-known to disrespect peers and adults. I was having none of it, if successful instruction and learning were to prevail, so I got to work reestablishing the team cited earlier, our Instructional Intervention Team. Composed of the assistant principal, school psychologist, and guidance counselor, among others, the IIT would zero in on those students who would benefit from the countywide alternative education program. Such a placement would see these youngsters receiving closer adult supervision, smaller class sizes, ongoing school and home partnering, along with learning strategies and approaches that would be individually designed to meet the needs of such students.[17]

There is a great deal of benefit that schools, families, and communities can derive by offering extended-day and extended-year programs. I was interested in applying for grants to extend both our school day (cited earlier) and school year programs to bolster our instructional efforts to engage and move the student academic performance needle. I spoke with different staff at school district headquarters to ascertain what possibilities existed, and the assistant principal would head up a committee looking into what was available. Ironically, I knew I also wanted to reboot the after-school program that had been offered the year before my arrival, the one that put us in a financial pickle. It was ill-managed, and staff said it was disorganized such that only a handful of staff wanted anything to do with it. That would change. I spoke to our local police and the governor's office in Annapolis to request a meeting, since we were, in fact, located in the heart of a designated Maryland State Police Hot Spot Community, and the grant we would be operating under was funded through the governor's office.

The extended learning opportunity would furnish both additional academic enrichment and supervised activities for our kids beyond the traditional school day. I would regularly observe school-age youngsters—elementary, middle, and high school—running about the neighborhoods all hours of the late day and evening; I recognized that a number of them were our cherubs. Well-planned and organized extended-learning programs could, I reasoned, support our academic efforts and provide safe, positive activities for our kids after school hours.

The research is clear; the hours after the school day are the riskiest for youngsters. The After-School Alliance, in partnership with the Met-Life Foundation, cites the following:[18]

> The gap in time between the ringing of the last school bell and when parents arrive home from work has long been a concern of families, law enforcement and community members due to the potential dangers and risky behaviors that take place after school. More than 15 million students—including approximately 3.7 million middle schoolers[19]—are alone and unsupervised between 3 and 6 p.m., the peak hours for juvenile crime and experimentation with drugs, alcohol, cigarettes and sex.[20]
>
> The hours after school when children are on their own are not just a time of risks, it is also a time of lost opportunities to help students grow and develop the skills and competencies to make positive life decisions that can lead to their future success. Strong support and guidance are critical to middle schoolers during a life stage that shapes their trajectory into high school, college, career and beyond.[21]

After-school programs are an environment where students can go to feel safe and find staff and mentors whom they trust. They also offer a space where students can express their creativity, find their voice, learn how to deal with challenging situations, and better understand how the choices they make will impact their lives and the lives of those around them.

Access to after-school programs can help keep middle schoolers safe, keep them engaged in learning, and help them take advantage of their full potential as they navigate school, peers and their surroundings.

Additional studies over the years reveal identical findings. The bottom line is this: Turning youngsters out onto the streets with neither constructive activities, nor adult supervision is wholly unwise; not only does criminal behavior spike, but they themselves become victims of bullying and violent crimes, and they engage in risky behavior. The reality for many is an empty house and fending for themselves, including hanging with friends while parents are working.[22] Far better to have children in a program where they can receive help with homework and can participate in wholesome activities; that was our goal at Harper's Choice.

We also had a sizable non-native English (ESOL) population, and similar surveys indicate that students with limited English proficiency achieve fluency at a higher rate than those not in such a program. The fact is that I was most interested in getting such a program underway at Harper's Choice, one we would ensure was organized and well-managed. The extended discussions, the presenting of successful in-school initiatives and results, and the wrangling that took place for some time proved beneficial. We received funding for our Hot Spot after-school program, which included partnerships with county police and county department of parks and recreation. We had quality school staff associated with the program, as well as police and parks and recreation department employees who connected well with kids. We saw to it that it was linked to the school day with enrichment opportunities, frequently involving activities for the families, and we would evaluate the program each year to look at strengths and weaknesses, making any necessary adjustments. As the years progressed, we applied for additional grants and were able to provide an even more extensive, wide-ranging after-school academic initiative.

In the interest of continuing our efforts to bolster instruction and learning, we wanted to ensure that any staff member new to Harper's Choice would have a mentor, and I asked a wonderful world language teacher of Spanish to coordinate the effort. She was great with kids and a good workplace team player, always smiling and enthusiastic. She was happy to do so, and she met with the administrative team to discuss ideas and coordinated staff to serve as mentors. Arriving new to a workplace, often unfamiliar with the community, can be a bit daunting, whether a beginning or seasoned teacher. There is nothing of value in expecting a new teacher to "sink or swim," which is generally the case in many schools. If I wanted to ensure first-rate instruction, it was paramount that these folks new to the school felt as comfortable as possible. This added feature augmented the confidence level of our new staff, which allowed them to adapt to their new environment more comfortably.

Over the course of the first week of return for all staff, we blocked out a few minutes each day for an orientation activity for our new staff. The first day might be breakfast and a tour of the school; the following days would see them receiving a presentation on rules, policies, procedures; a gift and sweets would be provided to help them through their initial week; lunch for both mentor and mentee to chat up the school and academic year; a potluck lunch with the administration on another day; and a PowerPoint presentation on who's who at HCMS, allowing them to associate a name and face with the staff member's responsibility so they would know whom to contact for any questions. Opening day of school for our students saw a treat and note of encouragement placed in the mailboxes of our newest staff members.

Recently hired staff believed that the program allowed them to feel more at ease, more productive, and more effective than they might otherwise have been. Each would say that the orientation and the fact that they were able to meet key personnel facilitated better communication between them and veteran staff. If there were questions or a clarification needed on a policy, an issue, it was nice to touch base with a trusted mentor. It turned out to be a tremendous idea, and we provided it every year that I was principal.

I advised our staff and school PTA that we would develop an end-of-academic-year annual report. We would begin producing end-of-year *State of the Content Area Reports* that would be the basis of the *HCMS Annual Report*. Each subject area description would serve to be a comprehensive report on our school's activities regarding our two major goals throughout the academic year. Much like any corporate report, the information would be shared with our community and with school district headquarters. The report would also include a description of our school's instructional and management activities, as well as provide a picture of our overall student academic performance. I would reference it as I would address various community business partners, including the Rotary, a group of successful businessmen and businesswomen who were especially supportive of our school turnaround. Teaching staff would zero in on their efforts and the results of those efforts, taking pride in their performance and the accomplishments of our students. I also accessed any available school district funding that would allow the School Improvement Team and me to plan our summer professional development activities. The annual report would be reviewed at these summer meetings and used in our planning of the following academic year's goals and professional development training.

I felt good about the school's initial progress. Many on the teaching staff knew their craft; they felt valued, respected, and supportive. They appreciated the direction we were heading and were "on board" to effect a positive turnaround in student academic and behavioral performance. I was determined, responsive, and laser-focused on our results, all with an eye for improving academic performance classroom by classroom.

9

A Focus on Continuous Improvement

Continuous improvement. What is it? *Education Week* describes it as "a cyclical process intended to help groups of people in a system—from a class to a school district or even a network of many districts—set goals, identify ways to improve, and evaluate change in a sort of continuous feedback loop. It became a buzzword in K-12 policy and practice, as states, districts, and schools strove for systemic, long-term gains in student achievement, instead of looking for the next, shiniest silver bullet."[1]

Others cite that "continuous improvement" is used across industries to describe a process or approach to problem-solving that represents an ongoing effort to improve outcomes.[2] There are multiple continuous improvement models, among which is one long-standing model called PDSA—Plan, Do, Study, Act. The four stages of PDSA usefully illustrate the continuous improvement process:

> *Plan:* A continuous improvement team studies a problem that needs to be solved, collects baseline data on that

problem, elaborates potential solutions to that problem, and develops an action plan.

Do: The team implements its action plan, collects data on its intervention, and records developments.

Study: The team gauges the success of the intervention by comparing baseline and new data, analyzes results, and documents lessons learned.

Act: The team determines what to do with its results. Depending on the success of its intervention, the team may choose to adopt, adapt, or abandon its tested solution.[3]

The idea of assessing, analyzing, adjusting, and trying again is the trademark of continuous improvement, and this was an approach that became an integral part of the school improvement turn-around at Harper's Choice Middle School.

No matter the endeavor, there is a certain grace in always trying to improve, whether you are improving a skill, a talent, your job responsibility, or yourself. In the position I accepted, quality teacher instructional performance and student behavioral and academic achievement were a direct response to the emphasis we placed on and the efforts expended in the area of continuous improvement. These three areas—teaching, learning, continuous improvement—were interwoven throughout my tenure as principal of Harper's Choice, and professional development became an integral part of our success equation. Organizations—be they local businesses, companies, foundations, corporations, or schools—must exert an ongoing effort to improve their product, their service, or their process if they are going to excel and be at the top of their game. I mentioned my years-long interest in quality management and how successful pioneers in a particular industry steered their particular company to distinction. Often it was their focus on improved customer service that propelled their product and their company to greatness.

Whether in the classroom, working as part of an administrative team in several high schools, or as principal of this school, I had an early interest in continuous improvement, and sought ways—quietly and personally—to improve my own craft. It was about providing a better service to teaching staff, students, and their parents. I wanted feedback from my high school students on the various classes that I was teaching, so I created a teaching evaluation form that I left in an area of the classroom to be completed voluntarily; kids could elect to sign their names or submit anonymously. I would ask for comments on my class preparation, my organization, whether they thought I designed assignments that made them problem-solve and think critically, whether I was clear in giving directions and graded fairly, whether they thought they learned or gained something from the course, etc. I would include their thoughts and comments as I made adjustments to my instruction. Likewise, when I was a school administrator and principal, I gained insights over the years from the feedback received from staff, students, and community. The idea was to improve daily, throughout the year, every year, our mission of caring for and teaching the scores of youngsters that came through our doors. I wanted the staff to understand that such evaluations are healthy and can be anonymous and kept within their own purview, a practice that potentially could well improve their own instruction.

Harper's Choice Middle was a particularly different challenge. As the reader well knows, the school had fallen on hard times, and the school culture was found especially distasteful to staff, parents, and more than a few students. According to staff at the time, there was little, if any, substance to or meaningful interest in pursuing professional development initiatives. There was a professional development school initiative that had gotten underway, only to be taken away because of the school's unsavory, disruptive climate. Parents and staff described a school too beset with, in their opinion, a "lack of organization, student disrespectful behavior, low teacher morale, and parent dismay." In their view, they would say, "we'd just be spinning our wheels," attending to professional development activities when the poor school environment would not allow for it, a problem they would go on to say was "not recognized by school administrators or the board of education."

It was my view that it required the perspective of first things first. I would continue contacting, meeting, and listening to various constituencies. I knew what I wanted in the way of change and results, and my immediate priority was to get a hold of the school's dreadful climate that needed to see a complete metamorphosis. I had in my mind that staff, students, parents, and the wider community needed to see, to understand, and to believe my sincerity, sense of purpose, and tenacity—a palpable sense of leadership—before we could begin talking about real, substantive teaching and learning. Accomplishing that would give us entree to talk about professional development as a vehicle to continually improving what it is that we would go on to achieve at Harper's Choice.

We worked hard on providing a school environment conducive to teaching and learning that would turn out to be an endeavor requiring our attention every day, every year, for the years I was their principal. I met with several of the school's constituents, and there were those I met with several times. Early on I sat down with key staff and assembled a professional development committee that organized meaningful activities throughout each academic school year. I had emphasized to staff early on that the professional development I had in mind had to be meaningful; otherwise, the sessions would have little effect and zero impact. So, we would want to solicit ideas from our staff, review the research, and ensure that our activities provided continuity between our professional development initiatives and what was happening daily in these classrooms; in other words, our professional development initiatives throughout the year had to revolve around answering those pivotal guiding questions:

- *What is it I want my students to learn?*
- *How will I provide it?*
- *How will I know if they have learned it?*
- *How will I respond if they don't?*

My initial go at this was to see that each of our monthly faculty-staff meetings featured a professional development segment revolving around accelerating student performance and strengthening instructional delivery. Each month saw a presentation and seminar of, for example, "co-teaching," usually pairing a general education teacher and a special education teacher working together with groups of students in one classroom; "every pupil response," which looked at techniques for getting all students actively participating in class sessions; and "quality inclusion programs" that could accommodate special needs youngsters in general education classes.

The emphasis on quality continuous improvement saw growing interest in professional development by all segments of the staff, both certified and non-certified employees. We capitalized on the opportunity to send various staff to out-of-state professional development seminars, the first of which was an instructional performance conference in Philadelphia, for which we were able to secure funding for five staff members. These attendees later made presentations at our school faculty and staff meeting, at which they cited "best practices" gleaned from their conference attendance.

As time progressed, I rearranged our monthly staff meetings, and we tailored professional development to specific subject areas. We would commence a monthly professional development strand called "Enhancing Instructional Practices and Student Achievement at The Choice," which saw all major academic departments meeting separately in the effort to collaborate on teaching-learning excellence in their subject area, to review and drill down on available student academic data, and to share "best practices," that colleagues were either currently using or were practiced elsewhere that showed promise, practices we would consider for our population here at Harper's Choice. In the interest of drilling down on available data, each staff member was touching base and coordinating with the school assistant principal, data clerk, and attendance secretary in the effort to assemble needed student data for these professional development meetings. Staff would review students' class quizzes and test scores, classroom deportment, student report cards, student attendance, student schoolwide disciplinary data, and local district functional assessments, all with an eye for crunching the data in such a way as to determine the kinds of instructional delivery that were working best, while deciding to jettison less effective instructional practices, all with the singular focus of reaching more students and excelling student academic performance. It was impressive. I recall school district subject-area supervisors touching base with me after they had observed our content-area team leaders and teaching staff in these meetings to inform me how impressed they were to see such professionalism at work, the organization and detail not something they said was typical in many schools they visited.

The reader will recall that continually improving our craft was among the three core values (Instruction, Continuous Improvement, Connections/Partnerships) that would serve to propel us to deliver first-rate instructional performance at Harper's Choice. Our North

Star would be those pivotal guiding questions that we would ask ourselves individually.

The professional development activities offered each year thereafter were based on input solicited from staff and might include, for example, extra training in the use of technology; strategies for working with special needs students in the effort to enhance their academic success; taking a reading course that might meet recertification requirements; differentiated instruction (providing one's classroom students a range of different avenues for understanding new information and concepts); peer coaching or peer sharing (a confidential process through which two or more professional colleagues work together to reflect on current practices); expand, refine, and build new skills; share ideas; teach one another; conduct classroom research; solve problems in the workplace; or look at how best to use available data to improve a teacher's efforts to see more students academically successful. This input, available data analysis, and relevant feedback would be discussed and reviewed by our overall school improvement team.

The ensuing academic years saw us ratchet up our fervor for continuous improvement through a sundry of professional development initiatives, including standards of improvement associated with professional learning communities; exemplary programs that showed promise in advancing academic achievement; accountability parameters that cited best practices in the areas of instruction, programmatic issues, and leadership; educator-level factors that impact student learning (teachers connecting, involving, reinforcing, and knowing the learning preferences of students, creating a positive learning environment); vision of exemplary teaching and learning, believing that *all students can learn*; and, as always, content area high-leverage strategies that were specific, research-proven approaches in one's subject area that teachers used to reach their students and improve student performance.

As principal, I also maintained close contact with school system headquarters professional staff development coordinators and staff members, who were always able and willing to offer meaningful input, guidance, and support for our various continuous improvement initiatives. Whether reviewing school improvement guidebooks, exemplary models of instruction, educator-level factors impacting learning, or how best to analyze data, I would frequently have school system staff development facilitators out to the school to assist us in our efforts to enhance instructional delivery.

I recognized that we had on staff select individuals who were excellent teachers, so I often tapped one of our teachers or another staff person to work with or share various instructional strategies with their teaching peers that we found facilitated improved instruction and resulted in promoting wider student academic achievement. This would be done frequently, initially at our monthly schoolwide faculty meetings, then at our more concentrated subject-area monthly continuous improvement meetings, as well as on those days when schools would close for professional development. Each month, each academic year a growing number of staff were incorporating new instructional strategies in their individual content areas, as a result of participating, sharing, and discussing with peers various instructional techniques that showed promise in moving the student academic performance needle.

An idea occurred to me, when one of our successful teachers indicated an interest in retiring, and I asked what her plans were and if working part-time as a professional development teacher—more of a new-teacher mentor—might be something that appealed to her. She liked the idea, and along with the school district curriculum office, I got to work on writing a grant. The following year, for three days a week, we had an on-site retired professional teacher who worked with individual teaching staff on their professional development needs. She related well with staff and students, worked with teachers on lesson planning, ensuring that teaching staff had appropriate materials, activities, and assignments that were thoughtful and engaging. She provided timely and meaningful feedback to the individual teachers with whom she was working. The idea of having an on-site professional development staff person was huge. It resulted in more teachers engaging students in instruction, which saw a more confident staff connecting with and enhancing overall student academic achievement.The passion for instructional excellence and continuous improvement and the teamwork throughout the school had taken hold and continued throughout my tenure as principal. Our teachers were now collaborative teams with the singular focus of improving their instruction and enhancing student achievement. They were drilling down on the metrics regularly, not only in English, mathematics, reading, science, social studies, and special education; the related arts classes regularly met, as well, and during those times they might have an academic representative share subject-area goals and strategies. The reader will recall that each of the related arts teachers, mindful of these goals, would incorporate them into their instructional delivery with an eye for advancing their subject area, as well as the students' skill area that would, in turn, benefit them in their academic subjects. All subject areas found beneficial the idea of drilling down on different metrics, various data relevant to their subject in the effort to improve overall student classroom performance.

I mentioned earlier that our metric was a focus on results, not race. It was a paradigm shift, a completely different tact from the philosophical bent of school systems today. It was also a culture change, in more ways than one, that I had in mind, and I was bent on raising the level of instruction throughout the school such that our performance would "lift all boats." The best-performing school districts provide high-quality education across the entire system so that, ostensibly, every student benefits from excellent teaching.[4] We would be doing the same within this specific school community, and the way to do that was through professional development, and at the time, I didn't think anywhere was practicing it better than we, better than the teaching staff at Harper's Choice. Below is a copy of one of the entries I would typically place on our electronic bulletin the morning of the day teachers planned to conduct these meetings:

Professional Development Activity

A reminder that content area professional development meetings take place this afternoon in the area designated by your team leader. Unless you have already done so, please forward to the assistant principal your agenda, followed by the minutes of your meeting, which allows us to review, stay abreast of, and discuss at our administrative staff meetings.

As you know, these meetings should generally center around those high-leverage strategies cited last year and again recently in a memo from me...strategies meant to enhance our efforts to accelerate the academic skill levels of our students.

Be mindful of how meaningful these meetings are to be, if we are to see an appreciable increase in student achievement. That, of course, is no easy challenge, but it's no less an admirable one that we can and will meet.

We CAN move these scores...and build the academic muscle that lies within these walls.

Again...my thanks for everyone's time and energy!

This was serious and meaningful professionalism—teachers collaborating, reviewing, and crunching data, all in the effort to see more youngsters succeed. We as an administrative team would often observe different subject area professional development meetings more out of pure interest; it became a joy to witness so regularly the hard work and effort that obviously was going into the business of teaching and learning in a manner that had not been done previously.

All of us, together, zeroed in on research-based best practices throughout the profession that a teacher or teachers in that subject area had employed to reach wider student academic performance, locally or in another part of the country. I would frequently speak with teachers and school officials around the nation on various successful student academic performance initiatives that I was researching or came across by way of the media that might have piqued my interest.

I recall one of my earlier conversations with a research institution and later with staff members at an Inglewood, California, public school. The school had a majority Hispanic and black student population, and I had read of their success boosting the scores of their at-risk student body. I was intrigued and particularly interested in what they were doing to raise their youngsters' mathematics scores. Children entered the school with very low scores, yet the school's mathematics scores we're the envy of schools in more privileged settings. As a later article on the study asks: How did they do it? By studying a traditional curriculum that emphasizes fundamental math; by teachers directly instructing children, not relying on cooperative groups; by limiting the use of calculators until students had mastered basic arithmetic; and by relentlessly pushing children to learn more and reach higher.[5]

I would share such information with the appropriate subject area team leader, as well as the contact information if additional discussion or clarification might be needed. The idea was to leave no stone unturned in our effort to renew, with a passion, instructional performance techniques that had the potential of improving our school's teaching-learning experience in a manifold fashion.

Reviewing and using additional proven, top-shelf instructional performance initiatives at times was the result of an individual teacher's own research, or that of school system professional development staff, who provided meaningful assistance. In that respect, the strategy was more in the vein of business leaders learning to steer their companies toward success; they take inspiration from others and then adapt lessons learned to their own situation.[6]

The school was being viewed in a different fashion, even forward thinking (according to school district central office staff), forging head-on into uncharted territory, given the school's previous reputation inside and outside of the building. That forging ahead was a blend of "boundaryless" sharing of ideas, an intense focus on people, and an informal give-and-take that, frankly, at times might have seemed to distance school headquarters (not a goal, but it might have seemed that way), as we pursued a path that best met our community-specific needs, not unlike that which might have been reminiscent of many successful business folks over the decades like Jack Welch, former CEO of General Electric.[7]

We would occasionally invite school district headquarters staff to participate in these monthly continuous improvement, professional development meetings to lend any critical perspective. Much like the subject area supervisors who earlier commented to me on their observations, these district staff members from testing, assessment, and research departments would see me and express their appreciation for the seriousness at which teaching staff were working so collaboratively to examine student work; to problem-solve; to crunch, to analyze, and to share data points with peers; and when appropriate, to develop, to decide how best to monitor, and to implement student support plans for those cherubs demonstrating below-grade level academic performance. This was teaching professionalism at its best. It wasn't long before Harper's Choice Middle School instructional performance gains were talked up at headquarters meetings, as relayed to me on occasion by a host of other school system subject area coordinators and supervisors.

We had become a professional teaching-learning community. Our teachers were meeting regularly with one another, collaborating on how best to reach specific students so they, and their teachers, would see marked improvement.

As mentioned earlier, the addition of the mathematics instructional support teacher (MIST) proved a boon for the mathematics teaching staff and our students, as teachers benefited from the MIST's years of experience and successful teaching, and our youngsters received extra instructional time, as she would pull out specific kids needing academic assistance and work with them as they began to see improvement daily in their mathematics skills.

Each end of the school year saw us meeting at a school-business partner's restaurant, where they would provide a room, breakfast, and lunch. Here we would have most of the day to review our annual end-of-year reports on all subject areas, taking note of our progress on our two major goals for the year, citing areas in need of strengthening, and outlining any professional development initiatives that would enhance our overall school efforts toward excellence. Each year I would lobby school district headquarters to access funding that would allow staff to work during the summer months on goal-related initiatives for the following academic year. We also capitalized on the two to three days each academic year the school district set aside for professional development.

Now that we were also operating as a Professional Development School, we were further enhancing our efforts to improve instruction and student achievement. We took pride in establishing this partnership with the university and appreciated the various benefits it brought to our entire school community. The partnership dovetailed nicely with the value we placed on and derived from continuous improvement. Above and beyond the practical training for teaching interns that was cited earlier, we realized some meaningful professional development opportunities that enhanced our continuous improvement efforts, and a number of those future teachers participated in our extended-day academic achievement programs. We conducted or attended various workshops, we developed curriculum, and we conducted action research. Some staff took specific graduate coursework; formed study groups; observed and modeled lessons for peers, everyone working together to refine and build teaching skills, critique each other, and share classroom research. It was a professional collaboration, the substance of which would pay dividends for years to come.

The level of success we achieved at Harper's Choice Middle over those years was due, in no small measure, to the emphasis we placed on continually improving our craft. The passel of professional development activities in which we found ourselves immersed year after year led to an instructional renaissance that took on a life of its own, resulting in renewed staff interest in, if not, a passion for excellence in the classroom, the beneficiaries of which were our students and their families.

As principal, I was regularly assessing, analyzing, and looking at various data, then making needed adjustments. Perhaps by osmosis, more and more faculty and staff would come to exhibit a gradual, seemingly unconscious assimilation of the components of continuous improvement. As time and years would go by, I would become proud of the strong, diverse faculty and staff that we assembled. The newer staff—some younger and always on top of internet technology, as well as older, experienced individuals—always seemed to add a measure of knowledge, a can-do spirit, and care to subject area and grade-level teams, and all came to recognize how important the idea of daily improving self and our school was to our overall instruction and student academic achievement.

Our success at Harper's Choice Middle quite simply would not have been as pronounced if we had not incorporated an emphasis on continuous improvement throughout my tenure as principal.

10

A Culture for Teaching and Learning

The reader well knows at this point my view that an appropriate culture for teaching and learning is key if schools at all expect to be successful. Parents agree. According to the 2015 PISA (Programme for International Student Assessment) results, when choosing a school for their child, parents are more likely to consider *important* or *very important* that there is a safe school environment daily, that the school has a good reputation, and that the school has an active and pleasant climate—even more so than the academic achievement of the students in the school.[1] As a prelude to the rest of this chapter, I offer the following:

Public schools are a microcosm of society, and the reader is aware that I share former senator Patrick Moynihan's years-ago assessment that American society "defined deviancy down." His analysis was accurate in 1993 and remains today, in my view, not healthy for our country.

I had not the slightest intention of tolerating at this school site the ill behavior I had observed being tolerated regularly in schools for years. My personal constitution and perception of our declining culture had an indelible impact on my high expectations for success in the behavior expected from our students, staff (including me), and community, and it therefore played a not-so-minor role in our culture change at Harper's Choice.

Let me elaborate. Many people in our society today seemingly have lost their moral compass, and the result is a culture that has coarsened. Our students behave the way they do because they get it honestly. Too many of our youngsters and their parents appear bereft of the values and mores once taught at home and reinforced in schools. These values were among those we included in our character component within our daily school schedule throughout each academic year: self-respect; courage, personal responsibility; respect for parents, family, teachers, the law, our military, first responders, and our country; and the belief that you cannot respect others if you, yourself, have no sense of self-respect.

I informed staff that I viewed every teacher, no matter the subject area, as an English teacher. Each of us should be expected to use appropriate English when speaking and writing, and it's particularly important for our students to hear their teachers and other adults speak English properly. Lord knows that their school should at least be the one place where the language, our language, is respected. The more they hear it, and perhaps begin using appropriate language themselves, the better chance that one day it may work in their favor of standing out among others and being selected for a workplace promotion, perhaps being among those selected for acceptance to attend their first-choice college or university, or being asked among other employees to represent a product line at a national convention.

I also asked staff to join me in routinely calling out poor student behavior in the hallways, in the cafeteria, and in their classrooms. That would include how they spoke; I did not want boys and girls using inappropriate, much less vulgar language and have it excused because their parents used it regularly. It was about how many in society elected to carry themselves, as though there was near nothing worthy of reverence or respect, and I would like to think the majority of Americans find such behavior disconcerting. As I will cite again in this chapter, it is also healthy to keep in mind that the majority of youngsters of every race do, indeed, carry themselves with dignity and a sense of self-respect. It is for them, as well, that I believe we need to care about "things that matter"[2]—a deferential nod to the late esteemed columnist and author Charles Krauthammer, who had spot-on insight on American culture, education, politics, and government.

I asked staff to be mindful of our earlier discussion of the concept of "broken windows" and, without going over the top, remind students of the importance of respectfully addressing one another, saying, "Good Morning," using the name of the student or adult, if they knew them, or using a firm handshake, while looking directly at the teaching staff member or administrator and saying, "Thank you," upon receiving a certificate or award. That is how pride is developed, and I wanted kids to learn to understand how important it was to carry themselves well and to develop respect for a job well done. It is how boys and girls become humble, respectful, and appreciative men and women, and that is how we would change the community for the better. I was well aware that, for some of our students, this change in how we would do things would be incomprehensible, well aware that the word "family" had a very different meaning for many of them. Nonetheless, I would use various avenues—from addressing kids in the cafeteria, speaking to kids during and after the school day, during our weekend ball games, using the school's public address system, or addressing the community at a public event—any avenue that allowed me occasionally to reference and to chat up the importance of family values, tradition, honesty, balance in one's life, caring, learning, thrift, leadership, standing on principle, compassion, respect for family and country. It would be, for all of us, a major lift, a formidable challenge, and we fought the good fight every day to promote civility, compassion, and a love of learning and succeeding. This endeavor, as much as anything else I specifically cite in this chapter, enhanced our efforts to promote a culture for teaching and learning.

Successful schools across the globe are those with a formula that values the individual and the importance of instruction and achievement—its mission, its reason for existing—and in so doing they actively cultivate a culture for instructional excellence and successful student academic and behavioral performance.

Assorted reasons account for those schools that have strayed from their mission of educating a community's students. As referenced earlier, today it would appear that we are too prone to accept ill behavior that would have been considered inappropriate in a previous, more ordered, and civilized society. It has created an intractable predicament throughout America, including in many schools, where teachers, students, and parents express abject frustration, a considerable number seemingly feeling that the die has been cast. As the reader has come to understand from reading this book, I refer to behavior too often exhibited by students *and* adults, including school and administration staff, parents, and community. Throughout the book, I want the reader to understand that I am unequivocally *not* critical of the vast majority of students, who are courteous, personally responsible, and respectful; staff, who are professional, creative, and hardworking; and the many parents who are loving and caring, raise terrific children, and are active in and supportive of their schools.

I have mentioned on a number of occasions over the years, and I have cited several instances in this book when caring, actively involved parents worked in concert with me and our staff and played a huge role in our school's positive teaching-learning school culture.

I emphasized to our parents my belief in a shared partnership with them and the wider community. I asked that they support unequivocally the school's mission, that it was important that they stay actively involved in their children's school years, and that they were welcome—indeed, I would ask them, please—to capitalize on opportunities to play an active role in helping us achieve our mission. As a result, we had parents in and out of the building regularly, volunteering in classrooms, serving on our school improvement team, tutoring and mentoring students, and chairing or participating in any number of PTA committees. It was gratifying to see a once-strained relationship wholly transmogrify into one that now saw parents, families, and the community engaged and supported as partners in the education of our youngsters. It had an overall positive and heartwarming impact on our teaching-learning culture.

Throughout the nearly forty years in this business, many parents have heard me urge youngsters at both the high school and middle school parent-student-principal conferences or in large group settings the following: "It's not a good idea to audit life; you should opt, instead, to get up every day, make your bed, find purpose each morning, show up, work hard, and play hard, making the most of each and every day. That is how you will succeed during your school years, and later in a trade school, college or university, the military, and the world of work." That kind of interrelationship with parents and their youngsters over the years had built a kind of familial trust between home and school, which translated in making our school, in effect, an extension of the home, which completely enhanced our efforts to promote a rich, caring, and successful teaching-learning culture.

Among the reasons we enjoyed a successful academic culture was my right-hand staff. During the time I was principal, I happened to be fortunate to know and work with three respectful, thoughtful, and excellent assistant administrators, two of whom served separately as assistant principals, the other as an administrative intern. Over the years, we were on the same page with regard to our shared philosophy of school, student, teacher, and community expectations, and we communicated regularly throughout the day. I would not have been nearly as successful were it not for having known and worked alongside these smart, capable, talented individuals. Together, we took on a considerable challenge, and along with staff, students, and parents, we transformed our school into a culture for teaching and learning that afforded each of us some of the best experiences in our professional lives. Principals ought well be grateful, when they find themselves as charmed and fortunate as I. Praise and support those assistant principals for the many talents they bring to the table daily, without which many principals I've known over the years would have been lost. As unfortunate as the situation was at the time when I was appointed principal of Harper's Choice Middle School, I shake my head when thinking of the daily challenges presented in schools located in cities throughout the country like Philadelphia, Detroit, Baltimore, St. Louis, Los Angeles, and Washington, DC.

Returning a failing school to solid footing is a formidable challenge, but no matter its location, it can be done, and it must start by examining its school climate or culture. A good starting point lies in recognizing the pivotal importance that *character* can play in a successful school turnaround. Such a recognition could well be the catalyst for promoting a kind of rebirth for students, teaching staff, families, and whole communities. I will clarify that a turnaround can occur no matter the zip code, but it takes passion, grit, organization, and some reasonable smarts—but by no means does it take a genius. It takes caring, personal and professional accountability, problem-solving skills, conflict resolution, communication, an ability to motivate and delegate, a recognition that everyone matters, and intestinal fortitude—you have to be willing to go toe-to-toe on principle in the fight to preserve the dignity of your students, staff, parents, and school programs, if you are to serve your community well.

At Harper's Choice Middle, the formula began with a recognition that character would be the soul of the school, from which every decision would emanate. It followed that if we were going to get our house in order, there would need to be a palpable recognition that every individual mattered, that decisions made would be on the basis of mind, heart, and gut and whether such would be in the best interests of our students, staff, parents, and community. That principle followed for the years I was at the helm of that school, as did our motto:

High Quality Teaching + Parental Involvement +
Student Academic and Behavioral Excellence
First Step: NO EXCUSES

The reader will recall that for many individuals, our school motto became more of a mantra; it spoke to our beliefs, our values, and our near-monomaniacal focus on establishing a culture of instructional excellence and student behavioral and academic achievement.

The combination of placing character at the core of our school and establishing our "No Excuses" motto gave us entree to an "appropriate teaching-learning culture," that philosophical foundation of norms and beliefs—academic and social—that informs every aspect of a school's daily operation. Recognizing those pivotal components was precisely why we were able to bring about such a total and complete turnaround at Harper's Choice, which gave entrée to uninterrupted teacher instruction, solid positive student behavior, and high-achieving academic performance.

How we did so is played out in each chapter of this book, starting with an acknowledgment of the fundamental importance that character would play in achieving a wholesome, productive, more complete school mission. Where character is the soul of a school, you have a positive, vibrant teaching-learning climate with high expectations. That was my focus; it remained our focus throughout the years, and we consistently zeroed in on results, forging ahead week after week, looking at avenues that would produce those results time and again. The reader will recall teaching staff advising me early on of their frustration with students who remained in the hallways during class time—"hallers," they were called—frequently disturbing instruction, yelling at friends in classes, and causing mayhem. We put the blitz on that nonsense in that opening week of school in my first year, and it never became a problem. I can well imagine how it must have destroyed instruction and learning regularly in those previous years. That action item alone, I was advised by more than one staff member, improved our school climate considerably.

The reader learned that I re-established the school's Instructional Intervention Team, in part to review the number of students who exhibited repeated disrespectful, disruptive, sometimes violent behaviors, individuals I knew needed to be out of our school, educated at the school system's countywide alternative education program, where they would receive close adult supervision, smaller class sizes, ongoing school and home partnering, along with learning strategies and approaches that would be individually designed to meet the needs of such students. As we were able to transfer these students gradually but steadily to a more suitable placement, the positive effect on our school's environment, of course, was dramatic, and we could observe and "feel" that we were well on our way to a far more positive school climate that was paving the way for steady and continual successful teaching and learning.

I have outlined in various chapters a number of ideas, issue positions, and actions that cultivated and nourished our renewed emphasis on creating an acceptable learning culture. I will expound on a few of those practices, and I will introduce other activities that were a product of the enthusiasm, hard work, love, and caring of teaching and supportive staff, all in the effort to create an improved, positive, and supportive daily school environment that enhanced instruction and overall student success. These academic and socialization initiatives were schoolwide in scope, others were administered by specific grade-level teams, and still other ideas were put forward by support staff.

One of our teachers was gracious enough to take the lead on putting together a Building Cougar Character initiative that would be interwoven into our daily schedule for all our grade levels. She and staff members worked over a summer to put together a sizable packet from which teachers could provide teaching lessons and group activities. My written introduction for the booklet summarized the initiative and what we hoped to accomplish:

Building character is at the heart of a youngster's education. It is through this moral lens that we as a staff determined our school motto:

High Quality Teaching + Parental Involvement +
Student Academic and Behavioral Excellence
First Step: NO EXCUSES

We've taken a comprehensive approach to infuse character development in a manner that informs every aspect of the school day, believing that our students will grow to appreciate throughout their lives the importance of respect, courage, honesty, empathy, understanding, dignity, personal responsibility, integrity, perseverance, and resilience, among other traits, committing themselves to a lifetime of forming caring relationships.

Together we were experiencing a complete renaissance, a renewal that fostered teaching staff appreciation and improved student academic and behavioral performance and parent satisfaction. The more we focused on instructional excellence, the more fulfilling was our school culture. We were a busy demographic community, and the attitude was that no matter the challenge, no matter the obstacle or setback that might confront the school community, we would be a different, stronger, smarter school community, and I affirmed that our focus would remain on producing first-rate instruction and top-shelf student behavior and academic achievement. While I will likely miss mentioning every initiative that we got underway, the point is that the entire staff was about continually improving what it was that we were about—successful teaching and learning.

Academic initiatives, some of which I cited earlier, alone consisted of my feeling the need to designate the assistant principal as "lead teacher" in coordinating and keeping track of every initiative that was underway, initiatives that she and I would discuss and review at our weekly morning meetings. Our mathematics instructional assistant and a testing instructional assistant worked in tandem to establish student schedules that allowed for direct assistance to students. Like the instructional intervention team that devised meaningful student support plans for underperforming students, these two instructional assistants would work with mathematics, reading, and writing teachers to construct comprehensive student support plans to address those cherubs performing below-grade level; each student operating below-grade level in a subject had an individual student support plan. I asked seasoned, respected teachers to assist in providing professional development specifically for our non-tenured teachers in the effort to boost their confidence, and feeling of competence, in constructing these student support plans.

We provided a mathematics-reading initiative for yet other students with skills deficits in these areas, students who would have mathematics and reading classes daily (the reader will recall that our school daily schedule had students taking ninety-minute classes every other day). Above and beyond what the instructional assistants were providing their students, specific seventh- and eighth-graders with skills deficits would take what we called an interdisciplinary studies course, combining reading, writing, and mathematics. Specific special needs students were enrolled in a small group (some fifteen children) Spell-Read Phonological Auditory Training literacy program for struggling readers, cited previously. The sixth-grade team offered a reading and support class, as well as tutorials for our ESOL students, mostly immigrant students whose primary language was other than English. The seventh-grade team had two staff members offering student "pull-outs" for mathematics assistance and reading support. The eighth-grade team followed with weekly after-school work sessions for their students, arranged student schedules to allow for mathematics state testing tutorials, and worked after the school day with any student needing assistance in any subject.

I would occasionally remind folks that our school was about the four Rs (the first three usually said as "reading, writing, and 'rithmetic"), including *respect*, which required the need to go about our instruction in a more holistic fashion. We recognized the importance of supporting the social-emotional component of our students, that teaching and support staff—in and out of the classroom—needed to be mindful that some students have, through no fault of their own, challenges, stresses, and emotions that make learning, at times, seemingly insurmountable. We wanted to be cognizant enough to be there for them—mind, body, and heart—again, a kind of *cura personalis,* care for the whole person. I was fortunate to have a support staff—some veteran staff, others I would hire—who were among the finest, in my view. Our guidance counselors, alternative education staff, pupil psychologist, and PPW conducted various group sessions for students dealing with anger management; those who were immature and had friendship issues; others with self-esteem matters; students who may have been a victim of a specific circumstance, event, or action; those whose parents were divorced; and yet other students who might be dealing with depression or obsessive-compulsive disorder.

Let me expand for a moment on the importance of support staff in a school community. These professionals were also actively involved in developing ideas and taking lead positions on initiatives that would further enhance our efforts to provide a quality culture for teaching and learning. Our school psychologist coordinated a high school mentoring program that saw students from the feeder high school coming to Harper's Choice regularly to work with our middle level cherubs. She did this in collaboration with our PPW, who the reader may recall, was assigned to work with both the community's high school and our school. A prince of a guy, this gentleman was a kind of Father Flanagan (a reference to the main character in the biographical movie *Boys Town*), who would work with staff, students, and parents in the ongoing effort to resolve or prevent problems and challenges that could have adversely impacted our students' education. They provided this mentoring initiative twice weekly after the school day. Our students developed relationships with the high school mentors, who worked with them to boost their academic standing. These high school mentors would provide their younger peers with insight into how best to study and how to navigate their high school years, emphasizing the required appropriate behaviors these youngsters would need to be successful high school students.

The PPW typically works at the direction of the school principal. He would stop in and provide updates on his caseload of students. We could depend on him to make contact with any parent who was unresponsive to teacher, guidance counselor, pupil psychologist, or administrator attempts to reach the home of a particularly troubled student. He facilitated a Boys' Group, tackling various issues teens face, as well as reinforcing the character traits that would put them in solid stead as they matriculated through high school and beyond. As a PPW, he had contacts and was resourceful in obtaining medical and mental health services, as well, for students and their parents, when parents themselves had been previously unsuccessful in doing so. In the spring of each year, he would don sneakers and play alongside the students for whom he had coordinated an after-school tennis camp. He and other staff would coordinate efforts each Thanksgiving and Christmas to provide food and gifts for our needy youngsters, giving those families a chance to experience the spirit of the holidays.

Among the reasons we were able to cultivate a culture for success was the belief that everyone attending or working at HCMS mattered, again *cura personalis*. In the case of those youngsters presenting individual social-emotional challenges, the student's predicament was always met with a sensitive, caring, commonsensical approach. The appropriate guidance counselor, school psychologist, PPW, and school health nurse worked in tandem with the youngster, the student's parents, and the family physician or other health care provider. It was at all times a comprehensive approach that attempted to ameliorate the child's predicament. In specific circumstances, where there might be issues involving use of school bathrooms, arrangements were made for the student to use the school health room bathroom, as needed or appropriate.

As regards the very serious and sensitive social-emotional challenges that weigh on some of society's individuals, I take a moment to exercise author prerogative and provide a career professional educator's viewpoint:

> Given federal court decisions and the current national conversation about gender identity, I believe it appropriate to address the issue of gender dysphoria as it relates to schools. I am not a certified psychologist; neither are the politicos and jurists who have dictated transgender students may use a school restroom that matches their gender identity. Biological males identifying as females, for example, may freely enter girls' bathrooms or shower areas, as well as participate on girls' sports teams. Regarding school bathroom use, a federal court stated in one case that "a public school may not punish its students for gender nonconformity."[3] Such a statement is condescending and dismissive, in my view, and I cannot imagine any school willfully punishing any student dealing with such an emotional dilemma. Courts and other proponents blithely and piously make such remarks while denying biology and science and showing a complete disregard for fairness, for common sense, and for the privacy and dignity of biological female students and participating biological female athletes.

> Having spent a career in education, I suspect that such ill-conceived decision-making will prove disastrous and needlessly invite chaos and tragedy into the schoolhouse, not unlike that cited in 2018 of a Decatur, Georgia, mother alleging that her daughter, a five-year-old kindergartner,

was assaulted by a "gender-fluid" classmate, a biological male who followed her into the school bathroom.[4] So the political establishment and courts knew well that such a policy had more than the potential to exact confusion and chaos, if not outright harm on a school community, and yet they still proceeded to make it law.

I would hope that one day such a mandate will be revisited with an honest and factual recognition of biology, keeping politics and social engineering out of the schoolhouse. Students dealing with social-emotional challenges, including gender dysphoria, deserve the respect and dignity that ought well be provided any individual, but such should also be accorded *the remaining student body*. I imagine every biological male and female athlete wants to see their fellow classmates, who identify as trans girls or trans boys, treated fairly. However, the cost of treating fairly those youngsters identifying as trans should not come at the cost of discriminating against those students who, for example, were born biological females and deserve to compete fairly with other natal females and vice versa.

Legislative bodies—in this case, school boards—immediately abuse their role when they self-righteously take a position that willfully steals honor, respectability, and dignity from the majority of the student population because they, as school officials, are craven and feel pressured to make a decision, no matter how foolish or hairbrained. Those adults in pivotal decision-making positions owe it to those they serve to be better stewards of the trust and latitude given them by using common sense and avoiding nonsensical extreme overreach.

The scope of our academic and socialization initiatives was comprehensive. Each related arts subject area participated with various measures that would reinforce our total school effort to promote academic and behavioral excellence. Our school's world language classes successfully participated in the countywide "It's Linguistics" celebration of language; students in our family & consumer science classes sewed newborn baby quilts for the area hospital; the media center facilitated our senior citizen mentoring initiative, book fairs, computer drawing contests, and extended-day initiative; our music department sponsored or participated in various music showcase performances; and physical education supported mathematics initiatives by incorporating student use of measurement in physical fitness objectives, while focusing on peer interaction with an emphasis on sportsmanship, as well as coordinating after-school athletic intramural activities. Our alternative education staff were all about assisting students with organizational skills, assisting students with projects, providing academic enrichment study sessions, and utilizing in-school suspension time meaningfully to complete studies.

I will add that the related arts play a significant role in our schools, without which students, overall, would not perform as well in the more academic, state-tested subjects. Over the years at both the high school and middle school levels, I would inform parents and students of the importance of looking at options in the physical and fine arts to complement the child's educational experience. Research reveals that students who take music-related activities achieve significantly higher scores in science, mathematics, and English than their non-musical classmates.[5] Such offerings in schools enhance our efforts to ensure a school culture for instructional excellence and wider student achievement.

University of British Columbia professor Peter Gouzouasis, one of three authors of a study examining some 113,000 public school students in Canada, cites the following:

> Students who learned to play a musical instrument in elementary and continued playing in high school not only scored significantly higher but were about one academic year ahead of their non-music peers with regard to their English, mathematics and science skills. Just as interesting is that these statistics were consistent across the board, regardless of socio-economic background, gender, ethnicity, or prior learning in science, math, and English. Learning to play a musical instrument and playing in an ensemble is very demanding, the study's co-investigator stated. A student has to learn to read music notation, develop eye-hand-mind coordination, develop keen listening skills, develop team skills for playing in an ensemble, and develop discipline to practice. All those learning experiences, and more, play a role in enhancing the learner's cognitive capacities, executive functions, motivation to learn in school, and self-efficacy.[6]

That kind of focus, effort, and motivation on the part of students, in my experience, makes for a more refined, calmer, and nurturing school environment, one that is much conducive to instructional excellence and student behavioral and academic achievement.

The school's new and improved culture saw veteran staff responding in the affirmative when asked to consider sponsoring a club or activity; new staff were eager to get involved. I suggested we start specific clubs that would allow kids to participate in countywide competitions. We held a schoolwide spelling bee, where the winning student would participate in the larger competitions, then a schoolwide geography bee. I tapped a new social studies teacher to sponsor a Boys' Book Club, the only one of its kind; more about that in the next chapter. We had a talented drama club; we started a school Scrabble Club; we participated in science fairs, as well as a host of other in-school and intramural activities. One of the science teachers started an Energy Alliance Club, which revolved around finding ways to reduce school energy costs and to engage students in environmental education through hands-on, project-based activities. The students were tapped to participate in a Public Broadcasting Corporation documentary on climate change that was shooting segments throughout the United States. Film directors, a unit manager, and members of the taping crew could not say enough about our school and were effusive in their compliments to staff, parents, and student members of the club.

We secured a grant that would pay four staff members, two reading and two mathematics teachers, to provide early morning, one-hour tutoring/mentoring to struggling students in those subject areas. It required the commitment of both student and parent/guardian, and the mentoring program would enhance the students' efforts to pass the statewide academic assessments in mathematics and reading.

We made contact with a black fraternity of businessmen to meet with a number of our male students once weekly in the evenings, an effort that would provide yet another avenue to reach these youngsters, enforcing the values of making good choices, working hard, being personally responsible, and being respectful if they were to achieve worthy goals in life.

Among our school-business partnerships was an engineering firm whose Hispanic male engineers initially addressed our Hispanic student males in the effort to steer our youngsters on the right path. As was done for our black males above, I requested that these gentlemen impress upon our youngsters the value of hard work, attending school daily, participating in class, being on time, studying hard, and making appropriate decisions. The engineers would coordinate with the Spanish teacher, whom I had freed for a class period daily to work with our Hispanic students. The engineers would occasionally return to address interested students, male and female, Hispanic or other minorities, about how best to impact their community by way of science, technology, engineering, and mathematics.

Another fine effort was an initiative we dubbed Girls' Group, also headed by the school psychologist. The students' selection was based on discipline referrals related to disrespectful behavior and insubordination. She ran an eight-week session, utilizing the book *7 Habits of Highly Effective Teens*.[7] The girls overall made favorable gains in behavior and report card grade improvement. Might the improvement gains have been made anyway? Perhaps, but my bet is that the girls saw a better self in the lessons presented by this professional educator, and they decided life was better to be recognized for their accomplishments. Another important initiative on this staff member's part was the formation of two groups of sixth-grade students, one involving those accused of bullying, teasing, or harassing; the other composed of those having reported being teased or bullied by their peers. The discussions revolved around defining teasing, bullying, and harassment, as well as discussing the characteristics of those who engage in such behaviors and ways to seek help. Those who were victims of such behaviors explored why they were being teased, considered how they might better handle rumors, learned how to respond to teasing and bullying, and gained skills that helped them make more friends. All the youngsters assisted in creating public service announcements for our in-school television program.

Often, as was the case with this staff member, youngsters began to turn the corner for the better when they perceived they had an adult "in their corner." The value of making connections was readily viewed time and again at this school site, emphasizing once more that "students don't care how much you know until they know how much you care."

I was fortunate to hire a stellar health room nurse who, along with the school's Instructional Intervention Team staff, initiated "New Student Luncheons," held once a grading quarter to acclimate students new to the school and to introduce them to support staff when they presented a specific need. Just as we developed a program for new staff, this program was designed to ensure that new students, as well, felt connected and that they belonged. Such a connection enhanced their chances of doing well academically and socially.

Staff were conscientious and on top of their game, again all in the effort to promote an environment conducive to instructional excellence and student behavioral and academic achievement—a culture for teaching and learning.

Our schoolwide efforts included nominating specific staff members for school district awards, as an avenue to recognize the tremendous professional performance of our staff, one of whom, our school psychologist, went on to win state recognition. Each year saw staff—in and out of the classroom—nominated for their professional accomplishments.

I may or may not have mentioned earlier that I worked for years as a vocalist with a Washington-Baltimore area society Big Band, with weekend performances at hotels, DC's "Embassy Row," and private homes for various events and affairs; we'd play various songs from the swing era up through Motown and current pop songs at the time. When the staff would organize our annual winter or Christmas celebration gatherings, the venue was usually an area hotel. I would sometimes ask the DJ if he had a karaoke version of the Temptations' song "My Girl." I'd ask for some backup, and three or so male teachers would jump up and join me, and it seemed to take on a life of its own, as I was asked to reprise it with each annual gathering.

The area high school band teacher would call me at the school, asking if I would join his jazz band for an evening's show, and I would do so barring any schedule conflicts. It was a hoot because I would be singing a Sinatra swing number with former Harper's Choice students, who, with their parents in the audience, seemed to love playing music onstage with their former principal as much as I enjoyed singing with them. Those performances made for some memorable, enjoyable evenings.

I stated that I regularly ate lunch daily in the school cafeteria with the students, eating with sixth-graders one day, seventh-graders the next, eighth-graders the following day. Excepting any meetings I might have had, this routine went on during my entire tenure at The Choice. When I finished my meal, I would occasionally meander over to the stand-up microphone that was used from time to time to address different audiences. I would stand about reading or glancing over whatever book or material I had with me, generally keeping an eye on a few hundred students. Every now and then, I would turn on the mic, back away from it, and subtly begin singing a tune, maybe "My Girl," as kids would look about the cafeteria wondering if what they thought they heard was, in fact, what they heard. When they would come to realize it was their principal, they would chime in, as well. The smiles exhibited by staff or parents who might be passing through the cafeteria at that moment were priceless, as they would stop to hear several dozen students singing,

"Well, I guess you'd say,

"What can make me feel this way?

"My Girl (My Girl, My Girl).

"Talkin' 'bout My Girl (My Girl!)."[8]

These kinds of interactions made meaningful, caring, enjoyable connections with students, staff, and parents, and that familial-like connection served as a kind of glue that allowed us, together, to make so many positive advancements academically and behaviorally.

We would hold "spirit days" that might see kids wear certain colored clothing or be able to wear a wacky hat, something fun and positive, that often allowed us to celebrate schoolwide successes and create a familial sense of "togetherness." Teachers would send out so-called positive postcards to the homes of students performing well in classes; all staff would issue Gotchas, where faculty and staff would "catch" a student exhibiting good character, random acts of kindness, courtesy, respect, or perseverance, perhaps helping another student, saying a kind word about another individual, or helping someone pick up dropped books and supplies. We had our own caped superhero, *Gotcha Man*, one of our teaching staff adorned with a Superman-like cape, who would surprise students with *Gotcha Slips*. They were encouraged to share this recognition with their parents and later to place the slips in a special "Gotcha" container so that the students could be recognized by having their picture taken with the principal; the students would receive a school T-shirt or lanyard and be featured on our schoolwide HCTV, the school's daily morning television show. We considered it important to recognize and praise good behavior, which enhanced a more inclusive, family-like atmosphere. We celebrated our Students of the Month for their academic achievements, and we supported and celebrated our spelling and geography bee participants, our school Math Olympiad, those involved in our countywide student book club and our St. Jude's Mathematics Fundraiser, the student thespians in our drama club, as well as those students attending a national leadership conference coordinated and run by a former successful high school teaching colleague and author.

Our PTA worked with school administration to sponsor an "artist in residence" activity that saw our sixth-graders work with a muralist to produce murals on planks that were displayed on school walls, each plank reflecting a character trait. We held occasional evening activities and discussions, one of which was called Human Sexuality, which featured parents who worked professionally in this field delivering a meaningful presentation on adolescent sexual development, teen risk behavior, strategies for parents to reduce youngsters' risk, parent-child communication, and the latest research at the time. We offered a Friday "Bingo Night," with pizza, snacks, and beverages. These kinds of activities helped create that sense of family, of belonging, that totally enhanced our efforts to create a warm, inviting, and success-oriented school community. Our data record-keeping saw an accompanying drop in disciplinary referrals each school year, a direct result, we believed, of our philosophy, our emphasis on character, and our renewed values, resulting in a total and complete teaching-learning school culture metamorphosis.

Another effort that reinforced the importance we placed on an appropriate school climate was how we organized and ran our school dances, the bane of many a school administrator, causing considerable stress and annoyance. Teaching staff and parents—and many youngsters—will cite that school dances are more about "grinding" and less about dancing. Many describe school dances today as "out of control." I recall chaperoning high school dances using a flashlight and giving one warning only before a couple was asked to leave. I was quite aware of and observed on multiple occasions school administrators eschewing any notion of actively enforcing appropriate behaviors at such activities, in many cases allowing for a darkened gymnasium, the only faint light coming from overhead door emergency exit signs. It was, in my view, peak stupidity that resulted in spineless, foolhardy decision-making that ignored any potential inappropriate or illegal drug, alcohol, or sexual activity. According to staff and many parents, school dances are generally viewed today as something to behold.

No matter, I wasn't having "crazy" at Harper's Choice, even if it meant having no dances at all. Given the school's condition when I took the helm, I wasn't entertaining a dance activity until the end of the year, when the traditional 8th Grade Farewell typically included such an activity.

I held discussions with key students, staff, and parents about the end-of-year activities that would occur, and that I very much wanted to see our youngsters enjoy an appropriate and enjoyable sendoff to high school, but I also needed to ensure that the entire program would be afforded dignity and proper protocol. I made up and presented (to everyone's amazement) a so-called No Freak dance "contract", thinking that some would, indeed, "freak out," as it were. There was some shaking of heads initially, and after considerable discussion, we found agreement. We were on our way to an 8th Grade Farewell Dance, with one additional proviso: The DJ had to play at least one Frank Sinatra song, and I said, "Take or leave it." They took it!

I placed the following in my "Principal's Corner" section of the school-community newsletter that went out monthly:

No-Freak Zone

As the 8th Grade Farewell approaches, it is a good time to remind students and parents that the farewell dance will be a NO-FREAK ZONE.

There will be plenty of snacks, good music, and fun, just no Freak Dancing. In case you haven't been introduced to this particular dance form, it is a type of dancing that typically involves the direct contact of bodies (pelvis to pelvis, or pelvis to bottom). Often more than two students are involved creating a sort of human dancing sandwich. Sometimes in extreme cases several male students surround a single female student.

Needless to say, it is not an appropriate dance style for an Eighth-Grade Farewell celebration. The PTA made arrangements for a DJ company that will include games and prizes, as well as a karaoke setup. We believe the activities will help keep the kids busy and entertained, and I hope they enjoy a terrific sendoff.

As the dance approaches, students will receive a "contract" to sign and have signed by a parent. The contract states that student and parent agree to the expectation of reasonable behavior at the dance (including No Freak Dancing). Students who do not honor the contract will be asked to leave the dance, and their parents will be called to come to the school and pick them up. We thank everyone for their support in our efforts to encourage our children to have a great time, while behaving in an appropriate manner.

As you well know, our evening and extracurricular activities have always enjoyed a successful record, because of our organization and the fact that they are well attended by adult chaperones throughout the activity, exhibiting a kind of "quiet" presence. We want our youngsters to feel safe, warm, and supported, without our having to stand right over top of them; they're great kids, and I believe our mere presence can be a source of comfort. Thank you for any time you may be able to give us.

Stephen Wallis, Principal

A humorous anecdote:

Disc Jockeys can be terrific with school-age youngsters. Over the years, however, I found that some DJ's could take a bit of license and play songs containing sexual or vulgar lyrics, which pretty much means the majority of music played today. On his contract and to his dismay, I inserted that the DJ forfeits total payment for the gig, should any such song be played. Imagine how challenging it was for him to cull through his playlist to ensure he played acceptable but still enjoyable music throughout the dance. At the end of the dance, he looked at me with a half grin, pleased that he was able to deliver. I appreciated his efforts, shook his hand, and gave him a check, along with a generous cash tip. He was our deejay for the years I remained at Harper's Choice.

I take a moment here to mention that there is a more principled, serious, and thoughtful concern regarding what many in society seem to have taken for granted but is worthy of introspection. In an issue of *Psychology Today*, a clinical psychologist stated the following:

> Many parents don't realize this, but high school students no longer dance. Instead, they "grind": A boy approaches a girl by rubbing his genitals into her buttocks. She responds by grinding back, as both partners move their hips in a circular or figure-eight motion. While grinding, the girl may bend forward to touch her knees or the floor, bringing her genitals in more direct contact with the boys'. Sometimes a girl initiates grinding on a boy. Teens grind in a tight crowd, with the raunchiest grinding taking place at the center of the crowd.
>
> Grinding happens en masse at high school dances throughout the country. It happens at my niece's Catholic school. It happens at my friend's daughter's Jewish camp. It's probably rampant at your local high school, too.
>
> Adults have objected to teen dance styles throughout the ages. The waltz was considered indecent when it first appeared. Is grinding anything more than today's version of Elvis' swiveling hips? Yes, it is. Grinding is explicit rather than suggestive. It's anonymous, rather than intimate. It reflects a lack of boundaries. Crowds of teens "dry humping" in public are a screaming declaration that nothing is private or personal.
>
> Teens argue that grinding is harmless—no one gets pregnant or even catches a sexually transmitted disease from grinding. But sexuality is about more than bodies; it's about feelings, and identity, and values, and, often, it's about another human being.

When adults do nothing to curb grinding at high school dances, it sends unhealthy messages. To girls, it says, "You should be comfortable with being used this way, because no one else is objecting!" To boys, it says, "Approaching anonymously, from behind, genitals first, is a popular and completely acceptable way to treat girls!" Grinding creates a climate of predatory sexual harassment and dehumanization.

However, grinding has become so pervasive in teen culture, that many school leaders feel powerless to stop it. A high school principal recently told me that when he tells one couple to stop grinding at a school dance, they stop temporarily, but then they start up again as soon as he turns his back to tell another couple to stop grinding. And it's not just established couples or troubled teens doing the grinding, he insists. It involves teens who barely know each other. It involves student leaders. It involves the majority of students attending dances.[9]

That first year's 8th Grade Farewell address followed by our end-of-year dance for the kids turned out to be a success, and God as my witness, we heard the Sinatra classic hit "New York, New York"—and each year thereafter for all the years I was at the helm! We would go on to have grade-level dances at the end of the first semester, a mid-year kind of activity. They would be three separate dances, one for each grade level, each taking place after school in the afternoon, each student in attendance presenting his or her "No Freak" contract. Those dances genuinely went well every year I was their principal, because we were organized, the expectations were clear ahead of time, and a growing number of our students, year after year, displayed an understanding of the importance of personal responsibility, self-control, and respect for one other.

Our once-a-week *Dress for Success* initiative was a welcome success, as well. I understand why many schools throughout the land incorporate a uniform policy year-round into their daily operating programs. Nearly 22 percent of public schools in the United States required uniforms in 2015–2016—up from almost 12 percent in 1999–2000, according to the National Center for Education Statistics.[10] The research is mixed as to the actual effect that school uniforms have on student behavior, attitude, and achievement; some schools report success, others not so much. Those schools that require it believe they have overall positive results, with students focusing more on a positive attitude and performing well and less attention to peer pressure and fashion. I thought it was a good idea, and I believe staff and many parents liked it and thought it made a positive difference. Many students appeared to enjoy it, and we would give recognition over our morning student-produced television announcements, as well as award a prize each week to select students. Awardees for that month would have their picture taken with the principal; it was fun, and the kids appreciated the recognition. Had I not retired, we would have stepped it up and gone with a twice-a-week program.

Throughout the academic year, I would place a notice in our combined school-PTA newsletter that typically read as follows:

> Our optional Dress for Success Day occurs each Wednesday of the week. We ask all students to participate in this one-day-a-week venture, when students may dress up a little special. No matter one's ethnicity, socioeconomic status, gender, or grade level, every student is asked to consider making each Wednesday just a little more special by dressing accordingly.

Perhaps males will consider wearing slacks and a golf shirt or a sport coat and tie; females may wish to wear a dress or attractive pants suit. My experience is that students feel different about themselves when they are "dressed for the occasion."

I have observed that such participation tends to impact school climate, students' behavior, and student image in a positive manner. Everyone likes to look nice, and we're hoping that every student "catches the spirit" and will want to participate. I would appreciate every parent's support in encouraging students to get involved in this effort. Anyone needing assistance in any manner with apparel is asked to contact me; the PTA and I will work together to see that interested students and families can, indeed, participate.

Stephen Wallis, Principal

On the topic of dress, there has been criticism for years on how students choose to dress, in general, for school. Parent expectations vary, from insisting that their child dress appropriately to those who say nothing, advising me that they would otherwise be suppressing their youngster's freedom of expression. Really? Only half of schools nationally indicate that they enforce dress codes;[11] that may be true, but likely it is not. My experience is that some school systems will include the issue in their so-called codes of conduct, but it's more a perfunctory point of information and generally not at all enforced at the school level. I had my own perspective and outlook on the matter, and as the reader likely knows by now, my philosophy on expected school behaviors, in general. I asked parents to reinforce our expectation for appropriate dress to school daily, that how students (and staff, for that matter) dress has an effect on the school's climate, that everyone ought well be dressed sensibly. The reader might think that such is a reasonable expectation and that all students and parents would be understanding; you would be incorrect. It is fair to say that I had considerably more than my share of "discussions" with students and their parents over how their kids were dressed; a number of these conversations became openly confrontational. I fully get why schools allow inappropriate dress because staff—including administrators—dislike fighting the good fight; they get frustrated, and many openly choose to avoid the potential confrontation and the labeling they would receive. I will cite only two examples of the myriad times over the years when this issue presented itself to me at various high schools and this middle school.

I kept a length of rope in the main office for those male students who could not—would not—wear their pants at the waist, regularly exposing their underwear or buttocks. They and their parents were reminded of the policy expectation by staff; some kids complied. Those who would not were immediately referred to an administrator. The assistant principal would confer with the youngster, note for the record her conversation with the student, and cut an appropriate length of rope that he could use as a belt for the remainder of the day, just as I would handle the matter. Some kids apologized, tied their makeshift belt, said they understood and that they would remember for the future, and be on their way. We don't doubt that some kids purposely wanted the attention and would show their "belt" throughout the day to friends.

Others, however, preferred to be noncompliant, liked wearing their clothes in that manner, and of course would refuse to use a rope for a belt. Those students would remain in the administrative area until a parent could either talk some sense into their child over the phone or come to the school with a belt, and we would have a more in-depth conversation at that point. If the parent was not available, the student would be escorted to the alternative education classroom for the remainder of the day, including his lunch time, and he could not return to school thereafter without his parent or guardian. Sometimes the parent conferences went well; other times, not so much. If no understanding was reached—and that happened frequently enough—I explained that the bottom line was that the youngster and parent didn't have to agree with me that his butt should be covered in school (imagine having to conduct such a conversation with an adult and his/her child); however, he either complied with our policy or the parent would return home with the youngster in tow. The parent would have to return with the youngster the following day, and we would have the same exact conversation; additionally, the student would be receiving an after-school detention assignment for his noncompliance with school policy. It usually turned out that when the parent or guardian was inconvenienced enough by having to take time from their workplace to address school matters, only then would they apply enough pressure on their insubordinate child, warning the miscreant to straighten up and behave accordingly.

Staff wanted to enforce healthy dress expectations but at times were skittish about approaching female students and sometimes were not certain that the youngster fell out of expected norms. I informed them that our rule of thumb would be the Three B's—No Boobs, No Belly, No Butts. If any of those areas was showing, within reason, we simply were not having it at Harper's Choice...period. They appeared to appreciate the clarification. I also understood the sensitivity of such things and knew that both male and female staff members expressed some discomfort with having to address the issue with any student, male or female. Nonetheless, I reasoned that if we were going to value our teaching-learning culture, we needed to uphold an appropriate and reasonable manner of dress for school. I informed them that they could also consider contacting an administrator, secretary, or school health nurse, who would summon the youngster from class and counsel the student to see if the issue could be resolved right then.

I recall another instance involving an older female student, an eighth-grader who had an ill-fitting top with an exceedingly short skirt that was obliterating our rule of thumb. When students are conferred with on such matters, they would be asked if they had other clothes that they could change into for the remainder of the day, as some students would wear one outfit out of their house that morning, but they'd hit the school bathroom stall on arrival and change into their other outfit. If the youngster answered, "No, I do not have another outfit," she would be given the option of wearing a school sweatshirt and/or sweatpants, items we kept on hand in the female assistant principal's office. This particular student was having none of that. I advised her that she would remain in the administrative office area as I would contact her mother to bring a pair of jeans and an appropriate top; additionally, the youngster could expect to serve after-school detention for her immature, noncompliant attitude. The mother was not at all receptive to my reason for calling her, much less to bring clothes up to the school; "I don't have time for this," she informed me. When I insisted that she come to the school posthaste, because her child was missing classes and would not be allowed to enter the hallway, much less attend class, until such time as she was properly dressed, she reluctantly changed her tune.

I was in another area of the building speaking to students who were rehearsing for a school play, when my secretary contacted me on the two-way radio, saying my expected parent appointment had arrived; in a lower voice, she said, "Be prepared." On entering the office, I introduced myself and asked both the mother and student to come into my office. I winked at my secretary, as other staff were looking at the three of us. Turns out the mother was dressed more inappropriately than the kid, and she was a knockout to boot. I noticed she had no bag of clothes, so I assumed this situation potentially was about to become a barn burner of a conference. I was correct. I explained the matter at hand, what we were trying to accomplish at the school, and why I needed every parent's support in understanding why, in this case, her child was dressing more like a twenty-three-year-old than someone who was fourteen, and that such attire would no longer work at this school. Well, she went at it, that no one needed to tell her how to raise her child, that she saw to it that her daughter had clothes on her back and a roof over her head, and furthermore, she'd had to take time off work to come to school for this...yada, yada, yada.

I then delicately and without fanfare placed the trash can nearer to her, thinking she might want to dispose of her equally inappropriate, annoying, and audible chewing gum. She looked at me, barely stopping her harangue, with a "No, I don't need that," as she continued inveighing against me and the school. This went on for a few more minutes as I delicately attempted again to explain the inappropriateness of her daughter's outfit, that while I understood she worked hard to "put clothes on her daughter's back," I stated that we would prefer that she had enough apparel to cover her front, as well, if that wasn't too much to ask. She was still going full speed when she took notice that I was unimpressed and not budging on this matter. She turned to her daughter and told her there was a change of clothes in a bag in the outer office area, but the daughter was still having none of it, and they proceeded to argue. The conversation was going nowhere, so I said I would step out for all of two minutes. I would reenter and her child would be wearing the change of clothes or be going home with her mother. When I reentered my office, I saw that the child had changed, reminded her of her after-school detention, and asked, please, that she dress appropriately for the remainder of the year. The mother surprisingly shook my hand and proceeded to sashay out past the secretarial staff and on out of the building with me shaking my head, as the secretarial staff looked up from their desks, smiling at the episode that had just transpired. Such events have a way of getting around the school, and it wasn't that long before everyone generally got the message that we were there to teach and to learn; that was our priority, with the goal being that students would go off to high school better prepared than when we received them; we all hoped and believed that they would one day realize how fortunate they were to have so many caring staff as their teachers.

The reader may recall that, on my arrival, the parent community had expressed exasperation with what they perceived as little to no communication between the school and home, and that which they could point to in the way of communication was ill written, at that.

Among the tenets of successful schools is cultivating positive home-school relations. Such was very much part of the "shared partnership" between the home and school that I touted frequently, and communication was key. We created multiple opportunities to communicate or otherwise share information with our parents and community. Every School Improvement Team (SIT) meeting included roles and responsibilities accorded to individuals. Among these were the recorder and minutes-taker. We ensured that the minutes of these meetings were distributed to all participants, including PTA officers. Additionally, these SIT discussions were shared by me with parents at PTA meetings. We used a number of additional avenues to share school improvement discussions and decisions with all stakeholders. Included among these were our faculty/staff meetings, Instructional Leadership Team meetings, grade-level team meetings, committee meetings, administrative staff meetings, daily morning student-produced HCTV announcements to the student body, afternoon principal announcements to the student body, and my "Evening Tea with the Principal" community-wide meetings held throughout the academic year. Grade-level teams would hold quarterly early morning "Coffee & Conversation" opportunities for those parents who were early risers or those interested in stopping by on the way to work to confer with teachers.

I initially wrote a *Principal's Corner* newsletter, available weekly to parents and community, which evolved into a combined school-PTA monthly newsletter that was made available on-line and in hard copy format. It provided information from academic departments, assessment dates, school health nurse reminders, guidance counseling department, music boosters organization, and the like.

I typically ended my section of the newsletter by telling the community, "We have some terrific students at Harper's Choice, and I thank our parents for doing such a wonderful job! I am delighted to be your principal, and I appreciate that you recognize the importance of a shared partnership in the education of (y)our youngsters! Here's to a successful and fulfilling academic school year!"

We provided each student with a folder that also served to communicate with parents. We called it a Monday Folder, and I would occasionally make reference to it in our school-PTA newsletter. Parents were advised that they should look for these folders in their child's notebook binders. The folder would be a stand-out color, blue and white, citing the character traits of *fairness, dependability, respect, trustworthiness,* and *cooperation* on the cover. We emphasized daily the importance of possessing these traits, building upon them throughout life. Students would place in these folders any important school notices and forms that parents were to see. Parents were advised to inquire of their youngster if there were important notices for the week that required their review and signature.

We also provided each student with an organizational agenda handbook that allowed them to note their homework assignments. It contained an outline of *The 7 Habits of Highly Effective Teens*, interesting and useful information on academic subject areas, study and test-taking skills tips, and a world map; it was also used as their pass to be out of class and would be carried with them. Parents enjoyed being able to look readily at their child's homework assignments for the evening to see whether their child was being excused from class, or if and when a particular project might be due.

The parents appreciated the various forms of communication, of being informed and remaining abreast of school items of interest all through the years. We developed a school website, courtesy of a parent, who would then turn it over to another parent with an incoming child so that we always had a go-to computer online guru. To go from nothing at the time to a full-on school website that looked sharp and was user-friendly was a terrific achievement, one that eventually allowed parents to communicate directly with their youngster's teachers and administrative staff. We coordinated a PTA email listing of parents that served as another avenue by which regular correspondence would be transmitted, regarding school-community events and notices.

Thanks to our robust school-business partnership with the Rotary, we purchased and frequently used our SchoolMessenger automated school dialer, which for years allowed me to leave a recorded message in English and Spanish on the answering machines or voice mail of all our students' homes, regarding various events and happenings about the school. There's a reason why positive home-school relations is cited among the correlates of successful schools, and open communication plays a singularly important role in a school's success and parent satisfaction. We knew that the more the school and parents shared information on our students, their children, the better equipped both of us would be in helping those youngsters succeed academically.

While we're on the topic of communication, I would find additional opportunities daily to interact with students, staff, and the community. Above and beyond my ordinary, sometimes impromptu conversations with kids, I would occasionally address the kids and staff briefly on our student-produced daily HCTV television morning program, just after our daily Pledge of Allegiance. I would remind our cherubs to step to the plate, get involved, and perform well at Harper's Choice, that it was the time to begin focusing on their own academic and behavioral performance, which would lead to personal success throughout their school years and beyond, always reminding them that "if they believe it, they will achieve it." I informed students that they could achieve anything they put their minds to, but they needed to believe in themselves, that it was tempting sometimes to believe that laziness paid off now, but such a notion was foolish, as they would soon realize that hard work paid off a lot more later, allowing them to enjoy a better, more enjoyable high school experience. One of our parents shared with me a quilt she made for her children, both of whom were attending Harper's Choice. She titled it "Quotes of My Principal, Mr. Wallis," featuring various inspirational, motivational, or everyday life quotes that I would articulate to students throughout each academic school year. She was among a number of wonderful parents, who consistently supported our school.

As mentioned earlier, throughout the year each Friday afternoon at the end of the school day would see me say a few words over the main office public address system. The idea was to thank staff and kids for their hard work, telling the kids to enjoy the weekend and to say to someone in the family, "I love you." I would tell them to do some chores around the house and yard or perhaps for an elderly neighbor, and to return Monday fresh and ready to "avoid the urge to be average."

I would also use the PA system to address our national holidays. I would take two to three minutes to address Veterans Day, Memorial Day, Martin Luther King Jr. Day, Columbus Day, religious holidays, and the like, informing the kids that it must be important for a nation to celebrate this particular individual, group, or idea. I thought it important for a fuller understanding of our country, a beacon of freedom to the world. In this book, I cite our Founding Fathers. Among many American patriots was Noah Webster, who was called the "Father of American Scholarship and Education." His "Blue-Backed Speller" taught generations of children how to spell and read, and in 1828, he published the *American Dictionary of the English Language*, later becoming the *Merriam-Webster Dictionary*. In his essay "On the Education of Youth in America," he stated that:

> But every child in America should be acquainted with his own country. He should read books that furnish him with ideas that will be useful to him in life and practice.
> As soon as he opens his lips, he should rehearse the history of his own country; he should lisp the praise of liberty, and of those illustrious heroes and statesmen, who have wrought a revolution in her favor.[12]

I always thought it an appropriate, if not, wonderful sentiment, and sage advice to all Americans, particularly in twenty-first-century America, and most particularly today. So, talking about these various holidays, even for a few minutes, promoted American citizenship, patriotism, and integration; we were a school representing a host of world cultures, after all. We are Americans, I would tell them, and it

is always healthy to celebrate our identity, cohesion, and the importance of tolerance, appreciation, and understanding of one another.

The following example is what I said to the student body on Veterans Day, November 11, 2005:

> Today we celebrate a day in which we honor all who served
> and/or continue to serve valiantly in our armed forces
> around the world. We recognize some twenty-six million
> living veterans, as well as thousands of those who gave
> their lives so that we might enjoy the freedoms we have
> today.
>
> It is a time to pause and reflect upon the sacrifices of these
> men and women, a time to recognize them, thank them,
> and learn from them. This year's holiday continues to hold
> significance in the hearts and minds of many because of
> the ongoing issues revolving around terrorism and the
> continued unrest throughout various parts of the world.
> We're honored to have among our staff those who served
> as military men and women, protecting our freedom and
> precious liberties, among whom are...(I would list staff
> members who were armed forces veterans). We rightly sa-
> lute them, as well as any of our parents and community
> members who have served proudly. God Bless America!

Years of mutual respect and appreciation for the fine professional work of the building and grounds maintenance folks provided
some terrific dividends. The reader is aware of the work that was
done on the grounds, including the initial landscaping around the
front entrance area of the building, as well as the refurbishment of
our flagpole, which had been ignored and was in a state of disrepair
and absent a flag for quite some time. The grounds and maintenance

staff not only installed a new halyard; they took pride in their work and installed a new flagpole truck and finial. Additionally, on their own volition, they bypassed attaching what would have been a suitable enough flag for one that was larger, which flew beautifully and proudly all those years I was at the helm.

I would regularly ask the staff if there were any needs that they might have within their subject areas that would enhance their instruction and student learning. The physical education staff said they had a few requests that had been made over the years, but they had seen no action taken on any of them. They were apparently without a telephone or a way to contact the main administration office if they had an emergency in the gymnasium area. I went over to observe the entire area. In order to access physical education equipment, they had to wrestle with a wide, heavy metal door that required their leaning over and lifting the handle, using their legs to pull the door up. They also informed me the school was the only one in the county that still had a concrete floor in the gymnasium, that it was less than forgiving on youngsters who would occasionally fall, not to mention the toll it had taken on their own bodies over the years. I recalled playing on that very floor years earlier in a countywide faculty basketball league. Within a week, building maintenance had installed communication service, ensuring that female and male teachers each had access to a telephone, as well as an emergency CALL button to provide communication with school administration staff. They uninstalled and jettisoned the large, heavy metal doors and installed new upright, wood double doors that allowed staff to access exercise equipment easily. The change from concrete to wood gymnasium floor was a capital expenditure and required some conversation and time. We were later able to secure needed funding, and over the course of a summer, the wood floor was installed, complete with beautifully painted boundary lines, free throw foul lines and circle, and three-point arcs. New electronic controls for raising and lowering the basketball backboards were also installed—as opposed to the time-consuming hand-winding of the boards into position.

I also noticed on arrival to the school that the school library was old, outdated, and had uncomfortable furniture and seating areas. That, too, was another major expenditure and took some haranguing, but we were successful in the end, and I was most appreciative to district staff for the results. The new "media center" was beautiful, with bright colors, attractive décor, new furniture and seating areas, as well as new books and periodicals added to our inventory. Later we would complete grants that allowed for mobile laptops that teachers could sign out for use by an entire classroom.

We commenced what we called Fat Fridays. Every other week a school department area and team would be responsible for arriving early and setting up breakfast treats for staff to mingle and socialize a bit. It added to our renewed good morale and *esprit de corps*.

I approached the PTA to inquire if it might be possible to offer a once-in-a-while spirited recognition of staff simply to reward them for their tireless efforts, and the result was monthly staff birthday acknowledgments and what became enormously appreciated, *Fabulous Fridays*, the first Friday of each month, when staff names were drawn from a hat and awarded gift certificates from our equally wonderful area merchants. On any given month, the PTA would have some thirty merchants participating in the program that would see lucky staff members receive movie tickets, restaurant coupons, dinner theater tickets, and certificates for massages and manicures. The entire staff was appreciative that the community would care enough to recognize their time, efforts, and talents. Such hard work and conscientiousness on the part of the PTA in so many areas of our school operations contributed significantly to our total school program.

Our health education teacher, an avid runner, offered to organize a school staff walk/run club, open to anyone interested in health and wellness. Upon my military discharge, I regularly ran and exercised for over thirty years and thought her idea was terrific and would add to our spirit of fellowship.

Our various school-business partnerships also enhanced our instructional-learning culture. The county-wide Office on Aging collaboration saw senior citizens mentoring our youngsters and providing one-on-one assistance weekly. To walk through a public school's media center and observe this intergenerational collaboration was fulfilling.

The years the students and I played football, jogged the neighborhood, and lunched each weekend on Saturday or Sunday were enjoyable and resulted in a meaningful connection that only added to the teaching-learning culture that we cultivated at the time. Such connections are at the heart of schooling and effecting positive change. Former students well into adulthood and I will occasionally run into one another, sometimes a far distance from the community, and they will smile as we chat about the school, those weekends, and sometimes a particular play or tackle they recall as noteworthy.

An incident of a different sort might come to my attention that would directly or indirectly impact our teaching-learning culture. I addressed an issue with a substitute teacher whom we had just hired for a long-term position in one of our academic subject areas. A colleague—a pleasant individual and an effective teacher, who happened to be of color—came to me to discuss an incident that had occurred only minutes earlier in a faculty lounge. The recently hired long-term substitute teacher, a white female, had made a disparaging reference, racial in nature, when responding to the teacher, who had approached me. The offended teacher was not at all looking to see the individual fired, only counseled on how the substitute might better address matters in the future. My discussion with the substitute teacher was disappointing, and I wound up letting her go. It was unfortunate, because we were a busy demographic school with some meaningful initiatives going on, after all, and I needed everyone on staff to be operating at a top-shelf level, making good decisions that honored the dignity of staff, students, and parents. I felt it best to do a full-on immediate search to find a suitable long-term replacement. It was the appropriate decision to make and reinforced our priority that our teaching-learning culture was sacrosanct.

I was fortunate that the many times I requested assistance with students, their families, or the community, I could count on my teaching staff. My support staff— guidance counselors, pupil psychologist, speech pathologist, health room nurse, and pupil personnel worker— were instrumental in working with me and my colleagues to support efforts to accomplish our goal of creating and enriching an appropriate teaching-learning culture. As mentioned earlier, they assisted me in carrying out any number of initiatives over the years that fully supported student achievement, providing differentiated services to assist students, their teachers, and students' families develop positive academic identities that always led to individual successes. They fostered positive, trusting relationships with staff, students, and our parent community, awfully important in making connections and, along the way, encouraging positive, wholesome parent involvement in the education of their children.

The goal was for staff, students, parents, community, and outside school building district staff to feel the shared partnership, that we were all in this together. Throughout the years, various individuals from these groups would ask that I write a personal reference or recommendation; it might have been a job placement or college recommendation for a student, perhaps a parent who was in need of a personal reference, or a maintenance or grounds staff person in need of a written recommendation for a lead position in one of those areas.

Occasionally, I would think about my initial day on the job, and after several hours of observing and listening, remembering how hell-bent I was on developing a culture for teaching and learning that would reduce instructional interference, enhance student achievement on a wider scale, and provide a better service to the citizenry. Turns out, we did a great deal more. We created a completely different school environment, one that felt familial— a "family" with the singular goal of producing students who would go on to high school and beyond, demonstrating achievement and feeling that they could contribute meaningfully to society. Not bad.

These schoolwide, grade-level team, and individual staff member initiatives were key in providing and ensuring a long-lasting, supportive, and nurturing teaching-learning environment at Harper's Choice Middle.

Understand that schools need to be about instructional excellence and student academic performance. That rules out any notion of tolerating mediocre or unsatisfactory teaching or ignoring and putting up with disrespectful, disruptive student behavior that destroys any sense of school and community cohesion. To act otherwise undermines the school's purpose, which is to provide teaching excellence so youngsters can learn, can grow, and can become model, productive citizens. To accomplish that goal, teachers must be able to teach, and youngsters must be able to learn in safe, warm, inviting, and first-rate schools.

The preservation of an appropriate teaching-learning climate— one that cultivates and promotes top-shelf instruction, respectful student and staff deportment, and student academic performance achievement—is critical to a school's success. The school principal is key to establishing and preserving such a climate.

11

A Focus on Partnerships

Attending a community event celebrating school-business partnerships, I was asked to comment on the nature of such relationships. I made the point that the most successful organizations are those that recognize the importance of the community they serve, that schools should be vibrant, welcoming places that invite active participation on the part of students, staff, parents, and the wider business community.

This perspective derives from my belief that the education of our students should be a shared partnership among students, their parents, our staff, and local businesses, a sentiment I openly expressed throughout my tenure as principal. I maintain that this belief was as much responsible for our successful school turnaround as any other philosophical principle or action that I had taken since my arrival to this school community.

Connecting with those I felt were part of the equation for educating this community's youngsters always seemed to make sense. My intention was to improve teaching and learning such that students would feel that they had a solid academic foundation that would enhance their personal efforts to perform well in high school, a foundation that would also serve them well in the world of work, perhaps right there in the community with a company that might well have been among our school partners.

I mentioned early in the book that Harper's Choice Middle was the quintessential public school. We served a diverse population of students representing a myriad of cultures throughout the world. We had a growing ESOL (English for Speakers of Other Languages) population with students speaking a wide array of languages. The academic skill levels were equally varied, with some of our students unable to read or speak English or compute well, while others were more accomplished, some of whom participated in the Johns Hopkins University Center for Talented Youth.

Two years earlier, the school had been described as "in crisis," with rampant student behavior problems, low test scores, a lack of vision, waning parent involvement, and no meaningful connections with area businesses. Why would there have been? It is one thing for a company to extend itself and want to work with a struggling school where its administration and staff work hard to take care of and to provide meaningful instruction to their students; it's quite another to expect any company to consider such a relationship, much less spending time and resources on a school where all hell seems to break out regularly, with no apparent direction or will to achieve calm and promote substantive learning. However, this was a different time in the school's history, and the business of schooling here had undergone a dramatic change for the better. We were ready and proud to go about presenting ourselves to the community, making our case for school-business partnerships that would advance further our goal of instructional and student performance excellence, academically and behaviorally.

The idea of a shared partnership was part of my DNA. The staff and I, together, would improve the teaching and school environment that I hoped they would come to enjoy and appreciate; my aim was to have them look forward to getting up each weekday morning to come to work. I would like to think those professional teaching staff with whom I worked over the years would be able to say they felt that we, together, were partners in educating our community's youth. It took a Herculean effort on the part of each staff member—all of us, each and every year—to achieve the kind of positive recognition they justifiably deserved.

I shared that same perspective with our student body, informing students that I wanted them, as well, to wake up each morning not at all dreading school, but with smiles on their faces, looking forward and enjoying demonstrating their academic prowess, while experiencing wholesome positive social interaction throughout the school day. I advised that I welcomed their partnering with me and their teachers to make this a vibrant academic setting. I have always found that in the most troubled schools, there are large numbers of students who are well-raised, are respectful, and value their education. Many students were excited and hopeful that school would once again be fun, that they could go to classes with friends and enjoy their classroom lessons without the kind of repeated disruptions that had characterized so many of their previous school years. I would not let them down.

I extended the same sense of shared partnership with our parents and the school Parent Teacher Association (PTA). Every year that I was school principal, parents extended themselves time and again in the effort to assist the school administration and staff in our efforts to see every child succeed.

Parents heard about or had attended my "Evening Tea with the Principal" gatherings, those occasions when I would be invited out to speak to the community. As the reader knows, these might be held on the front lawn at one of the parents' homes, as was the case for my first meeting with the community, perhaps the living room or backyard patio of another home, as well as in a parking lot of an apartment complex among one of the federal Section 8 subsidized housing areas, where I would set up a table with unsold Back-to-School supplies that had been donated by a grocery store manager who approached me for assistance earlier in the school year; one morning he had wheeled over to the school entrance door a shopping cart filled to the brim with various unsold school supplies. As I would address a crowd, parents would freely take any needed notebooks, folders, pencils, and pens from a table I had set up for the evening activity.

At one of my evening greets in an apartment complex parking lot, a young mother, with a smile, yelled out to remind me that I had suspended her in high school years earlier. She laughed when I called her by name, telling her she shouldn't have been smoking in the bathroom at the time (caught for the fourth time, I recall). I admonished her, stating that I hoped she had since quit, when she said, "I'm still trying," as she was exhaling smoke into the night air. I asked for her daughter's name, and she was thrilled that I knew her and could state how well her daughter was performing in school. It was always nice, if not, heartwarming to see her with her child at school events throughout those years.

I would hold several such get-togethers as a way to introduce myself, to meet the community, and to talk about how we were working hard to provide the best education to their children. I enjoyed answering any questions they might have about me, the school, or our school system, as well as provide suggestions to those parents asking how best to address a challenge they were having with their child or school district. It was an opportunity to get up close and clarify the importance of regular student school attendance, of parents setting high expectations for their children, helping their youngsters with homework, and establishing communication with their child's teachers. I would distribute a sheet containing the dates of important school events and testing, as well as the contact information for school administration, guidance department, and health room staff. Those gatherings were mutually beneficial, for certain. On the basis of those evening meetings, scuttlebutt about the community, or interactions with me, parents felt the school was turning a corner, and they were all in.

It remained an actively involved PTA throughout my tenure as principal. The notion of a "shared partnership," describing the pivotal relationship of home, school, and community in furthering the success of this community's youngsters, was something I regularly expressed to families. It was encapsulated in a large, painted wooden sign beautifully created by parents that was affixed to a wall at the front entrance of the school, signed by that academic year's PTA president and me. It read as follows:

A Shared Partnership

Harper's Choice Middle School is a partnership of students, staff, parents, and community committed to providing a school culture that is safe, nurturing, inviting, and academically stimulating.

We actively cultivate a climate where respect, teaching and learning, appreciating differences, and service to others are modeled and valued. We are committed to a focus on instruction, acceleration, shared partnerships, and continuous improvement.

We believe that every child can and will be successful as we continue to develop and foster responsible, productive, and respectful lifelong learners.

Principal   *PTA President*

On my initial arrival, I recall asking the secretary for a PTA list-ing, which contained some forty or so names; fewer than a handful, staff advised me, could be counted on to assist staff, due to the poor school climate. Parents throughout the community had decided to enroll their children in area private schools. In fact, our school was listed among the ten worst schools in the school district by the teach-ers' union.[1] That would change.

The school year was in session some three weeks or so when we held Back-to-School Night, a ritual marking the beginning of a new school year, where parents meet their youngsters' teachers, learn about the curriculum for each course of study, and obtain a glimpse of daily life at their child's school. The attendance was overwhelming, standing room only, in the school cafeteria. I was bowled over with the enthusiasm, interest, and support shown by so many parents. It made me smile as I welcomed everyone and introduced myself and my administrative colleague, and our grade-level teams of teaching staff. I spoke briefly about my background and experience and pro-ceeded to talk about the school. I did not dwell on the past, but I felt obligated to describe the results of the previous year's state testing. I was enthusiastically pleased with the turnout and presented my view, my philosophy on schools, teaching, and learning. I clarified our two major school goals for the academic year centering on student aca-demic and behavioral performance, and that such could only occur in an environment conducive to teaching and learning. I informed them that such a school environment was precisely what they could expect from here on out, at which point people stood and applauded. I emphasized the importance of a "shared partnership" and asked that they be actively involved in their child's academic achievement, both at home and in their school. I welcomed their involvement, as staff excused themselves to their instructional areas to prepare for their students' parents.

Our parents were actively involved each school year, in and out of the building daily. On special occasions, like American Education Week, they would take the opportunity to come in and observe teacher instruction and student participation in action, something they had stopped doing previously. A number of PTA fund-raisers would be held that would assist the faculty and students, particularly in the area of providing cultural arts assemblies and guest speakers throughout the year. One such fund-raiser saw parents purchasing "stock certificates," as an "investment" in their child, which another business partner offered to match. This kind of hard work and interest on the part of our parents would continue for the years I was at the helm.

Having developed a vibrant shared partnership with our students, staff, and parents, we would pursue the potential of developing school-business partnerships. I believed we were more than ready—hungry, really—to establish some business contacts and make our case. I contacted a host of different entities in the county, various companies, service organizations, corporations, and foundations.

Given the increasing demands on schools to ensure that students are well prepared, it should be acknowledged that we do not work in isolation, but in collaboration with our community. Schools throughout the nation—including Harper's Choice Middle—are asked daily to accomplish more with seemingly fewer resources. I reasoned that when we remain focused on our mission, continuously improving, and meeting satisfactorily the goals that we have established, it makes sense to forge a strong bond with our business community. In that vein, I suggested that we change the way we think traditionally about education and begin to impact our school in ways that the school system was unable to do.

We were well on our way—in fact, at that point we were establishing a reputation—to improve teacher instructional excellence and student academic standing and looking to form a mutually benefi-cial relationship with area businesses. Such a partnership would be a mutually supportive relationship between Harper's Choice Middle and a business, each committing to specific goals and activities in-tended to benefit students, staff, and business community. It could be recognized by way of a formal proclamation and run through the school system, or it could be a low-key relationship between the busi-ness and the school, where the company, in essence, would "adopt" Harper's Choice Middle. We eventually developed a combination of business relationships, resulting in a record number thirty-two school-business partnerships.

Our needs at the time varied from chocolates to computers, and I believed that our business community would realize gains, as well. The business was welcomed to stop in and have lunch—on me—in our cafeteria with our students or staff at any time. We presented free tickets to their employees for any evening band and or musi-cal performances, and I offered to have our music department play or perform at one of their holiday functions. Any business or foun-dation would, in turn, see public recognition by me through our school-PTA newsletter that we got underway, as well as any addition-al media outlets, realizing the benefits of enhanced goodwill and a stronger presence throughout the community. I surmised that such partnerships would have a profound effect on our students' learning and our teachers' instructional success. Ideally, such a partnership would lead to businesses realizing improved, stronger prospects for a future labor pool.

As a result of our interest in and aggressively going after opportu-nities, we would occasionally have community members out to speak with our students. Some were business owners; others were profes-sionals working in a host of varying fields. We might invite them to address students in a school assembly or provide a presentation in a classroom setting. We coordinated with a local bank and invited bank volunteers to teach the importance of saving and money management. I always found it a bit foolish over the years that so many kids "graduating" from high school knew little, if anything, about economics and financial literacy. This particular partnership saw bank employees instilling sound saving and spending habits that our youngsters would take with them to high school and beyond, and the lessons were designed to accommodate a normal class period.

Students and parents asked me to accept a suggestion from a parent to have his friend, an NFL player, come out and speak to our youngsters. I didn't believe the player was a particularly good role model (since, among other things, he refused to cooperate with a highly publicized police investigation into the deaths of two others at a location where he was present and alleged to have been involved). I made the decision that our youngsters would be better served hearing from a successful owner (also of color) of several businesses. They heard an emphasis on the importance of acquiring a good education, working hard, and being generally responsible, as the hard work now would most certainly pay dividends later. It was a message well worth our students hearing. Turned out he was terrific, and the youngsters appeared to enjoy his address (or maybe the fact that he spoke over his allotted time and caused some kids to miss a portion of their mathematics class). Depending on the topic and opportunities, it was entertaining and enjoyable occasionally to welcome an athlete or celebrity to address students, and we did so at times. As a school administrator, and later as principal, I thought it more of a priority to welcome successful men and women who distinguished themselves in technology, medicine, trades, arts, law enforcement, communication, management, engineering, and science, to cite career areas from which speakers came out to address students.

Business partnerships are very much needed to acquaint students to the various careers that await them after high school graduation, post–high school training, or college graduation. How terrific it would be if schools throughout the country enjoyed their fair share of school-business partnerships that also provide educators with a heads-up on the skills, education levels, and training that is or will be required by companies, locally and nationally, when students exit high school and beyond, frequently providing students with real-world relevance.

Among the many partnerships we enjoyed was an engineering company that provided speakers to our classrooms; a martial arts studio that offered to provide activities to kids after school; a community athletic club that donated weight training and cardio equipment, including a stationary bike and chest-press machine that both students and staff enjoyed; a restaurant that offered, as the reader knows, a meeting room with breakfast and lunch each June for our School Improvement Team meetings, at which we would review the school's Annual State of the School Report, clarify summer continuous improvement professional development funding and activities, and plan for the following academic school year initiatives.

We enjoyed valuable, productive partnerships with a local church, that saw members and students periodically spruce up our campus grounds; a community village shopping center, on which I sat as a member of their board of directors; a tech-surveillance company; the community college; the community hospital, where, as cited previously, students in our family and consumer science classes would make newborn blankets; the local McDonald's, whose owner, the reader will recall, approached me one weekend, offering to provide me and my weekend ballplayers and runners a free lunch meal each week; the local Safeway grocery store, whose manager sat on our school improvement team, and was the gentleman, the reader will also recall, who approached me early in my arrival as principal and asked for assistance in ending the years-long loitering, threatening behavior, and thievery that the store had experienced, the same gentleman, once again, who would later provide the school with unsold back-to-school supplies that I would share with the community on my "Evening Tea with the Principal" gatherings. A partnership with another restaurant saw the owner ordering extra boxes of nutritious snacks that she would share with our school nurse, who kept a supply of snacks on hand for those students arriving to school hungry.

As I would observe the students reading to themselves in the cafeteria or in the hallways between classes, I would occasionally approach them and ask what they were reading and to describe to me the plot of the book. A number of these kids were boys, and the idea of starting a boys' book club occurred to me. I approached a social studies teacher I had hired and asked if he would be interested in sponsoring such a club after school. He connected well with the kids, and I thought he'd be a good fit. It turned out to be a wholesome, terrific idea and a welcome addition to our extended-day activities. I coordinated the effort via a partnership with local county library staff, and a representative worked with the teacher on book selections. Once the boys decided on a specific title, she would bring enough books to the school, and if there was any cost, I would take care of it with available funding. She, too, had not known of such a boys-only book club and was completely taken with the idea. She and the teacher worked together on this effort with the boys. It was gratifying to observe, and the boys and their families benefited greatly.

The police department was a solid partnership, as well. They were part of our daily extended-day program, and since the community was a state-designated Hot Spot area, I was asked to participate in weekly justice department meetings with the police, prosecutor's office, and sheriff's department representatives, regarding matters of import that involved our community, some of which affected our school population. Regarding this specific school community, one law enforcement incident remains noteworthy. I received a telephone call during the school year, regarding a joint task force operation involving additional Baltimore-Washington area police agencies, working in concert with the FBI, and the Bureau of Alcohol, Tobacco, Firearms, and Explosives. The county-state coordinator asked if I would approve their holding a community-wide meeting on a specific weekend in our school cafeteria, where they also posted the photos of some forty-five criminals dealing in drugs, firearms, and robberies. It gave one pause to see that a number of the photos featured Harper's Choice area individuals, among whom were those with a direct family connection to our student population. It served as a reminder of how fortunate we are that there are men and women, who willingly risk their lives confronting issues that most people would rather not think about, and they do so humbly in cities, towns, and communities throughout the country.

One particularly noteworthy school-business partnership was with a computer refurbishing company. The owner contacted me after hearing some "really positive things" about our school. He said that he was "intrigued," wanted to visit the school, and asked if I might have time to confer with him about a potential partnership. I was enthusiastic, to say the least. We walked the building, going in and out of classrooms, as I talked about the school's recent history and our efforts to effect positive change. Turns out he was familiar with the school community as his wife worked with a county agency within close proximity of our school and was familiar with the school community. The conversation turned out to be a years-long partnership where staff received much-needed computers and printers for a nominal charge. He was more than happy to work with us and simply asked me to ensure that the computers were not hooked up to the school system's network. The request worked for me, and his company also would service and maintain the computers. We started by placing two staff computers in the mathematics department. Eventually, we received additional computers for both staff and student use. I would periodically ask staff to provide me with the names of students in their classes who indicated they had no home computer. Over the years, we would hold "Technology Evenings," and I would invite a host of parents and their students. I had already spoken to select parents by telephone to obtain their support and commitment to a contract I would have them sign, along with the signature of their child the evening of the event. Specifically, students were held to three conditions:

1. Attend school every day, unless they were legitimately ill.
2. Receive no disciplinary classroom referrals from their teachers.
3. Receive no lower than a grade of C in each and every course.

The students and parents were advised that I would also sign the contract, and as long as they were willing to make that commitment, they would go home with a computer, printer, modem, and library card, as I also asked the local library staff to be present to address the gathering, a number of whom had never visited a library. These were enjoyable, beautiful evenings for families and our school. Over the years we gave out several hundred pieces of technology equipment, and only once did a police officer and I need to visit a home and confiscate the equipment, which I then provided to a more deserving family. The partnership was especially rewarding, and we continued our relationship for as long as I was at the helm. It turned out that Harper's Choice staff and students would become that much more computer-savvy, as a result of such a wholesome and worthwhile partnership, and I remained appreciative of the hard work, talent, and generosity of such partners.

We enjoyed a wonderful partnership with the county Office on Aging, which saw twelve to fifteen senior citizens come to the school weekly to tutor and mentor a number of our students in need of reading and mathematics assistance. Their experience and wisdom added a welcome dimension to our school and the efforts of our students and staff. The activity included a member of our PTA, who assisted by hosting the sessions weekly. Our reading and mathematics specialists conducted a training session for the senior citizens on how best to present and "teach" prepared lessons; the following week they were on their own. Paired for an hour with their students, these "seniors" informed me that they simply loved getting involved in the program and working with the kids. Those retirees working with our kids on reading skills asked if they could call their group the Readers Club; the name worked for me, and that's how it remained for years. A review of the students' academic progress indicated that the weekly opportunity to work alongside our senior citizens was proving beneficial, and it became quite a centerpiece at Harper's Choice. I was grateful for the staff and PTA participation and support that proved to be a positive intergenerational endeavor that continued to enhance the academic skill levels of our students.

The countywide senior center's annual Thanksgiving dinner was yet another terrific example of the value of wholesome partnerships that would see a number of our students serving meals, waiting tables, and eating with these older—and great—Americans. I would attend, as well, and it was a delight to see the interaction and forging of connections between the generations.

One among several interesting and beneficial partnerships was our relationship with a local chapter of Rotary International, a service organization of businessmen and businesswomen who provide humanitarian service and generally advance goodwill throughout the world. One of our parents was a member, and I recall making an initial presentation to the organization, explaining the school's previous poor condition, as well as the kinds of actions we had taken and were continuing to take in our efforts to turn things around for the better. I advised that if they were interested and thought they would like to work with us, I would be happy to suggest ideas that they might consider supporting us. It was soon thereafter that they contacted me, expressing their "complete and enthusiastic interest" in working with Harper's Choice; I was elated. In a follow-up conversation, I made mention that not a single teacher had a comfortable, professional desk chair, that staff had always used student-type chairs. Our Rotary parent advised me of a company moving to another building, whose owner said he would be happy to donate their current desk chairs to us, as the building into which they were moving had suitable chairs. The parent then orchestrated a moving truck and assistance in moving the chairs—unbelievable! I also joined them in the effort to load chairs, and over a weekend we placed some eighty or so adjustable desk chairs in the school corridor that greeted teaching staff on their arrival that Monday morning. You had to be there to realize fully the sheer joy and expressions of appreciation shown by the staff. Such a simple gesture meant the world to them and seemed to validate the role they played daily in working with the community's youngsters.

The Rotary parent was a caring, get-things-done kind of guy, and the organization remained enthusiastic supporters of the school well after his child had moved on to high school; in fact, the Rotarians were the reason we were able to purchase an electronic automated computer dialer that allowed me to contact the homes of students, a great tool then to communicate with a wide audience. We used it to contact parents whose youngsters were late or absent from school and had not notified the school earlier. I used it regularly to send any number of important messages to the community, including upcoming state testing dates or scheduled meetings that parents might wish to attend. I also sent messages out in Spanish, after asking the Spanish teacher to listen to my pronunciation to ensure that I was communicating clearly and was pronouncing any word or phrase correctly. It was a huge success, and I used it regularly over those years.

I would occasionally attend the Rotary meetings to provide an update on our continued improvements and success. They would conduct their meetings, on occasion, in our school media center and were met at the front entrance area by male students in shirt and tie and female students wearing dress or slacks, always remembering to greet the individual businessman or businesswoman with a "Good morning, sir/ma'am. I'm so and so, and I'll walk you down to your meeting location." Our youngsters enjoyed meeting and interacting with our various business partners; students began to see the benefits of an education in a different light, when they saw first-hand how it correlated with success.

We were most fortunate to achieve such success in the area of school-business relationships. Our business partners were seen for what they were, good corporate stewards. They played an instrumental role in our academic, literacy, physical education, and general wellness initiatives, while we benefited appreciably from much needed support and assistance.

The idea of a shared partnership between the school and the home and wider business community turned out to become a hallmark of a Harper's Choice Middle School education. We were better citizens because we recognized that all of us throughout the community were, together, stakeholders in this school's transformation to one of instructional excellence, positive student behavior, and demonstrated student academic performance.

12

Results

The reader will recall that the summer of my arrival saw me poring over a variety of available statistics on the performance of Harper's Choice Middle. It occupied the bottom rung in standardized test scores. Disrespectful, disruptive student behavior was rampant, the school dubiously leading the entire county with nearly two hundred suspensions. Staff morale was at an all-time low, placing it on the teachers' union Watchdog List of the ten worst schools in the district. PTA involvement had dropped off dramatically, with parent frustration at a record high. As it would turn out, that was just a portion of the litany of concerns that the school community would bring to my attention on my arrival.

Early on, I wrote an abbreviated list[1] of at-a-glance facts regarding the school I was about to lead. I scrawled it on a sheet of notebook paper after I had the opportunity to confer with school district officials, staff, parents, and students in those first few days of my arrival. I kept it in a drawer in my desk, and from time to time over those years, I would occasionally read through the list of academic and behavioral concerns, smile, and shake my head. That list I made earlier noted the following:

July 2000

- School described as "in-crisis," by superintendent and central office administration; "dead last" in the view of school system officials, teaching staff, and teacher union representatives
- Among ten worst schools on teachers' union watchdog list
- Teaching staff express racial unease
- Low-to-failing test scores, including all student subgroups
- Small PTA membership (forty-three on paper, but only 1-2 active parent volunteers)
- Basement-low faculty/staff morale
- Building and grounds neglected, with no flag flown for years
- Staff and parents describe student behavior as disrespectful, disruptive, and violent w/bullying and thievery; excessive amount of truancy from classes/students occupying hallways during classes
- Parents/staff/students complain about number of students from all area schools (HCMS, SES, WLHS) causing continuing problems in village center and community weekday afternoons and weekends
- High rate of district suspensions; staff/parents (and some students!) feel there should have been far more suspensions
- School in arrears, owing money to state
- No dress code enforced (student and faculty), expressed by parents and staff
- "Inconsistent" teaching practices, expressed by district school administrators, staff, and parents
- Staff and parents cite little-to-no meaningful academic intervention
- No formal business-education partnerships, according to district administrators

- Parents cite little, if any, communication (what they did receive was "meaningless and poorly written")

It was comforting to look back and know that each one of those
noted concerns on that sheet of notebook paper had been completely
replaced with solid accomplishments on the part of staff, students,
parents, and business community.

As was made clear in each of the chapters of this book, our emphasis on character, our *No Excuses* mantra and the plethora of actions, policies, programs, partnerships, activities, and instruction-
al/behavioral interventions put in place to enhance overall student
achievement together had a dramatic positive effect on our school
community for the years we were together. The Herculean efforts
on the part of our staff, our students, and our parents catapulted
the once-failing school into a caring and accomplished professional
teaching-learning community that went on to receive regional, state,
and national recognition.

Each successive year saw improvements, academically and behaviorally—if only at times, seemingly glacial. The school would go
on, notwithstanding, to become a completely different education
story. The school community's success revolved around collaboration, trust, satisfaction, and commitment.

Each academic year's annual report noted, for example, a drop in
suspensions from school, the first three years reflecting 102, 93, and
75 suspensions respectively, and each year thereafter continued to
see fewer behaviors requiring suspension. Our School Improvement
Plan for the academic year 2008–2009, the year I would retire, saw
a total of thirteen student suspensions for the year or a whopping
94 percent decrease in student suspensions from the year I took the
helm of Harper's Choice. [2] My assistant principal and I regularly reviewed our school data, academically and behaviorally. Noted in the

September 2006 *Building Cougar Character* staff manual was the fact that we experienced an overall drop each year in student discipline referrals, particularly in the areas of disrespect and insubordination,[3] a spectacular accomplishment on the part of staff, students, and parents, given where we were when I accepted the position.

The reader will recall my conversation with a couple politicos at the time I arrived at Harper's Choice and my stated prediction—my hope at the time—that we would see a diminution of ill behaviors, including disrespectful, disruptive, and violent behavior, as well as a drop in suspensions, when staff, students, and parents began to understand the importance of placing character at the center—the heart—of the school, that if they wanted a genuine rock-solid education at this school, everyone would need to give his or her best effort, acknowledging the values that were put in place. In fact, that is precisely what occurred. There were also the predicted additional academic benefits.

The overall tenor of instruction and professional development at Harper's Choice Middle changed for the better; there was a deeper appreciation and respect for one's instructional excellence; the research-based high-level strategies used throughout the school could be viewed and felt in every content area, every subject being taught in every classroom in the school. There was a respect for the idea of continually improving one's teaching craft.

Our reading content area high-leverage strategies were paying huge dividends, thanks to the professional leadership in that subject area and the fine efforts of the reading team. Students were involved in a number of various reading program interventions cited earlier in the book, and our students each grading quarter were demonstrating substantial improvement gains in their ability to read, to comprehend, and to demonstrate active strategic reading that saw them provide text evidence to support oral and written responses to questions asked about a work of fiction or nonfiction. They could be observed gradually throughout the school year moving beyond text evidence to interpreting and critically analyzing text; more and more of these students could be observed using Before-During-After reading strategies without prompting.

Teaching staff could witness the fruits of their labor, observing so many students learning to read on their own and appreciating their personal accomplishments. Teachers reported in the 2004 annual report that, of those students who previously performed below-grade level in reading, 77 percent received grades of C or better by the end of the first-quarter grading period; at mid-fourth quarter of that year, a full 81 percent of students in our reading classes obtained a grade of C or higher; these were markedly different measures of advancement than had been experienced previously. We observed an increase, as well, in report card grades and district assessments for our students who participated in our Readers' Club, our intergenerational effort that saw senior citizens working weekly with students on vocabulary, comprehension, fluency, and building relationships.[4]

We eventually found ourselves frequently encountering various successes, large and small, successes all the same. Among the interventions was a retention program for kids having failed to be promoted the previous year. The cherubs in our retention program saw 98 percent of them receiving no D or E grades in their core content areas; we tried to remain humble, but we were ecstatic, and we would continue to monitor their individual performances.

The entire staff delighted in the academic and behavioral improvements made by our students every year we worked together. Our mathematics teachers could report proudly that their instructional strategies and academic interventions were seeing results throughout the year, every year. We saw substantial improvement in our so-called local assessment scores each grading quarter, particularly in our lower mathematics sections and our pre-algebra classes in all grades. We saw steady improvement each grading quarter in the number of below-grade level students moving to on-grade level status, again in all grade levels. The October 7, 2003, *Principal's Corner* section of the school-PTA newsletter cited the recent state functional testing results at that time. The school system report at the time cited Harper's Choice Middle on more than a few occasions for its student performance improvements.

Among the highlights from the state report provided to the school system were these:

- Maryland Functional Mathematics Test: "One SIU school, Harper's Choice, experienced growth of 5%. Pass rates at all other SIU schools decreased."
- Maryland Writing Test: "The greatest growth was experienced by two SIU schools, including Harper's Choice, which increased 12 points."
- Maryland Functional Reading Test: +4 increase in the Pass-rate Growth over SY: 2001–2002.[5]

Harper's Choice was recognized by the state on multiple occasions over those years for "improved academic performance and your recent recognition in the state School Performance Recognition Program,"[6] along with a several-thousand-dollar award. It was a major accomplishment, and we wore such recognition proudly. We were supremely prepared each year for these test administrations, with a terrific assistant principal and data clerk taking the lead and parents volunteering their time to assist as school hallway area "monitors," ensuring that all was quiet for students taking these tests. Each time we received such recognition, I would share the news with staff, students, and parents. At times, we would surprise students with a treat, usually in the form of ice cream sandwiches that parents and I would distribute to students during the students' lunch hour in the cafeteria. A growing number of our students seemed inspired to learn, our teachers were dialed in and challenging students to grow, and the wonderful efforts on display daily occurred in a completely renewed environment, one that was engaging, supportive, and now, successful.

As was cited early on in the book, the federal education law *No Child Left Behind Act* dictated that all schools throughout the country were expected to meet annual yearly progress (AYP), a measure of the extent to which students, schools, and school districts demonstrated proficiency in at least reading and mathematics, and at this level, schoolwide student attendance. Such was a big deal for all schools, and it meant a great deal for all those schools designated as in need of school improvement (SIU). We received the results from the 2002–2003 state assessments, which indicated that Harper's Choice had *met* or *exceeded* AYP in all areas—including student attendance—for all subgroups. This would include our racial/ethnic groups—Asian, American Indian, Black, White, and Hispanic, as well as our Special Needs youngsters and our FARMS (Free and Reduced Meals, a federal measure of poverty) students.[7] We crushed it! We were overjoyed, and when I made the announcement over the school's public address system, I believe the entire community heard the enthusiastic applause of our students and staff. We would repeat our performance of meeting or exceeding AYP in all areas, including student attendance for all of our student subgroups. Such was an achievement that schools with so-called stronger demographic communities could only hope one day to achieve. Soon after, we had shed "SIU" status and stood on our own continually working toward academic accomplishments. We would go on and repeat our performance, receiving state recognition again on the 2004 statewide assessments for meeting all AYP measured areas.[8] In the results for the 2008–2009 Maryland School Assessments, when I would retire at the end of that academic year, we again scored huge gains, increasing our student proficiency percentages by large margins.[9]

The school continued its march toward instructional excellence and student behavioral and academic achievement. The Johns Hopkins University Center for Talented Youth recognized eleven Harper's Choice Middle School students for their program offering.

Harper's Choice Middle was recognized in December 2006 as a State Character School of the Year. It was a humbling affirmation of our philosophy, as well as the time, talent, and hard work of staff, students, parents, administration, and the business community. It was a tribute to our recognition of character as the soul of our school, our high expectations throughout the school community, as well as the various programs, policies, and activities that we put in place, including such initiatives as our "Gotchas" and Dress for Success to our anti-bullying assemblies, character education lesson plans, and the myriad other activities that enhanced our efforts to develop in our students their full potential as adults and responsible, caring, contributing citizens.

On arrival to the school years earlier, I was poring through various documents, one of which cited PTA membership with few active members, staff stating that parent volunteers numbered "fewer than a handful" because of the school environment. Our focus on instruction, student behavioral and academic achievement, and a shared partnership with parents resulted in our hosting hundreds of parents at our Back-to-School Nights each year, with any number of parent volunteers in and out of our building daily. In fact, our PTA membership rolls numbered closer to five hundred members, a spectacular 1,000 percent increase in active membership. Many supportive parents played roles, large and small, in advancing our students, our staff, and our entire school. All our efforts were rewarded. Our "early commitment in identifying and implementing an action plan for school improvement," and our "transformative family engagement" resulted in our being designated a 2003 "National PTA School of Excellence." Harper's Choice Middle was one of twelve schools in the state of Maryland, one of 251 nationally to be acknowledged.[10] The award recognized those schools whose parent involvement practices were the "gold standard" across the nation. It bestowed this honor in recognition of those schools that demonstrated dedication of staff and community for a school to excel, as well as for successfully implementing the National Standards for Parent/Family Involvement Programs. The national recognition that came with this award was humbling!

Each successive year saw increasing numbers of teachers wanting to work at Harper's Choice, either from outside the system, inquiring if we might have a vacancy, or school district staff requesting a transfer to our school. The reader will recall that on my arrival, the folder for transfer requests was empty, no one expressing interest in working in such a dispiriting school environment. I would smile approvingly each end of the academic year, when I would review the folder filled with telephone messages, official transfer requests, and letters from teaching staff in and outside of the state, expressing their enthusiasm and their wish to be interviewed, should a vacancy in their subject discipline occur.

School climate is a particularly good measurement of the quality of one's professional teaching workplace, an indicator of job satisfaction or dissatisfaction. It stands to reason that the happier staff are at their school, the more motivated they will become, and the more productive they will be. Studies show links among employee job satisfaction, productivity, and corporate financial success.[11] At the time of my arrival to Harper's Choice Middle, the school was on the teachers' union "Watch Dog" list of the "Ten Worst Schools" in the district. The emphasis on *character*; our two major goals focusing on student academic achievement and student behavior; our no-nonsense approach to the school's mission; and the emphasis on a shared partnership with staff, students, parents, and community resulted in our leaving that list behind us very quickly. In fact, where the annual union-sponsored job satisfaction or school climate survey produced a countywide average of some 70 percent, Harper's Choice Middle would average 98 percent.[12] The annual survey results typically cited "good morale among staff, open communication and trust, opportunity to speak openly without repercussions, working conditions that were conducive to success, and administrators who always respected the Negotiated Agreement (union contract)."

I have been a critic of national teachers' unions, often viewed as ineffective in improving teaching conditions and student achievement, more concerned with money, power, and preserving jobs (including NEA/AFT union-specific jobs) than improving the day-to-day conditions of students and teaching staff. I've always condemned their political activities, particularly their support of political candidates and bad government policies that have had a deleterious effect on schools, teaching staff, students, and their families, including worsening the plight of minority youngsters in failing communities typically overseen by politicians beholding to union donations of money, time, and resources. My experience over the years found that many individuals active in teachers' unions were at one time classroom teachers but had long since lost the perspective that our enterprise should revolve first and foremost around children and what is in the best interests of youngsters. I always felt that if children became the focus of the unions—national, state, and local—many of their teaching concerns would be resolved.

A further editorial comment on teacher unions:

Though I was certainly respectful of teaching staff, my perspective on teachers' unions throughout the years was no secret. It has been my view that national teachers' unions have forsaken the lives of many thousands of students for the purpose of self-aggrandizement, power, and influence. As just mentioned, I disagree with union use of agency fees for political activity, doling out hard-earned teacher dollars almost exclusively to politicians who care not a whit about youngsters or the in-the-trenches classroom teacher, but care very much for high-dollar donations to their campaigns and offices. Dues-paying members agree to join, knowing how their money is spent; extracting agency fees from non-consenting teaching staff to use their dollars in that fashion is wrong and unfair, as has since been declared by the high court. Even in light of what many consider questionable opt-out clauses regarding paying of political lobbying, the 2018 Supreme Court *Janus* determination was an appropriate decision, in my view.

While strong unions over the years have resulted in higher pay, improved health care, and retirement benefits—all important items—they have shown little-to-no concern for students. They support and defend incompetent teachers; they fail too often to protect good teachers from inept school officials; and they have placed excessive time, effort, and hard-earned dollars over the years on political and social engineering activities that many Americans find objectionable. As an illustration, the NEA adopted resolutions stating its support for abortion, incorporating "white fragility" in trainings and literature, calling for an "exit strategy" for the Iraq war, wanting amnesty for illegal immigrants, and using digital communication tools to educate members and public about the struggles of Palestinians. However, the NEA elected to *defeat* a business item calling to "re-dedicate itself to the pursuit of increased student learning in every public school in America by putting a renewed emphasis on quality education."[13] Picture me shaking my head when hard-working dollars could otherwise go to supporting bona fide classroom teaching and learning rooted in truth and historical accuracy.

All the same, I nonetheless enjoyed a respectful relationship with the local teachers' union, its succeeding union presidents, staff representatives, and state union lawyer publicly commenting on the high regard that teachers and the union itself had for me throughout the district, as I was respectful of union contracts and due process rights in legal teaching staff matters.[14] All the more appreciative I was, since I was sitting across the table from union representatives on more occasions than I can count, regarding holding unsatisfactory teachers accountable for what I felt was their inferior teaching or other less-than-professional behaviors. In every instance—and the teachers union knew this to be true—my evaluations that brought us to the table were fair, thorough, and professional; and due process was very much always accorded the union member working at my schools.

I never took these union school community climate survey ratings for granted, as there are a host of troubling school workplace environments throughout the country. I would advise our staff and parents regularly that I was open to suggestions on how we might improve on any area of the teaching-learning process, that the more my staff enjoyed coming to work every morning, the better chance that they and our students would be successful. I would often use the school newsletter or publicly address the staff to express my appreciation for the inordinate time and effort that so many of them gave to each other and to our community's youngsters.

There often exists an adversarial relationship between labor and management, between teachers' unions and school administration. In the early years of my career, there existed a strange twist in that the teachers' union in this district, called an "education association," represented both teacher and administrator. It was odd in that, as a school administrator, who was a dues-paying member, I conceivably could find myself confronting my own union representative and lawyer, who were representing a teacher that I, a school administrator, was trying to hold accountable. On the other hand, there were any number of times, as a school administrator, when it was a union representative and/or lawyer supporting me, when I felt the need to defend my honor or hold a higher official's feet to the fire for an action taken against me that was without merit or unethical. In each instance, the dispute or issue brought before a hearing was ruled in my favor, though they were Pyrrhic victories.

There developed a sense of esteem and mutual respect between a particular union representative and me. He was smart and a fighter, and I occasionally called him "Bulldog," one who was often in my corner and waged solid arguments; he was a respected foe, as well, when I would find myself on the other side of the table and he was representing a teacher or other staff member whom I had called on the carpet.

On a different note, our school was proud and humbled to be asked to host a Chinese delegation visiting the United States. They wanted to visit a number of American schools and stated how impressed they were with their conversations with Harper's Choice staff, students, and parents. They were visibly impressed with the magnitude of the school's turnaround, stated that they "understood and admired" our philosophy, our emphasis on *character*, and were impressed with the organization that they saw evidenced in their classroom visitations, thanking staff for their "kindness" and their "hospitality." Such a visit, of course, would have been out of the question and not at all entertained years earlier.

The numerous partnerships with our community businesses, government agencies, and organizations enhanced the overall educational experience for our students, our staff, and school administration. Given the value and the long-term relationship that we cultivated with some of our partners—and over the years we had anywhere from twenty-seven to thirty-two active partnerships—it would be difficult for me to imagine why any school—certainly a community's public school—would not want to reach out and make that valuable connection. I never sensed that any of them saw our relationship as a marketing opportunity, though such connections in the community certainly are useful advertising and an avenue to promote a product. No, it was because we proudly and sincerely extended ourselves and, in the case of our partnership with the local Rotary, connections were made and businessmen and businesswomen saw an opportunity to connect with and to serve in a way that would benefit their school community, specifically its students and their school teaching staff. The interaction and genuine interest in understanding each other's core values and purpose led, as cited earlier, to our hosting some Rotary meetings in the school's media center as a way to show our appreciation and give our youngsters a chance to intermingle with and to speak personally with some of the community's most successful individuals; the students always saw such opportunities as rewarding.

I was contacted by the district public relations office, advising me that the *Washington Post* was soon producing their annual *Education Review* of schools. The newspaper had heard or read of our school turnaround and was curious to learn more. The school system public information officer provided information and statistics to them. The result was our being cited among the "Top Thirty schools in the Virginia–Washington, D.C.–Maryland area," stating, in part:

> ...even rich suburbs such as Howard County MD have pockets of poverty, and Harper's Choice draws many of its students from them.
>
> When Stephen Wallis arrived six years ago, he found the usual pathologies of schools with many disadvantaged kids: low test scores, poor teacher morale, racial tension, disruptive behavior, vandalism, few PTA members, and no business partnerships.
>
> Now test scores are up; suspensions are down; the PTA has more than 400 [500] members; and 27 businesses have established partnerships with the school, tops in the county...."[15]

Results was a focus throughout my tenure as principal of Harper's Choice Middle, and our accomplishments were a direct reflection of the hard work, time, dedication, and effort of so many: our students; our staff, in and out of the classroom; our parents; our community supporters; and the organizations and businesses that contributed treasure and human resources. All had a direct and palpable impact on our staff's workplace—the students' school.

As I look back, it is as important today as it was then to recognize and express appreciation for their talents and their caring, which, for me, served as a tremendous source of energy. I remain most satisfied with all our efforts, and I hope our students—today's young men and women—look back with an equal amount of satisfaction, fondness, appreciation, and pride. Though I'm reluctant to say, given the fact I was a high school English teacher at one time, I am reminded of my granddad's use of a Philadelphia colloquialism: "We done good!"

13

Leadership

Given the unique challenge that I accepted in taking the helm of this school community and the successful results of school staff, students, parents, and wider business community, it seems appropriate to share a perspective on leadership.

Leadership is about setting an example—a solid, pragmatic, positive standard of behavior; it is about working harder than the hardest worker on staff. It's about *character*, it's about *passion*, it's about *teamwork*. The most successful leaders in any industry are those who have a passion for what they do. I mentioned earlier that leading this school community was more about duty, and that was true. It is also true that no matter the scope of one's job, no matter the duty, one derives a great deal more satisfaction out of a challenge when you have a passion for what you are doing. It was about not asking anyone to do anything I had not already done or would not be willing to do. It was ensuring that every staff member would be personally responsible for his or her position, and that always started with me. The leader should be a solid individual—kind and considerate, but tough and resolute—someone who is confident but humble and principled, someone who is empathetic, a professional who exercises decisiveness and good judgment. All of us would be expected to walk the talk, as it were. A decision would be made on the basis of how it improves instruction and learning, how it impacts kids, staff, parents, and community. It follows that decision-making would be based on analyzing data and drilling down on that data, looking at available information and resources.

How leaders conduct themselves daily gives a window to observers that allows them to make immediate judgments on how leaders think and what they value. I found it important as a school administrator to be upfront, honest, and transparent with professional staff, students, parents, and their respective communities. I encouraged my administrative team and instructional team leaders to share with me their perspective on issues, including dissenting viewpoints, as I respected them and valued their frame of reference on matters, that only then could I make the kinds of decisions that were in the best interests of the school community. My abilities, my results, would be our results—staff, students, parents, and the wider community— and I had no problem checking my ego at the door. My mindset was that we, together, would make what needed to happen, happen.

The leadership style that always suited me, that was comfortable for me, revolved around a combination servant-transformational approach. It is important to listen, to be empathetic; it's equally important to provide an inspiring vision for the future of the school community, motivating staff, students, parents, and the wider business community to fulfill the vision of building a vibrant, successful, academically strong school community. So I recognized the importance of the people with whom I worked, the students and families we served. My approach would revolve around *cura personalis* and a principled compassion, by which I mean I would strive to be sensitive to and address the needs of individuals, while not undermining the integrity of the operational or instructional program of the school. As an example, if a teacher was not performing satisfactorily, I would ensure that the individual received a fair shake and was given every opportunity to improve, any absence of which would find me recommending his/her firing. I would not follow those schools that retained unsatisfactory teaching staff year after year. The genesis of that leadership style was likely experiential. My exposure to the fire service allowed me to see directly how delicate and fragile the fabric of life can be. My military service and training reminded me that life is temporary, and I believed it important to be purposeful daily with one's life, making a contribution and, if possible, a palpable difference in whatever endeavor I might find myself, be it family, business, or personal area of interest.

Merriam-Webster defines leadership as "the office or position of a leader, the capacity to lead, and the act or instance of leading." While that is true, a clearer definition to me is that leadership is the art of motivating a group of people to act toward achieving a common goal. Whether my role as among five company squad leaders within a battalion at a tender age in army boot camp or someone the likes of Lee Iacocca, who was among the inventors and often regarded as the father of the iconic Ford Mustang, a guy who would later, as CEO, be fired by Ford Motor Company, hired at the failing Chrysler Corporation, and deliver one of the greatest corporate turnarounds in history, the fact remains that leading and motivating people to achieve a common goal is a nonnegotiable requisite of leadership. Such would be required if we were going to be successful in turning around this failing school community.

When discussing leadership, I would guess that many individuals may think of people like Dwight Eisenhower and Winston Churchill, both leaders and heroes of World War II; Mahatma Gandhi and Martin Luther King Jr., one who employed nonviolent resistance to lead the successful campaign for India's independence from British Rule, the other whose nonviolent resistance was a hallmark of this most visible spokesperson and leader in the civil rights movement; New York City mayor Rudy Giuliani and retired police commissioner

William Bratton, one known as "America's Mayor," well-recognized for his leadership throughout his tenure as mayor of the "city that doesn't sleep,"[1] including the aftermath of the September 11 terrorist attacks; the other, Bratton, among the most successful police leaders anywhere in the country—ever— who was responsible, along with Giuliani, for decreasing crime and improving the quality of life in New York City, via the use of the "broken windows" theory of urban decay and the introduction of the CompStat system, where crime data was used to redirect police personnel, and precinct commanders were held accountable for their crime numbers;[2] Geoffrey Canada, whose Harlem Children's Zone has provided hope for over twelve thousand urban poor youngsters, with 95 percent of these children attending college; and Malala Yousafzai and Donald Trump, to name a few, one a Pakistani activist for female education and the youngest Nobel Prize laureate, the other a "disrupter," who, after years of marked decline in public confidence in those holding high political office, invoked a wave of change that millions welcomed from this first commander-in-chief who was a career businessman,[3] entering office with no prior government or military experience.

I would also guess that many folks would ascribe to leaders a number of various attributes and traits, among which would be honesty, integrity, knowledge, passion, and excellent communication skills; they might say that leaders are ethical, objective, fair, reasonable, and responsible for their own actions; that they provide clear direction and are solid decision-makers; that they own their position and exhibit personality and professional accountability, among any number of additional characteristics. Such traits are what most people look for in their leaders, in whom many place their trust.

A leader has a vision, a plan, and the ability to lead others in that vision and in carrying out that plan. Years of experience in the field of education afforded me the opportunity to meet both sharp, innovating school administrators, as well as those who were poor at what they did in their schools, designated "school leaders" with no particular vision and lacking any plausible plan for leading a school community to greatness. I recall as a young high school administrator realizing that, rather than grouse at having to work with a mediocre or poor school principal, I would learn from that experience, as well, determining what not to do were I to lead a school community one day. I would then continue to apply myself daily, giving the staff, students, and community my best effort. I found it a noteworthy irony and disappointing commentary that in a nearly forty-year career in the education profession, one that frequently touts itself as having a lock on leadership, I encountered so few genuine leaders, and the greater percentage of those were classroom teachers and coaches. The remaining appeared to be in two camps: those who simply went along to get along, i.e., they would conform to the bureaucratic expectation so as not to disrupt or endanger their own sense of security or "belonging," and those—arguably a bit strident, but I think, accurate—who were mere sycophants who would follow the latest fad or politically correct policy, no matter how spurious the research, if any, no matter the harm that such direction might befall students and staff, with the hope of being noticed, hoping to be seen among the anointed, and tapped for a higher paying position among the bureaucracy to spread the message, via their own mediocrity and sense of self-importance.

Let me take a few minutes to share additional observations on the matter of school- and district-wide leadership. School communities—their staff, students, and parents—deserve top-shelf leadership; it makes no difference what the leader looks like, as long as he or she is a strong, capable, and forward-thinking leader. In my professional career I have observed more than my fair share of incompetently run schools and school systems. Unenlightened, disingenuous individuals who occupy pivotal decision-making positions frequently hire equally unserious individuals who often are correspondingly unimpressive to take the helm of individual schools or a school district, a not-so-minor reason for our continuing national education malaise.

Where school officials discard merit and appoint leadership positions based on race or favors to friends and family, major risks are incurred, frequently resulting in harm to the education experience of school youngsters, professional staff, and communities. It is wholly unfair but done regularly throughout the profession. Whether a race-based or gender placement, where school officials believe the appointment will make them look righteous, or in the case of nepotism or a favor to a friend, where they hope to be seen in a generous light, these officials are quite willing to sell their souls to the devil, no matter the consequences endured by a school community that otherwise potentially might have thrived prosperously with a more qualified and deserving candidate.

Such appointees to a district headquarters or school-site position typically had no problem taking such a position, no matter that they failed to earn the position by demonstrated high-caliber performance, competence, or leadership qualities. You might think that the individual accepting the job would not rest comfortably knowing that he or she was appointed because of whom the person knows, or was that "diversity" hire or "token minority," occupying a position for which he or she was clearly less qualified than another, especially when their staff and community dismiss their appointment as having resulted from a tilted playing field. You would be wrong. These individuals regularly fill school district positions and proudly remain, even though their incompetence regularly results in low staff morale, poor student behavior, and failing academic performance, sometimes resulting in the unfit individual being "promoted" to a higher position in the administrative bureaucracy.

On the other hand, where you will not find anything close to malaise or school official incompetence, is in the countless number of schools and districts that are posting exceptional student behavior and academic achievement performance, where you will observe on display daily, outstanding instructional excellence on the part of teaching staff, active parent involvement in their children's schools, where you will see an entire school community devoted to instruction, continuous progress, and partnerships. You can bet that such schools are led by strong, vibrant, dedicated men and women of every color, ethnicity, and background, because that particular school district performed its due diligence in providing a deserving school community a first-rate school principal. Such schools dot the American landscape, and as a parent, school-age youngster, or teaching staff member who may well work in one of these schools, you best count your lucky stars!

I wasn't interested in being—and the staff at Harper's Choice didn't deserve—an average school administrator; they didn't need a manager; they needed a leader, and I was confident in myself, my skills, my background, my experience, and my talents to lead and quite willing to confront any issue and make the necessary decisions that would propel this school community into the stratosphere. I was prepared to take responsibility for those decisions, just as I expected staff members, students, and parents to take their share of responsibility regarding the individual roles they played. As school principal, it was important to me that all staff members felt that they mattered, no matter their position, that each of us was expected to make a difference. That is how you connect with your entire teaching staff—in and out of the classroom; be upfront, be transparent, listen to and value the input of your constituency. Doug Pederson, former

NFL coach, who led the Philadelphia Eagles to their first Super Bowl championship, encapsulated nicely his role as a leader when he said, "For me, it was just about staying the course, staying true to who I believe that I am, being open, being honest, being transparent with the players, being firm with the players but at the same time listening to the players. And I think that's been the difference for me, is listening to the guys and that's what helped us win this championship.... It was just the connection that our team had all season long that helped us win."[4]

I had met and spoken with various school system officials and Harper's Choice staff, parents, and students during those first few days of my arrival. I had read and reviewed a number of documents, surveys, parent letters, and state department of education assessment reports. The vision and goals, as well as the results that I was focused on obtaining, had been made more than clear to the staff and community. We, together, now had purpose, a direction, that Harper's Choice now stood for something. That kind of no-nonsense plan and direction, accompanied with my clear expression of caring and support, was huge for the staff and community, huge. It was important that staff, students, parents, and area businesses knew that I cared, that I had a passion for supporting and turning this school community around in a positive, winning fashion. It wasn't long before I felt that various school constituencies began to feel the passion.

My daily goal was to focus on ensuring that staff and students enjoyed reporting to work and attending school every day. It was important that staff and students understood my shared vision and had complete buy-in. Once I was assured that folks genuinely understood what was required for us to be successful, I got out of the way, let the good teachers teach, and the administrative team would work with the less-than-stellar staff in a positive but firm professional development fashion. It was important to me that they knew they were being led, not managed, and we were going to turn this situation around together. Of course, I wasn't going to have it any other way, so I was willing to—and did—fight issues of race, unions, and the like, when it was warranted. I might add there were a number of those kinds of confrontations, and I was successful in every one of the encounters. That is noted with not the slightest bit of swagger; it is to say that when you are organized, methodical, and right—that the decision you made was done in the best interest of students, staff, parents, and community—your chances of winning these kinds of challenges are supremely enhanced.

I had a high regard for my staff, students, and their parents, and as I pointed out earlier, I needed to conduct myself in a fashion that guaranteed their respect for me. As time went by, I felt that staff, students, and parents were willing to do most anything for me, and I can't think of anything I would not have done for them. We had begun to make successes, then we began to win awards; they had begun to think of themselves as winners, they developed a sense of pride, and they were willing to go the extra mile.

When addressing the public, I made it a point to share or give credit where it was due, and the teachers, students, parents, and business community deserved a great deal of credit for the success we enjoyed.

In an address to Tufts University graduates several years ago, former secretary of state Madeleine Albright stated that "humility and critical thinking, when combined with courage and determination, are indispensable qualities of leadership."[5] I believe that is absolutely true, and we worked at cultivating those traits in our entire staff, starting with me. The Harper's Choice staff and community, in my view, needed to know that my leadership style revolved around trust, a sense of fairness, and transparency, that our philosophy would be one of teamwork and family, that those defining characteristics would support the compelling vision I offered to them. I was driven, and I believe my demeanor, my organization, and the vision I had for this school community was becoming infectious. I was reminded of the motion picture *The Shawshank Redemption*, and the mantra uttered twice by separate characters that you either "get busy living or get busy dying." We were driven, and we would get busy realizing our dream, right then, right at that moment, and each day thereafter, every academic year.

It was apparent to me that within the first few days, and then into the academic year, that I would need to move folks out of that school building. It was how certain staff carried themselves professionally, how they addressed other staff and students, the shallowness of their classroom planning and the less-than-satisfactory instructional delivery in their classrooms. I would wind up moving a number of certified and noncertified staff from the building over the years. Such is another important aspect of leadership, surrounding yourself with good people, smart people, creative people, and over those years, I was able to hire genuinely smart, sensitive, creative, and hardworking staff who made a seamless transition to our school community. These men and women, in and out of the classroom, worked hard and well with other staff members, connected beautifully with our student body, and delivered solid instruction that was focused on advancing our students, academically and behaviorally.

Much like many coaches—former college and NFL coach Lou Holtz comes to mind—there were certain attributes that I thought always served me well, traits that became more pronounced the day I was drafted into the military and remained with me throughout my professional life. *Attitude* can be a useful, positive characteristic for anyone, certainly for a leader. I held a positive, forward-leaning mindset, which was saying something given the condition of the school, the campus grounds, and the school climate upon my arrival.

We would not dwell on the problems and challenges. I was *focused* and *results-oriented*, two additional attributes that served me, served us, well. In fact, leaders and their staff cannot help but be successful when they are laser-focused and know the results they're after. It was not a one-man operation; I made it a point to ensure that staff throughout the years—in thought, word, and action—knew and felt that we were in this together, a kind of Harper's Choice family, "The Choice," as we later called our place of work. As challenges presented themselves, we elevated teamwork and together resolved to meet the challenge head-on, deciding firmly on a course of action and continuing toward our goal of getting results. It's fair to say that I was passionate about what we were doing and the results we knew would make such a difference in the lives of our students, their families, and the community. In that respect it was more than achieving results that reflected academic measurements; it was about making that kind of human connection, again, *cura personalis.* I believed that if I took good care of my staff, they would take good care of our students and their families; I just felt that if they perceived how willing I was to step to the plate for them, individually or collectively, they, in turn, would extend the same to our students; it certainly seemed that way to me.

We appreciated our gains in student improvement performance, though small at times, and one could argue if "the punch was worth the squeeze," yet we would entertain "no excuses," because all of us acknowledged that we had skin in the game and we were hell-bent on being better tomorrow than we were today. We adopted a "whatever it takes" disposition. It was more than a culture change in how we did things at this school; we felt it was a kind of renaissance. Staff, students, and community could dream again. The school was anchored safely with a clear vision, purpose, direction, and goal, and there was no question in my mind that we would persist with a singular focus on results. It was reassuring to hear from staff and parents from time to time, that they felt the energy, the direction, and appreciated the support.

Many education and school administrators believe they are leadership proficient, believing they are instructional leaders. No matter how school administrators have come to occupy the positions they hold in the field of education, they are presumed leaders, and many of them are, as cited earlier, leading successful schools throughout our country. However, many people—among whom are scores of teachers—believe that it is often not at all true, that to work for a successful school leader is a rare occurrence, one to be valued, respected, and appreciated.

Experience and observation in the profession have proven the importance of hiring smart, capable, and sincere professionals for various leadership positions. Otherwise, as cited earlier, you undermine the purpose and scope of the job to be handled, giving short shrift to staff, students, and the school community. Among the key elements that saw such a positive transformation at Harper's Choice was being given the full responsibility for leading the change in total school performance and the accompanying latitude to get things done, to get the job accomplished. Equally important, however, is to transfer, if appropriate, or fire those who do not get the job done. Therein lies the rub, because too often inept school officials remain in their respective positions for far too long.

The issue of appointing competent leadership warrants elaboration. As I earlier mentioned, my years of professional experience afforded me the opportunity of working with or observing some terrific educational leaders. I also encountered mediocre, if not, incompetent school administrators, whether in my own school district, through work I did with the state legislature in Annapolis, by way of writing and researching for think tanks, viewing and reading of various school districts at the center of national media coverage, as well as through my research and conversations with professionals for the testimony on American schooling that I gave before the United States Congress.

These ineffective school officials held school district system-wide assignments, frequently positioned high on the administrative ladder; others occupied individual school site-based leadership positions. It would be one thing if they were titular in nature, holding the title but having no real authority. The unfortunate rub, again for emphasis, is that these individuals frequently occupy decision-making positions that directly and negatively affect professional staff, students, and often the parent community in some capacity in neighborhoods and cities across the country. These men and women do not possess and therefore cannot appreciate the full professional understanding of their position, seemingly completely unaware and devoid of the principles required for effective leadership. While that may sound harsh to some, sundry examples occur daily in school communities, with only off-the-chart maladies garnering headlines in local and national media: teachers en route to out-of-building meetings, for example, observing district-level officials using professional workdays for personal business, from shopping to hair salon appointments; a school principal who routinely arrived to work some thirty minutes late daily, almost always after the students entered classes and the school day had begun, a principal whose motto she proudly proclaimed to fellow administrators was "The less parents know, the better," the same individual who had scores of teacher grievances filed against her, with the union representative pleading, "What's the use, when the superintendent refuses to take any action," and the same principal whose school was allowed to fall into state-designated "failing school" status, a school where she was allowed to remain until retirement; another principal who completely botched an investigation that saw the wrong student suspended, denying the youngster due process because he wouldn't reveal or didn't know the names of students actually involved in a disciplinary incident; the parents demanded an open hearing with the local school board, with the ensuing legal sparring resulting in the student being cleared, and the matter costing the school system thousands of dollars in legal fees.

Such personal anecdotes are typical of too many K-12 education "leaders," individuals who occupy school administrator positions of trust and responsibility but who fail to deliver in many communities. These unserious individuals are embarrassments to the profession and the many outstanding school administrators who work alongside these slackers. They are an insult to staff, employees, and the communities they are entrusted to serve. My view is that much like universities today, K-12 schools—public and private—often are top-heavy with administrators, a good portion of whom should find other work, with the money spent on these positions going directly to classroom instruction and needed academic instructional interventions.

Mayor Rudy Giuliani, who was also a former United States associate attorney general and United States attorney for the Southern District of New York, knows something about personal and professional responsibility and cites the following in his book, *Leadership*:

> A lot of leaders have catchy slogans on their desk; many believe in them. The two-word sign on my desk genuinely summarizes my whole philosophy: I'M RESPONSIBLE. During my time at City Hall, I did my best to make those words a signature theme for every employee, starting with myself. Throughout my career, I've maintained that ac-

countability—the idea that the people who work for me are answerable to those we work for—is the cornerstone. And this principle starts with me.[6]

School principals frequently receive the results of annual state testing prior to public release. School district administrators may take the opportunity to examine areas that were problematic, as well as review areas where their students performed well. This is important feedback, providing relevant information and insight to school-based administration and staff. We had fallen short and had not made state annual yearly progress one year in the area of reading and special education. Upon reviewing the information during the summer recess, I called relevant staff members in those departments, along with staff support personnel, and they agreed to meet. We reviewed the data, gathered additional information on specific students, and discussed instructional practices in place. We conferred further and analyzed how best to address these areas in need of improvement, reviewing research-based best practices, and we proceeded to plan the professional development of staff that would take place the few days before the academic year would get underway. The planning saw each of us organized, prepared, and confident with the manner in which we would work with our cherubs on their return for the new school year. The following year's state tests, as a point of interest, saw us meeting our state annual yearly progress goals in *all* areas for *all* our student subgroups, an accomplishment that, as cited earlier, schools with so-called stronger demographics had not attained; the student (and teaching staff) performance results were, once again, huge for us.

I noted at the time that when the annual district-wide meeting of several hundred staff would take place at the end of summer, there were school principals raising their hands anxiously asking school system headquarters administrators when affected principals were going to receive direction on addressing their school's failing the previous year's state testing. They were sincere— helpless, lost, and looking forlornly, but sincere— and waiting for direction, their instructions, if you can imagine, and their students would be returning to their schools in a few days. All were making well north of $100,000 annually and sat there with their hands raised asking when they would be told what to do. District officials didn't see the irony, stating that they would provide direction soon enough. You shake your head that such people serve in critical leadership positions throughout the profession.

A cursory examination of American education reveals failing practices in school districts, as well as at individual schools within these districts. For all the criticisms—some fair, others unfair—that we see plastered across newspaper headlines and featured on national media news broadcasts, few school administrators—whether superintendents, local board of education members, or school principals—seem to learn anything from past failures. Why would they, really, when there is often no palpable, meaningful sense of personal responsibility. Meanwhile, these individuals continue to go about their jobs, making poor decisions, daily, year after year, with no professional accountability.

Leaders must learn from their mistakes; that's what leaders do. Failures are humbling, but they can strengthen you. It's not that any of us is immune from making mistakes; I'm certainly among those who have made their share of mistakes in life, but you learn from them, and you use the lessons learned to motivate yourself, your staff, your students, and your wider school community. Such a practice provides the motivation that allows one to go on to future challenges with that much more confidence.

I am reminded of Navy Admiral William McRaven's book, cited earlier, in which he references "The Circus," held every afternoon after U.S. Navy SEAL training. It consists of additional calisthenics, combined with nonstop harassment by SEAL combat veterans, who wanted only the strong to survive training. If you failed to meet the standard on any event that day, your name was put on the list to attend that afternoon's *circus*. Most of the Basic Underwater Demolition/SEAL candidates—each one a top-shelf American patriot—reach their breaking point and, as described earlier in the book, "ring the bell," voluntarily dropping out of the program; others gain insight, strength, and reach down to find the grit, determined to graduate from SEAL training.

I am not recommending similar treatment of civilians, who happen to work in the field of education, though it is too bad that substandard school administrators and boards of education bear no responsibility for their ineptitude in how specific school districts and individual schools are operated that fail to serve their respective community's children and parents. As McRaven notes later in his book, none of us can avoid *the circus*, making our own individual share of failings, but we ought not be afraid of *the circus*. I would advise those school "leaders" to acknowledge the fault, where and when it occurs, sooner rather than later, dig in, and make the necessary corrections, advancing your school community, or. . . "ring the bell."

I join those who are critical of what passes for education in many classrooms throughout America today. Any discussion of school improvement in many of these districts is pure folly, given what is standard fare both in the classroom and how schools are run, how they are "led." Wholly unwise it is, in my view, to entertain notions of erasing the achievement gap or raising graduation standards in these school communities that ignore the very reasons why such goals are unachievable. Many an educrat will take umbrage at such criticism, but hard truths are truths nonetheless, as I have learned and observed over the many years I have spent in this business. Imagine, however, if the importance of character were recognized and practiced by the management and staff in each community's school across the country, the effect such would have on teacher instruction and retention, student behavior and academic achievement, as well as parent and community satisfaction with our schools.

I have stated that I've no lock on any of the principles or initiatives that I have cited or elaborated upon that were responsible for our success. The fact is that our success was the result of teamwork—staff, students, parents, and the wider business community. We earnestly and continually looked to work smarter, work harder, and work better. I feel good about the people I assembled over those years, who did what many could not, and all these years later, I suspect they still feel proud; I know that's how I feel about each of them. I appreciate that I was able to stand on the shoulders of a number of humble, smart, caring, and terrific people over the years, whether they were family, colleagues, and friends, or people I had come to know and become friends with because of our mutual interest in improving American education.

My leadership perspective over the years was shaped, in part, by my youth and how I was raised, my military service, my experience with a busy fire department, and my years as a classroom teacher and educational leader. Early on I developed an interest in and a respect for those leaders in whatever field of interest—politics, sports, military, business—people who improved in a notable fashion their community, individuals who possessed a passion for improving the condition of things, the lot of everyone within their purview, leaders who understood instinctively the meaning of integrity, vision, courage, gratitude, duty, as well as personal and professional accountability.

School districts need to understand the principles of meaningful, substantive leadership if communities are going to see their fair share of successful, safe, and caring schools that are individual professional teaching-learning communities that can promote the best of teaching excellence and student behavioral and academic achievement. Hooah!

14

School Safety and Security

Given the precarious state of many schools that have made news headlines over the years, this bears repeating: The home is considered a safe place (notwithstanding the fact that many homes, sadly, are not), and since, by law, the government is mandating children be enrolled in schools, the expectation is that educators act in *loco parentis*, "in the place of a parent." I mention such, yet again, for emphasis for it cannot be emphasized enough. It refers to the legal responsibility of a person or organization to take on some of the responsibilities of a parent. Therefore, because students must be in school, we must ensure that the school setting is safe and secure. If you think it would follow that all school officials understand this principle, you would be mistaken.

I have found for over three decades in the profession that the response to school safety and security events—particularly violence—by educators, school administrators, local and state boards of education, and school district headquarters officials is typically partial, cosmetic, and ad hoc. We know that far too many schools across this great nation demonstrate daily that they are neither safe nor secure, and not for a single minute should such be tolerated in any community.

This issue is why I scheduled that meeting with the district school security coordinator upon my arrival the summer of my appointment, alluded to in an earlier chapter. Being aware of—and following through by taking school safety and security measures—is hugely important when charged with leading a school community, and in our case, among the reasons we all but eradicated inappropriate to uncivilized behaviors that had gotten in the way of student and faculty performance, behaviors that today are rampant throughout too many of America's schools.

There were a number of security initiatives that resulted in a safer Harper's Choice school environment. A major factor in our success to create such a school atmosphere was our recognition that our school culture and student behavior itself needed to be among our two major schoolwide goals, not just to be cited as another district goal, but to be proactively addressed throughout the academic year, every year. Both our academic and student behavior school goals were district-wide goals, as well. However, we tackled both goals differently, and we did so with vigor and a degree of personal and professional accountability typically lacking in the schools throughout the district in which I worked, which was no different from the manner in which many school systems nationally address these issues. Our School Improvement Plan cited an at-a-glance view of various statistics relevant to our student behavior or school culture goal, among which were suspension data, disciplinary and threat management referrals, student participation in extracurricular activities, as well as parent/community participation and outreach efforts. The plan went on to show how we would go about improving student behavior, featuring sections that answered questions we would ask ourselves: Objectives–What do we want for our students? This area would cite specific statements of desired and measurable yearly student results: Strategies–How will we provide it? We would cite methods, procedures, techniques, and program interventions; Milestones/Time-lines: this area would include statements that identified students or staff who were expected to achieve results and when they were to be achieved; and Evaluation–How will we know that we've done it well, and how will we respond if we haven't? These statements identified the results achieved. The overarching, almost monomaniacal purpose of our schoolwide school improvement plan was to ensure an appropriate teaching-learning environment that gave teachers a reason to get up in the morning and enjoy coming to work at this specific school, a place that provided a secure, warm, and inviting place for students to learn, to interact, and to grow, a school that parents might boast about throughout the community. While every neighborhood across the country deserves such schools, this community was overdue for a community-wide makeover, including this specific school.

The governor's office and local county police had designated the area a Hot Spot Community,[1] a locally designated neighborhood, among several throughout the state, suffering from a disproportionate amount of crime, commenced in the Clinton administration, under the Justice Department's "Reclaiming Our Neighborhoods" program. The designation would provide additional police monitoring, including state police presence; increased prosecutions in the area; federal funding, as well as services for at-risk youth and substance abusers, which, it was hoped, would see a strong deterrent effect on crime.[2]

The neighborhood development included high-density, low-income housing, a sizable portion of which was federal Section 8 subsidized housing, clustered near the village center where stores, a community meeting hall, and recreation facilities were located. While there are good reasons for such a design, such can frequently be a magnet for crime, including robbery, rape, drugs, theft, and gun violence. Despite its well-planned origins and suburban character, the area was not immune to the kinds of problems that affect other urban cities,[3] which is why this specific school needed a wholesale makeover.

Above and beyond an actual schoolwide plan to highlight the importance of and promote school safety and security were a host of other actions. I mentioned earlier our Citizens on Patrol (COPS) program that would see senior adults (wearing T-shirts with a prominent school logo and carrying clipboards and two-way radios) walking and monitoring the various paths leading to and from the school in the morning and afternoon throughout the year. Having established earlier an earnest and trustworthy relationship with the neighborhood grocery store manager, I was also asked by the local merchants' association to sit on the Merchants Board, which met regularly in the evenings and included various store owners, managers, and representatives of the corporation that owned the shopping mall. I made it a point to attend weekly meetings at the community police substation, along with various representatives of the county police, the state's attorney, representatives from the state court system, and juvenile justice departments.

At the school itself, I insisted that we keep exterior doors closed, locked from the outside, unlike previously, when the building was like a sieve, with various doors that might or might not have been locked, some kept open by way of chairs or other items, allowing people to gain easy access. We would have only one entry through which one on the outside could enter the school; this would be a front entrance door closest to the main office. Staff were to secure classroom doors at the start of each instructional lesson period. The reader will recall that any student wishing to leave a classroom was to sign out and sign back in, having an identifiable hall pass from that teacher's class in their possession when outside the classroom.

The beginning and end of each school day saw staff manning the hallways and exterior grounds, monitoring activity and interacting with students arriving to and leaving school grounds for the day, far different from employee reports that noted most staff previously remaining in their classrooms or faculty lounge. Staff were advised to intervene immediately at anything even slightly perceived as bullying, notifying the appropriate parent and/or an administrator just as quickly. If such behavior were going to disappear, it would only happen if students felt the entire staff was on top of the issue, as well as the youngsters themselves gradually understanding and becoming more sensitive and caring about one another.

I cited the scourge of bullying earlier in my separate addresses to staff, students, and the PTA. Given that the chapter you are reading focuses on safety and security, the issue warrants emphasis, as I have shaken my head over the years at the number of schools where naïve, if not, inept administrators and school system officials tolerated nauseatingly poor student behavior, all the while fancying themselves as "leaders," daily exhibiting little, if any, knowledge, of a single leadership quality. Such was the case with the egregious behavior surrounding school bullying, which, according to students, parents, and researchers today, continues to be routinely ignored, allegedly not recognized at all, and if it is, handled dismissively and inadequately by educators, school administrators, school system officials, and local board of education members, in spite of some school systems touting their concern and offering online reporting that is then forwarded to administrators.

How serious is this menacing behavior in our schools across America? Following up on the statistics cited in an earlier chapter of the book, research studies vary on the issue; the National Center for Education Statistics states that more than one out of five students reports being a victim of bullying at some point in their schooling.[4]

K12 Learning Liftoff, an online education resource, cites a recent survey of twenty-seven states by a San Francisco nonprofit that asked students about their experiences with school bullying during the 2017–2018 academic year.[5] A third of the students reported that they had experienced bullying, an increase over previous years' surveys, in which one-fourth of students report being bullied. Whatever the results of various surveys, we're talking millions of cherubs, the sons and daughters of tax-paying parents, who rightly should expect that their children are cared for and kept safe while attending school daily.

These millions of students are subjected to being made fun of, called names, insulted, made the subject of rumors, and made to do things they wouldn't ordinarily do; they are purposely excluded from activities, they have their property destroyed, they are threatened, pushed, shoved, tripped, spit on, and written upon—you read that correctly; a couple years earlier, while an administrator at a high school, I suspended and involved the police on a case where a bully physically assaulted a special needs student, then used a pen to write derogatory and vulgar words on the youngster's neck and arms. The victim, his special education teacher assistant, and his mom said they had reported previous incidents of bullying by this same offender and others since elementary school, stating that the reprobates continued to do so with impunity. This same incorrigible offender regularly made life difficult for his teachers, all of whom were attending or working in a so-called Blue Ribbon School, a designation "too often awarded to schools for impressive paperwork and fashionable instruction methods, and too infrequently a measure of academic achievement," according to a 2000 Brookings Institution report and cited in a September 6 *Washington Post* article by Jay Mathews titled "Study Tests the Meaning of Blue Ribbon Schools."

On this specific occasion, however, the result of meaningful action taken by a school administrator to address the ill behavior meant that the harassing behavior stopped for this victim, who finally was able to go on enjoying his last three years of high school, free of torment. He gained self-confidence and started participating in school extracurricular activities, including playing a role in the school play. An added effect was the expression of appreciation by teachers, saying they could finally teach without having to stop instruction periodically to address the offending student's repeated ill behavior.

Above and beyond the sometimes-indescribable pain of a youngster being bullied, these kids understandably increase their absence from school; their academic grades suffer, and they develop difficulties in learning.

RethinkEd's director of research Christina Whalen cites that bullied students often suffer sleep difficulties, headaches and stomachaches, as well as mental health issues such as anxiety and depression.[6] She cites the research of Gianluca Gini and Dorothy Espelage, who found that bullied students are two times more likely to have suicidal ideation or attempts.[7] Whalen goes on to state that students who are bullies also have long-term issues, such as academic problems, substance use, behavioral issues, and problems with the law. They are less likely to obtain meaningful employment and often struggle with independence and relationships as adults.

One cannot emphasize enough how important the issue of bullying behavior must be on the radar of every educator and school official in American schools across our land.

There were additional practices put in place at Harper's Choice that I believed would enhance our efforts to provide a safe and secure school environment. Any evening activity saw me contacting county police well in advance to arrange police visibility to ensure there was zero loitering, much less drug dealing or potential violent behavior. The idea was always to anticipate possible negative incidents that might vitiate the quality of a school's evening program or any school-scheduled parent-student event, such as a technology education evening described earlier, featuring one of our business partners, a computer refurbishing company, and I presenting computer and electronic equipment to select families. The idea of having the police patrol parking lots, moving loiterers on from the school grounds, and stopping in to greet school staff and community was always welcomed and seen as a healthy, positive measure that provided a sense of security to staff, students, and families.

It wasn't too long before I introduced a Dress for Success program once a week that saw our boys wearing shirts and ties, sometimes a suit, while our girls wore dresses, skirts, and blouses. The reader will recall that I advised parents that if an economic issue prevented their youngsters from participating, I would be happy to provide the apparel; the PTA was fond of the idea and offered to provide assistance, as well. Each year we would see additional students get involved in the program. The practice dovetailed nicely with our schoolwide goals revolving around academic performance and student behavior excellence. Individual students would say that Wednesday's Dress for Success made them feel important, respectful, and confident. That kind of attitude allowed students to start off the day in a positive manner, seeing themselves as more mature and taking their studies that much more seriously. Schoolwide behavior improved, and students were far more focused academically, while being less concerned with what they or other classmates were wearing, when such might be a concern other days of the week and regularly in those schools without such a program. We displayed posters throughout the school advertising the program, and students could—and often did—elect to have their picture taken with the principal, sometimes in a group photo, which was then placed in our school yearbook and daily morning schoolwide television announcements. Weekly we would draw the names of those participating Dress for Success students and present them with a school monogrammed lanyard, T-shirt, or similar gift to recognize their participation and spirit.

My military and fire department background likely subconsciously keeps me aware that crisis situations can occur with nary a moment's notice. I put together at the time a safety/security group, representing various staff and community. We would meet at an appropriate time in an administrative conference room to conduct tabletop "what if..." emergency scenarios, which allowed us to review current procedures and practices in place. This was above and beyond the monthly fire drills that schools conduct (or should conduct), and later, the so-called lockdown drills that would also be practiced. The gathering included the assistant principal, my secretary, a school psychologist, a guidance counselor, our chief custodian, a parent, a teacher, at times the school system security coordinator, and a grade-level or subject area team leader, who, in turn, would share any info with appropriate staff. I usually tried to include an area police officer, and when we would later win approval, our own school resource officer.

We went about it in a low-key fashion, not wanting to make staff nervous or stressed out. I advised folks that we wanted to feel prepared—to the extent possible, given an emergency situation—for whatever emergency occurred. Whether the issue involved fire, an active shooter, an angry parent over a child custodial concern, or an emergency weather occurrence, the idea was to review our practices and establish new procedures, as appropriate, so that we limited student and staff exposure to danger or injury during crisis situations. I invited a school district headquarters staff person, whose purview included emergency management. Following one morning's exercise, he expressed his appreciation for the invitation, saying he was "bowled over at the seriousness, preparation and organization" that he had observed that morning, adding that he wished other schools would be as conscientious as the staff at Harper's Choice.

I spoke to our students and addressed our PTA and all parents attending our fall Back-to-School Night about the importance of the above planning, stating that it was part of our culture, the principle of *cura personalis*, of caring about one another and realizing that emergency events occur, and that we wanted to be able to respond accordingly and in a way that substantively benefited our youngsters, staff, and community. The presentation was seen as positive by the majority of parents and community. As the school system produced its school emergency procedures handbook, we made it a part of our school safety protocols.

Now, years later, such exercises are more comprehensive and streamlined (or they should be) since schools over the years have witnessed so many nationally publicized emergency events, but what we had in place at the time was purposeful and meaningful. Looking back at the approach we took, I'm proud that we always strove to be on top of our game. Police and emergency preparedness folks expressed their opinion that we were ahead of the curve, having taken time to think about and take substantive training action on the issue of safety and security sooner and more meaningfully than they had observed or were aware of with schools in the area, if not in the nation. The staff and I were appreciative of their comments, particularly given the responsibility each of us felt as guardians of the community's children.

It would turn out that our training and experience provided sound decision-making regarding actions taken during various emergency events, including the occasional school lockdown for police-reported criminal behavior in the neighborhood; the dreadful September 11, 2001, terrorist attacks, when scores of parents arrived unannounced to retrieve their children; again during the October 2002 Washington

Beltway Area Sniper Attacks, when a series of coordinated shootings occurred in the Maryland-Virginia-DC area. Parents and available staff, outfitted with school-identifying vests and two-way radios, volunteered during that time to walk the school grounds throughout the school day, observing parking lots and looking for anything or anyone causing suspicion. I recall that one of my parents was nearly arrested when an officer approached him and would only let him go when the officer heard my voice on the parent's two-way radio.

I made mention earlier of a School Resource Officer position, known in and around schools as an SRO. In an earlier chapter, I referenced a talented, terrific beat officer, whom we had the pleasure of working with for years. An SRO position is an in-house assignment. I expressed an interest early on in acquiring such a position for our school, and it took some time before we were able to make it happen. These are career law enforcement officers, in our case, a county police officer, assigned to work in collaboration with the school principal and staff. We were the first middle school in the county at the time to have such an officer assigned, albeit part-time, which meant three days a week. I was grateful and welcomed the staff position. While the officers are responsible for safety and crime prevention, our officer, a black female, and I had a terrific working relationship, and she was more than willing to accept, among other roles, mentoring a number of students and making various presentations to classes and groups of youngsters. She would also look in on students serving a Friday Twilight School assignment. I valued this position, and I do not doubt that over the years I was that community's principal, a number of staff, including the SRO, reduced the likelihood of a host of students acquiring a criminal record; the school resource officer's presence in the lives of our students was impressive. Having an on-site SRO on board—and actively engaged with our students and staff—enhanced the feelings of safety and security among students, parents, and staff, which in turn enhanced the quality of instruction and learning. I will cite later in this chapter additional examples of why it's important to have such a position assigned to schools today.

By way of a Department of Justice grant, we made application more than once and eventually won approval, receiving funding for a security camera system that allowed for surveillance of the school's interior and exterior, as well as a closed-circuit television (CCTV) that allowed main office staff to view the entire building and the exterior areas. We would later see a buzzer notification system installed that allowed secretaries to give entry to those visitors identified via CCTV.

However, on our way to making use of surveillance cameras, there occurred a weekend vandalism incident, which felt like a punch to the solar plexus, that I observed on arrival one Monday morning. We had just received the funding for cameras and had hired a company to commence installation. They started with the front exterior and would continue after the weekend. However, they failed to anchor the exterior cameras and outfit each with protective screening that might have otherwise prevented their destruction. On my arrival at 6:30 a.m. the following Monday, I observed that all the cherry trees that lined our walkway up to the school had been destroyed; each had been hacked in half with a machete or similar tool. My heart sank. I noticed that the lenses of two cameras out front had been painted, and the cameras themselves had been torn from their positions. I called the police so a report could be completed. I stewed and thought about the now unsightly front entrance. Had it been perpetrated by our students, maybe the older students who could no longer sell their dope or harass our students, or perhaps others just traipsing through the school grounds looking to vandalize? I shook my head and later made mention of it on the PA morning announcements to our staff and student body, asking that anyone with information or hearing anything around the community touch base with me. I was taken aback by the number of students who expressed their disappointment and sorrow at the destruction that occurred. I called the company to express my dissatisfaction that the cameras had been left so vulnerable and their failure to recognize the importance of installing them in a more secure fashion, including with protective screens. I ended the contract with the company and proceeded to secure another company that would later install a far more comprehensive and effective, near vandal-proof camera operation.

I reviewed the grounds and building perimeter with custodial staff and the security coordinator to determine how vandals had accessed our building's roof. We made the necessary modifications that would prevent future unauthorized access.

The interior cameras were a welcome, and they provided a comfortable layer of security for our students and staff. I asked that hallway cameras be mounted in a way that took in bathroom entrances. Having spent a lengthy career in public school education, I can say that when vandalism occurs—let's say in a bathroom—the administration typically paid little, if any, attention to the matter. Writing for Arizona State University's Center for Problem-Oriented Policing, Kelly Dedel cited research finding that school administrators may hesitate to report all cases of vandalism, break-ins, or arson because they viewed some as trivial, or because they feared it would reflect poorly on their management skills. Such is too often accurate; the reader will recall the fraudulent actions by school staff for similar reasons, regarding academic issues cited in an earlier chapter.

Partially because of the failure to report incidents of vandalism, few perpetrators are apprehended, and even fewer are prosecuted.[8] This was a familiar refrain throughout my tenure in education. Such was the case in one high school where one principal, who lived within close proximity of the school and was out for a walk, entered the school and noted a considerable amount of vandalism. A classroom American flag lay burnt on the floor, opened cans of paint were thrown about classrooms, and one particular teacher's social studies classroom was demolished. Her desk was turned over, and classroom textbooks, student desks, papers, and instructional equipment destroyed. Instead of notifying the police, he called the school custodian and directed him to report to the school building and clean the entire area so no one would notice come Monday morning. Speaking to the custodian that morning, I was incredulous. He expressed no surprise, stating that it had not been the first time such had occurred and handled in the same fashion. I spoke to the principal that morning, confirming the events over the weekend, and he was comfortable with his actions; I wasn't. Shaking my head, I stated that such a coverup destroyed evidence crucial to any investigation, making it next to impossible to identify any suspect(s), that for all we knew at the time, another school might also have been vandalized, and a proper investigation of the schools targeted—together—might well enhance police efforts to weigh the evidence from each school site and potentially make an identification.

I suspect more to get me off his back than recognizing the utter wrongfulness of his misdeed, he said, "Well, go ahead, you call them; I'm not." Both the custodian and the principal spoke to the investigating officer, who promptly notified his duty officer, a lieutenant, of the principal's actions. To make matters worse, as the lieutenant entered the building, the lead administrator, in a dismissive-sounding, abrupt fashion, told the officer, "I don't need any kids being arrested in the school." At that very moment, I thought to myself, "Not smart." The lieutenant directed him to enter my office, where both had been standing, telling the principal, "I should be arresting you, based on my officer's investigation thus far; how dare you! You're not in a position to dictate to me how to do my job," at which point the principal returned to his office, while the officer and I spoke. Coincidentally, the lieutenant and I had a respectful professional relationship for years in other school communities, and when it turned out to be him who would follow up on the initial officer's report, I well suspected that the principal would likely have his rump handed to him. (A postscript: A nearby school, indeed, was also vandalized that weekend, and the investigation later saw two of our own high school students arrested and charged accordingly for the damage to both schools.)

The destruction in many schools—toilets purposely stopped up, urinals and/or stalls pulled from the wall, graffiti scrawled about—was often enough to warrant closing off use of a particular bathroom until it was repaired. There was little, if any, investigation, and no real interest in finding the culprit(s); generally, the only action was notifying school system maintenance to repair, end of story. Only it is frequently not the end of the story, with such vandalism repeating itself time and again in many of these buildings. Research indicates that the willful defacement or destruction of public and private property, including schools, homes, businesses, and others costs some fifteen billion dollars annually.[9] It is estimated that yearly school vandalism costs, alone, are in the hundreds of millions.[10] Imagine the glorious effect of those dollars being otherwise put toward classroom instruction, student achievement, and school activities.

We were having none of that at Harper's Choice. When vandalism occurred in these restrooms, the custodian, now accustomed to checking bathrooms on the hour throughout the school day, would present his/her clipboard to an administrator, which we used to zero in on the time the defacement or destruction occurred. We would review the camera footage and identify the individual(s) using the bathroom at the time of the vandalism. Students would be disciplined accordingly, their parents would be notified to meet with an administrator, and the family would be financially responsible for the materials and labor to repair the area. In those instances that a police report was made, an officer would meet with all parties at the school, clarifying appropriate charges and making any arrests, if warranted. Routine damage to restrooms all but disappeared to the point where it was no longer among our concerns.

Above and beyond concerns for the school building and grounds, it is also important to be cognizant of student and adult erratic behavior or emotional unease, agitation, or distress. Students were regularly reminded that the school was our school, belonging to each of us—students, parents, staff, and community. Being mindful of "broken windows" and our principle of *cura personalis*, it was emphasized that if they saw someone behaving unpredictably, if they caught any scuttlebutt of inappropriate, dangerous, or illegal actions on the part of others, that would be the time to demonstrate their character and privately inform an adult immediately—parent, teacher, staff, or school administrator. Likewise, faculty and staff were advised to contact straightaway the administrative team, school counselor, school psychologist, or school nurse when they personally believed any student or adult was exhibiting stress or behavior they perceived out of the ordinary. Once advised, I informed them, we would activate specific protocols that would immediately allow school/school system staff to assess the perceived mental health problem or uncivilized social behavior; depending on the issue, it sometimes included making contact with the area local police officer and/or our future school resource officer. Where there have been throughout the country major school disruptions or school shootings, it is often noted that warning signs more frequently than not were there, if only earlier action had been taken.

This was confirmed, as well, in my impromptu discussion with Columbine High School staff and students during the week of a Colorado vacation, when my wife and I found that we were close enough to the town of Littleton.[11] The students and teachers shared with me that all the signs were there: repeated troublesome behaviors, how certain kids dressed, frequent disparaging and/or threatening comments made by the offenders and their ilk both online and to other students and staff. It was their opinion that "everyone knew about these guys," and a couple staff members said they did not perceive that any noticeable action had been taken to hold these kids, and kids like them, accountable. Indeed, newspaper accounts cite any number of harrowing incidents on the part of the two murderers that officials simply refused to follow up on with any degree of due diligence. "The families of victims have gone to court—they've filed nine separate lawsuits against the sheriff's department, the school district, and the parents of the two murderous students," cites correspondent David Kohn. His investigative piece goes on to cite the following:

> A year before the attack, Joe Schallmoser and Howard Cornell were worried that Columbine was just the kind of place where a school shooting might happen. They were in charge of security for the school district that included Columbine. After the shootings in Paducah, Ky., and Jonesboro, Ark., they were afraid that one of their schools might be next.
>
> In August of '98—a full eight months before the attack on Columbine—Cornell and Schallmoser wrote a security plan that required school officials to notify and meet with parents and law enforcement officers as soon as they learned of "a threat by any student" to "commit any act of violence." They say Columbine didn't follow the plan.
>
> When Cornell and Schallmoser presented their plan to Columbine, the school had already been alerted that one of its juniors, Eric Harris, might be dangerous. At night, Harris and his friend Dylan Klebold had been building

an arsenal and making plans to use it—plans that Harris wrote about on the Internet, on his Web site.

In 1998, Brooks Brown was a junior at Columbine. That March, he found his name on Harris' Web site. Harris was threatening to kill him. "When I first saw the Web pages, I was utterly blown away," Brown says. "He's not saying that he's gonna beat me up, he's saying he wants to blow me up and he's talking about how he's making the pipe bombs to do it with."

Brooks' parents, Randy and Judy Brown, say they were horrified by the Web site and frightened of Harris, who lived nearby. They decided to take pages from the site to the Jefferson County Sheriff's Office, where an investigator told them that Harris already had a criminal file. He and Dylan Klebold were on a form of probation, for breaking into a van and stealing equipment. "I was utterly dumbfounded that they did nothing with the Web pages," says Brooks Brown. "Eric was saying how he was gonna blow people up. 'Hey, I'm making pipe bombs. I've got the designs for them on my Web site. I'm gonna kill these people. Here's why.' That's a level beyond making a joke."

At first, the sheriff's department denied its investigators had even met with the Browns in person. But we obtained this police paperwork, showing those investigators not only "met with Mrs. Judy Brown," but then worked on a warrant to search Eric Harris' home. Even more surprising, one document shows a sheriff's deputy found "a pipe bomb...consistent with the devices" Harris described on his site. But the sheriff's department never searched—or even visited—the Harris home. It was April of '98—a full year before the Columbine massacre.

"People are covering up everything that went wrong and I want those lessons out there," says Judy Brown. "They're doing studies, they're getting profiles. Everybody's trying to get programs going and what we can do. Well, guess what? All the signs were there. You know what the lessons are? Do your job."

...In February of '99, Dylan Klebold turned in a story he wrote about an assassin in a black trench coat who shoots down students and bombs the city. "The man unloadeone (sic) of the pistols across the fronts of [the] four innocents," Klebold wrote. "The...streetlights caused a visible reflection off of the droplets of blood.... I understood his actions."

Klebold's teacher later called it "the most vicious story she'd ever read," and voiced her concerns about it to Klebold's parents and his school counselor. But no school official ever looked into the matter, and it ended there. It was two months before the shootings.[12]

I am aware of other tragic occurrences at schools where school officials maintained that they had no indication, only for such statements to be proven false. I do know that a healthy teaching-learning school climate can go a long way in heading off mischief, much less tragic, catastrophic occurrences, as students will often tip off an adult about their suspicions or direct knowledge of an impending act they know is foolish, wrongheaded, or potentially dangerous. As recklessly dismissive as it sounds, it is not uncommon for school administrators to avoid taking time to investigate, much less taking aggressive action that might otherwise ensure the safety of everyone. I have known—and we have read accounts of—those who eschew any notion of having to deal with confrontation, much less a potentially disrespectful, disruptive, or violent student, parent, or colleague. I get it, but such craven scruples allow behavior that might well place in peril the lives of other innocent staff, students, and community members. Every individual needs to recognize the importance, the vitally sound practice of taking immediate action and notifying appropriate staff of anything inappropriate, much less something that might prove harmful to another. If students, staff, or parents find that their reporting such a concern to a school's administration falls on deaf ears, they should well follow up and go to the next higher level, including outside the confines of a school by contacting the police or the media, if necessary. Why any school official would not act posthaste on such expressed concerns is as incomprehensible to me as it is reprehensible.

You see, when policies governing school behavior are weak or inconsistently enforced, the mission of schooling becomes amorphous, and sensible expectations are eroded. The culture in these schools is ruled initially by a kind of silent chaos and, as cited earlier, a laundry list of behavior problems emerges—the "dissing" of peers and adults, pushing, fighting, alcohol and drug activity, tardiness to class, inappropriate sexual displays, truancy, indifference to class participation, disregard for proper dress, pervasive use of vulgar language—often with no corrective behavior or consequences. It is as though such schools are waiting until youngsters are at the edge of the cliff before they act. The wake-up call for too many officials is a tragedy that might well have been averted.

Our character education infusion within the schoolwide schedule routinely introduced characteristics surrounding expected appropriate student and adult behaviors, including respect, compassion, grit, determination, perseverance, patience, diligence, courage, honesty, gratitude, and optimism, to name a few.

My view is that it remains at all times important to tend to any "broken windows," allowing others in need to get the attention, concern, care, and support that otherwise may well be lost.

I referenced earlier the importance of having on staff a school resource police officer, at least in specific schools with busy demographics or identified behavior challenges. As a school administrator and principal at both the high school and middle school levels, there were any number of times when my administrative colleagues and I had to deal with a myriad of behaviors that jeopardized the safety and security of a school community. Among those would include vulgar, disrespectful student behavior to teaching staff, classmates, or other adults; violent, threatening behaviors to student peers and staff; and violent physical assaults on other students or staff. A number of occasions dealt with the issue of weapons on school property, including taking guns or knives from students. One morning at one of the high schools, a student alerted me that he observed what appeared to him to be a gun in another student's locker. I located the alleged offending student, an otherwise nice, polite kid whom I would not ordinarily associate with such a violation. He was standing within close proximity of his hall locker, and I asked him if there was anything in it that would disappoint me. I could see the fright, anger, and sadness in his face as he replied, "Yes, Mr. Wallis, I'm sorry," and started crying, saying he was tired of another bigger boy threatening him, and recently, his girlfriend. I waited until the hallways were clear, then asked another administrator to remain with and later escort the youngster to the main office as I removed a 12-gauge shotgun from the student's locker.

On another occasion at a different school, a colleague and I wound up wrestling a student in a school corridor for several minutes in the effort to secure a .38-caliber handgun strapped to his ankle.

One morning a teacher in yet a different school walked into my office and placed a .45-caliber pistol atop my desk that he had just taken from a youngster.

In another high school, a world language teacher expressed her dismay to me regarding her inability to obtain support from one of my colleagues, her administrator (at times administrators are assigned to various subject/departments), as well as the principal. Three girls were harassing her because she had given one of them a failing grade. She stated that she had also received no assistance from the student's mother. The repeated harassment came in the form of the girls following her in the school hallway, walking past her classroom between and during class time (which meant that each had planned ahead of time how to get out of class at a certain time) shouting threats like, "We're gonna f*** you up, Ms. _____." On two occasions, the teacher had been hit by a water bottle that she believed had been thrown by one of them in a crowded school corridor. Having spoken to both administrators about the matter, I determined that their unenthusiastic handling of the teacher's concern and their general incompetence necessitated going a different route. Bottom line was that I facilitated the teacher's being able to obtain a Peace Order from a District Court Commissioner, dictating that the girls remain a specific distance from the teacher at all times, and that any future threatening behavior would see them in court. Given the complexities of fulfilling such an order in that school building, it resulted in the three students being administratively transferred to another school. You can imagine how grateful she was for the assist, which allowed her to go about the job of teaching without enduring the stress that came with the students' previous harassment and threatening behaviors.

Still on another morning, at a different school, an administrator and I were conversing in a high school hallway when I observed a student who, minutes earlier, was identified by another youngster as having sold drugs to some students in a parking lot. I knew the alleged dealer well, called his name, and asked why he was wearing such a long heavy coat on a warm day, as well as why he was out of class without a pass; it turned out he hadn't attended classes yet. He was six feet in height and weighed north of 220 pounds, and he was known for running from authorities. (Quick aside: I had always been interested in case law regarding public schooling and was generally on top of various lower court and Supreme Court rulings. Keeping in line with the Fourth Amendment to the U.S Constitution, law enforcement follows a "probable cause" standard regarding searches of individuals. Not so with school administrators, who operate on the lower standard of "reasonable suspicion." It is argued—correctly, I believe—that schools, after all, daily must strike the balance between a student's right to privacy and the need to maintain school safety for all students and staff.)

His refusal to accompany us to an administrative office area prompted our commencing a search right there of his belongings, when he chose to kick violently at us and run, spilling several dozen packets of so-called dime bags of dope on the floor that had been wrapped around his legs. One of us hurriedly picked up the contraband, while the other kept observation on the direction the student was headed out of the building so police could follow up.

Years earlier in another area high school, I interrupted some serious drug dealing in a school auditorium, which resulted in my suspending the students, all of whom were well known by staff as causing an inordinate number of problems each school year. They would later stab to death—for thirteen dollars—an elderly gentleman delivering papers to a neighborhood store.

It is quite dismaying that such serious, at times, uncivilized occurrences can occupy a school administrator's time on any given day.

On another occasion in yet a different school, I suspended a number of athletes for use of cocaine, when an officer greeted me the following morning, closing my office door. He advised me that a police informant had been present the previous evening among suspended students, all of whom were smoking dope and allegedly paid or offered to pay a thug to shoot me. It was a sobering few minutes to be informed of such a thing. For the next couple of weeks, a police officer was assigned to keep a close eye on me, my home, and my travels. I was advised by the police to consider carrying a weapon, and the police department command staff wrote letters in support of my application to obtain a concealed carry permit for a weapon I planned to carry on my possession away from my day job; picture me shaking my head, sobering alright!

In a separate incident, I suspended a student who had threatened, then physically assaulted, his science teacher, only to return to the campus the following morning hell-bent on stabbing me (and presumably anyone getting in his way), according to his mother, who called the school to warn me that he had just stabbed his father that same morning, stating that the police were at the home at the time she was calling. Like any high school about to start the school day, this high school's hallways were busy, congested with students and staff going to their lockers, classrooms, restrooms, or faculty lounges. The police arrived about the time I hung up the phone. I met the officer, who was six foot four, tough and seasoned, a terrific professional and gentleman. We proceeded to walk the school corridors, when he asked that I take off my jacket and prepare to wrap it around my hand/arm as protection, which was a bit disconcerting to hear. I alerted a guidance counselor who was standing in the hallway conversing with students; he stated that he had seen the offending student moments earlier. A few minutes later, I observed the student in the hallway and calmly cleared the corridor area of students and any staff. I addressed him in an even, reasonable tone, when he placed a hand in his pocket, at which point the officer swiftly had him on the floor, taking the weapon from him.

Each time I encountered such tense situations over a period of three decades in education, I found it to be solemn, dour, and sad. This student—and thousands like him throughout the country—needed far more help than the typical public school could or can provide. Such individuals cannot be allowed to continue attending a typical community school and behave so erratically, so disrespectfully, so violently, yet many such students remain in schools across the nation.

I will reiterate that schools are a microcosm of our larger society, and they, too, have defined deviancy down. Much like many of today's communities, schools accept ill behavior that would have been considered inappropriate in a previous, more ordered and civilized society. Teachers regularly observe the inept handling of students' disrespectful, disruptive behavior by school administrators attempting to placate different constituencies. Meanwhile, scores of conscientious students are cheated out of learning. The net result are schools in which many teachers report having to perform in "combat conditions." While that may sound bizarre, read on.

Just as research finds that school administrators may hesitate to report all cases of vandalism, break-ins, or arson because they view some as trivial, or they fear it will reflect poorly on their management skills, the same can be said—and, indeed, has been observed and cited by others—for disciplinary data.[13] Many a feckless school official—from school-based administrators to superintendents—are inclined to make deceitful, foolhardy decisions in order to produce the "data" they know will please school district supervisors, local or state policymakers, or that the school district's superintendent's office knows will please the community it serves. They don't get—or worse, don't care to get—that students for whom the abdication of personal responsibility brings no disgrace, and distressingly, no disciplinary consequences from school staff, will likely continue to go on and potentially commit more serious offenses, which, at the very least, will steal teaching, learning, and dignity from teaching staff and other students; at worst, they will continue to exhibit behavior that could result in catastrophic injury or death.

Within the book, I make mention of alternative education or alternative schools, sometimes referred to as centers of alternative studies. I explained earlier the positive difference in our school's overall teaching-learning climate that occurred when I was able to procure an alternative education teacher and assistant to work with some of our students who needed more attention to skills deficits but who did not necessarily need to be removed to another school site.

More important is the need for separate alternative education centers. Whatever school districts prefer to call them—centers for alternative studies, alternative schools, alternative evening education—these alternative schools are essentially initiatives within public school districts that serve at-risk youngsters whose needs are not being met adequately in the traditional school setting. We would never have achieved our level of success at Harper's Choice had I not insisted and ensured over the years that a host of troubled, violent students be removed from Harper's Choice and placed in such alternative school settings.

You can well bet that many of the students responsible for tragic school events causing mayhem, injury, and death and garnering national attention had a record of behaviors that should well have seen them placed early on in alternative school settings, providing them with emotional and behavioral services.

School districts, in fact, have such alternative programs to service these youngsters, students for whom the traditional school setting is not working. Particularly unseemly, however, is the fact that school officials are reluctant, if not unwilling to place what they believe will be too many students in them, especially when their focus is often on race. They will offer what they believe (or say that they believe) are high-minded reasons for their actions; they lie, they posture, they put on airs. School officials need to be less concerned with their image and looking self-righteous and become more concerned about their teaching staff and their students—every student's education, every student's life.

School districts should have in place first-rate, well-designed, and well-run alternative education centers that offer school day as well as evening school programs. Such schools are not necessarily meant to "fix" students so much as to shape instruction in such a way as to meet the needs of these kids through individualized instruction, personal attention, and a modified curriculum that simply cannot be expected to be done in a standard public school. The process for such placements should be a well-organized, professional review of these students' school academic and behavioral records, which, if appropriate, would see these youngsters placed in such an alternative setting. While attending such schools, these students also receive the services of the various specialists on staff who can address the emotional and behavioral components that trigger disrespectful or disruptive behaviors. Students will sometimes receive their diploma, having remained in the alternative school. Often, however, student progress is substantial and may allow them to transition, re-enrolling at their assigned school to continue their education and matriculate through their lower grade level school or graduate from their home high school.

As a high school administrator, I would look beyond local resources for lost kids, students who were flailing in school, especially when they and their frustrated parents were not able to access the district's alternative programs. On several occasions I was successful in getting these students enrolled in either of two separate and life-affirming programs for troubled kids. The Department of Labor administers a program called Job Corps, a no-cost residential education and vocational training program where the students can work toward their high school equivalency diploma (GED) and obtain counseling or related assistance.[14]

A second viable option for kids was the U.S. Army–funded Freestate ChalleNGe Academy that provides students a second chance at an education.[15] A twenty-two-week course, it is another residential program, a structured, disciplined, quasi-military environment. The students, now called "cadets," follow a strict schedule and are monitored 24/7. During the residential phase, teens receive an education toward their GED, and they are administered the Armed Services Vocational Aptitude Battery (ASVAB). They learn life skills such as money management, leadership, résumé writing, and interviewing skills. The program also includes a post-residential phase, where the cadets work closely with mentors in their community. They are placed in jobs, continue their education, or enter the military. The students and their parents were extremely grateful that these opportunities were presented to them, often inviting me to their graduation from these programs.

The point is that there are no "throwaway" kids, and given the current problems faced by so many schools, families, and youngsters in communities throughout the country, it is important that public schools, no matter how large, be places of instructional excellence and student achievement. School officials should be expected to cultivate—and parents and communities should demand—a school culture conducive to academic study and wholesome extracurricular participation. That will require that school officials find the *cojones*, the intestinal fortitude, to step up and clarify the school's mission and put an immediate stop to any student or staff behaviors that detract from an academic setting. Such may well mean finding another venue for particularly problem students and, where appropriate, problem staff.

There are state statutes and school laws by which public schools can control egregious behavior. The valuable, worthwhile effect of such policies and statutes, of course, is contingent on the degree to which school officials employ them consistently, and too often they do not. The acceptance of or the acquiescence to ill behavior has a negative cumulative effect on the school community that lays the groundwork for still further escalating incivility and violence.

A nurturing yet aggressive advance on this menacing behavior would provide a consistent, safe, and secure environment that students and staff would find conducive to academic and extracurricular achievement. Such would restore a school culture in which the sense of decorum, combined with substantive, achievable standards, would well give meaningful hope for long-term payoffs: less interference of instruction, lower drop-out rates, reduced reliance on costly social programs, and a better educated workforce. America's parents, schoolchildren, and their teachers richly deserve our national attention to this matter. As it is, we are reaping what we have sown, and given what has been standard fare in many schools, it should be no surprise that many of these schools will, at times, erupt violently.

Broward County Schools' February 2018 tragic shooting at Marjory Stoneman Douglas High School in Parkland, Florida, was yet another outrageous example of how political correctness can play out in its worst manifestation, this time at the expense of the remaining student body, teaching staff, and community.

Lindsey Burke, education policy analyst at the Heritage Foundation, cites the following in a commentary on the tragedy in Parkland:

"This incident that occurred, this outrageous tragedy that we have had to deal with, we really had no signs, no warning, no tips," announced Broward County School Superintendent Robert Runcie on CNN on Feb. 15, 2018.

Runcie was speaking of the tragic school shooting at Marjory Stoneman Douglas High School that had left 17 students and staff dead the day before.

"No signs, no warning." Well, that's simply not true.

The confessed shooter in Parkland, Florida, had a long history of violence that school officials were well-aware of—a history that should have alerted them to the potential risk.

Andrew Pollack and Max Eden document this in their new book, *Why Meadow Died: The People and Policies That Created the Parkland Shooter and Endanger America's Students.*

Pollack is the father of Meadow, a girl who lost her life on the third floor of Stoneman Douglas that day.

The warning signs were abundant—from animal torture and attempted suicide, to bringing knives and bullets to school and an overall obsession with guns. Police had been called to the shooter's home 45 times to deal with incidents involving him or his brother.

Pollack and Eden identify the shooter throughout by his prison number, 18-1958. 18-1958 had been in a fight in school, repeatedly issued death threats to other students, and was prohibited from bringing a backpack to school so as not to be able to conceal weapons in it.

Yet as Pollack notes, when the shooter bought his guns, "he had a totally clean record. On paper, he was a model citizen."

How did his record stay so clean?

Pollack and Eden meticulously document that district and school officials did not stop 18-1958 because of the district's policy to limit student suspensions and expulsions. That policy—the PROMISE Program—also deterred educators from referring students to police.

Such leniency, Eden argues, meant that officials neglected opportunities to refer 18-1958 to law enforcement, allowing him to avoid arrest, which ultimately made it possible for him to buy a gun.

While the media at large focused on lack of "gun control" as the major problem, Pollack and Eden explain that PROMISE and the related rules on student discipline— which the Obama administration had then promulgated in school districts across the country—are undeniably at the center of this tragedy.

The PROMISE Program "deters teachers from reporting disciplinary problems and makes administrators less inclined to trust teachers' intuition and more inclined to make decisions that produce the disciplinary 'data' that their district-level superiors want to see," Pollack and Eden write.

At every possible turn, the adults in the system ignored glaring warning signs. Pollack and Eden write that 18-1958's story is "a cautionary tale of what can happen when everyone in a school system has an incentive to do the wrong thing."

Pollack and Eden's book is difficult to read because Pollack's pain, sorrow, and frustration is present on nearly every page. Furthermore, the detailed recounting of the tragedy pulls no punches in identifying the policies that allowed this disaster to happen.

"Every step of the way, [district officials] had a choice: do the responsible thing and help [18-1958], or do the politically correct thing and ignore him. They made the wrong choice every single time," Pollack writes in one section.[16]

The so-called Promise Program is more than a misnomer; such poorly titled policies, whether in Broward County or in any of a host of other school systems throughout the country, are wrongheaded and willfully make inaccurate use of a term. Benighted school and district officials cravenly and wrongly focus on race rather than look at how best to eradicate ill behavior so that all students—including those of color who strive for excellence daily—may do so free of disrespectful, disruptive behavior and instructional interference.

Further, other critics of the discipline guidance echo Senator Marco Rubio's concerns that "disturbing reports have indicated that federal guidance [read the Obama administration 'Dear Colleague' letter and 'guidance' issued to school districts in 2014] may have contributed to systemic failures to report [the former student perpetrator's] dangerous behaviors to local law enforcement.[17] It is as indefensible as it is contemptible that so many adults in key decision-making positions (members of the Broward County board of education, teachers' union, principals' association, school superintendent, chief judge, state attorney, public defender, sheriff, police chief, state secretary of juvenile justice, and NAACP local president) chose to flaunt such disregard for, and to fail, their youngsters and the entire school community.

They should have known better, or worse, they knew but still chose to enter recklessly and irresponsibly into a so-called Collaborative Agreement on School Discipline,[18] gleefully agreeing with the false premise and equally irresponsible federal "guidance" issued to school districts.

Amazingly, the agreement literally cited that "the use of arrests and referrals to the criminal justice system may decrease a student's chance of graduation, entering higher education, joining the military, and getting a job." They believe that the arrest and referral—*not the abhorrent, often illegal, behavior of the individual that led to the arrest*—is what reduces a student's chance of a successful life. How did this despicably ill-considered nonsense of a decision work out for the student murderer, his victims, and their families? Records show that the sheriff lied, insisting his office received no more than twenty-three calls (as though that were not enough), when the investigation proved the police were called forty-five times to the perpetrator's home.[19] Students themselves repeatedly warned school staff and others about the danger they saw in this student's behavior.

Columnist Ann Coulter, author of multiple *New York Times* bestsellers and known for her depth of research, states the following:

> If Cruz [the perpetrator, 18-1958] had taken out full-page ads in the local newspapers, he could not have demonstrated more clearly that he was a dangerous psychotic. He assaulted students, cursed out teachers, kicked in classroom doors, started fistfights, threw chairs, threatened to kill other students, mutilated small animals, pulled a rifle on his mother, drank gasoline and cut himself, among other "red flags."
>
> Over and over again, students at Marjory Stoneman Douglas High School reported Cruz's terrifying behavior

350

to school administrators, including Kelvin Greenleaf, "security specialist," and Peter Mahmood, head of JROTC.

At least three students showed school administrators Cruz's near-constant messages threatening to kill them— e.g., "I am going to enjoy seeing you down on the grass," "Im (sic) going to watch ypu (sic) bleed," "iam (sic) going to shoot you dead"—including one that came with a photo of Cruz's guns. They warned school authorities that he was bringing weapons to school. They filed written reports.

Threatening to kill someone is a felony. In addition to locking Cruz away for a while, having a felony record would have prevented him from purchasing a gun.

All the school had to do was risk Cruz not going to college, and depriving Yale University of a Latino class member, by reporting a few of his felonies—and there would have been no mass shooting.

...Just a few months ago, the superintendent of Broward County Public Schools, Robert W. Runcie, was actually bragging about how student arrests had plummeted under his bold leadership. When he took over in 2011, the district had "the highest number of school-related arrests in the state." But today, he boasted, Broward has "one of the lowest rates of arrest in the state." By the simple expedient of ignoring criminal behavior, student arrests had declined by a whopping 78 percent.[20]

In the view of this professional school educator and administrator, and in the opinion of those who have studied and reported on this horrifying ordeal, the tragic loss of life was in no small measure a result of perilously reckless actions by those cited above, most all of whom are those with the responsibility for ensuring the education and safety of Broward's children and community. To think that this catastrophe was spurred on all the more because of the twisted political view of race and the misguided, nefarious myth of the "school-to-prison pipeline" pedaled by a number of individuals is tragic. Their answer, though they are loath to admit: End a sensible and effective school discipline program, and *Voila!* Problem solved!

The expression "school-to-prison pipeline" is, in fact, a myth, a lie, and its related so-called restorative justice policy together fail to address individual will and personal agency, youngsters who choose to be kind, respectful, caring, and responsible, as opposed to those kids who elect to be unkind, disrespectful, irresponsible, disruptive, and too often violent. Proponents of this nonsensical tripe state that the only reason so many "black and brown bodies" are in prison is because they were disciplined in school, diminishing their opportunities. "The next time you are inclined to seek scapegoats, stupid slogans, and simplistic 'solutions' for complex educational issues, please keep this fact in mind: Schools and teachers, both individually and collectively, are not the problem," says author Anna Deavere Smith. In her article entitled "The Myth of the School-to-Prison Pipeline," posted by educator and author Robert Ward on his blog, she states the following:[21]

> Schools and individual teachers can frequently do a better job at all of this, but they are too often distracted by, reacting to, and trying their best to remedy factors not of their making and not wholly within their control.
>
> ...The sad fact is that too many schools are not fully equipped or funded to properly educate the youth they serve. Now they are called upon to be professional mental health clinics and medical centers, too? Where are the personnel, facilities, and funding for that???

Instead of suspending students, schools are now supposed to support them through the trauma that causes them to act out in the first place. And doesn't this sound like the compassionate and correct thing to do? But during what part of the instructional day? And carried out by whom? By school guidance counselors, who are nowhere near trained or licensed to conduct ongoing therapy to a caseload of hundreds of students for whom they already valiantly struggle to provide basic academic assistance and routine coping skills? By classroom teachers, who are even less prepared as child psychologists and who have literally no dedicated time to meet with students privately and one-on-one to conduct regular therapy sessions?

Educators already sincerely honor and dauntlessly attend to the needs of the whole child, which certainly includes active attention to each child's social-emotional development. But to place entire blame on public institutions that were created only to educate students, and then to foist complete responsibility on teachers and schools for the psychological well-being of children who grow up in homes and communities that do some kids more harm than good, is wrongheaded, mean-spirited, and patently unfair.

When was the last time you heard people talk about the guns-and-gangs-to-prison pipeline; the drinking-and-drugs-to-prison pipeline, or the abuse-and-abandonment-to-prison pipeline? "Data shows that more than half of all U.S. children have experienced some kind of trauma in the form of abuse, neglect, violence, or challenging household circumstances—and 35 percent of children have experienced more than one type of traumatic event, according to the Centers for Disease Control and Prevention."[22] And yet the public and politicians want to point the finger only at schools??? Clearly, schools are not the main cause of the unconscionable number of people behind bars. Yet somehow, schools and teachers bear the blame and shoulder the stigma—and are saddled with becoming the sole solution.

Those who support the school-to-prison pipeline nonsense will, as cited earlier, often talk of so-called restorative justice, which they purport is a kinder, gentler way to mete out discipline. Proponents of restorative justice misunderstand appropriate disciplinary action and portray traditional discipline as barbaric and only looking to seek retribution against the offender.

In my experience, that is simply not true—and it never has been, when applied appropriately. The school's disciplinary procedures should be comprehensive and seek to apply a sanction commensurate with the offense and always seek ways for the victim and offender to make amends, including mediation. Such will enhance the school's teaching-learning culture and further cultivate a climate of respect for the rights of each individual, which will help promote a healthier community and a better, stronger, and more civilized society.

Beyond the issue of school discipline, schools should ensure that presentations—including classroom instructional lessons; explanations; actions; and processes, in general—always be rooted in truth and historical fact, including appreciating just how exceptional a country America is. It is unfortunate that there are school officials often influenced by those who have their own agenda, so they will focus on race and look for ways to adjust school statistics. School districts that employ "restorative justice" discipline procedures should be monitored to ensure that the community's schools are, in fact, safe, secure, warm, and inviting places for students, teachers, and parents. If the school community's evaluation finds them rendering a favorable opinion on how discipline, in general, is handled, no matter the nomenclature, then run with it, but parents should be vigilant and monitor their school's overall delivery program to ensure that *all* students are treated fairly and are provided an authentic, historically accurate, and meaningful wholesome education experience.

I understand and "get" why the Parkland tragedy authors would determine that the imbecilic Broward County Program and the equally mindless Obama administration 2014 "Dear Colleague" discipline guidance letter to schools were "at the center of this tragedy." While the authors are correct, the fact is that far too many schools have tolerated for years—decades, really—nauseatingly poor behavior, often disruptive and violent, on the part of far too many students. The 2014 "Dear Colleague" letter to schools—directing them to reduce racial disparities in how they discipline students—lent credibility, I am certain, to the manner in which school districts were already conducting themselves regarding all of their students; the administration's letter served, in effect, to throw gasoline on an already out-of-control "burn" in these schools.

Thankfully, following a federal commission's December 2018 report determining that the Obama administration guidelines "made schools less safe," the Trump administration education and justice departments rescinded[23] the previous administration's "guidance," stating,

> "Every student has the right to attend school free from discrimination. They also have the right to be respected as individuals and not treated as statistics." Education Secretary Betsy DeVos went on to say, "In too many instances, though, I've heard from teachers and advocates that the previous administration's discipline guidance often led

to school environments where discipline decisions were based on a student's race and where statistics became more important than the safety of students and teachers. Our decision to rescind that guidance today makes it clear that discipline is a matter on which classroom teachers and local school leaders deserve and need autonomy."[24]

Amen! If only a larger percentage of school officials exercised meaningful leadership and common sense, making decisions on these matters that reflect a care for all students and faculty under their purview, instead of attempting to look politically correct.

Let's analyze for a moment the rationale behind so many schools' seemingly deliberate myopic focus on race over how best to obtain excellent academic and behavioral performance from all our school youngsters.

Yes, national statistics demonstrate that a high number of those anti-school, anti-success behaviors are committed disproportionately by black students, but that doesn't mean black students are, by their very color, disruptive students; far from it. Every school will have its share of academically productive students representing every ethnicity, just as poorly behaved students come in all sizes, shapes, and colors. The idea is to stand up and recognize this fact, go toe-to-toe with it, and do what we can to eradicate ill behavior from the American school so that every student can reap the fruits of excellent instruction. We will always encounter the need to address human behaviors, good and bad, but the daily abysmally poor behavior that rocks so many schools need not be standard fare. It can be changed, and we proved it at Harper's Choice. More on this aspect in the chapter dealing with the national achievement gap.

Suffice it to say that it is irresponsible and reckless on the part of school officials who advocate and/or support efforts to keep such emotionally unbalanced students in our schools, when they present a clear and present potential danger to entire school communities. When students present emotionally unstable, disruptive, and violent behavior, school staff—in conjunction with resource school system professionals—immediately must work together with community, medical, first responders, and family crisis social agencies to get these students the help they need. It may mean that the student on suspension must also be directed to an alternative education setting, while undergoing treatment or therapy, but I reiterate that such students must not be allowed to remain in the comprehensive public school; it isn't fair to the remaining majority of students and staff, and it is entirely unfair to those troubled, unstable students, who need serious, substantive professional care that cannot be provided by public schools.

Given the rampant, serious nature of this issue across the country, and the fact that too many schools insist on keeping such troubled youngsters in school, I cannot drive this point home enough: Disrespectful, disruptive, violent behavior is nothing less than that, and consistent meaningful teaching and learning cannot occur in an environment that allows it; it must be eradicated if schools are to serve the needs of all their students and their families, as well as teaching staff.

Still, there are those who refuse to accept the idea of suspending students from school, a number of whom are school and school district administrators; they would not work for me. They will declare suspensions are associated with academic failure, school dropout rates, and involvement in the juvenile justice system; for a number of young adults in society, that may well ring true. That is why it is important to have programs in place to address student emotional and education needs, when a student's actions have jeopardized the safety, teaching, and learning environment for others. Those adults who feel otherwise must understand—but often do not—that their naivete or ax-to-grind agenda places school staff, innocent students, as well as the ill-behaving student in potentially great peril.

Many misguided school officials refuse to recognize and accept the absolute priority of ensuring the safety of the school's student body and its staff. Nearly every one of the mass shootings over the years at our schools around the country bear this out. Instead, critics of sensible disciplinary policies will stand in front of a camera or behind a microphone and pompously inject race, so-called social justice, or identity politics into the equation, which invariably proves destructive to teaching and learning, wholly dismissive of the emotional needs of the student perpetrator, while recklessly endangering the remaining student body, teaching staff, and community. Further, they alienate the community and defer any meaningful discussion that might otherwise lead to a comprehensive resolve. Such individuals have no business working in American schools. There are instances when you must exercise prudence and exclude that student from school if you are to provide a substantive measure of safety and calm to your school constituency. When you avoid taking such action—and a number of school systems do so routinely—you risk the welfare of your entire school community, which is foolhardy and a dereliction of duty that should result in the school official's removal.

Whenever I found that a student needed to be suspended from school, whether at the high school level or at Harper's Choice, I ensured that a host of individuals and professionals were notified: the parent/guardian, of course; his/her teachers; guidance staff; school psychologist; and pupil personnel worker (as the reader may recall, our link between the school and home, a school system staff worker familiar with outside agencies and community service providers that might assist homes). Sometimes the behavior, if criminal, also involved contacting the police. A long-term suspension would generally see me work with school and school system staff to ensure that the youngster was placed, once again, in a county alternative education center.

School administrators will also, from time to time, encounter behavior issues with adults, sometimes a staff member, a parent, a guardian, or a community member. One morning at Harper's Choice, prior to our receiving the security camera system, I was notified by a staff member walking down a school hallway that she had just observed a gentleman who appeared to be drunk walking into a social studies class. I entered the class and asked that he speak to me in the hallway; he initially declined, until I informed him calmly and quietly that his decision was a very big and unnecessary mistake. He followed me out to the corridor, and I clarified our policy that those wishing to observe a class or speak to a teacher must first report immediately to the main office, preferably not drunk; the smell of liquor was strong. He said that was what he had always done previously, and I escorted him out, telling him that he would receive a No Trespass letter. I advised him that, in the future, he would need to contact me first, before visiting a classroom. I then asked if he was getting assistance, or if he thought he needed any help for the drinking, given that it was 8:30 in the morning; he declined and went on his way. I would later address the issue with the teacher, whose classroom the gentleman entered.

On a number of occasions, I found it appropriate and necessary to issue No Trespass letters to various folks, a number of whom were parents who had been prior to my arrival—and thought they would continue to be—routinely abusive to staff or would demonstrate behavior that disrupted the orderly operation of the school. On those occasions when such a letter was issued, I would notify and/or provide a copy to the police department or the officer assigned to our school community. Issuing such a letter is an unfortunate action, because in the case of a parent or guardian, the individual has a youngster attending the school, and it makes for an awkward situation. Nonetheless, if one is to preserve student, staff, and instructional dignity, it is a necessary action that many school administrators simply will not consider, much less take, which is among the reasons why some school environments are chaotic, as well as why many teachers, not feeling respected or supported, leave the profession annually. I would shake my head in amazement that such action was needed on more than a few occasions those first few years after my arrival.

In fact, it would turn out that over the years, over thirty parents would receive such letters for disruptive behavior, at times displaying a threatening, disrespectful bearing toward staff. Most of those letters went out within the first two years of my arrival, and those wishing to return to the school were given one option. They would be required to make an appointment to meet with me and a police officer together, at which time we would review the reason they received a letter, discuss appropriate social discourse, and clarify how they generally needed to conduct themselves when meeting with school staff. Some of my most ardent supporters over those years were two parents who had earlier received such letters from me for belligerent behavior. We became close, and there was nothing over those years that we would not do for one other; it was gratifying. Their youngsters went on to succeed in high school and beyond, with both parents crediting my tenure as principal for their academic and behavioral turnaround, when, in fact, we each worked steadfastly together to enhance their youngsters' chances for success.

On another morning, a "parent" of a repeatedly disrespectful, disruptive youngster was upset with the assistant principal and came to the school to make a ruckus over the child being assigned after-school detention. As I addressed her respectfully and professionally in the main office, in the presence of some eight to ten people, she began berating the school, calling me a "white cracker mother******" whereby I told her to hold that thought, as I needed a quick moment to pick up something in my office. What I picked up was a telephone to summon the police.

I returned, asking her please to be respectful and to discuss her issue with me in my office; she refused. I directed her to leave the school building and not return until such time she could be civil; she refused. The officer had been within close proximity, and he entered the main office fairly promptly. He knew me well, and when he looked at her, I stated I wanted her charged with trespassing and disturbing the orderly operation of a school. She put on a show as he placed her in handcuffs. I quietly requested that the officer hold tight for a moment, until the tone rang for lunches, at which time he could march her out in front of several hundred students, staff, and community members. And yes, I issued a follow-up No Trespass letter. In this specific matter, I looked further into her situation and found that she had also registered in our school an equally poorly behaved nephew whom she had somehow passed off as one of her sons. There was paperwork in the file indicating that the youngster had been living in New York City at one time. I worked with another officer, whose family member was a NY Transit Officer. Together we were able to confirm that the nephew had been thrown out of a school in New York City, where his legal mother, the woman's sister, was still residing. The individual arrested had hoodwinked the school when registering the child and she had no legal custody, so the student was withdrawn from school that afternoon. It wasn't long before she returned to school to withdraw her own frequently disrespectful, troubled son, as well. The teachers smiled and appeared relieved when they received these students' withdrawal notifications from classes, stating that they were tired of having to deal with the woman's harassing behavior.

These incidents are a sampling of the scores of times over the years when students, and at times, adults, presented disrespectful, disruptive, incorrigible, sometimes life-threatening behaviors in the schools where I've been assigned—no different, generally, from what many teachers and school administrators encounter daily in our country's schools. In today's world, it makes sense for communities to consider the addition of school resource officers to complement the staffing at many of our schools.

Schools, and the learning that takes place in them, should be held sacrosanct, and parents should view the teaching of their youngsters as a shared partnership with classroom teachers and school officials—responsible school officials. To continue operating schools as we do in too many cities and suburbs throughout the country is to risk losing a generation of children, and we will do so at our own peril.

It doesn't have to be that way. And we—students, staff, parents, school administrators, and community partners—proved it at Harper's Choice, by employing the various ideas and programs put into action and outlined for you in this book.

15

Wokeness and Critical Race Theory

Given the tenor of the times and the fact that this book is a treatise on teaching and learning, I will share with the reader my professional view on issues that, while they have been around in some form or another for years, are very much part of our current national conversation, and as I write this book, have a direct impact on America's school communities.

The term *woke* refers to being aware of or well informed in a political or cultural sense, especially regarding issues surrounding marginalized communities, and in that vein, it dates back to the early sixties.[1]

Today it is part of the larger mainstream conversation regarding transgenderism, critical race theory, and issues of social and racial justice that fly in the face of experience and well-documented research, a falsehood based on a lie and a denial of our country's history. Nonetheless, these issues have found their way into school curricula, spawning community protests throughout the country.

It is one thing for such topics to comprise classroom discussions, debates, and conversations in social studies, psychology, and economics classes. It is quite another that such issues are now hardwired into school curricula—kindergarten through twelfth grade. Such nonsense that passes for education is much like a cancer and has a corrosive effect on American culture, including American schools.

Critical Race Theory is a Marxist theory, a divisive ideology that turns every aspect of society into racial conflict, categorizing individuals—students—into groups of oppressors and victims. There are specific anti-American terms, organizations, and pejorative descriptors associated with today's wokeness and critical race theory that make up the nomenclature, among which is jargon used recklessly to assign fault and guilt to innocent, everyday American school–attending youngsters. Among these are *white privilege, white supremacy, identity politics,* so-called *unconscious bias, equity* (demand for equal outcomes, discarding any regard for equality, as outlined in the U.S. Constitution), *Black Lives Matter, systemic racism, the "1619 Project"* (revisionist American history that every leading historian has labeled a lie),[2] *restorative justice, reparations,* calls to *defund the police, social* or *racial justice,* along with the promotion of radical views of family, gender, and sexuality. Schools and school districts willfully using taxpayer money to fund such divisive, anti-American issues either for classroom instruction or systemwide staff training is wholly inappropriate.

This nonsense is based on fabrications and is without merit, all meant to drive an anti-America agenda in which we are to suspend our sense of disbelief. Imagine, for example, teaching classroom youngsters that colorblindness, a once-cherished idea that sprang from the civil rights movement, is a "myth"; yet such is part of the critical race theory venom presented and taught in many of our schools today. Misguided school administrators from Pennsylvania to California, Texas to Minnesota, know full well—yet they fail to appreciate and defend—the extent to which all educators have gone to be inclusive in virtually all aspects of instruction. And yet teachers' unions, school district officials, state and local board of education members, activists, and policymakers appear hellbent on pushing diversity, social engineering, and equity at the expense of perspective, honesty, historical accuracy, and rigor. They adamantly refuse to recognize that stable two-parent families, educational attainment, workforce participation, and the resultant economic prosperity account for the large bulk of observed racial differences.

Such divisive claptrap and the attendant identity politics passing for education is injurious to our youngsters and their families. It steals meaningful time and attention from the academic lessons students need in reading, writing, mathematics, science, and social studies, as well as the additional academic and related arts disciplines. In those school districts that have cowed to activist pressure, school leadership has been replaced with advocacy. They willingly elect to sow seeds of division by pushing harmful critical race theory on their communities, and they do so with utter disregard for facts, dignity, family, and country.

It is all the more disgraceful when such destructive schemes are deceptively called and implemented by school districts as "cultural literacy," "anti-racist curricula," or "anti-racist professional development training sessions." These schemes are, in fact, racist, and such indoctrination is an assault on our country's culture, history, customs, and traditions. It is hate-filled propaganda that deliberately distorts both American history and present-day society. It steals from the meaningful time that ought to be spent on providing students a concerted, thoughtful, balanced, and accurate portrayal of U.S. history that reflects the contributions of all Americans who make up the mosaic of this truly exceptional nation that we call America. Should this craziness continue, students will matriculate through their school years confused, insecure, bitter, and possessed of a false and meaningless portrayal of the world. They will find themselves devoid of a meaningful, accurate, and substantive education, bereft of the knowledge, skills, and talents that would otherwise have made them employable, confident, secure, and happy in twenty-first century America.

K-12 school youngsters very much want to opine on various issues in classrooms, but only in an environment that is free and open and that welcomes diverse viewpoints. Proponents of woke critical race theory curricula—among the worst people imaginable—intentionally stifle free and open inquiry, using race and identity politics to divide people; it is destructive and harmful to students, staff, parents, and entire communities.

As for the promotion (read teaching) of woke radical gender and sexuality viewpoints, leave such topics to parents, who raise and educate their children according to their own beliefs and values. School districts have no legal or moral standing to usurp parents' rights, and parents neither cede nor lose those rights at the schoolhouse gate. It is confounding that school systems and political policymakers continue not to understand that our schools should be about promoting excellence in teaching reading, writing, and arithmetic, revolving around ideas and values that are rooted in truth, historical fact, and principles that enrich America and embrace a meaningful sense of patriotism. Radio talk show host and author Dennis Prager rightly asks, "Why would you send your young child to a school that sponsors a 'Drag Queen Story Hour' or that dwells on 'non-binary' gender identity? Do you think such things do not damage your child's innocence? Do you want your child to be challenged about his or her sexual identity?"[3]

It makes one exclaim, "What the hell!" How on God's earth could hard-earned taxpayer money find itself funding such destructive, mind-numbing decision-making in any school's curriculum? How did we get to this point, particularly when schools throughout America need so desperately to focus their efforts on meaningful teaching and learning in the spirit of compassion, a can-do attitude, and respect for one another and our country? It is wholly inappropriate when political officials or school district staff take it upon themselves to push political ideologies into the schoolhouse and impose their own personal or political biases onto a captive student audience. Such is well outside the purview of an educator. Government and political activism should play zero role in dictating curricula to school communities. Millions of Americans correctly note that such ideas rooted in the social and political realm are skewed, divisive, and anti-American. When such ideas play a prominent role in a school system's philosophy, funding, or curriculum, it is a horribly misplaced priority, forsaking meaningful, first-rate academic instruction for all students. Such drivel is described as brainwashing, propaganda, indoctrination, or proselytizing; it is not an honest, meaningful, and substantive education. It is a complete and total distortion of the idea of equality under the law.

It is bizarre that we find ourselves as a society having to deal with such anti-American insanity, such nefarious foolishness, in any American city, neighborhood, or town, much less in our schools. We should not be in the business of needlessly forcing whole communities to take sides, while its school system's mission becomes more amorphous, something closer to social engineering. Schools should be about providing worthwhile, purposeful academic classroom instruction. At Harper's Choice, we committed to provide our youngsters with top-shelf teaching in the various disciplines, including English/language arts and English for speakers of other languages, mathematics, reading, science, social studies, world languages, the related arts, and physical education...in my view, a kind of classical liberal arts education. The role of such instruction was to teach our youngsters, and in the process show them how to learn, how to think...not what to think. Why on earth would any school district knowingly bastardize teaching and learning by injecting a divisive political agenda into its curriculum offerings that would promote a society motivated by cultural tribalism? Hardly an appropriate vehi-

cle for investing in our nation's future. What say you that we simply
let our kids be kids, for God's sake. It also makes not a whit of difference that celebrities, athletes, and corporate America have adopted
such a toxic stance; it remains entirely improper, no matter that the
national teachers' unions approve of such destructive malevolence.
American educator, author, and orator Booker T. Washington said
that "a lie doesn't become truth, wrong doesn't become right, and
evil doesn't become good, just because it's accepted by a majority"
(or what may appear at times to be a majority). Schools need principals who possess character, and schoolhouses large and small should
be in the business of academic instruction and character-building,
fostering respect for each other and for our country. Those in key
decision-making positions throughout this nation's cities and communities should strive to be better, more responsible stewards of
hardworking taxpayers' dollars. Besides, our youngsters deserve
better. The majority of Americans know well that such ill decision-
making is misguided, and in my view, they should not abide such
education malfeasance on the part of school leaders, nor from those
holding local, state, or national office. We are in a dark place when
the worst of humanity is allowed to infiltrate our schools and willfully rob American youngsters of the American dream, which allows
youngsters to be agents of their own destiny, no matter their color.
It is a dream well worth fighting for, but it requires strong families,
first-class schools, and equally unshakeable faith-based organizations that will demand excellence, set high expectations, shape character, and build self-sufficiency. "The antidote to racism is not anti-
racism [especially regarding the twisted manner in which the word
anti-racist is used in the Marxist ideology of Critical Race Theory], it
is a philosophy of humanism that celebrates and uplifts the inherent
dignity in each individual. And the antidote to inequity is not diminished expectations for all. It is equal opportunity and a belief in each
person's capacity for upward mobility, no matter their race, ethnic-

ity, or skin color," cites American Enterprise Institute's Ian Rowe in a *USA Today* op-ed.[4]

Throughout America, many rightfully believe that our K-12 schools and universities have gone off the rails, losing sight of their primary mission to help students gain the requisite knowledge and skills that will allow them to function in the world of work and afford them opportunities throughout society.

Our focus should be, as singer/songwriter Graham Nash wrote, "to teach the children well," providing every child opportunity and fairness. Such requires that we teach our students to read, to write, to compute, to think critically. Every American should hope to be on the same page if we are to improve our education stature throughout the industrialized world. We can hardly afford to hamstring our children, our staff, and our communities with such destructive woke rubbish, when the emphasis should be on shoring up our school-age youngsters' and their schools' academic well-being. Our sixteenth president, Abraham Lincoln, once stated that "America will never be destroyed from the outside. If we lose our freedom, it will be because we destroyed ourselves." If we continue to tolerate such nonsensical progressive political indoctrination in our schools, as well as from our elected or appointed officials at local, state, and national levels, we will do so at our own peril and that of America.

So, what action might parents and communities consider, when encountering such destructive foolishness in a school district? Make your protests clear and reject all content that teaches racial discrimination, reminding school districts and local governments that such teaching violates Title VI of the Civil Rights Act of 1964.[5] Attend local, state board of education, and town hall meetings, and remind them that the first amendment protects us from compelled speech in addition to granting us the freedom to speak; request copies of school instructional materials, as well as teacher professional development training particulars and examine them fully; develop a social media platform and ascertain the number of other families within the community who are in agreement with you; establish a community listserve to send and receive emails; hold community events to increase awareness; and demand that your schools stay out of politics and return to a more connected and significant focus on providing a first-rate education to all its youngsters.

As was cited earlier on the issue of student bullying and the need for parents to hold school officials accountable for their youngsters' safety, parents need to stand tall and push back on the issue of critical race theory and defend in the public square both American history and traditional family values. Insist that the school district be transparent regarding the content taught throughout the curriculum at every grade level. Parents should be well aware of everything taught in their children's classrooms, no matter the subject area discipline. If your concerns fall on deaf ears, work hard with others to remove from office those with an agenda, by way of a recall, if necessary. I will reiterate for emphasis that radical national, state, or local lawmakers and unenlightened or cowardly school officials willfully using public taxpayer dollars to fund the indoctrination of a community's school-age youngsters is a slap in the face to American citizens, including hardworking parents, who pay their fair share of these taxes. Such an evil practice is wholly against the values of parents, against the values of America itself, and is entirely wrong and unprincipled.

If you are financially able to consider another education option, do so immediately, and find a school that clearly understands its mission of offering its families a quality, honest, and first-rate education for every youngster. Get online and contact national grassroots organizations and think tanks that are working to reclaim schools from moronic activists all too eager to promote toxic curricula and corrupt programs that so damage our children and divide our communities. Talk to like-minded state lawmakers about the idea of promoting legislation to outlaw critical race theory, as well as withhold federal and state funding from school districts that practice, promote, or attempt to compel students to believe that any sex, race, ethnicity, religion, color, or national origin is inherently superior or inferior. Suggest—perhaps assist—in designing legislation proposals that offer other school opportunities, for example, education savings accounts, like those in Arizona, Florida, and North Carolina, for those students attending schools that discard wholesome, meaningful teaching for indoctrination of racially discriminatory content.[6] How utterly bizarre that such overt critical racial discrimination, as that found in critical race theory, would find advocates of such poison, of all places, within our American schools. Any educator or school official responsible for espousing such divisiveness or allowing such to be part of a school curriculum should be removed, and where appropriate, summarily fired.

The schoolhouse is no place for activists and policymakers, and the willful bastardizing of school curricula will continue the practice of providing a fraudulent education to American youngsters. Further, such will consign tens of thousands of students to a life of ignorance, insecurity, and failure. The intentional denial of their future prosperity is unconscionable. Moreover, know for certain that where character is the soul of one's school, meaningful teaching and learning rooted in truth and historical fact is the surest route to an informed patriotism. The best policy is to keep politics and one's personal or social agenda out of the schoolhouse and instead focus on instruction, continuous improvement, connecting with one another, and establishing partnerships—a proven winner for youngsters, their families, and our American communities.

16

The Achievement Gap

Given that this book is about our success in turning around a challenging and troubled majority-minority public school, affording the school community the opportunity to find its fair share of success, it is appropriate to discuss the "achievement gap," a seemingly age-old education and social conundrum. It is a term that refers to a significant—and persistent—disparity in academic performance or educational attainment between or among students, such as white students and minorities or students from higher income or lower income, as examples. Over the years, as achievement gaps are discussed—particularly when the groups are white and black—the issue does not result in answers that are black or white, so to speak, but the answers should be that clear. I suspect they are not because of the very issue of race. Issues can be complex, with no easy solutions that appeal to all sides that would resolve any particular predicament or matter. On this issue, we do know there are specific traits, elements, or characteristics that must be in place in order to enhance one's chances for success—academic or otherwise. As regards schools, it starts with a philosophy, standards of excellence, policies, and actions much like those outlined in this book that saw us achieve elevated classroom teaching, improved student deportment, successful student academic performance, and unqualified support from our parent community. Achievement gaps can be dealt with meaningfully, if only incrementally, and it is entirely possible for schools throughout America to take substantive steps in minimizing the gaps that communities currently experience in student academic achievement and deportment. Attempts to close these gaps, however, stand zero chance if the way we continue to run many American schools remains standard fare. As you have gleaned from reading this book thus far, schools need to be about teaching excellence and student achievement, but a review of the literature and media on any given day would indicate that such is all too often absent from many of them. Two reasons are often put forward to explain poor minority school performance—funding and discrimination, both of which, in my view, are irrational and lack substance.

Average U.S. per-student spending for students pre-K through 12th grade is over $12,000. Some of our most poorly performing schools spend far and above the national average: Baltimore at over $16,000; New York City at $23,000; and Washington, DC, at $22,000 rank among the nation's highest per-pupil educational spending. The charge of discrimination, however, to explain away poor student performance is more pernicious. That would have to change. I suggest that school communities across the nation divest themselves of their focus on race, victimization, and blame, and instead begin to adopt a *can-do, no excuses* mindset, not unlike the many students and families from identical circumstances who do so daily...and with success.

Let's stay for the moment with this issue of race, behavior, and school academic performance and examine it in a manner that traditionally is not generally done, maybe even getting our hands dirty.

We revisit my view that public schooling is a microcosm of society, where one will observe and come in contact with good and not-so-very-good human behaviors that life offers; that's the reality of any profession, any job, where one is immersed in and dealing with the public on a daily basis.

Our country's annual criminal justice statistics reveal a disproportionate percentage of blacks who come in contact with law enforcement. Many individuals seemingly automatically cite the cause as racism, when they clearly have not read, much less understand anything about the issue, because if they did, they would know that such is blatantly untrue, and their knowledge of this would then allow them to add constructively to the conversation. The matter is well worth taking the time to review, to study, and to become informed about, because it is an important issue in our culture, and every American should feel that he or she matters. When looking at how the criminal justice system works, from policing to prosecution decisions, judging determinations to sentencing decrees, it turns out that the system responds to crime, the heinousness of crime, and individuals' criminal records, no matter their color. It is a factual lie to say that racism accounts for the high percentage of blacks having trouble with the law in this country. Stay with me on this issue.

The myth, the false narrative that a biased legal system accounts for the black incarceration rate in this country, has been exhaustively researched by criminologists, both liberal and conservative. As a matter of fact, "the black incarceration rate is overwhelmingly a function of black crime. Insisting otherwise only worsens black alienation and further defers a real solution to the black crime problem," cites Heather MacDonald, a Manhattan Institute fellow and contributing editor of City Journal.[1] Her well-researched writings cite the work of criminologists Robert Sampson and Janet Lauritsen, who reviewed the massive literature on charging and sentencing, concluding that "large racial differences in criminal offending," not racism, explained why more blacks were in prison proportionately than whites and for longer terms.[2] Yet another criminologist—easily as liberal as Sampson, she notes—reached the same conclusion in 1995: "Racial differences in patterns of offending, not racial bias by police and other officials, are the principal reason that such greater proportions of blacks than whites are arrested, prosecuted, convicted and imprisoned," Michael Tonry wrote in *Malign Neglect*.[3] The evidence is clear: Black prison rates result from crime, not racism.

Likewise, a disproportionate percentage of black elementary and secondary school students receive out-of-school suspensions and are expelled from schools across the country at rates far higher than the percentages for students of all other racial/ethnic groups.[4] The pattern of antisocial behavior mirrors that of black school-age youngsters' older peers.

In 2013–2014, about 2.6 million public school students (5.3 percent) received one or more out-of-school suspensions. A higher percentage of black students (13.7 percent) than of students from any other racial/ ethnic group received an out-of-school suspension, followed by 6.7 percent of American Indian/Alaska Native students, 5.3 percent of students of two or more races, 4.5 percent each of Hispanic and Pacific Islander students, 3.4 percent of White students, and 1.1 percent of Asian students. The percentage of black male students who received out-of-school suspensions (17.6 percent) was the highest of male students from any racial/ethnic group. This percentage was nearly twice the percentage of the next highest racial/ ethnic group—American Indian/Alaska Native male students with 9.1 percent—and was more than twice the percentage of male students from any other racial/ethnic group. A similar pattern was observed among female students, with black female students receiving the highest percentage of out-of-school suspensions (9.6 percent). About 111,000 students were expelled in 2013–2014, amounting to 0.2 percent of public school students. The percentages of black and American Indian/Alaska Native students who were expelled (both 0.4

percent) were higher than the percentages for students of all other racial/ethnic groups.[5]

Academically, we look at the National Assessment of Educational Progress (NAEP), the "Nation's Report Card." I explained earlier that NAEP is the largest nationally representative and continuing assessment of what America's students know and can do in various subject areas. We find that a disproportionate percentage of black elementary and secondary school students are retained in grade. This ethnic cohort lags behind most or all of the other racial/ethnic groups in the NAEP-assessed areas of reading and mathematics in grades four, eight, and twelve, with the achievement gap widening as the youngsters progress through those grade levels, with the largest reading discrepancy at grade twelve. Similarly, the same pattern emerges at all grade levels in the area of mathematics, with black students falling ever more by grade twelve, averaging a scale score lower than all other racial/ethnic groups. It is no surprise that black students represent a disproportionate percentage of elementary and secondary school students retained in grade. NAEP notes that retention can be related to both disciplinary and academic issues; a student might be retained because of behavioral issues or because the student is not academically ready to progress to the next grade level.[6]

Just as there are those who cite racism as the cause of our country's high black incarcerations, so, too, do many cite discrimination to outright racism as the cause for black academic failure and high incidents of ill behavior in our schools across America. It is as though willful and erroneous preconceptions are all that matter. Disappointingly, many school officials have jumped on board, exhibiting a craven submission to political correctness.

Does the scourge of racism exist throughout the world? I believe so. Is America itself a racist country? Of course not, and I would hope the majority of the nation would concur. That does not mean there are not individuals throughout the world, including in the United States, who hold views of prejudice, bias, and antagonism toward others; the human species is not infallible. If you are smart, moral, and fair-minded, you steer clear of such people, take an appropriate stand against such behavior, and raise your children to be principled, thoughtful, caring individuals, respectful of everyone. That is how you improve the living condition for everyone on our planet. There are those in society, however, who seemingly feel this need to promote racial differences, identity politics, and victimhood. That, too, is equally anathema and contributes equally to lives of closed opportunities.

Over the years, I have enjoyed the thoughtful and insightful commentaries of Walter Williams, the esteemed economist, commentator, and academic. In a piece entitled "Blind to Real Problems," he stated the following:

> For several decades, a few black scholars have been suggesting that the vision held by many black Americans is entirely wrong. Dr. Shelby Steele, a scholar at Stanford University's Hoover Institution, said: "Instead of admitting that racism has declined, we (blacks) argue all the harder that it is still alive and more insidious than ever. We hold race up to shield us from what we do not want to see in ourselves."
>
> Dr. John McWhorter, professor of English and comparative literature at Columbia University, lamented that "victimology, separatism, and anti-intellectualism underlie the general black community's response to all race-related issues," adding that "these three thought patterns impede black advancement much more than racism; and dysfunctional inner cities, corporate glass ceilings, and black edu-

cational underachievement will persist until such thinking disappears."

In the 1990s, Harvard professor Orlando Patterson wrote,
"America, while still flawed in its race relations...is now
the least racist white-majority society in the world; has
a better record of legal protection of minorities than any
other society, white or black; (and) offers more opportunities to a greater number of black persons than any other
society, including all those of Africa."

During an interview in December with *The Daily Caller*,
Steele said the anti-Americanism that started during the
1960s and has become mainstream and visible in the black
community is "heartbreaking and sad." That anti-Americanism that so dominates the American black identity has
been "ruinous to black America, where we are worse off
than we were under segregation by almost every socioeconomic measure."[7]

Having served in this profession for over three decades, including working in majority-minority school communities, I speak from
personal and professional experience. Over this period of time, I
have read or pored over a good deal of research and public policy,
at times producing published writings on the subject. I have inter-
acted with and have had multiple dialogues or conversations on race
regularly with people of color—colleagues, students, parents, and
those who found success in business. I have reviewed with various
communities of color scores of public school documents, policies,
and actions taken by school administrators, regarding various disciplinary matters involving students of various races and ethnicities.
The opinions, results of research, and scholarly deductions on this
topic are conclusive: assigning any excuse other than one's own per-

sonal poor judgment in committing discipline infractions is simply irresponsible. Using the race card is a hackneyed, destructive lie; in today's America, it is foolish. Black student school suspension rates reflect not a whit of discrimination; they do reflect school behaviors committed by specific students that result in suspension, and these students own that ill behavior. Moreover, my experience and the view of many in and outside of the profession maintain that the total number of discipline referrals and suspensions belies the actual degree of school ill behavior exhibited by students of all races. This is because school officials generally and willfully ignore a good deal of the disrespect and disruption that steals dignity from staff and other students (including better-behaving black students). Why? you may ask. Again, for appearances. There are those school officials who willfully disregard the facts and boast that their school or district has fewer suspensions; therefore, that must mean that these schools are well run and operating swimmingly, when the fact is that nothing could be further from the truth.

We're now looking at years of failing schools and the high percentage of "graduating" students of every race needing to take remedial course work at universities. This is sobering, very serious stuff, accompanied by continued failing black academic performance, disproportionate black disciplinary referrals and suspensions, along with cries of discrimination or racism. Why on earth do we continue this circular argument year after year after year? Opting to ignore facts and truth, school and university officials, as well as those with a political ax to grind, have made a cottage industry out of critical race theory which, as cited in the previous chapter, is itself racist. They hold seminars that fulminate against so-called white privilege, where educators are told that they hold racist views and harbor "low expectations" for black students, hammering home to teachers and school administrators that they, in fact, are the problem. It is a sinister, twisted point of view that is promulgated throughout the profession in communities across the country, a poison to society that fosters resentment and division. Race hustlers need to understand and take to heart what many successful blacks know and have been saying for decades. The continued failure in behavior and academic performance of too many black students throughout America is a black cultural problem. It will require deep cultural introspection and reassessment of student attitudes and behaviors toward learning that continue to affect so negatively the behavior and academic performance of millions of black students, both male and female.To call it anything else is slanderous to classroom teachers and other educators throughout the country, the majority of whom work hard daily to prepare lessons they believe will lead to academic success for their students—all of their students; further, it completely red-pencils the role of individual will, of personal agency. On numerous occasions over the years, I found it necessary to clarify to problem students—and their sometimes equally uncooperative parents or "advocates,"—no matter what they looked like—that there were many youngsters in the neighborhood of identical color, age, economic, and family circumstances who chose not to engage in repeated disrespectful, disruptive, violent behaviors, making life so inordinately difficult for the remainder of the student body and staff. I would emphasize to them that such behavior could not be tolerated, that our instruction and the benefits to the community's students and their families on the part of our hardworking staff were simply too important. American economist and social theorist Thomas Sowell is easily one of the smartest, most insightful observers of American culture, American society. In a piece on race, politics, and lies, he is critical of this "us against them" vision or mentality, stating the following:

That vision is nowhere more clearly expressed than in attempts to automatically depict whatever social problems exist in ghetto communities as being caused by the sins or negligence of whites, whether racism in general or a "legacy of slavery" in particular. Like most emotionally powerful visions, it is seldom, if ever, subjected to the test of evidence.

The "legacy of slavery" argument is not just an excuse for inexcusable behavior in the ghettos. In a larger sense, it is an evasion of responsibility for the disastrous consequences of the prevailing social vision of our times, and the political policies based on that vision, over the past half century.

Anyone who is serious about evidence need only compare black communities as they evolved in the first 100 years after slavery with black communities as they evolved in the first 50 years after the explosive growth of the welfare state, beginning in the 1960s.

You would be hard-pressed to find as many ghetto riots prior to the 1960s as we have seen just in the past year, much less in the 50 years since a wave of such riots swept across the country in 1965.

We are told that such riots are a result of black poverty and white racism. But in fact—for those who still have some respect for facts—black poverty was far worse, and white racism was far worse, prior to 1960. But violent crime within black ghettos was far less.

Murder rates among black males were going down—repeat, DOWN—during the much lamented 1950s, while it went up after the much-celebrated 1960s, reaching levels more than double what they had been before. Most black children were raised in two-parent families prior to the 1960s. But today the great majority of black children are raised in one-parent families.

Such trends are not unique to blacks, nor even to the United States. The welfare state has led to remarkably similar trends among the white underclass in England over the same period. Just read "Life at the Bottom," by Theodore Dalrymple, a British physician who worked in a hospital in a white slum neighborhood.

You cannot take any people, of any color, and exempt them from the requirements of civilization—including work, behavioral standards, personal responsibility and all the other basic things that the clever intelligentsia disdain—without ruinous consequences to them and to society at large.

Non-judgmental subsidies of counterproductive lifestyles are treating people as if they were livestock, to be fed and tended by others in a welfare state—and yet expecting them to develop as human beings have developed when facing the challenges of life themselves.[8]

Moreover, making such specious claims defers a more substantive examination of the reasons for black failure, as well as any potential meaningful resolution that would otherwise see these youngsters achieving at their optimum level. I referenced the issue of academic remediation at the outset of this book. In Baltimore, not unlike various communities and cities across the country, 80 percent of incoming students at Baltimore City Community College need remedial education—80 percent! Public two-year and four-year institutions in Maryland report that 56 percent of students going directly from high school to college need some form of remedial education, in a state, by the way, honored three years in a row by *Education Week* as having the top public education system, cites Marta H. Mossburg, a senior fellow at the Maryland Public Policy Institute and a fellow at the Franklin Center for Government and Public Integrity, writing in the *Baltimore Sun*.[9]

Rather than take the logical step of ascertaining how it is that a significant number of black students in similar circumstances throughout America find it within themselves to perform well, by making good choices, respecting others, and committing to those character traits that will propel them to success, many educators, lawmakers, and so-called activists choose the disappointing, lazy, and reckless easy option of blaming society and its phantom systemic racialism or bigotry.

As I described earlier, a number of school officials have grasped the racism canard, insulting educators and costing taxpayers millions of dollars annually on a manufactured industry of race-based seminars and cultural literacy programs. These programs often contain wildly unsupported generalizations, frequently defame individuals, disrespect America, and disunite the very populations that should be bridged and supported. Professional school administrators throughout America would find more meaningful success, be better stewards of taxpayer money, and provide a better, more substantive service to the citizenry if they stuck to the research that actually impacts meaningful teaching and learning. Hard truths are truths nonetheless, and while there are many fine school administrators fighting the good fight daily, communities should not abide such foolhardy decisions on the part of those insecure school officials who fall prey to such nonsensical farces. Similar programs have been among discussions with a number of public school officials over the years, and it is telling that many have been quite willing to jump on the bandwagon of political correctness, hoping to appear self-righteous, all the while chasing an elusive and costly mirage. Political correctness cannot begin to assuage critical race theorists. These so-called "anti-racist" and diversity seminars are anything but anti-racist; as cited previously, they are, as a matter of fact, racist and push ugly, hateful concepts that all of America should spurn. We are so much better than that. It is astonishing that so many school officials either do not understand or fail to grasp the toxic nature of such anti-American sentiments. More nefarious are those who do understand and buy into such destructive ideology; they have no place educating American youngsters.

In my over thirty-five-year career in education, I never—not once—had the displeasure of encountering another professional with a bias against a particular race; that is not why anyone enters the teaching profession. Frankly, it would be hard to cite a profession more dedicated to inclusivity over the last several decades than the field of education. Generally speaking, schools and the teachers within them go to great lengths to make appropriate accommodations for any student's personal, social, or socio-economic status; such is in a good teacher's DNA. Still, craven school officials feeling insecure or self-righteous or hoping to be seen as virtuous—men and women who lack character— willingly sell their teaching staff down the road and dictate that schools invest is such divisive and malignant curricula.

I have met teachers of all races who had disdain for disrespectful, disruptive behavior exhibited regularly by many black students; those same individuals equally abhorred the ill behavior of white students. Repugnant behavior is not indigenous to any one particular race of people any more than intelligence is reserved solely for another specific ethnicity. Years ago, in one high school, I had to discipline a particular Asian student who was later arrested and taken out of the school in handcuffs. His father heartbroken, the student was more interested in dealing drugs than he was working for and one day taking over his family's business. There were those who thought it amazing that an Asian student could get in such deep trouble. The fact is that no matter how busy we are as parents, we must love, care, and stay on top of what our children are saying, feeling, and doing; somehow this family lost that connection, and the result was costly. Such destructive behaviors are seen across the spectrum of race, just as successful character traits are also shared across all ethnicities.

Our fortieth president, Ronald Reagan, stated, "We must reject the idea that every time a law's broken, society is guilty rather than the lawbreaker. It is time to restore the American precept that each individual is accountable for his actions." This would apply to school disciplinary codes of behavior, requirements for school academic success, or U.S. laws and regulations meant to protect American society.

I have met those black staff members who I thought were overly race-conscious. My position has generally been that one has to walk in another's shoes to appreciate that individual person's life experience. As long as the professional teacher was exercising appropriate and satisfactory teaching and staying well within expected professional norms, I was fine with that colleague's disposition. Those types of individuals, I often observed, were generally kept at arm's length by other staff members of color who saw life through a different lens. So, while race may or may not present itself throughout the course of one's job, that's a far cry from the issue of racism. The point is that, just as I do not believe that police, prosecutors, and judges wake up each morning hell-bent on making life difficult for American blacks, it is also true that teachers and school administrators occupy the positions they do because they want to teach, and they want very much to assist youngsters—all youngsters—to be all they can be. It simply makes no sense that everyone, from cradle to grave, is out to make life difficult for those who are black.

On separate occasions over the years, I convened meetings of parents to review student disciplinary referrals from teachers, as well as the action taken by administrators to address the disrespectful, disruptive behaviors that can destroy a teacher's lesson plan on any given day, and in the process can ruin the instructional time for the remaining responsible students. The relevant concern with respect to race, discipline, and school suspensions of black students is whether the rate at which blacks are disciplined and suspended is the result of prejudice or because of a higher rate of offenses subject to discipline and suspension being attributed to the ill behavior of specific black students. The exercises proved insightful.

The earlier meeting was at the high school level; the gathering held years later was at the middle level. Both schools served a majority-minority population, and most parents (in fact, all the invited parents at the high school level) were black. On both occasions, I redacted the names of students and staff but revealed the race and gender of each individual referral, and I asked parents to pore over all the documents, some two to three hundred or so different referrals. The offenses were dramatically different from the garden-type classroom issues of yesteryear, regarding chewing gum, not raising one's hand, and talking out of turn. No, the parents saw actual referrals regarding behaviors that interfered with instruction, frequently stealing one's dignity too often in their school. The referrals ranged from deliberate class disruption, disrespectful or insubordinate behavior, bullying, vandalism, bus behavior, inappropriate sexual behavior, fighting, use of drugs, assaults on staff, harassment, threatening staff, weapons, alcohol use, and arson (setting clothes and trash cans afire in a classroom), to name several among the various offenses that are dealt with each school year. They were surprised and generally shook their heads that such behavior had occurred so regularly, some of the parents attempting to guess the identification of several of the ill-behaved. Interestingly, they acknowledged the stressful environment that goes with a teaching assignment today. They also agreed with almost every administrative action, including out-of-school suspensions, stating that more than a few of the students should have received tougher sanctions. Not one parent or guardian in either meeting felt that black students, who made up the bulk of the discipline referrals, were given disparate treatment or were otherwise handled differently than any of the other student referrals. When the statistics and documents were analyzed, it was shown that racism and bias were not at all a contributing factor; the school sanctions meted out to all students were fair, and the discipline referrals were overwhelmingly a result of black ill behavior.

It's about deportment, how students comport themselves in school and in the community. I frequently engaged in conversations with immigrants—students, parents, colleagues, and those in business—wanting to learn more about their culture, how another country educates its young, and the role that family plays. A number of Africans—Nigerians mostly—would tell me that "we are successful here because we do not accept failure, nor do we accept violence. We have grown up with and have seen too much violence that degrades the individual and family. We teach our sons and daughters a totally different view of life, including the importance of treating others with respect, obeying one's elders, working hard, and striving for success; if they do these things, they will find success here in America." As principal, on more than one occasion, I was asked by an immigrant parent to "try and keep my kids (usually boys, but occasionally, girls) away from those American black kids in the school," youngsters who were not seen as upstanding individuals. While I found their perspective an interesting commentary, I would inform them that there are specific youngsters, kids of every ethnicity, that loving, protective parents would not want around their own children. Moreover, I stated that their sons and daughters would surely find and make friends with a host of American blacks who were raised well and who took their education as seriously as anyone in the community. Nonetheless, I clearly understood what they meant, and I would share those views with other school-supportive and hardworking parents of color, and they, too, advised that they understood such comments, saying, "I don't want my kids around them, either."

Offering seemingly endless manufactured claims and spurious arguments to explain away ill behavior and academic failure, no matter one's color or racial makeup, is intellectually bankrupt, pure bunkum. Disrespectful, disruptive black students—no different from ill-tempered, disrespectful students of any color—cannot succeed; worse, tolerating these students and their enabling parents or guardians interrupts instruction and academic success for the remaining responsible and deferential student body, including those students of color who do know how to behave, who do have caring parents, and who are respectful of others. You will recall from an earlier chapter the extent to which even one student's troublesome behavior negatively impacts teaching and learning for the remainder of an entire classroom of well-behaved students. Nonetheless, enablers will offer ad nauseum that racism plays a role in the education of black students, whether these students live in well-to-do areas or in poverty and crime-ridden areas, so it follows that their chances of being disciplined and suspended from school increase, thereby setting them on a destructive life path, a kind of, as the myth goes, "school to prison pipeline," so we should be more understanding and tolerant of ill behaviors. Again, wrong...and an equally bogus excuse that condemns so many black kids to a life of failure. No matter one's zip code, those who bellow such an ugly rationale as a cause of high black student failure and discipline referrals ignore the very real fact that many black kids in identical circumstances choose not to fail academically and elect not to misbehave. It's a matter of grit, will, and self-efficacy—"that character thing again"—which finds these students making better decisions, demonstrating caring, compassion, and a respect for the dignity of others. They go on to attend universities, enter the workplace, join the military, start companies, or become neurosurgeons, frequently finding ways to give back to their communities.

Given that this chapter zeroes in on the country's achievement gap, I take a few minutes to cite the unfortunate ridicule that young, black, academically successful students can endure, as well as some interesting research done in one community at the behest of its black residents.

Youngsters will sometimes kid those who are particularly given to academic interest and accomplishment, sometimes calling them "nerds" or "geeks"; such might at times be annoying, but typically it is innocent enough (unless intentionally committed repeatedly or with malice). However, my sundry conversations with a host of multicultural students over the years reveal that such kidding, ribbing, or ridicule is not generally done in some other countries; in fact, students who are intelligent, respectful, serious about school, and academically accomplished in those countries are considered, they contend, "cool and respected" by society.

I have also observed, have read, and have talked to numerous students and parents over these years in education about a social phenomenon experienced by minorities—more specifically studious, respected, academically successful black students—about another kind of ridicule a bit more pejorative, biting, and pernicious. These kids are sometimes told by other less successful black peers that the accomplished black student is "acting white," as though scholarship is reserved only for those who are white, implying—if not, outwardly stating—that the successful, respectful, and accomplished black student is somehow betraying his own culture. Twisted? Yes, but clearly an unpleasant, if not, debilitating social experience that too many youngsters unnecessarily endure as they make their way through adolescence and beyond, including their college years. Minority and non-minority parents, educators, and the larger society need to admonish those who possess such a low regard for knowledge, education, and individual accomplishment and who are quick to mock successful students or otherwise subject another peer to such derision.

Interestingly, as cited in a piece by Celeste Headlee,[10] former host of the NPR podcast "The Takeaway," the term "acting white" doesn't have roots in the black community. She cites Stuart Buck's book, *Acting White*, in which he shares that the expression was used contemptibly by whites toward blacks in the days after the Civil War and the Jim Crow era and evolved as a derisive charge later picked up and used by blacks toward other black peers.[11]

There are those who falsely declare that such a phenomenon does not exist and, in fact, maintain that it never existed. Instead, like those who offer different excuses to explain others'—perhaps their own—sense of insecurity, inferiority, and lack of success in life, they will blame "equity" issues, "implicit" racial bias of white teachers, and the myth of "school-to-prison" discipline handling as an excuse for black failure. Such denials only sow discord and continue to attempt to mask over a phenomenon that many good, respected, and accomplished black parents and their youngsters find debilitating. Those who deny the existence of such a mean-spirited and demeaning phenomenon needlessly, recklessly, and endlessly defer an appropriate recognition of the problem that would allow for clearer, concrete action toward a resolution that potentially could improve the academic progress, as well as the quality of life, for scores of black youngsters and their families.

Author, *Wall Street Journal* editorial board member, and senior fellow at the Manhattan Institute Jason Riley touches upon this blight in his book, *Please Stop Helping Us*.[12]

> The kind of ribbing that I experienced as a child would follow me into adulthood, where my older sister's children would take to deriding my diction. "Why you talk white, Uncle Jason?" my niece, all of nine years old at the time, once asked me during a visit. Turning to her friend, she continued, "Don't my uncle sound white? Why he trying to sound so smart?" They shared a chuckle at my expense, and I was reminded of how early these self-defeating attitudes take hold. Here were a couple of black third graders already linking speech patterns to race and intelligence. Moreover, they had determined that "sounding white" was something to be mocked in other blacks and avoided in their own speech.
>
> The findings of academics who have researched this "acting white" phenomenon are thoroughly depressing, and demonstrate that my experiences are neither new nor atypical. Here is basketball great Kareem Abdul-Jabbar describing his experience as a studious kid at a predominantly black Catholic school outside of Philadelphia in the 1950s:
>
> "I got there and immediately found I could read better than anyone in the school. My father's example and my mother's training had made that come easy; I could pick up a book, read it out loud, pronounce the words with proper inflection and actually know what they meant.

When the nuns found this out they paid me a lot of attention, once even asking me, a fourth grader, to read to the seventh grade. When the kids found this out I became a target...

"It was my first time away from home, my first experience in an all-black situation, and I found myself being punished for doing everything I'd ever been taught that was right. I got all A's and was hated for it; I spoke correctly and was called a punk. I had to learn a new language simply to be able to deal with the threats. I had good manners and was a good little boy and paid for it with my hide."[13]

In a *New York Times* article by Felicia Lee entitled, "Why Are Black Students Lagging?"[14] she cites writer John Ogbu, anthropology professor at the University of California at Berkeley, a well-known figure in the field of student achievement. His book, *Black American Students in an Affluent Suburb: A Study of Academic Disengagement*, highlights a study of blacks in Shaker Heights, Ohio, an affluent Cleveland suburb, whose school district is equally divided between blacks and whites. As in many racially integrated school districts, the black students lagged behind whites in grade-point averages, test scores, and placement in high-level classes; black students were receiving 80 percent of the Ds and Fs. Professor Ogbu had been invited by black parents in 1997 to examine the district's five thousand students to figure out why.

As Riley accurately points out in his book, "Nationwide, the racial gap in education is well documented. Black kids are over-represented among high school dropouts and students who are not performing at grade level. Black scores on the SAT and other standardized tests are far lower on average that those of whites. The achievement gap begins in elementary school and widens in higher grades. By the end of high school the typical black student is several years behind his white peers in reading and math. The usual explanation of this is class inequality. Blacks don't perform on the level of whites because they come from a lower socioeconomic background and their schools have fewer resources, goes the argument."

Professor Ogbu finds, however, that this problem transcends class and persists even among the children of affluent, educated black professionals, as he and his team observed in Shaker Heights.

"None of the versions of class-inequality can explain why black students from similar social class backgrounds, residing in the same neighborhood, and attending the same school, don't do as well as white students," wrote Ogbu. "Within the black population, of course, middle class children do better, on the average, than lower-class children, just as in the white population. However, when blacks and whites from similar socioeconomic backgrounds are compared, one sees that black students at every class level perform less well in school than their white counterparts."[15]

The professor's team were given access to Shaker Heights students, teaching staff, school administrators, and parents. His conclusion: More than anything else, black culture explained the achievement gap. The black kids readily admitted that they did not work as hard as whites, took easier classes, watched more television, and read fewer books. "A kind of norm of minimum effort appeared to exist among black students," wrote Ogbu. "These students themselves recognized this and used it to explain both their academic behaviors and their low academic achievement performance."[16]

Due to peer pressure, some black students "didn't work as hard as they should and could." Among their black friends, "it was not cool to be successful" or "to work hard or to show you're smart." Ogbu found that black high school students "avoided certain attitudes, standard English, and some behaviors because they considered them white."

The behaviors and attitudes to be avoided included, for example, enrolling in honors and advanced-placement classes, striving for high grades, talking properly, hanging around too many white students, and participating in extracurricular activities that were populated by whites. "What amazed me is that these kids who come from homes of doctors and lawyers are not thinking like their parents; they don't know how their parents made it," Ogbu said in the New York Times piece. He continued, "They are looking at rappers in ghettos as their role models, they are looking at entertainers. The parents work two jobs, three jobs, to give their children everything, but they are not guiding their children."

He found that few black parents were members of the school's parent-teacher association. Participation in early-elementary school programs designed primarily for black children was spurned by black families. And the white parents tended to have higher academic expectations for their kids. "From school personnel reports of school authorities, interviews with students, discussions with parents themselves, and our observations, we can confidently conclude that black parents in Shaker Heights did not participate actively in school organizations and in school events and programs designed to enhance their children's academic engagement and achievement," he wrote. Riley cites that Ogbu also faulted the school system itself for the achievement gap.

> It turned out that "teachers were passing students who did not perform at grade level. The practice was widespread, particularly in kindergarten through eighth grade, and well known among students. And the teachers who were setting lower standards for black kids had 'good intentions,'" Ogbu reported. But it had the effect of lead-

ing some black kids to believe that they were doing better in school than they really were.

Other kids simply didn't try as hard as they would have otherwise. When Ogbu asked students why their grades were poor, "they would say that they did not take their schoolwork seriously because they knew they were going to be passed into the ninth grade anyway."

Ogbu's team of researchers also noted that in classes where most of the kids were black, teachers expected less of the students in terms of homework, even going so far as to de-emphasize its importance.

Obviously, school officials aren't responsible for the poor attitudes and lack of effort among black kids, but ignoring or indulging this isn't going to help close the learning gap. There was a time when black leaders understood the primacy of black self-development. They fought hard for equal opportunity, but they knew blacks have to be culturally prepared to take advantage of those opportunities when they arrive.

Speaking to a black St. Louis congregation in 1961, Martin Luther King Jr. stated, "Did you know that Negroes are 10 percent of the population of St. Louis and are responsible for 58 percent of its crimes? We've got to face that. And we have got to do something about our moral standards. We know there are many things wrong in the white world, but there are many things wrong in the black world too. We can't keep blaming the white man. There are things we must do for ourselves."[17]

Over the years, I have observed school officials routinely offer a panoply of excuses for poor student behavior and failing academic performance, particularly for the performance of black students. I am reminded of the British physician I cited earlier, Theodore Dal-rymple, author of the book *Life at the Bottom*, and his perspective on liberal intellectuals, when I say about such school officials that they "tend not to mean quite what they say, and express themselves more to flaunt the magnanimity of their intentions than to propagate truth." We know, for goodness' sake, what is required to address ill behavior, as well as the requisites needed to kick-start academic achievement. Instead, as Riley makes clear, we have people on this issue who are trying to help blacks by making excuses for them (perhaps, though I believe he's being a bit kind here, as many such people appear more interested in calling attention to themselves and generally looking to make the most outrageous incendiary comments that will get them noticed), offering the idea that the achievement gap is not the product of a black subculture that rejects attitudes and behaviors conducive to academic success, but rather a product of other nonsensical reasons, among which would be that it results from "racist" standardized tests or "Eurocentric" teaching styles. As an illustration, multiculturalist Geneva Gay, professor of education at the University of Washington-Seattle, holds that "standards of 'goodness' in teaching and learning are culturally determined and are not the same for all ethnic groups." Expecting black kids to "pay close attention to teachers for a prolonged, largely uninterrupted length of time" is apparently onerous, according to her. Judging student attentiveness in class "based on nonverbal communicative cues, such as gaze, eye contact, and body posture" is likewise unfair. Instead, we are told, the U.S. system should accommodate "cultural orientations, values, and performance styles of ethnically different students" instead of "imposing cultural hegemony." If schools did so, then black kids would "feel less compelled to sabotage or camouflage their academic achievement to avoid compromising their cultural and ethnic identity."[18] Imagine anyone with common sense entertaining such blather.

In other words, Riley clarifies, black kids are being asked to sit still in class, pay attention, follow rules, and complete homework assignments—all of which is a huge imposition on them, if not a racist expectation. One major problem with this theory, he reveals, is that it can't explain the performance of other nonwhite students, including black immigrants, who readily adjust to the pedagogic methods of U.S. schools and go on to outperform black Americans. Even black immigrants for whom English is a second language have managed to excel in U.S. schools.

As students, as parents, as teaching staff, and as school officials, everyone at Harper's Choice needed to recognize his or her own individual responsibility; teachers were there to teach well, and students were to put forth effort in the classroom, persevering and understanding that nothing replaces hard work. We consistently emphasized those characteristics daily throughout the years I was principal, and we worked hard to correct or ameliorate the conditions holding back successful student performance, both behavioral and academic. In the end, we were able to reach most of our cherubs and see the great majority of students reach their fair share of potential and achievement.

What many individuals find maddening, including successful minorities, is the degree to which so many blacks—enabled by benighted school officials, activists, and political officials—are rendered helpless or crippled by the notion that they have little to no responsibility for their own underachievement. Such a thought pattern is more than crippling— it redlines the self-efficacy of individuals, it reduces their humanity, and in so doing, it diminishes society.

Any number of reasons can account for one's success or failure. One in particular has always been a determinant that figures prominently in whether a youngster excels behaviorally and academically, and that would be *parenting*—caring, responsible, loving, and supportive parenting. It's been a time-honored truth and remains a truism no matter one's race, socioeconomic status, or zip code. A youngster is sitting on a pot of gold if he or she has a caring mom and dad...or a single mom, single dad, or caregiver who is loving and benevolent, someone whose world revolves around the child and who teaches the youngster about character, respect, empathy, the importance of making thoughtful, good decisions, and how to be self-reliant and law-abiding; someone who takes the time to provide steadfast wholesome values that will last the youngster a lifetime. It is about the degree to which parents insist their boys and girls hang with good, trustworthy friends who are equally respectful and law-abiding, and who understand the importance of getting an education. These are among the values that parents must model and inculcate in their children if they are to become respected, productive, and successful as they mature into adulthood.

A 1966 national report titled "Quality of Educational Opportunity" is among the largest research studies in history, including more than 650,000 students and teachers in more than 3,000 schools. Known as "The Coleman Report," named after the lead researcher, James Coleman, a Johns Hopkins sociologist, the survey and report cite a number of interesting findings, among which is that funding "has little effect on student achievement," and that there is "little difference" between white and black schools when it comes to physical buildings, formal curricula, and other measurable criteria. They found that a significant gap between white and black kids existed in first grade, and the gap became wider at the end of elementary school. Among the consistent variables explaining the differences in scores within each racial group or ethnic group was *the educational and economic attainment of the parents*, that student background and socioeconomic status are wholly important in determining educational outcomes of a student. But are those variables enough to propel student achievement? The years-later research study performed in Shaker Heights, Ohio, cited in this chapter proved that background and socioeconomic status were not a guarantee of student success. Why? It's not enough to be the children of doctors, lawyers, and engineers. What is necessary is another Coleman Report finding, emphasizing specifically the critical importance of *attitudes of parents and caregivers at home and peers at school of students toward education*,[19] similar to that which was evident in the Shaker Heights study. While it is clearly important that parents are successful and value education, it's not enough; you must also be on top of and actively involved in your child's schooling. This is most consequential in the early years, showing your youngster how best to study, as well as taking the time to review and check his or her homework assignments. As kids mature and advance in each grade level, this will become less necessary as you will have developed in your youngster successful study and test-taking preparation habits for a successful school experience.

Schools frequently feel outmatched by the societal social challenge faced by too many children, whose fathers are unknown, whose mothers are overburdened, where the exhausted grandmother frequently is the stabilizing force in the family. The achievement gap would appear to be due more to societal challenges and personal or family poor judgment than any form of witting or unwitting discrimination on the part of educators, so it stands to reason that we would gain immeasurably more in this area by zeroing in on those very real challenges that actually create and further exacerbate this dilemma. More specifically, I would recommend the strategy we used to make a difference in the Harper's Choice community. I jettisoned the metric of race altogether and focused our efforts on results; again, it was an unconventional viewpoint, a completely different approach from the philosophical bent of school systems today. We steadfastly pursued instructional strategies that were seeing success in advancing academic achievement for all students. The reader will recall that I often spoke with teachers and school officials across the country on various successful student academic performance initiatives I was researching or came across by way of the media that might have piqued my interest. The idea of continuous improvement became infectious, as teachers were also doing individual research on promising practices in the effort to advance their students' knowledge base and skill level; they would, in turn, share those successful instructional practices with their in-house colleagues, and our students were the direct beneficiaries.

There are a number of additional suggestions and considerations that we will explore on the subject of this chapter. The achievement gap remains a formidable challenge; the odds are long, and the history of attempts at closing the gap is checkered. These insights are a product of considerable research and a near-forty-year successful career in education working with various student populations. Parents, school districts, policymakers, and those in the media would be well-served to consider what is offered throughout this book.

Well-run schools have program offerings, policies, and procedures in place that should "lift all boats." At Harper's Choice Middle our daily focus was to do just that, and we proved remarkably effective accelerating our disadvantaged populations, as well. As with the instruction cited previously, we looked at what might be among the more productive, meaningful ways to spend time thinking about resources, actions, and programs that would enhance efforts to obtain the results all of us wanted for our school youngsters, their parents, and our teaching staff. That meant employing instructional research-based best practices, mentoring and tutoring by senior citizens and neighboring high school students, commencing an after-school academic and recreational program and summer "bridge" camp for our youngsters, providing student leadership training (by a former colleague, a social studies instructor and author), creatively scheduling a Spanish teacher to mentor and work with our Hispanic youngsters and their families, providing a substantive and meaningful Instructional Intervention Team of carefully selected staff, all of whom focused on those students needing academic, social, or emotional supports. The newfound sense of professionalism was electric, and the students, parents, and wider community were talking about Harper's Choice in a very different light.

We remained steadfast on the results we were after at Harper's Choice. The focus would remain setting kids on a path to success that would allow them to participate responsibly in their communities, which would lead to greater community prosperity, increased public safety, and an enhanced quality of life.

You have to believe in your goal, your mission, the results you are after, and you have to stay true, determined—with grit, fortitude, perseverance, and duty. This book outlines how we specifically changed the failing culture to one of teaching excellence and student academic success. The initiatives we ensured were in place revolved around instruction, continuous improvement, connections, and partnerships, all within the concept that character would lie at the heart—the soul—of our school. The philosophy, policies, and actions taken by the Harper's Choice School community proved instrumental in its effort to turn around a failing school to one recognized for high performance. All of these initiatives and ideas figured prominently in our efforts to minimize achievement gaps.

We listened to the feedback we received from students and where appropriate, we adjusted our instructional delivery accordingly. In an earlier chapter, I shared with the reader the results of a school district student questionnaire on "The Keys to Academic Success,"[20] which I included in my presentation on instruction to my faculty and staff at the time I took the helm of Harper's Choice. I remind the reader that the results of the research survey were from the perspective of students, grades three through twelve. Their responses provided keen insights into the minds of school-age youngsters and how they see themselves, their parents, their teachers, their schools, and their individual performance. The reader may recall that among the findings were the following:

- More white students than black students in the above-average group turned their homework in on time.
- More black than white students in the below-average group usually quit when their schoolwork was too hard.
- While most all students perceive that their parents think school is important, they cite a far lower percentage as ever talking to them about how they are doing in school; many parents do not check to see if youngsters have completed their homework.
- Only one-third of students think they are being given assignments that are challenging.
- Fewer than 65 percent of all students believe they are given enough time to answer a question, are helped to locate and correct errors, are praised when they do good work, are given as much attention as they need, are called on as much as other students, and are asked questions that require an explanation of reasoning.

On the issue of race, the following is noteworthy:

The primary difference in performance between students who achieve in the below-average quartile and those who achieve in the high-average quartile is not a factor of ethnic group or socioeconomic status. Performance differences are the result of differences in academic values, expectations, and commitment behaviors which the two groups demonstrate. High-achieving students value education, have high expectations for achieving academic success, and put forth the commitment and effort to ensure that they succeed academically.

The research project reaffirmed the belief that academic success is dependent on the following:

- Students valuing learning and working at acquiring knowledge
- Parents setting high expectations, communicating those expectations, and seeing to it that they are met
- Teachers providing support and continuously engaging students
- Administrators structuring learning environments so that student commitment behaviors result in learning, good grades, and post–high school success.

The above is near everything a parent needs to know—and when you become a parent, these things must be taken seriously. When actually done, youngsters will believe in themselves and understand that they can go as far as they can dream. Amazing things happen for youngsters when parents, guardians, schools, and communities work together in harmony. I cited earlier that some of the findings in the survey were not all that surprising, but they were reaffirming, and they particularly apply when the subject is the country's achievement gap. A variant of the above finding on performance differences is their conclusion that "students who value learning and work hard at acquiring knowledge, generally earn A/B grades and do well on standardized tests regardless of race or socio-economic status."

This is a particularly cogent fact, given my earlier statement that it's a matter of grit and will—"that character thing again"—that finds so many successful black males and females, sharing identical circumstances as those students who cause problems in their communities and schools, nevertheless making better decisions, demonstrating caring, showing compassion, and respecting the dignity of others.

We know as adults what needs to be done, no matter the community in which we live across America. It is worth emphasizing that students, parents, and teachers must work together to reduce the achievement gap, bearing in mind the following recommendations cited throughout the book:

- Strong links between home and school must be established and maintained to ensure that students are achieving expected outcomes.

- Students must accept responsibility for their own learning by demonstrating academic value, setting reasonable or high expectations, and demonstrating commitment behaviors; the three go together. Saying that one values education and has high academic expectations but doing little to make it happen will not result in the attainment of desired or expected outcomes. Students must follow through with academic behaviors that support their belief statements.

- Parents must support and monitor their children's activities to ensure that home and school expectations are being achieved. In addition to communicating that school is important and expecting their children to get good grades, parents need to talk to their children about what they are doing in school and check and/or help with homework. This consistent monitoring will ensure that parents know how well their children are doing in school.

- Teachers must demonstrate behaviors that communicate support to students. Specifically, teachers need to praise students when they do good work, give students attention when it is needed, try to balance the number of times that students are called on in class, and give students assignments that are challenging.

- Teachers must implement the interventions in their classrooms, which most students indicated would help them be successful, including providing clear expectations of lessons, using the chalkboard when presenting lessons, providing time for students to practice the skills they are learning, identifying and implementing a variety of ways that students can receive help in doing their homework, and going over homework in class.

These very kids were among those who responded to the survey questionnaire, citing the importance of family. As I emphasized throughout the book, what a difference in a youngster's life when a child, no matter his or her economic circumstances, has a loving, supportive, and actively involved mom and dad, or at least an equally loving and caring single mom, dad, guardian, or caregiver. I often found that the grandmother was the one stabilizing influence in a child's life in some of our busy demographic neighborhoods. Many a grandmother made certain that the child felt loved, supported, and understood self-discipline; she visited or was supportive of the school; she talked about school with her child; she talked about the fun of making new and good, well-behaved friends; she arranged for the child to ride or walk to school with another neighborhood young-ster; she found out about wholesome after-school activities that the youngster could join. She cared and was on top of her job of nurtur-ing a strong, independent, loving, and caring future adult...and she always lived in the same neighborhood, living within identical social and economic circumstances as those adults who elected not to pro-vide a loving, caring, and responsible home front. It can be done, and in fact, it is played out regularly in neighborhoods across America.

The research survey questionnaire also found that low-achieving students want individual help from adults and/or teachers, as well as small-group instruction, so we incorporated into our delivery of instruction at Harper's Choice the thoughts and opinions shared by students. We were steadfast in our pursuit of instructional and student performance excellence. The survey's data confirmed that which is required for optimum student success, illustrating what students, parents, teachers, and administrators must do to support academic excellence:

- Students should work at acquiring knowledge.
- Parents should set, communicate, and see to it that high ex-pectations are met.
- Teachers should demonstrate behaviors that are perceived as providing "most of the time" the support defined in the questionnaire.
- Administrators should provide the delivery system students say they want or prefer; should structure the learning envi-ronment so that student commitment behaviors result in learning, good grades, and post–high school success; and should help parents set, communicate, and see to it that high expectations are met.[21]

These are the kinds of beliefs that are held and the meaningful actions that are taken by successful schools throughout the country, if students are to succeed, *regardless of race or poverty.*

On the idea that "administrators should provide the delivery system students say they want or prefer; should structure the learning environment so that student commitment behaviors result in learning, good grades, and post-high school success," school officials would do well to employ use of "ability grouping," tailoring specific instruction to a small group of students based on a youngster's academic ability level. In my view this method differs from so-called "tracking" that over the years has fallen out of favor and, in fact, is in violation of Title VI of the U.S. Office of Education Office of Civil Rights, because of reports that, historically, educators steered students of color into non-academic coursework. Whenever and wherever that was done, such a practice was or would be wrong. It was felt that these classes had diminished expectations and an altogether impoverished learning environment. That may or may not have been accurate, but then schools offering such a failing curriculum were likely staffed by less-than-stellar educators and school officials that allowed such malfeasance to exist. As the reader now knows, I have found that when groups of lower-ability kids are taught by great teachers, where there are high expectations, while targeting academic deficiencies, kids respond and grow strong academically. In my view, *ability grouping* is the prescription for addressing students' instructional needs and is an acceptable and appropriate practice, when based on an effective, sound, and comprehensive curriculum.

As a sound academic teaching convention, the instructor has to start at a skill level that youngsters understand, so they can build on that knowledge base to further understand concepts that will lead to achievement. The use of ability grouping can be very effective. Harper's Choice staff were becoming more adept at differentiating instruction, looking at various ways to tailor instruction that would accommodate children's learning experiences and levels of performance. We offered extra classes, as appropriate, to accommodate small groupings of students who were devoid of the basic skills needed to be successful in, say, mathematics or reading. Some may see use of tracking or ability grouping as a matter of semantics; I do not, and the opportunity to group students in need of remedial assistance proved very successful throughout the years. There are those school officials who will avoid such practices, based on ignorance or timidity, and when communities and their schools lack sound reasoning or kowtow to political correctness, they undermine excellence in teaching and learning.

In a Brookings Institution op-ed, author Tom Loveless cites a Washington, DC, area school system that paid consultants $100,000 for a study on how it teaches mathematics. The culprit for the persistent gaps in achievement—white and Asian students scoring significantly higher than black and Hispanic students—was tracking, and they recommended that it be abolished. The author goes on to explain why the conclusions of the consultants were faulty, that citing tracking as responsible for the achievement gaps was purely a fiction:

> The consultants provided no evidence that putting everyone in the same classes will close the achievement gaps but nevertheless recommended abolishing the high schools' three-track system, which includes advanced placement classes for seniors. But they didn't investigate whether students who struggle with arithmetic will benefit from taking classes in higher math.
> They also didn't ask whether students ready for calculus are held back by being in the same classroom with stu-

dents learning fractions. And they didn't see whether the race gap has narrowed in neighboring jurisdictions that claim to have reduced tracking.

Would getting rid of tracking help? It's doubtful. The best research has found that tracking has no significant effect on achievement. As James A. Kulik of the University of Michigan has demonstrated, *the best results come when curriculum is tailored to different levels, targeting the academic deficiencies of low-performing students* and allowing high performers to accelerate to a level at which they're challenged. So how do we get more minorities into upper-level courses and close the achievement gap? Better preparation in the lower grades is key.[22]

In reiteration, when we had a specific number of students in need of shoring up basic skills in reading or mathematics, we provided a specific class to address those learning deficits. These teachers provided direct instruction, not the cooperative grouping that is often practiced, where students learned to master basic arithmetic and were pushed relentlessly to reach higher. Such was how they would later find themselves in high school on par with student classmates, feeling more confident about their academic experience.

At Harper's Choice Middle, we recognized the importance of solid preparation, and as a professional learning community, we recognized that for both student and teacher, parents, and school administrators, nothing replaced hard work, grit, and passion. School administrators indeed should provide the delivery system and structure the learning environment such that student commitment behaviors result in learning, good grades, and post–high school success. I differ with some of the prevailing research done in education, and with regard to this issue, I maintain that offering a multitrack course selection system is a proven strategy that school systems should consider.

Interesting and encouraging, as well, were students' opinion that family, from their point of view, is the backbone for providing student encouragement. Family is followed by teachers and friends at the elementary and middle school levels and by those high school students receiving A/B grades. Those high school students receiving D/E grades rank order family, friends, then teachers.[23]

In light of school-age youngsters citing the importance of family, it is important to emphasize that marriage, education, work, and personal responsibility are basic yet solid requisites that lead to a productive, fulfilled life for every person of every race, and this will build stronger, more productive, and caring communities.

Realizing all the time, effort, love, and caring that so many expend on educating and raising our youth, bolstering student lives, renewing communities, and instilling hope in so many, society can ill afford the continued poor judgment exercised on the part of so many men and women—too often young boys and girls. Arguably, nothing is more unwise, more damaging to communities and our country's social fabric than the repeated issue of having children out of wedlock. It is foolish, it is reckless, and it denies so much of what life has to offer to those infants born into this world without a father, and frequently, a caring, supportive, and competent mother. Society is all too familiar with the pathology of problems that await a child born out of marriage, including the fact that for children living in single-parent homes, the odds of living in poverty are great.[24]

Good mothers are smart, talented, and driven. They teach their children the value of confidence, they are patient, they give unconditional love. Stay-at-home moms are multi-tasking organizers, social planners, shoppers, housekeepers, chauffeurs, a kind of all-purpose family glue. So mothers are instrumental to a child growing up. It is equally important and equally true that fathers matter—a lot. Manhattan Institute's MacDonald clarifies that fathers, on average, bring a set of values and norms to child-rearing, such as self-reliance, discipline, honor, and courage that complements what mothers bring to the table. Loss of that symmetry has an overwhelming negative effect on children, far more important than the economic support that fathers bring to a marriage. A marriage that is whole has twice as much kinship, allowing each of the two parents to spot the other when one is exhausted. The current unrest regarding the anarchy, looting, rioting across the country is preceded by a breakdown of the family; prisons are filled largely with fatherless men, cites MacDonald.

It should be said up front that all youngsters need to be cared for by someone—no matter the family composition—who loves, supports, and provides them with a stable, loving, beautiful home. Boys and girls who are fortunate enough to have such a life often go on to live wholesome, productive, happy, and successful lives.

Having said that, my experience as a school administrator and married father has been that a youngster's ideal living condition is, in fact, having and being raised by a loving, caring, and supportive mom and dad, both of whom are actively involved in their child's life, interacting with one another, with the child going places with mom and/or dad, watching mom and dad go off to work, a marriage and life entirely devoid of drama, absent of any family disruption, and where a child grows up, in the words of author, columnist, and radio personality Larry Elder, "with a solid moral, spiritual, and financial foundation."

Not all children, of course, have such a storied, beautiful existence. The issue of absentee fathers is a big deal. Many of our problems in crime control and community revitalization are strongly related to father absence. We know, for example:

- Sixty-three percent of youth suicides are of children from fatherless homes.
- Ninety percent of all homeless and runaway youths are from fatherless homes.
- Eighty-five percent of children who exhibit behavioral disorders are from fatherless homes.
- Seventy-one percent of high school dropouts are from fatherless homes.
- Seventy percent of youths in state institutions are from fatherless homes.
- Seventy-five percent of adolescent patients in substance abuse centers are from fatherless homes.
- Eighty-five percent of rapists motivated by displaced anger are from fatherless homes.[25]

Without fathers as social and economic role models, many boys try to establish their manhood through sexually predatory behavior, aggressiveness, or violence. These behaviors interfere with schooling, the development of work experience, and self-discipline. Many poor children who live apart from their fathers are prone to becoming court involved. Once that occurs, their records of arrest and conviction often block access to employment and training opportunities. Criminal histories often lock these young persons into underground or illegal economies.[26]

America has a national out-of-wedlock birth average of 40 percent, the proportions of which are 29 percent for white, 53 percent for Hispanic, and 71 percent for blacks, cites Joseph Chamie, a demographer and a former director of the United Nations Population Division.[27]

It is especially pernicious in cities like Baltimore; Washington, DC; Detroit; St. Louis; Chicago; and other cities across the nation.

Take Chicago, as an example, where 2016 data from the Cook County Department of Health show that in suburban Cook County, an astounding 86 percent of babies born to black women between the ages of eighteen and twenty-nine were born out of wedlock. It's been said that making a child is not hard to do; raising a child and conveying the values and rules that make for a successful life and responsible adulthood is. It's particularly important, now that popular culture largely dismisses these truths, says Star Parker, founder and president of the Center for Urban Renewal and Education. She goes on to cite that "in black communities, politics and the Left dominate with the message that life is unfair because of racism, that the answer is big government."[28]

According to Gretchen Livingston, senior researcher at Pew Research Center, about one-third of U.S. children are living with an unmarried parent, and about one in five of those children is living with a solo mom. All told, twenty-four million U.S. children younger than eighteen are living with an unmarried parent. The share of children who are living with an unmarried parent varies by race and ethnicity. More than half (58 percent) of black children are living with an unmarried parent—47 percent with a solo mom. At the same time, 36 percent of Hispanic children are living with an unmarried parent, as are 24 to 29 percent of white children. The share of Asian children living with unmarried parents is markedly lower at 13 percent.[29]

The same Pew Research Center statistics reveal that only 36 percent of black children under eighteen years of age live with married parents, as compared to 62 percent of Hispanics, 74 percent of white, and 85 percent of Asian kids.[30]

The issue of out-of-wedlock births is alarming and, in my view, arguably a national crisis. The matter figures prominently among the reasons why so many newborns start out in life with their hands tied behind their backs, and should this irresponsible behavior continue unabated, we will continue to see news stories similar to this attention grabber: A Maryland local Fox45 News investigative team, Project Baltimore, reported their paging through sixteen thousand lines of data, noting that of Baltimore City's thirty-nine high schools, thirteen had zero students proficient in math, another six high schools where 1 percent tested proficient. In half the high schools in Baltimore City, some 3,804 students took the state test; fourteen were proficient in mathematics.[31] These are shameful statistics that are repeated in cities throughout the country. We can do better!

The reader will recall in an earlier chapter my "weekend ball-playing" with students at times asking me, "Mr. Wallis, what do you have to do to be successful, to make money?" Sometimes the question would result in a lengthy conversation, in which they would actively participate and always seemed to enjoy. I would talk about the "success sequence," a commonsense rule of thumb that actually turns up in research about the requirements for achieving middle class success. Again, for the reader, I clarified that the youngsters needed to do well in school—academically and behaviorally—and graduate from high school, get a job, marry (if they chose to do so) after the age of twenty-one, then have children, should they choose to become parents. If they knocked any of those out of sequence, they were likely heading to poverty.[32]

Decades of research and reporting tout the importance of marriage, education, work, and personal responsibility as keys to a vibrant, productive, and successful life. "One key fact that keeps getting ignored is that the poverty rate among black married couples has been in single digits every year since 1994. Behavior matters and facts matter, more than the prevailing social visions or political empires built on those visions,"[33] says author and economist Sowell, citing a truth often ignored in our conversations on American culture today. He rightly cites the research (and common sense) that the drivers of poverty—and inequality, for that matter—revolve around family structure, education attainment, and workforce participation.

Any in-depth study of American education will always reveal the ever-important role that family plays in a child's school success. The reader is aware of the emphasis that I, as school principal, placed on a "shared partnership" with parents and families in the education of their youngsters. You will recall the results of the fifty-year-old Coleman Report and the years-later Shaker Heights study that the consistent variables explaining the differences in scores within each racial group or ethnic group were *family structure and the educational and economic attainment of the parents,* as well as the pivotal importance of *the attitudes of parents and caregivers at home and peers at school of students toward education.*

Schools can and should do a lot more to strengthen the educational outcomes of children, but they can only do so much, and if we fail to do more to strengthen families in terms of structure, process, and economics, we will not get as far as we could in bridging racial divides as well as emerging economic divides in American schools, says Heritage Foundation education research director Lindsey Burke. She cites research indicating a "growing kind of gender gap, where boys are more likely than girls to be floundering in our schools today, particularly lower-income boys."[34] She continues:

> These reports suggest that family structure plays an important part in the creation of this gender gap. Lower-income boys without fathers in the home are particularly likely to be floundering at school and to be suspended in school, as evidenced by studies conducted in Florida and Arizona and elsewhere.[35]
>
> If we are interested in addressing both the economic divide and the gender divide in our schools, we need to be

thinking much more about strengthening families and figuring out ways to get more and more fathers back into the home to help raise and to be good role models for their children, and their sons, in particular.

Unless and until we do that work of strengthening the family, of bringing more fathers into the picture, we will not make as much progress as we otherwise might in bridging the economic divides, the racial divides, and the gender divides in American life when it comes to the schools.

That is why we need to think more about how to strengthen families.

We need to think about ways in which schools can talk more about the success sequence and educate children in both public and private schools about the importance of finishing high school, working full time in their 20s, and then marrying before having any children.[36]

Circumstances do not determine destiny, but attitudes and decision-making do. Many single moms turn out decent, law-abiding children, often without the assistance of the child's father. But pressures of time, energy, and money make it more difficult for a single mom to inculcate the values necessary to create a healthy, well-adjusted adult, says Elder. He further posits that "caring, loving parents remain the greatest factor in creating a self-reliant, upwardly mobile, confident adult. A society ignores these lessons at great cost."[37]

The ESPN documentary *The Last Dance* explores the childhoods of basketball greats Michael Jordan and Scottie Pippen, clarifying how parental figures loomed large in both of their lives, speaking of lessons learned from examples set by their parents—both parents.

Nationally syndicated radio host Armstrong Williams, wrote a commentary on the documentary, in which he stated the following:

> Core familial stability is something that, sadly, is sorely lacking today, especially in African American households. The replacement of husbands and fathers by "baby daddies" has been outright destructive for the social fabric of the black community. What a difference it makes when role models live under the same roof, and young black men feel a deep sense of connection and commitment to both of their parents, as well as their siblings.[38]

The bottom line is that anyone unable to support herself should not start a family, as it will likely lead to hardship and heartache for the mother, family members, and the community. The child is very likely to be poor, have low educational attainment, and have a generally difficult life. On the other hand, if we can stanch this scourge, we will have a better educated, more productive workforce, wealthier families, and more stable households, which will make for improved communities and a stronger, ever-more-vibrant American society.

A vigorous economy throughout the country is yet another factor that can well figure meaningfully in the creation of strong(er), potentially high performing schools, including in our urban neighborhoods. But first a note:

> It is necessary and important to comment on the worldwide outbreak of a disease that occurred as I was writing this book. Countries throughout the world, including the United States, experienced rapid transmission of COVID-19, the disease caused by the novel coronavirus, within Asia and to Europe and North America from the Chinese

city of Wuhan. As a result, the United States has since been dealing with one of the greatest political, social, and economic challenges since the Great Depression. Among the challenges were so-called lockdowns, which affected schools, businesses, travel, education, worship services, sporting events, social gatherings, restaurants, entertainment, and other activities.[39]

President Trump at the time established "Operation Warp Speed," a program designed to produce and deliver three hundred million doses of safe, effective vaccines by January 2021, as part of a broader strategy to accelerate development, manufacturing, and distribution of COVID-19 vaccines, therapeutics, and diagnostics (collectively known as countermeasures).[40] News that pharma companies could secure authorization for a COVID-19 vaccine in weeks sparked hopes that the global economy could bounce back strongly.[41] Investors' hopes for a stronger economy sent stock markets soaring. According to the international weekly newspaper *The Economist*, "even before the news of a vaccine broke, the speed of America's economic bounce back was exceeding forecasts and surpassing others in the rich world."[42]

A robust economy figures greatly in the lives of all Americans, affecting all aspects of work employment, savings, schools, investments, housing, marriage, and personal responsibility. A major boon for the country is the fact that the economy under the Trump administration had been off the charts. The Bureau of Labor Statistics' September 2019 Economic News Release cited an increase in the number of people employed. The U.S. unemployment rate was at a near-historic low of 3.7 percent for the third month in a row, with unemployment rates among the major worker groups at 3.4 percent for adult men, 3.3 percent for adult women, 12.6 percent for teenagers, 3.4 percent for whites, 5.5 percent for blacks, 2.8 percent for Asians, and 4.2 percent for Hispanics.[43] Major media outlets cited favorable, if not, glowing reports on the economy. CNN Business reported black unemployment fell to a record low, citing an Economic Policy Institute report of "prolonged strength of the U.S. labor market, where employers had been adding jobs for 107 straight months, and unemployment nationwide was near a 50-year low."[44] Black Enterprise, a black-owned multimedia company, stated that "unemployment among workers who identified themselves as Hispanic or Latino fell to a whopping 4.2%." The U.S. economy at the time reflected "the smallest gap on record, regarding unemployment rates for blacks and whites."[45]

Other national news outlets—*The Associated Press, Census Bureau,*[46] the *Washington Post,* Reuters, the *New York Times,* the *Washington Examiner,* Daily Caller, CNS News, and the U.S. Bureau of Labor Statistics—all reported positive trends in the American economy.[47]

In line with the country's vigorous economic climate at the time was a particular national market that was offered called "Opportunity Zones," part of the Trump administration's 2017 Tax Cuts and Jobs Act. I believe such ideas hold great promise for communities, their schools, and education in general throughout the country. Such a program would appear to show assurance in addressing the multigenerational nature of neighborhood inequality throughout cities and communities.

An opportunity zone is an economically distressed community where new investments, under certain conditions, may be eligible for preferential tax treatment.[48] Localities qualify as opportunity zones if they have been nominated for that designation by the state and if that nomination has been certified by the Secretary of the U.S. Treasury via his delegation of authority to the Internal Revenue Service. Such communities are dealing with low quality education, crime, and low median income. These opportunity zones serve to answer the question, "What is being done to help underserved communities?" The idea is to unleash private capital and to partner with public investment for the revitalization of these communities. Such would provide tax incentives to encourage those with capital gains to invest in low-income and undercapitalized communities. As it is, many of these communities have few, if any, businesses, providing less, if any, revenue, resulting in low property values. A well-thought-out plan, however, that would secure one's investment and ensure that future employees could work in a safe and secure area could well mean providing to these areas more successful businesses, which pay local taxes, which help to pay for local schools. Community leaders, public officials, faith-based leaders, developers, and education leaders (including community area school principals) should capitalize on such a potential opportunity to look at ways that, together, an entire community can work in concert to spur meaningful economic development and job creation, and thereby see these communities—and the schools located within—come alive and be safe, warm, rejuvenated, and welcoming places for parents, their youngsters, and their teachers.

This kind of economic expansion affects in a positive manner the issues surrounding race, education, work, poverty, personal responsibility, marriage, and out-of-wedlock births, because each is among the issues that impact families, students, schools, and the achievement gap. As men find themselves out of work, suffering the loss of a steady income, families tend to fall apart; women naturally are not as interested in someone who cannot provide for them and a family. It snowballs and becomes disastrous for communities, negatively affecting schools and any notion of safe streets. Such a booming economy is very promising and will require that everyone—together—look at how best to provide the greatest opportunities for our children.

No matter the political party or political figure occupying 1600 Pennsylvania Avenue, healthy national policies that look at neighborhood investment and revitalization throughout the country hold out the potential—and hope—for building successful, more high-performing schools. Such will lead to healthier families, stronger communities, and an increasingly more competitive, more promising America.

Our schools throughout the country must accept the cards dealt to them, in spite of less-than- favorable societal or community conditions. I argue that staffing schools should be done according to community-specific needs, rather than a kind of one-size-fits-all budget or staffing allocation. National, state, and local leaders responsible for funding schools should do so with an eye for ensuring that specific schools have adequate materials, equipment, resources, technology, extended-day programs, as well as "wraparound" social services supports needed, including additional school-based counselors, pupil psychologists, pupil personnel workers, and the like to ensure that such things as counseling, health checkups, food, mentoring/tutoring, clothing, and appropriate housing are being met. As principal of Harper's Choice Middle, not a single academic year went by when I was not arguing for additional staffing to meet the needs of my school community.

Nationally, we might take a page from the Pentagon's schools, cited earlier in the book, as these schools have taken on the challenge of minimizing achievement gaps with some positive results. The reader will recall the unusual academic success of those schools on our military bases throughout the United States, a favorable outcome enjoyed at our military compounds throughout the world. Harper's

Choice mirrored, with success, some of the traits exhibited in these schools.

We should also avoid wasting time, resources, and millions of taxpayer dollars on a cottage industry targeting a specific race; as I have maintained, the better, more meaningful metric is results, the effect of which will promote a more meaningful human connection among staff, students, and their families. On that note, the U.S. Department of Education should ensure that any funding to schools is, in fact, supporting research-based best practices that meaningfully advance instruction and learning and not ineffective and misguided programs like the race-based programs cited earlier. And most importantly, not a dime of taxpayer funding should be released to any school district that has infused into its curriculum offerings the poisonous, anti-American critical race theory nonsense. In fact, schools and American citizens that fund them would be well-served if such toxic programs were outlawed.

The Title I school program would be an example of one such avenue at the disposal of national officials to ensure that such anti-American venom does not infect our school-age youngsters and their families. Title I is outlined in the Elementary and Secondary Education Act (ESEA), our oldest and largest federally funded education program, according to the U.S. Department of Education. It dates from 1965, and its main purpose has been to help underprivileged children meet challenging state academic standards. Schools with a student base that is lower income are provided with Title I funding in order to help those who are behind or at risk of falling behind, aiming to bridge the gap between low-income students and other students. The financial assistance is provided through state educational agencies (SEAs) to local educational agencies (LEAs) and public schools.

There are thousands of Title I schools nationwide, and they provide students with extra instructional support beyond the regular classroom to help low-achieving children meet state standards in core academic subjects. They coordinate and integrate resources and services from federal, state, and local sources. To be considered for Title 1 school funds, at least 40 percent of the students must be considered low-income.[49] The fund provides over $14 billion a year to school systems all over the country for struggling students (students who are at risk of failing or living at or near poverty), and it reaches over six million students, primarily in the elementary grades.[50] All the more reason why American taxpayer dollars should be well spent. Funding for school improvement should be aimed at worthwhile, research-based best practices that have been shown to move the instructional performance needle in a manner that will enhance community efforts to change dramatically the trajectory of teacher instruction, student academic performance, and parent satisfaction with their schools nationwide.

Schools and school districts experiencing failure year after year might well consider reading and digesting the contents of this book to understand how professional teaching and support staff, together, accelerated instruction and student academic achievement. They need to put their noses to the grind and research, review, and contact successful schools. As outlined in the chapter on continuous improvement, find what accounts for both schooling and corporate success, and try to replicate the philosophy, programs, and actions taken in a manner tailored to their specific school community. The idea is to commit oneself to a goal (read results), ask hard questions, expect honest answers, and begin to take meaningful action.

Recognize that youngsters frequently provide perspectives that can be insightful and helpful in our efforts to better meet their needs. Focus on what the research shows is essential to increase student achievement over the long term for all students: quality school and school system leadership; an emphasis on character education; well-trained teachers; Effective School Correlates, including clear and high expectations and regular monitoring of student progress. The idea is to be focused, determined, and responsive to improve student academic performance—classroom by classroom, school by school.

Such conversations and deliberations should include the subject of alternative education, specifically ensuring that alternative school venues are available to serve at-risk youngsters whose needs are not being met adequately in their current school. School districts must ensure that they have top-shelf, well-designed, and well-run alternative education centers that offer both a day school and an evening school option. This alternative setting should shape instruction and instructional delivery, which will mean more individualized instruction and personal attention for these youngsters. These schools must have on staff various specialists who can address the emotional and behavioral components that trigger disrespectful or disruptive behaviors in these youngsters. Alternative schools provide much-needed services to those students whose needs are not—cannot—be met in the traditional public school. Meanwhile, those students who attend the regular community public school will feel less anxiety, will feel better about themselves, and will be readily able to commit to their studies without feeling intimidation or fear from other disruptive miscreants who otherwise regularly make the intimidating student's life hellish.

Districts should consider "benchmarking" individual schools, establishing "growth targets" and measuring each school against past performance. Police departments across the country have used numbers—and data-driven statistics—to reduce crime in various precincts. The use of comparative statistics, or CompStat, alluded to earlier in the book, has provided enhanced information sharing and accountability, allowing police to zero in on crime and crime prevention. Similarly, school districts should look with a jeweler's eye at the academic and behavior statistics of individual schools, with an eye for holding school administrations accountable for a school's success. A key element in successful organizations is placing only highly qualified individuals in leadership positions. Provide them with the appropriate support and latitude, then let them do their job. Various interventions and research-based practices can be initiated and supported by school district headquarters staff, and if students' overall academic and behavioral stats remain poor, replace the school principal with someone hungrier, someone with the leadership acumen willing to step to the plate to advance teaching and learning.

School districts regularly fail the total quality management goal of a school's continued successful leadership, uniquely important, in particular, for those previously failing schools that have since made measurable positive gains in the areas of academic performance and student behavior. As a successful principal retires, school system headquarters staff should meet with the succeeding principal before he or she takes the helm. District administrators might clarify the hard work and specific achievements accomplished by the former school principal and administration, the staff, and student body, as well as cooperatively agree on future growth targets and avenues that likely would best reach those newly set targets. The idea is that headquarters staff should want to see no slippage in test scores, student behavior, or parent satisfaction with their school. What a school district should want is continued growth, but goals must be established and measured with appropriate timelines throughout the year if continued success is to come to fruition. Disappointing it is that schools and school systems fail to exercise such quality management practices. Instead, typically when one school principal retires, another is appointed, with the new administration citing standard goals and objectives that they individually set and send to school system headquarters staff, who generally provide a rubber stamp.

The school year ensues, and before you know it, you're looking at the end of another academic year, only to find less-than-stellar student academic achievement, poor student deportment, and low staff morale. Benchmarking, as a quality management measurement indicator, would lend clarity and a more meaningful sense of professionalism that school officials, staff, and the parent community should welcome.

School districts should recognize that academic achievement gains may require smaller class sizes along with additional staff; again, staffing according to community-specific needs. There is considerable research on both sides of class size and its impact and effectiveness on academic achievement. I have found over the years that smaller class sizes can enhance an individual teacher's ability to better manage and more successfully reach those students in need of academic attention. My experience has also been that when schools are serving a "busy demographic" community, it is important to get out there frequently and engage the community. Listen and be responsive to them, and always encourage public participation. Combine that with high standards and expectations, ongoing meaningful professional development, research-based best practices, and accountability—real accountability—and the community is well on its way to improved student academic achievement.

The best-performing school systems worldwide provide high-quality education across the entire system so that all students benefit from excellent instruction, again, "lifting all boats." In a research tract for the Organisation [sic] of Economic and Co-operation Development entitled, "What Makes High-Performing School Systems Different," statistician and researcher Andreas Schleicher elaborates:

> This requires that they set ambitious goals and are clear
> about what students should be able to do.... They encour-

age their teachers to be innovative, to improve their own performance and that of their colleagues, and to pursue professional development opportunities that lead to a better practice (a focus on continuous improvement).

In many education systems, different students are taught in similar ways. Top school systems, however, tend to address the diversity of student needs with differentiated pedagogical practice—without compromising on standards. They realize that ordinary students can have extraordinary talents; and they personalize the education experience so that all students can meet high standards.

Moreover, teachers in these systems invest not just in their students' academic success but also in their well-being.... This requires attracting the strongest principals and the most talented teaching staff to the most challenging classrooms,[51] if these less-than-successful schools are to enhance their chances for teacher proficiency and retention, instructional excellence, parent satisfaction, and student academic performance.

All schools require top-shelf leadership and a first-rate teaching staff, all the more important when staffing a challenging—much less failing—school community. Mistakes happen in the hiring of school officials, both at the district and school levels. Excusing repeatedly poor judgment, however, is misguided and devoid of any sense of principled compassion. Successful organizations understand the pivotal importance of competent leadership. Every school community deserves a strong leader, who creates a vision, motivates staff, and inspires all within the organization to reach high and produce their very finest effort. Only then do schools have a chance to play an active role in creating stronger communities and a healthier society.

We've wasted time in American education emphasizing our racial differences instead of extolling our "similarities," our "sameness," our "oneness," and as we focused too often on the former, we have exacerbated a growing divide. Again, in all things America, *e pluribus unum*, "out of many, one." It's high time we put race and differences aside and look at what binds us, look at what we can do, together, that will increase each individual's trajectory for success. It's high time schools focus on results as the metric toward improving academic achievement and a more fulfilling life for our youngsters and families. We have failed too many times for too many years not to have learned this lesson, and in the process, we continue to fail those we profess to care about, our students; they deserve better. It seems fair to say that the achievement gap will remain in some form for some time, but it is equally fair to recognize that we can—together as community and faith-based leaders, public officials, education officials, and whole communities—take appreciably more meaningful steps in closing or minimizing these gaps by steadfastly zeroing in on community revitalization and, in our schools, ever more solid instructional performance, as we listen and connect with students.

So, yes, we made progress at Harper's Choice Middle, often incremental, in advancing the academic skill level of our students. It was a continuing Herculean effort each day of every academic year. It bears repeating that schools and their communities together need to reflect, to review current practices, to look with a jeweler's eye at what makes for a high-performing school of excellence, and to re-commit, providing an education that will in effect substantively produce youngsters academically prepared for the world of work. That's a formula that can well be applied in one's neighborhood school, from South Central LA to Boston, from Milwaukee to New Orleans; we proved it so at "The Choice."

17

Parents and Schools

My experience as a high school teacher, administrator, and school principal proved time and again over the years that a school's parents are among the most important elements in any school community's success. The parents at Harper's Choice Middle School were as instrumental, if not more so, than any other facet in our school's turnaround. On my arrival to a broken school, I spent time speaking to more than a few emotionally spent, frustrated parents, and I informed them of my educational philosophy and the value that I placed on a shared partnership with the school's parent community. Each time it was like they were breathing in a breath of fresh air.

The reader may recall in the chapter citing the importance of character, former United States Secretary of Education William Bennett observes in *The Book of Virtues* that "there is nothing more influential, more determinant in a child's life than the moral power of quiet example."[1] It is important that parents, teaching staff, and school administrators send a consistent positive message and "walk the talk" when we are working to influence the character of our children. This should begin at the birth of one's first child.

Raising well-adjusted, well-behaved, good children is a remarkably wonderful achievement, singularly more important than any other accomplishment. Years ago, I noted that golf legend Arnold Palmer, so emblematic of that Greatest Generation, remarked on the subject of parenting that "it isn't enough to simply provide the basic necessities, that a parent needs to offer strong direction in attitude and behavior." Former First Lady Jacqueline Kennedy Onassis once remarked that "if you bungle raising your child, I don't think whatever else you do well matters very much." Both she and "The King" were spot-on!

Being a parent isn't easy, as anyone with children is well-aware, but it's not supposed to be easy. It's a loving challenge, one that needs to be met with intelligence and strength. Good parenting is the most important endeavor a person can undertake, and the rewards surpass anything else you do in life. Experience, research, and countless other surveys and studies for years show the correlation between good parenting, student achievement, and school success. Involved parents produce academically successful youngsters, they boost student attendance, they impact their child's social functioning and peer interaction, and parent involvement boosts a child's mental health and sense of self-efficacy.

In my address to parents at our school's first Back-to-School Night (BTSN) the year I took the helm of Harper's Choice, I shared my education philosophy, one that I said they might find different from many school officials throughout the nation. I expressed my high regard for the sanctity of schools and their classrooms. I conveyed to them my respect for the long-held traditional American values of liberty and self-reliance, which required, I informed them, a sound education; for opportunity and competition, which required a good education; and achieving the American Dream, a better life, and a higher standard of living, each of which also required a solid education. I stated that it was our expectation that parents send their children to school prepared and ready to learn, and when they did not, they put an undue burden on the school that affected staff and other students. We, in turn, would pledge to work in concert with parents to provide an effective, quality education to their youngsters.

I mentioned earlier that the list of those parents registered as active members in the PTA was small, and all but a handful had simply stopped volunteering. Imagine our surprise to see that the first year's BTSN was literally several hundred, standing-room-only attendees, parents hungry for a new beginning. Parents in all our schools should well attend those Back-to-School Nights and take the opportunity to get to know your child's teachers and gain a glimpse of the school's organization, resources, academic support initiatives, and direction. It's a good idea to attend the November American Education Week, as well, and take a portion of the day, if possible, to visit classes and to observe instruction and student performance in action. I would regularly advise parents how appreciative we were of those who were able to find time to visit us; further, I would remind parents they were welcome to visit the school anytime.

I remained thankful throughout my years in education that the majority of parents raised terrific children. Many of these parents understood the importance of staying actively involved in their children's lives as they matriculated through high school. In the chapter dealing with partnerships, I wrote about the pivotal importance that parents played in our school's turnaround.

The truth is that parenting—both good and bad—affects a school's environment, a school's teaching-learning culture. Poor parenting is the reason why many school administrators spend an inordinate amount of time dealing with disrespectful, disruptive, frequently violent student behavior. Poor parenting is the reason such a large swath of teachers leave the profession annually. As a society, we can do a better. Too many of our youngsters have poor role models at home, where the culture in the home and community seemingly revolves around athletes, entertainers, and celebrities. The choices made as a family and what families decide to do in their house is far and away more important than what is done in the halls of congress or in the White House. There is a perceived lack of motivation, a kind of apathy on the part of these "parents," and no apparent recognition of the importance of schooling, much less active support of academic excellence in the lives of their children. If only they realized that a more unified approach between the school and home could well result in their children likely understanding the importance of their studies, watching less television and spending less time on social media; developing a positive attitude about their schooling, thereby increasing their regular school attendance; and meaningfully applying themselves in a manner that would find them succeeding that much more in school.

My education career has afforded me the opportunity to observe poor parenting upfront and close; the adult ineptitude of these parents, I reiterate, has a deleterious effect on their children and their academic standing in school, as well as their neighbors' children and the academic instruction occurring in classrooms. Married couples who divorce present still greater emotional burdens on children. There are few threats to this country's future greater than family disintegration, the root of so much of society's ills. Those of us in education have seen more than our share of the sheer sadness in the eyes of students whose mom or dad has left the family, a recognized building block of all great societies.

Schools have our country's youngsters for six hours a day, and the world has them for the remaining eighteen; parents must be the heart of that world! It is critical that we realize our youngsters only get one childhood. Neither teachers nor school administrators can force youngsters to turn off the television at home, to put down the telephone and electronic devices, to do their homework; nor can they force parents to help with and review their child's homework and to ensure that the youngster attends school daily throughout the academic year. As columnist Walter Williams said time and again, "For somebody to do well in school, somebody needs to make him go to bed on time and get a good ten hours of sleep. Someone must make him do his homework. Somebody must feed him breakfast in the morning, and somebody must make him mind his teacher. If those things are not done, I don't care how much money you put in the school system, education will not occur."

Several years ago, at one of the high schools, a married couple stood at my office door, just after having left another administrator's office, looking forlorn and asking me, "What can we do to raise better kids?" I was thinking to myself at that moment that it was too bad they hadn't pondered that question years earlier; their kids at that point were fifteen and seventeen years of age. The question was asked in abject frustration over the repeated challenges they were having with their son and older daughter. While I can't say I knew the family well, as most of their dealings had been with another school administrator, I was aware that there were "issues" between the husband and wife. I told them that kids didn't need drama in their lives, as they encountered enough of that naturally as growing adolescents. I then said that it was important that moms and dads were on the same page, that they were in agreement ahead of time on how best to raise a son or daughter, that it was certainly less confusing to the child, when the parents, together, sent one loving—if not always welcomed or appreciated at the time—message or expectation to their youngster(s).

I then informed them that there were three elements that I always held in high esteem, that I believed were critical, and since they were asking, I said, "As a family, always eat dinner together; second, 'the best thing to hold onto in life is each other' (particularly when the goin' gets tough); and third, 'the most important thing a father can do for his children is to love their mother.' Likewise, (looking at the mother), the best thing you can do is love their dad." The first piece of advice was something my wife and I and our children had always practiced as a family and found to be wholesome and worthwhile; dinner proved a meaningful time for discussions on school or life in general. The second piece of advice came to me by way of a favorite actress when I was growing up, Audrey Hepburn, whom I always thought was as classy as she was smart and insightful, and I always thought it was a wonderful, if not, valuable sentiment. The third piece of advice came by way of an interview I saw of Father Theodore Hesburgh, former president of Notre Dame University some fifty years ago; it struck a chord, and on more than one occasion as a school administrator and principal, I would find myself sharing that advice with others.

There is no question that good parenting plays a positive role in the health of a community's school. As a parent, you are your child's first, most important teacher. Youngsters who feel loved, feel supported, and feel valued, who come from a strong and nurturing home, will likely do extraordinarily well as they matriculate through their school years. That love, guidance, and support from home will add immeasurably to the academic and behavioral climate of one's school. Further, such a home front can only enhance school staff efforts to ensure that students reach their academic potential.

Truth be told, the real role models are those parents who hang in there through the years, who pore over and check their children's homework, demonstrating to their kids that such a process is important and valued; there's a genuine expression of love and care. Parents who demonstrate a positive attitude about schooling and getting an education make an impression on a youngster; what we say and do helps children form their own opinions about school, and in the process, builds self-confidence in themselves as learners, enhancing their chances for academic achievement. Set goals with your children, and work with them in accomplishing those goals. Ensure that you are communicating with teaching staff and that you are accessing and reviewing your youngsters' academic standing in his or her classes by directly communicating with the school or using your school's electronic portal that provides parents an opportunity to stay on top of their children's academic workload and accomplishments.

Thank God there were a number of parents, who jumped at the chance to assist me in rejuvenating our school. Throughout this book, I make mention of the time and effort given by parents assisting teaching staff in classrooms, tutoring students, volunteering in our main administrative office, and serving on various school and PTA committees, all with the purpose of doing their fair share, to be a role model for their kids, and to assist in the total community effort to advance our school.

Parenting is a blessing, and we have but one chance to do it successfully. I will reemphasize that those who do it well have an impact—sometimes huge—on the schools serving their community.

Education blog writer Juliette Sivertsen notes that when parents make the commitment to get involved, they provide a support network for youngsters, particularly important when children face academic hurdles and challenges with friendships. Further, children whose parents stay involved are more likely to have higher self-esteem, be disciplined, have more self-motivation, and achieve better grades, regardless of their ethnic, social, or racial backgrounds. Your involvement allows you to stay on top of and be more sensitive to your child's emotional and social needs, and it will boost your confidence in parenting and any decision-making when it comes to the education of your child.[2]

Students and their families throughout the world are unique and come from different backgrounds, so I would not presume there is only one correct way to raise a child. I can only offer my view of what I believe is appropriate, as a married father of two and Papou to four grandchildren, as well as from my experience and observations in a nearly forty-year education career. There are, however, some generally accepted tried-and-true suggestions that are healthy and loving practices, some of which turn up in the blog "The Military Wife and Mom,"[3] which I share here with the reader:

> You should know something; change starts with one parent and one child at a time. You have a beautiful window of opportunity to build the foundation that your child desperately needs but also craves. The foundation for things like generosity, responsibility, appreciation, warmth, kindness, helpfulness and a hard-work ethic starts during the early years. Here's the hard part. It starts with us—*the parents.* Kids cannot even think at the maturity level needed to break a behavior cycle, let alone do anything about it. So, as the parents, it has to start with us. The foundation for well-adjusted kids always starts with us.

> Here are 13 simple ways that help raise well-adjusted [perhaps "grounded" is a better term] kids. Let's get back to basics.

> *1. Boundaries:* No-brainer, right? But... It's hard to set boundaries for kids and stick to them. This is especially true when kids push back, scream endlessly or threaten things like, "I hate you." Remember that when kids act this way, they are meeting their own needs in the only way they know how. Depending on the boundary, it can take a long time before a child lovingly accepts a parent's boundary

When kids start to push back or scream less, this is actually your child moving towards acceptance of the boundary. If your boundary is like a wall (and not a door that confusingly swings open from time to time), your child will bounce and eventually work to meet his or her need in an alternative way. The world is a very chaotic place. Boundaries help your child, not only feel grounded, but thrive. Check yourself and think about what your real boundaries are. Then remember, they're brick walls, not doors.

2. *Routines:* There's so much of childhood that is new and challenging for kids. Learning self-control and empathy. Learning how to be a friend and interact with others. These are all very BIG things for kids. Using something as simple as printable routine cards can help kids feel grounded and relaxed. In fact, knowing what to expect at mealtimes, mornings and bedtimes can bring a sense of relief to even the most carefree child. Have a strong-willed child? Even better. Routines allow kids to feel a sense of control, something that is very important to a strong-willed child.

3. *Early bedtimes:* Sleep is the building block for healthy brain development. It helps us process the day's events and learn from it. Kids' brains are constantly developing and creating new neural connections. They absolutely must get sleep to nurture these connections. Between kid activities, school and always squeezing in tech time, kids are going to bed later and having a difficult time settling before sleep. One of the most basic things you can do for

your kids' behavior, health and well-being is to help them get the sleep they need.

4. *Empathy:* What do kids really need to be happy and successful? The answer surprises most: Empathy. It's the trait that allows us to "walk in another person's shoes." New research shows that empathy plays a major role in predicting kids' happiness and success. Though kids are hardwired to care, they aren't born empathetic; it's a learned behavior. "Empathy promotes kindness, pro-social behaviors, and moral courage, and it is an effective antidote to bullying, aggression, prejudice and racism. It's why Forbes urges companies to adopt empathy and perspective-taking principles; the *Harvard Business Review* named it as one of the 'essential ingredients for leadership success and excellent performance,'"[4] states psychologist and parenting expert Michele Borba.

5. *Hugs:* [. . .] Pamela Li, creator of Parenting for Brain, says that "hugging triggers the release of oxytocin, also known as the love hormone. This feel-good hormone has many important effects on our bodies. One of them is growth stimulation. Studies show that hugging can instantly boost the level of oxytocin. When oxytocin is increased, several growth hormones, such as insulin-like growth factor-I (IGF-1) and nerve growth factor (NGF), are increased as well. The nurturing touch of a hug can enhance a child's growth."[5]

6. *Playful parents:* Children don't say, 'I had a hard day. [...] Can we talk?' They say, 'Will you play with me?'"[6] says psy-

chologist Lawrence Cohen. We don't reserve much room in our lives for fun and games anymore. Our days are filled with stress, obligations and hard work, and without realizing it, we are more disconnected from our kids than ever. Play is the work of the child and to connect with our kids, we must play with our kids. Taking the time to put down our phones and realize that our *kids need us to play*. It sounds silly, but all the mindless funny cat videos and random tasty recipes will still be there years later; our children won't.

7. *Outdoor time:* Author of *Enlightened Parenting*, Meryl Davids Landau [actually Landau correctly attributes this next quote to pediatric occupational therapist Angela Hanscom, who was interviewed by Landau for an article appearing in the Huffington Post] believes that "movement through active free play, especially outside, improves everything from creativity to academic success to emotional stability. Kids who don't get to do this can have so many issues, from problems with emotional regulation—for example, they cry at the drop of a hat—to trouble holding a pencil, to touching other kids using too much force."[7]

8. *Chores:* Even though it is more difficult at the time to persist in having children do chores, kids benefit from the experience. Research indicates that those children who do have a set of chores have higher self-esteem, are more responsible, and are better able to deal with frustration and delay gratification, all of which contribute to greater success in school. Furthermore, the research shows that involving children in household tasks at an early age can

have a positive impact later in life. In fact, the author of the research states, "the best predictor of young adults' success in their mid-20s was that they participated in household tasks when they were three or four."[8]

9. More screen-time limits: "In order for the brain's neural networks to develop normally during the critical period, a child needs specific stimuli from the outside environment. These are rules that have evolved over centuries of human evolution, but—not surprisingly—these essential stimuli are not found on today's tablet screens. When a young child spends too much time in front of a screen and not enough getting required stimuli from the real world, her development becomes stunted,"[9] writes psychologist Liraz Margalit.

10. Experiences, not things: Parenting writer Sally White states that "children require less [sic] things and far more meaningful experiences. When they grow up, it's not the stuff in their life they will remember, it's that time you tried to catch tadpoles at the lake, or that sandcastle you both built that the wave knocked over at the beach. [...] The best life experiences cost little to nothing, like a picnic in the park, blowing bubbles in the backyard, making chalk drawings on the sidewalk, or tossing a football around, but they all have one thing in common: you do them together. What kids really want in life is quality time spent with their parents."[10]

11. Slow moving days: Clinical psychologist John Duffy advises parents "to take some time to just watch their children, whether they are playing, doing homework, or eating a snack. Take a moment to drink them in. Remember and remind yourself how remarkable your children are. That pause alone, even if momentary, can drive a shift in the pace."[11]

12. *Books—read to them:* "One of the most important things parents can do, beyond keeping kids healthy and safe, is to read with them," according to parenting writer Amy Joyce. "That means starting when they are newborns and not even able to talk, and continuing well beyond the years that they can read by themselves. Study after study shows that early reading with children helps them learn to speak, interact, bond with parents and read early themselves, and reading with kids who already know how to read helps them feel close to caretakers, understand the world around them and be empathetic citizens of the world."[12]

13. *Music:* "Science has shown that when children learn to play music, their brains begin to hear and process sounds that they couldn't otherwise hear. This helps them develop 'neurophysiological distinction' between certain sounds that can aid in literacy, which can translate into improved academic results for kids."[13]

Ongoing research shows that family engagement in schools improves student achievement, reduces absenteeism, and restores parents' confidence in their children's education. Students with involved parents or other caregivers earn higher grades and test scores, have better social skills, and show improved behavior.[14] Further, it is said that being involved also boosts the mental health of children. It encourages communication between children and parents, which can foster higher self-esteem and confidence. It can also help children interact better with their peers and advance their social skills.[15]

Your active, caring involvement is a cornerstone in your youngster's education. Conscientious parents who have lovingly worked at developing, supporting, and raising well-grounded children have also provided their community, our society, an enormous benefit.

18

A Final Word

School communities throughout America have a template for transforming less-than-successful schools to those that can well reach the vast majority of students and their families. I was privileged to work with hard-working staff, students, and parents. We took what was handed to us in the way of ill behavior and failing academic performance and created a first-rate, student-engaged, teacher-respected, parent-proud, and community-appreciated academically strong school setting.

Our country is facing its share of challenges for certain. Yet, I remain hopeful and cautiously optimistic. We have faced larger, more threatening challenges throughout our history, and we have risen to such challenges with determination and resolve. We need to muster that same sense of patriotism, that love and respect for traditional American family values that revolve around caring for one another, courage, guidance, self-reliance, perseverance, support, and love of country. We need to take back our schools and universities and return the focus to their original purpose—learning and valuing the acquisition of knowledge, connecting with one another, appreciating inquiry, and respecting differing perspectives. Only then will youngsters learn to think for themselves and feel equipped to contribute, compete, and participate meaningfully in a democratic society.

I hope that the ideas, suggestions, and policy prescriptions presented within these pages will lead to a more meaningful discussion of how best to improve American education, one that will foster more confident, thoughtful, self-reliant, and balanced students.

A Carnegie Forum on Education and the Economy task force stated that "Success depends on the whole of society coming to place a much higher value not just on schooling but on learning."[1] What happens daily in our K-12 schools should matter—a lot. Schools must be settings that feature first-rate teaching and an atmosphere conducive to scholarship and wholesome extracurricular participation; far too many are not. As a nation, we can produce a higher quality graduate; it's more a matter of will than it is any other challenge or obstacle. As it is presently, it's seemingly right out of The Wizard of Oz—the scarecrow doesn't need a brain; all he needs is a diploma,[2] to borrow a line from humorist Jim Mullen; only there is no humor here, as this is serious stuff.

The public school is a microcosm of our larger society; stay with me for a moment and let's follow this theme, the idea that we should well recognize the noble and important responsibility of educating our citizenry to the best of our ability.

No less than Founding Father and third president of the United States Thomas Jefferson wrote, "I look to the diffusion of light and education as the resource most to be relied on for ameliorating the condition, promoting the virtue and advancing the happiness of man."[3]

I would like to believe that the Harper's Choice community felt that all of us did our level best to carry out Jefferson's notion of education. Given the condition of many of our country's schools, it would be difficult to argue that everyone recognizes this awesome responsibility, and our children, as well as their families, deserve better.

Author's Note: Some of the quoted material that follows will contain variant word spellings and usage common at the time.

Many Americans believe that our Founding Fathers saw freedom and liberty as the cornerstone of our nation, and public schooling as a vehicle to secure it. They also believed that such schooling should be available to rich and poor. Jefferson believed that public education could create more of a meritocracy than an aristocracy, saying:

> Instead of an aristocracy of wealth, of more harm and danger, than benefit, to society, to make an opening for the aristocracy of virtue and talent, which nature has wisely provided for the direction of the interests of society, & scattered with equal hand through all its conditions, was deemed essential to a well ordered republic.[4]

American statesman Samuel Adams much valued the importance of citizens acquiring an education, stating,

> If Virtue & Knowledge are diffused among the People, they will never be enslav'd. This will be their great Security.[5]

Our forefathers undeniably believed in an educated citizenry, again, for the rich and the poor. The colonialists were among the most educated people of their time. This belief on the importance of education and a growing literacy rate in society continued through the Civil War era, when thousands would travel, for example, to hear the Lincoln-Douglas debates. In fact, the United States had one of the highest literacy rates in the world at the time, exceeding 90 percent in some regions, quite extraordinary for the time period.[6] One can argue, and it appears generally accepted, that our Founding

Fathers were talking essentially about public schools, even though most schools in the middle colonies were run by a variety of religious groups.[7] Our second president of the United States, John Adams, on addressing education and democracy, famously stated in 1785 that,

> The Whole People must take upon themselvs the Education of the Whole People and must be willing to bear the expences of it. There should not be a district of one Mile Square without a school in it, not founded by a Charitable individual but maintained at the expence of the People themselvs they must be taught to reverence themselvs instead of adoreing their servants their Generals Admirals Bishops and Statesmen.[8]

Fast-forward some 245 years. I believe that our Founding Fathers never would have envisioned, nor imagined, never believed, never would have understood how any school should so forsake its awesome sense of responsibility and provide such a poor education, producing such an inferior product that is evident in so many cities, so many communities throughout America today.

I would hope that a number of communities throughout the country would well consider the philosophy and practices cited in this book, looking at Harper's Choice Middle at the time and the scores of other schools throughout the country that are successful and turning out educated, well-adjusted students as they look to turn around their own challenging school settings. While our efforts produced some very favorable results as compared to where we were when I took the helm of Harper's Choice, the efforts are only what worked for us, and we felt fortunate and proud. Though I believe much of what we employed and accomplished can be replicated in countless school communities, they are not a cure-all, and many schools may well have other ideas and approaches that have worked and continue to work well for them; indeed, as the reader of this book well knows, a number of instructional ideas that we employed at Harper's Choice with great success were, in fact, tried successfully in other locations throughout the United States and discovered by way of our relentless focus on continuous improvement.

As the Founding Fathers were about providing what we would call an education for the general population, the public, they were also very much about an individual's unalienable right to life, liberty, and the pursuit of happiness. They were about market freedom, competition, and choices afforded to individuals. The annual paltry results of the National Assessment for Educational Progress would appear to argue for expanding educational choice throughout America, if we are to enhance efforts to improve overall student academic achievement. Further, given the hue and cry today cited earlier over the recklessness of schools pushing identity politics and a poisonous curriculum on innocent school-age youngsters, citizens and lawmakers should well weigh the benefits of offering school choice throughout America. School Choice is an issue that has been bandied about for decades. It is a term that represents various ways that students may access their K-12 education; in essence, it would allow public education funds to follow the students to schools that parents feel would best fit their child's needs. Traditionally, youngsters are assigned to a specific public school, but school choice would give parents the power and opportunity to make a different school selection.

Most immediately, however, what might we do about those communities that year after year appear not to "get it" and continue to operate persistently failing schools? What to be done with those communities, towns, and cities that continue not to make their schools safe, warm, inviting venues for teaching excellence and student academic achievement? Specific communities with persistently failing schools must provide these children and their parents another school choice option, if their youngsters are to receive what they rightfully deserve—a fair, meaningful, and complete education. As offered above, school choice alone brings with it the efficiencies of the marketplace. Our youngsters' first teachers, their parents, ought well be afforded the right of choosing what is in their child's best interest, particularly when it would appear to parents in so many cities and neighborhoods across the country that community-elected and unelected "leaders" care not a whit about the hordes of children trapped, "stuck" in failing schools. Certainly, our Founding Fathers would not have approved of forcing kids to remain in such conditions.

There are those who might see a public school educator supporting school choice as an apostate. Not at all. This is not about abandoning public schools. Public schools are here to stay; they can and do provide a meaningful education throughout our country; we did so at Harper's Choice. The reality, however, is that until such change evolves in some of these communities, we need to throw a life preserver to those children, thousands upon thousands of children, who are drowning in a sea of despair. Compulsory attendance laws and a ready supply of youngsters in cities, neighborhoods, and rural communities across the country provide no incentive, much less competition that might otherwise serve to improve many public schools. Add to that the overwhelming number of myopic or incompetent political leaders, feckless school officials, and incompetent teachers too often found in these settings (though there are those professionals who are hard-working and doing the best they can within very challenging circumstances) and you have a recipe for continued failure that is inherently and patently unfair to thousands of parents and their youngsters.

States have a few immediate reasonable options that should be entertained to address the scores of American students attending failing schools. Provide an immediate taxpayer refund to parents of school-age youngsters who are not receiving an appropriate education. This would be a prorated portion of their property taxes that might be placed in a restricted-use, education-only account that is student-centered, allowing parents to use these dollars to choose a specific school for their child, a school they know to be safe and that will provide a meaningful, enriching education.

Absent a taxpayer refund, the introduction of formal school choice expansion as cited above could well be another option, one that should be viewed as complementing traditional public schools, providing alternatives to parents and children who are wholly deserving of another alternative, another course of action. Such options, including charter schools, work hard at attracting parents and their youngsters; they understand the importance of competing daily to hire excellent teaching staff, to insist on student behavioral and academic excellence, and to increase a parent's commitment and support of schooling that they know will provide safe, warm, and inviting venues that win the support of and enhance the overall quality of life in these communities.

State governments, in fact, have the constitutional authority to enact school choice policies. Since schools are generally funded on a per-student basis, state lawmakers, for example, could offer and pass legislation on education savings accounts for K-12 students, allowing parents, as cited earlier, to have their education dollars follow them to the education program of their choice, be it a private school setting, or pay for individual courses, on-line learning, private tutoring, or a variety of other education services. Taxpaying parents deserve this financial leverage. Those who argue against school choice maintain that somehow those who advocate for such options to public schools (vouchers, individual tax credits and deductions, charter schools, tax-credit scholarships, the education savings accounts just explained, among a dozen or so options that have been developed) "ignore the collective interests as a society," that such a program would lead to "educational inequality."[9] For goodness' sake, those making such arguments seem not to mind the loathsome, offensive, often frightful conditions that so many of these families face daily.

Many of these naysayers send their own kids to other "choice"—read private—schools, and then have the unmitigated temerity to chastise school choice advocates. Meanwhile, those youngsters trapped in failing schools continue to brave trying conditions walking to and from school, while regularly enduring disrespectful behavior, intimidation, and repeated interrupted instruction during the school day, every school year. Our forefathers would have seen our current dilemma as such a stain on American society that they would never have tolerated such a condition. It is as though many in society—including those overseeing many of our school districts—have embraced an overly indulgent, tolerant, dismissive philosophy that makes everything relative, with no moral anchor that clarifies right from wrong. However, a decision of right and wrong made from a philosophy of relativism is innately unfair to the scores of students, teaching staff, and families who do live their lives with an inner moral compass. Their rights, their feelings, and their liberties ought well be affirmed and respected, as well.

Choice detractors often bellow that the answer lies in providing still more money to schools, but that is not an appropriate argument in my view. It is not about providing more funding for schools, though I admittedly and feverishly fought every year for our share of funding, staffing, and programs. The majority of our improvements, in fact, were a result of a different philosophy regarding how schools should operate, electing to utilize our resources in a more efficient fashion as to how I would choose to use teaching allotments, how we would make better use of human resources in the way of instructional teams that would result in additional and more meaningful student interventions, as well as how I employed outside partnerships to enhance our instructional efforts.

It is worth noting that taxpayers have spent north of two trillion dollars since President Lyndon Johnson launched the education component of his War on Poverty in 1965.[10] Beyond annual federal dollars toward K-12 education, the National Center for Education Statistics cites that state and local taxpayers anted up another $706 billion just in school year 2015–2016 alone,[11] which makes our federal expenditure a fraction of the total spent on schools annually. What have the American taxpayers received on their investment? Academic achievement outcomes that have been generally flat, with only 12 percent of twelfth graders testing proficiently in U.S. History, 25 percent testing proficiently in mathematics, and 37 percent testing proficiently in reading, according to the National Assessment of Educational Progress.[12]

As a public school principal, I would have put our program up against any other school choice option at the time, but if these public schools continue not to be able to provide safe and successful teaching-learning environments, for heaven's sake, give these children a shot at success by providing them a viable option and investigate how school choice might result in offering focused, substantive, and meaningful teaching and learning that could well be their ticket to lifelong productivity, success, and happiness. Our nation's leaders need to review the plight of these youngsters and their families and respond affirmatively in their favor.

I mentioned the issue of vocational education in an early chapter of the book, not because the issue played any major role in this school's turnaround, but because any discussion of American education should include the trades and fine arts programs, and I shared my perspective earlier on the fine arts.Originally passed by the United States Congress in 1917, the Smith-Hughes Act authorized federal funding for vocational education in American schools. At the time, our country was experiencing enormous economic and social change as factories were facing a shortage of skilled labor in a rapidly industrializing society. Vocational-technical programs in schools across the nation filled the void for decades. My years as a school administrator included exposure to successful "vo-tech" programs that catered to those families whose youngsters were not interested in the more rigid academic programs, who had no interest in attending a college or university, many of whom were smart and possessed unique talents or potential in the trade skills and often were offered employment upon graduation. They served internships with local employers, and a number of them later went on to start their own companies. Just as I believe youngsters should have access to the fine arts, so, too, should those with an interest and aptitude for the trades have opportunities to explore those areas, as well.

However, benighted school administrators, local boards of education, and politicians have provided a disservice to the country with their feeling of superiority and an unenlightened, disparaging, and condescending view of the vocational trades; many of these individuals decided it best to jettison vocational-technical trade programs that were very much a part of the public school curriculum and served many communities well. Educators, students, parents, and employers criticized the action as senseless, a decision, they voiced, that would come back to haunt communities. The exercise in poor judgment proved foolhardy, and today is seen by many as a needlessly self-destructive overreaction to criticism of schools needing to boost academic rigor. Many educators, counselors, and school officials had this supercilious, disdainful, and misguided viewpoint that youngsters absolutely had to attend college or university if they planned to make anything of themselves in this world, no matter that scores of folks with college degrees are often unable to find work and are saddled with college debt. Welders, for crying out loud, make more money than philosophers. Georgetown University's Center on Education and the Workforce found that thirty million jobs in the United States do not require a bachelor's degree and they pay an average of $55,000 a year. Many of these positions are found in the technology sector, as well.

Presently we've a serious skills gap throughout the country. Manufacturing and construction industries are struggling to find qualified carpenters, truck drivers, diesel mechanics, painters, construction managers, welders, electricians, HVAC technicians, and bricklayers. The Great Recession of 2008–2009 saw a drain on the trades industries, and when the subprime mortgage crisis resulted in the collapse of the housing bubble, over a million construction workers changed careers or retired, creating an ever-more imperative that we provide opportunities for those interested in these fields. Contractors cannot find laborers who can build competently. Finding skilled labor isn't only a problem for building new homes and infrastructure; it's also a major issue after any natural disaster. A sufficient number of trained workers simply couldn't be found to help with the reconstruction of water-damaged cities following Hurricanes Harvey, Irma, and Maria.[13]

When I was a youngster growing up, many who were employed in trade-skills were very much part of the foundation of middle-class prosperity that allowed them to own homes, own a car or truck, send their children to college, and take reasonable vacations—nothing glamorous, but then many could not have cared less about glamour. They lived a good, decent life and felt they had dignity and worth. We need a return of those values that seemed ingrained in those post–World War II men and women we call the Greatest Generation.

Certainly, we can urge our local, state, and national lawmakers to take action based on solid research and best practices to provide opportunities for every citizen to achieve the American dream—that if they work hard and obtain an education, all citizens can make a good life for themselves and their families. A very good start would be to return a technical and trades curriculum to high schools as another option of study within the curriculum. Such a move will immediately impact youngsters, their families, and the surrounding communities, presenting these kids at graduation with opportunities to extend training, or with the requisite training and knowledge, grasp onto any one of the millions of jobs available to those prepared to work. That's how we'll provide a better standard of living, allow better job security for all, and begin to build a larger middle class. Doing so would be a far better bargain for Americans than enduring a welfare state and mentality that continues to steal a person's dignity, provides no incentive to work or to improve one's stature, and puts a drain on society.

I appreciate the various people associated with organizations like SkillsUSA, a partnership of students, teachers, and industry working together to ensure America has a skilled workforce.[14] Television host Mike Rowe is among those who have made it their mission to recognize the need for youngsters to be presented more fully, more honestly, and with a degree of respect the millions of opportunities that await those who have a penchant for, or an interest in, opportunities other than the university or military arena.[15] Our economy very much needs a different, fairer, and more accurate beneficial view on this issue if we're to confront in a meaningful manner any discussion of income inequality, poverty, and opportunity in our country.

Every year a minimum of several hundred thousand students (some researchers cite estimates as high as 1.2 million, which equates to 1 every 26 seconds, or 7,000 a day) drop out of high school.[16] Over the years a number of high school student dropouts expressed to me their frustration or disdain for academic-level coursework. I also knew that an effective vocational-technical program could be uniquely effective in stanching the exodus of many of these youngsters. As cited by the Alliance for Excellent Education, most people recognize the heavy yoke that high school dropouts place around their necks. What few understand, however, is the negative affect that hundreds of thousands of high school dropouts have on a community's economic, social, and civic health. Those without a high school diploma account for the overwhelming majority of individuals serving time in local jails, state prisons, and federal correctional facilities. High school dropouts are also generally less healthy, require more medical care, and die earlier. Dropouts earn about $8,000 a year less than high school graduates and approximately $26,500 a year less than college graduates. On the other hand, fewer annual school dropouts would result in a decrease in criminal behavior and realize substantial savings at the local, state, and federal spending levels. Moreover, ensuring that additional students remain in school and receive the knowledge and skills necessary to be successful at the university level, in the military, or in any of the millions of jobs available in the trades and world of work would have tremendous benefits for the national economy.[17] Who knows how many of our students who dropped out of school might well have stayed if they felt people cared enough about them and their future. An effective vocational-education program could be a key component in connecting with many of these students.

As the reader of this book well knows, the work of schools—teaching and learning—is about relationships, connecting, and at times communicating hope; the school, its teachers, and its leadership must genuinely have the students' interests at heart. These are among the ways to keep students in school and actively pursuing a diploma or certification that will see them gainfully employed when they leave school; vocational training programs are one such avenue.

Everyone of sound mind wants to work, wants to feel that he or she is contributing to family and a community. The issue—in this case, the need to ensure that our school-age youngsters are employable upon graduation—is more than financial or economic. One of the institutions that holds a nation together and gives people their identity—a shared identity, a sense of belonging—is the dignity of work and the importance of family and community. It contributes to the soul and health of our nation. When multiplied by thousands of American citizens, we're talking about our nation's identity, the character of our nation.

People have asked me if having spent a professional life in teaching was worth it. There have been any number of times when I've been reminded of heartfelt moments that have made it more than worth it, and I'm grateful for the many connections made with people I otherwise would have missed out on had I made a different life decision many years ago. More than a few stand out:

> Several years ago I was conferring in my office with a high school student and his father regarding yet another disciplinary referral on the kid—he was not a bad youngster, but he had his share of problems with schooling in general. I conferred with the student and his dad for several minutes; the issues surrounding the referral and how it would be handled administratively were discussed, when I asked the youngster to wait in the main office while I spoke to his dad. I had made an earlier reference to the teacher's disciplinary classroom writeup that the father was holding, and I sensed that he was trying to read it, but he could not comprehend it. I wanted to avoid any

perceived slight or sense of embarrassment but decided it was important enough to take a chance. I asked if he was able to understand it, and we danced around the matter for a moment or so, when I finally asked him if he could read. I said it was certainly okay, that any knowledge of it would remain in my office, but if he was game, I knew of a resource that wouldn't cost him a dime (they were financially disadvantaged). I proceeded to advise the gentleman that I knew an older female, a retired reading teacher and a volunteer at a local library. She was also the parent of a high school youngster, whom I had disciplined years earlier but had later connected with before he graduated, and she couldn't thank me enough for his positive turnaround, saying if there was anything she could do, etc. Long story short, he thanked me and left my office, only to stop by the school several days later to say he would like to "give it a shot." I set up the arrangement, and they worked for months. His boy graduated; it was a year or so later when the father approached me at a shopping center. We chatted for a moment, and then he took out his paycheck and started reading slowly a sentence or two from the attached salary statement. I smiled and shook his hand, when he said he "really, really appreciated the help." He was still working with the volunteer, and he practiced reading a newspaper daily, something, he said, "I ain't never done before."

It is always a pleasure when I encounter students years later as grown-ups in their thirties, forties, fifties, and, though it is hard for me to believe, their sixties.

In Maine, while at a wildlife sanctuary with my wife, Elaine, the forest ranger yelled my name, recognizing me as her high school administrator some twenty-five years earlier, stating that she was grateful that our lives had intersected, and refusing to allow us to pay for any of the sanctuary events.

At a gas station, also out of state, a student yelled my name, came over, and hugged me, saying he was vice president of a bank in New York. We were smiling, chatting away, when he mentioned my having to discipline him and the "near-major physical altercation with my crazy mom," he added smiling.

The evening one of my former English students, today a Catholic priest and pastor, was providing premarital counseling to a couple, when it was discovered that they and the priest knew me. At that moment he decides to pick up the telephone to call me---this is some 35 years since high school---and initially does not reveal his identity. He didn't have to. I immediately recognized the voice, which brought joy and laughter to the two us and the happy couple. He is also a fire department chaplain, which is close to my heart, and continues to lead a community in faith, worship, love, and the gospel of Jesus Christ.

I was at a restaurant where dozens of educators assembled to honor a colleague's retirement, when a young gentleman, a former student, approached me, in his late-thirties, to shake my hand and thank me for "knockin' some sense in my head, as a junior in high school, and straightening me out." At six foot three and 230 pounds, he could take care of himself, but unfortunately in high school he was often disrespectful to staff and bullied other students. He reminded me verbatim of what I told him one day, saying, "You might be six foot two and 220 pounds, but you're still your momma's boy, and if you bully another student, if you disrespect another teacher in this school, you'll be yanked off the football team, you will have seen your last days in this high school, and you'll be escorted out and charged by the county police. Do you get that?" He shook his head approvingly and smiled, continuing, "Or words pretty close to that. I never forgot that conversation, Mr. Wallis, and I appreciate it to this day." I smiled back at him, saying, "You've got a good memory. I very much recall that somewhere in there was a good kid, and I remember being happy shaking your hand at your graduation." He was on the executive track with an oil company and was on his way to Texas at the time.

A few years prior to retiring, I ran for political office and was jogging in the community, when cars would honk, former students well into adulthood yelling that they were voting for me.

And the time a student, now a father of three, saw me out in public and took a few minutes to approach me, thanking me for the time he came to me while in high school, remembering that he was interrupting a conversation I was having at the time with a parent. He'd had his wallet stolen. I recall the youngster was emotionally upset at the time, because he had a picture of his grandfather in the wallet, which was all he really wanted, not caring about the few dollars he had been carrying. He recalled that I excused myself from the parent, summoned a few suspected miscreants, and checked a couple bathrooms, eventually locating the wallet sitting in a toilet. I told him that I, indeed, remembered the incident. I remembered observing that a couple of the wallet's items were photographs. I scooped the items out, used paper towels to dry the pics, one of which was an old photograph of his grandfather; the photo was still suitable enough to keep. It made enough of an impression on this former ninth-grader that, years later as a grown man, he recognized me in a crowd and made it a point, with his children in tow, to thank me again, and show me the very grainy, water-stained picture of his granddad that he was still carrying after all these years. Good stuff!

Or the time a really first-rate student overlooked the reverse-page portion of an application for his first-choice school, The United States Military Academy at West Point. He was beside himself, not realizing how he could have done such a thing, and sure enough, he was not appointed. I called the commandant office and spoke to a number of folks, including one particular captain who said he'd sincerely look into what, if anything, could be done. The student could not thank me enough, and later he was fortunate enough to be offered an appointment to another of the service academies.

Then there are those situations, challenges that present themselves, that are different—some sad, some poignant—one involving a student brought to my attention by a staff member, who had been conferring with the student over an emotional crisis. The school psychologist escorted the student to meet me directly, advising me that she contacted the county social services office, that representatives were on their way, and she knew that I'd likely prefer to meet the student and confer with her. I pulled a chair out for the youngster and asked a few general questions about school and her life, when she confirmed that she had spent most of her life in Ghana, coming to the United States some three years earlier when summoned by her mom and dad. She initially attended another school in the county, and she had only recently registered at our school. The girl was twelve, and I casually asked when she would be thirteen, when she said her birthday was the following day. I asked what the plans might be for a celebration, when she responded, "We don't celebrate my birthdays. My mom won't allow me, but that's okay." I said, "Really, alright, tell me about your current situation and how we can help you enjoy a better day." At that point, I asked her to hold her thought for a moment; I stepped out of my office to grab my secretary, asking her if she could stop what she was doing and jump over to the nearby grocery store to purchase a birthday cake, candles, a card, any party plates, tablecloths, etc., and to do so immediately and return in a few short minutes, making sure to have the birthday card signed by the school psychologist and any additional staff members present. She was a bit taken aback, but she understood something must have been up for me to make such a request, at which point she dashed to the grocery store and returned minutes later.

I noticed that the girl had some swelling and abrasions above her eye and on her forehead. The youngster continued, saying that, "We do celebrate my brother's birthday, though. It's kinda hard at home, because my mom calls me the devil, and says she didn't really want me to come to this country. She thinks I'm trying to break up their marriage, and it was my dad who wanted me to move here, not her. I don't know why she says that, but I'm tired of getting hit." She went on to explain how her mother, at times, beat her with the post end of a vacuum cleaner, then would turn the cleaner on, making a back-and-forth motion over the child, as if she, the mother, was vacuuming up dust or dirt. I looked at her, horrified at what this child was enduring. So important it is that youngsters grow up in a caring, loving, supportive, and stable home. This child was getting none of that, and it occurred to me that someone—of all people, her mother—didn't think she, her daughter, mattered. The youngster did matter, however, in countless ways, and one day, I thought, she will matter very much to her husband, her children, and her grandchildren, and who knows what she'll go on to do or the impact she may have in the future here in America. I went on to say that she seemed a pretty terrific youngster to me, that we were going to help her, that her mom was wrong and needed help (and perhaps her dad, as well), but that there was a process in place to help her through this, and that I would keep tabs on her and follow her situation closely. I could see out my office window that social services representatives had arrived, and I asked the child if she would mind if we celebrated her birthday; she seemed a bit stunned. I opened my door to see five staff members, organized with items that would soon turn the round table I use for conferencing into a birthday table, all of us singing "Happy Birthday" as they set up the table, presenting her with a cake, ice cream, and a birthday card. Again, it was good stuff—sad, as well—but good stuff, nonetheless. Social services representatives conferred with the youngster and accompanied her to their office, where she would also be interviewed by the police. It turned out the mom was later arrested and went to court; the family was awash in dysfunction and moved from the area. The father transferred the youngster to yet another school. I later received a card in the mail from her, a heartwarming, appreciative thank-you, informing me that she was doing better and hoped that we would see each other again one day. I would like that.

One of my weekend ball-playing youngsters was a tough kid from D.C. She attended Harper's Choice as a sixth-grader, had her share of run-ins with peers and staff, then moved to another location, transferring to another school. She reappeared as an eighth-grader, asking if she "could play some ball again with the principal on the weekend." She knew the drill, deciding to behave herself and apply herself academically so she could go to high school and graduate, and she did just that. I would not see her until several years later, by chance, when she saw me out in the community, walked over, and gave me a prolonged hug. She was attending college in the Northeast, was in pre-med, and hoped one day to become a doctor.

I also had a gifted special education teacher who worked hard, was a real team player, who participated in and appreciated the meaningful strides we were making to turn the school around. She came in one day to inform me that she was being treated for brain cancer, a scourge that had taken my mom's life when I was young, just prior to my being drafted into the military. I decided one day, when my teacher was receiving treatment, to make a visit and spend time with her. The hospital treatment center looked like a salon, with several women sitting with their heads beneath hooded hair dryer-like medical equipment that exposed the glioblastoma cells to a rapidly alternating sequence of low-intensity electric currents. I surprised her and greeted the other ladies. All of us were chatting, at times finding some humor in our conversations. She and I held hands and talked for the next three hours. I recall addressing her life and death over the school public address system to the staff and student body. She was another kind, good, and caring individual, and her students were so very grateful that she had graced them with such love and care during her time on this earth.

There are also those times when, as principal, I would attend memorial viewings or funerals of the various family members of my students, and they were always so appreciative, always wanting to introduce me to their family. It was always, of course, a somber occasion, but family and neighbors always managed a smile, when I engaged them in conversation about my student—their son or daughter—and an anecdotal story that might have included the deceased family member.

Among the single most important character traits that one can demonstrate is the ability to connect, to care that another in your life matters, really matters. In the field of teaching, it has been particularly important and rewarding, and it gives so many of us in the profession so many wonderful opportunities to make such connections.

The results that we achieved at Harper's Choice Middle were predicated on the extent to which the school recognized the pivotal importance that character, passion, and teamwork—a shared partnership—would play among the staff, students, parents, community, businesses, government agencies, and school administration. The benefits that we accrued as a school in recognizing—and putting into practice—this shared partnership for our entire school community were huge.

As outlined throughout the book, our business partners recognized and supported our efforts fully, providing their time, their resources, and their expertise directly to our students, staff, and school operations, without which we would not have been as successful.

Our parents—our ever-supportive group of parents—I'm not certain I can ever thank each of them enough for their unconditional support, love, caring, and hard work throughout the school and community; they were tireless defenders and supporters of our kids, our teachers, and my administration.

The various teaching staff over those several years, who gave so much of themselves, who recognized how much we could—with enough will, caring, grit, direction, faith, and support—move past formidable challenges to succeed as they did, making life so much more improved for students and their families; they have my respect and admiration.

And the students—thousands over a career in education, as well as the hundreds and hundreds of Harper's Choice students over the years who walked through our doors and recognized that they, too, wanted to be part of something special, who worked so hard to prepare for high school and beyond. I remain proud of all these former students, some of whom are among today's young adults; others are in their mid-sixties, many of whom are grandparents themselves today.

It goes a long way when the majority of students understand the real meaning of school and learning, understand and practice those very character traits that will place them in solid stead no matter the choices they make after high school; all of them provided a good reason for my staff to want to get up every morning and enjoy coming to work.

It's absorbing, insightful, and affirming to look back on the vast amount of time, care, commitment, and effort that went into that particular school community's renaissance, and you confirm what has always been a truism: nothing replaces hard work; nothing replaces character, faith, family, love, caring, determination, passion, teamwork, patriotism, and a good education...nothing!

So, when I am asked, from time to time, about having chosen teaching as a living, I am thankful for the many times when I felt enriched by knowing and connecting with so many students, their families, teaching staff, and other individuals. I think about those weekends playing ball with and seeing students daily in the school hallways, only to learn that a particular student had suddenly moved and transferred to another school. We were a transient school, where a number of our students changed schools multiple times. I hoped that such students would remember our emphasis on character, a vitally important element in their lives, and I thought how nice it'd be if these youngsters' next school was one that exuded success, caring, passion, teamwork, and accomplishment, an inviting school environment, where staff realized that their connecting with students was at the heart of instruction. I was fortunate to be presented any number of opportunities to make a positive difference in the lives of students, staff, or a community, and I'm happy enough with the choice I made years ago.

I will state again that if the reader is a first-rate educator, or an intelligent, caring, courteous, and hard-working student; or a strong, top-shelf school administrator; or a loving, responsible, caring parent—know that this book is an homage—a tribute—to you. Together, it is you who make for strong, vibrant, accomplished school communities, which will only strengthen the America we all know, respect, and cherish.

Writing this book provided me the opportunity to relive, in a manner of speaking, my years in and out of the classroom; at times it was as though I was very much still there in the moment. As I reflect on what I've shared with the reader, I am reminded of what I also stated in the introduction, that on the whole, it was a rewarding experience, and I am happy to have shared a good piece of that experience with the reader. I hope the preceding pages adequately expressed that sentiment and that the reader has taken away some useful insights as to how communities across this land might improve American education for our youngsters and for America as a whole.

I sometimes think all that really matters is that we care, we love, we show up, and we do our level best. At the end of my tenure as principal of Harper's Choice, I looked back on the sheer professionalism, hard work, daily sincere intentions, care, and love expended by so many staff and believe that we were able to "ameliorate the condition, promote the virtue, and advance the happiness" of the majority of our students, their parents, and the community.

I think about the decisions made over a lifespan and wonder how a different choice, during and following my military service, or perhaps upon receiving my undergraduate degree, when I was twenty-five years old, would have altered my life's path. I recall having several spirited conversations with my dad, who, the reader will recall, was divorced from my mom and in and out of our family picture as we were growing up. He would suggest on more than a few occasions that I consider accounting, his chosen career, or perhaps finance and "become a Wall Street stockbroker," he would say. He then urged me to look at medicine, or to consider engineering. No; mathematics and the sciences, while interesting and often fascinating, did not hold a professional interest for me. I did consider law school; I interviewed with the Federal Bureau of Investigation; the Secret Service; the Bureau of Alcohol, Tobacco, and Firearms; I contemplated a career in professional firefighting (given my previous association with a Washington, DC, area fire department), as well as television journalism, and was offered the position of on-air journalist with a Washington, DC, news station.

As it would turn out, I wound up exceeding my dad's, and later my own, expectations; I became a teacher.

Know for certain that where character is the soul of the schoolhouse, meaningful teaching and learning rooted in truth and historical fact is the surest route to an informed patriotism.

—Stephen Wallis

About the Author

Stephen Wallis was born in Philadelphia and raised in the Washington, DC, metropolitan area. A Vietnam-era veteran, he served in the United States Army with USAEUR and 7th Army and stationed in Heidelburg, West Germany. He is a decorated chief line officer with a Washington, DC, area volunteer fire department.

He taught high school English and was a school administrator in the Washington, DC–Baltimore area. The recipient of numerous awards throughout his career, he received the National Distinguished Leadership Award from the American Federation of School Administrators, citing him "among the top eight school principals in the nation." He received Honorary Life Membership in the National Congress of Parents and Teachers in "recognition of his devoted and distinguished services to children and youth."

He has provided his K-12 education perspectives on television and radio broadcasts nationally, including National Public Radio, CNBC, NET, and WABS. His writings have appeared in national periodicals, including Insight Magazine, Education Week, USA Today, the Los Angeles Times, the Baltimore Sun, the St. Louis Dispatch, the Washington Post, the Chicago Sun-Times, and the Cincinnati Enquirer. His "no excuses" philosophy, emphasizing character, high quality teaching, parent involvement, and student behavioral and academic excellence, is a professional mantra that results in meaningful school success. Among his publications is a contributing chapter in the book Making America Safer, published by the Heritage Foundation, and a chapter in the book Trimmings, published by the Calvert Institute of Public Policy. He has over thirty years' experience as a teacher, secondary school administrator, principal, and guest lecturer at the university level.

Mr. Wallis was asked to take the helm of an "in-crisis," problem-plagued public school in the Baltimore–Washington, DC corridor. Upon arrival, he found the usual pathologies of schools servicing a diverse spectrum of students, many of whom are disadvantaged youngsters: failing state academic test scores, poor teacher morale, racial concerns, disruptive student behavior, vandalism, few Parent Teacher Association (PTA) members, and no business partnerships.

His leadership resulted in markedly improved student academic and student behavioral achievement, teacher satisfaction, active parent involvement, and community-wide satisfaction levels. His efforts boosted test scores and improved student behavior, decreasing student suspensions from school by 94%, along with a school climate survey that averaged 98 percent, in a school district averaging 70 percent. School PTA membership saw a 1,000 percent increase, and nearly three dozen businesses established partnerships with the school, tops in the school district, turning the once-blighted school community into a National School of Excellence and a Maryland State Character School of the Year. The Washington Post's Education Review magazine cited the school "Among the Top Schools in the Virginia-Washington-Maryland Metropolitan Area."

Mr. Wallis has worked on education bills with state House and Senate legislators, providing testimony to the Maryland General Assembly, as well as to members of the United States Congress on national education reform proposals. He appeared before the United

States Senate Committee on Government Affairs hearings, providing expert testimony on the role schools can play in the effort to combat crime and violence throughout our nation's communities.

He was co-founder and president of the proposed Business Preparatory Institute, a charter high school for urban youths.

Mr. Wallis and his wife, Elaine, have two grown married children and four grandchildren. They share their time between Ellicott City, Maryland, and St. Petersburg, Florida. He can be reached at stephenwallisauthor@gmail.com

Notes

Introduction

1 Kelley Holland, "Why Johnny Can't Write, and Why Employers Are Mad," CNBC Jobs, November 11, 2013, https://www.cnbc.com/2013/11/08/why-johnny-cant-write-and-why-employers-are-mad.html.

2 Karsten Strauss, "These Are the Skills Bosses Say New College Grads Do Not Have," Forbes, May 17, 2016, https://www.forbes.com/sites/karstenstrauss/2016/05/17/these-are-the-skills-bosses-say-new-college-grads-do-not-have/.

1. Current Condition of American Schools

1 National Assessment of Educational Progress, NAEP Report Card Results, Office of Educational Research and Improvement, U.S. Department of Education, Washington, DC, as cited in Anya Kamenetz and Corey Turner, "The High School Graduation Rate Reaches a Record High—Again," NPREd K-12, October 17, 2016, http://www.npr.org/sections/ed/2016/10/17/498246451/the-high-school-graduation-reaches-a-record-high-again.

2 Ibid.

3 Stephanie Banchero, "High-School Graduation Rate Inches Up." *Wall Street Journal*, January 22, 2013, as cited in www.dosomething.org, "11 Facts About High School Dropout Rates," http://online.wsj.com/news/articles/SB10001424127887323301104578256142504828724; https://www.dosomething.org/us/facts/11-facts-about-high-school-dropout-rates

4 The National Center for Public Policy and Higher Education, "Be-

yond the Rhetoric: Improving College Readiness Through Coherent State Policy," 2010, http://www.highereducation.org/reports/college_readiness/gap.shtml.

5 Ibid.

6 Complete College America, http://completecollege.org/wp-content/uploads/2014/11/4-Year-Myth.pdf.

7 Mary Nguyen Barry and Michael Dannenberg, Education Reform Now, RELEASE: "Americans Spending at Least $1.5 Billion in College Remediation Courses; Middle Class Pays the Most," report commissioned by *Education Post*, April 5, 2016, https://edreformnow.org/accountability/release-americans-spending-at-least-1-5-billion-in-college-remediation-courses-middle-class-pays-the-most/.

8 Ibid.

9 Peter Cunningham, executive director, *Education Post*, cited in *Education Reform Now* research study, "Americans Spending at Least $1.5 Billion in College Remediation Courses; Middle Class Pays the Most," April 5, 2016.

10 The Reagan Administration, *A Nation at Risk: The Imperative for Educational Reform, A Report to the Nation and the Secretary of Education, United States Department of Education, by The National Commission on Excellence in Education*, April 1983.

11 U.S. Department of Education and the National Institute of Literacy, 2015, as cited in Bradley Blakeman, "Literacy Is Fundamental to a Free Society," *The Hill*, May 8, 2017, https://thehill.com/blogs/pundits-blog/education/332236-literacy-is-fundamental-to-a-free-society.

12 Angel Gurria, OECD Secretary-General, PISA 2015, Results in Focus, Organisation for economic Co-operation and Development (OECD) Programme for International Student Assessment, PISA, https://www.oecd.org/pisa/pisa-2015-results-in-focus.pdf.

13 National Assessment of Educational Progress, NAEP Report Card Results, Office of Educational Research and Improvement, U.S. Department of Education, Washington, DC, 2017, 2019, https://www.nationsreportcard.gov/reading_2017/nation/achievement?grade=4, and https://www.nationsreportcard.gov/

highlights/mathematics/2019/.

14 Alison Doyle, "Hard Skills versus Soft Skills," February 4, 2019, https://www.thebalancecareers.com/hard-skills-vs-soft-skills-2063780.

15 Solving the Talent Shortage, 2018, https://go.manpowergroup.com/talent-shortage-2018#.WKrYrRIrJo4.

16 Centers for Disease Control and Prevention, Understanding School Violence, Fact Sheet 2016, National Center for Injury Prevention and Control, Division of Violence Prevention, https://www.cdc.gov/violenceprevention/pdf/School_Violence_Fact_Sheet-a.pdf.

17 Cyberbullying Research Center, January 3, 2017, article by Justin W. Patchin entitled, "Millions of Students Skip School Each Year Because of Bullying" based on their survey of some 5,700 middle and high school students from across the United States.

18 Kristen A. Graham, "It's Official: Report Says Philadelphia Schools Fall Short on Dealing with Crime," Assault on Learning series, *Philadelphia Inquirer*, January 18, 2012.

19 Council for American Private Education (CAPE), "Cape Outlook," Germantown, MD, January 2015, No. 401.

20 National Commission on Teaching and America's Future (NC-TAF), as cited by Education Resources Information Center (ERIC), sponsored by the Institute of Education Sciences, U.S. Department of Education, 2007, Washington, DC, https://eric.ed.gov/?id=ED498001.

21 Elizabeth Mulvahill, "Why Teachers Quit: Lack of Respect, Abominable Working Conditions, and More," We Are Teachers, an online media brand for educators, Shelton, CT, June 24, 2019, https://www.weareteachers.com/why-teachers-quit/.

22 Kathleen Cotton, "School-wide and Classroom Discipline," School Improvement Research Series (SIRS), Northwest Regional Educational Laboratory (NWREL), based on work sponsored wholly, or in part, by the Office of Educational Research and Improvement (OERI), U.S. Department of Education, under Contract Number 400-86-0006. The content of this publication does not necessarily reflect the views of OERI, the Department, or any

other agency of the U.S. Government. December 1990, http://web.archive.org/web/20080212033545/http:www.nwrel.org/scpd/sirs/5/cu9.html.

23 C. Stephen Wallis, "How State and Local Officials Can Restore Discipline and Civility to America's Public Schools," Backgrounder 1018/S, The Heritage Foundation, February 9, 1995.

24 Edwin Meese III and Robert E. Moffit, *Making America Safer: What Citizens and Their State and Local Officials Can Do to Combat Crime*, The Heritage Foundation, 1997.

25 Grace Chen, "Why 82% of Public Schools Are Failing," Public School Review, September 3, 2020.

2. Character

1 William J. Bennett, *The Book of Virtues*, (New York: Simon & Schuster, 1993), 11.

2 Moriah Balingit, "U.S. High School Graduation Rates Rise to New High," Washington Post, December 4, 2017, https://www.washingtonpost.com/news/education/wp/2017/12/04/u-s-high-school-graduation-rates-rise-to-new-high/?utm_term=.eeec6f980e84.

3 Ashley Fants, "Prison Time for Some Atlanta School Educators in Cheating Scandal," CNN US, April 15, 2015, https://www.cnn.com/2015/04/14/us/georgia-atlanta-public-schools-cheating-scandal-verdicts/index.html

4 Richard Fausset, "Central Figure in the Atlanta Schools Cheating Scandal Dies," *New York Times*, March 2, 2015, https://www.nytimes.com/2015/03/03/us/central-figure-in-the-atlanta-schools-cheatingscandaldies.htmlaction=click&module=RelatedCoverage&pgtype=Article&region=Footer.

5 Donna St. George, "How High Can Graduation Rates Go? The Story of One School Rocked by Scandal," Washington Post, July 27, 2017, https://www.washingtonpost.com/local/education/how-high-can-graduation-rates-go-the-story-of-one-school-rocked-by-scandal/2018/07/27/98a3c34e-3ab0-11e8-8fd2-49fe3c675a89_story.html?utm_term=.fc17fba8bcbb.

6 Kate McGee, "What Really Happened at the School Where Every

Graduate Got into College," nprEd, How Learning Happens, National Public Radio's All Things Considered, November 28, 2017, https://www.npr.org/sections/ed/2017/11/28/564054556/ what-really-happened-at-the-school- where-every-senior-got-into-college.

7 Nick Anderson, "Five Colleges Misreported Data to U.S. News, Raising Concerns about Rankings, Reputation," Washington Post, February 6, 2013, https://www.washingtonpost.com/local/ education/five-colleges-misreported-data-to-us-news-raising-concerns-about-rankings-reputation/2013/02/06/cb437876-6b17-11e2-af53-7b2b2a7510a8_story.html?utm_term=.2e4736c1a436.

8 David Wagner, "Which Schools Aren't Lying Their Way to a Higher U.S. News Ranking?" *Atlantic*, February 6, 2013.

3. Principal's Arrival and Initial Impression

1 Howard County (MD) Public School System, "Comprehensive Plan for Accelerated School Improvement," March 2002.

2 Maryland School Performance Program, "How MSDE Determines a School's AYP," Maryland State Department of Education, 2001, https://reportcard.msde.maryland.gov/Definitions/Index.

4. Preparing for Opening Day

1 Admiral William H. McRaven (U.S. Navy Retired), *Make Your Bed: Little Things That Can Change your Life…and Maybe the World* (New York: Grand Central Publishing, 2017).

2 James Q. Wilson and George L. Kelling, "Broken Windows: The Police and Neighborhood Safety," *Atlantic Monthly*, 1982 (based on earlier research by Philip Zimbardo, Stanford University, 1969).

3 George L. Kelling and William H. Sousa Jr., "Civic Report, Do Police Matter? An Analysis of the Impact of New York City's Police Reforms," Center for Civic Innovation at The Manhattan Institute, December 2001.

5. Teachers Return for the New School Year

1 Roland S. Barth, "The Culture Builder," *Educational Leadership*,

Association for Supervision and Curriculum Development, May 2002.

2 John O'Rourke, superintendent (former), Howard County (MD) Public Schools, "Comprehensive Plan for Accelerated School Improvement (CPASI)," 2001.

3 George T. Doran, *Management Review*, "There's a S.M.A.R.T. Way to Write Management's Goals and Objectives," 1981.

4 Peter Drucker, *The Practice of Management* (New York: Harper and Row Publishers, Inc., 1954).

5 O'Rourke (CPASI), 2001.

6 Ronald Edmonds, Larry Lezotte et al., *Effective Schools Correlates*, 1979, 1991.

7 2010 Maryland Code Education, Title 7—Public Schools, Subtitle 3—Attendance and Discipline of Students, Section 7-301-Compulsory Attendance.

8 Ministry of Education, Guyana, "Negatives of Disruptive Behavior in the Classroom," September 2015, https://www.education.gov.gy/web/index.php/teachers/tips-for-teaching/item/1674-negatives-of-disruptive-behavior-in-the-classroom.

9 Scott E. Carrell and Mark L. Hoekstra, "Domino Effect," EducationNext, Summer 2009, Vol. 9, No. 3, https://www.educationnext.org/domino-effect-2/.

10 Ibid.

11 Naomi White, "I Taught Them All," Clearing House, a journal of educational strategies, issues, and ideas, 1937, 151.

6. Opening Week for Students

1 Phyllis Utterback, Planning and Support Services Student Questionnaire, "Keys to Academic Success, General Findings for Grades 3–12, Howard County (MD) Public Schools, November 1994.

2 Ibid.

7. Game On!

1 Daniel Patrick Moynihan, "Defining Deviancy Down—How We've Become Accustomed to Alarming Levels of Crime and Destructive Behavior," *American Scholar*, Winter 1993.

2 Peter Roff, "The Bottom of the Deviant Barrel," *American Spectator*, May 10, 2018.

3 Robert L. Woodson Sr., *The Triumphs of Joseph: How Today's Community Healers Are Reviving Our Streets and Neighborhoods* (New York: Free Press/Simon & Schuster, Inc.,1998), 5.

4 Preeti Varathan, "The U.S. Is Having a Hard Time Keeping Teachers in Their Jobs," QUARTZ, June 1, 2018, https://qz.com/1284903/american-teachers-leave-their-jobs-at-higher-rates-than-other-countries-with-top-ranked-school-systems/.

5 "Why Are Teachers Leaving the Profession?" retrieved from *Education World*, https://www.educationworld.com/a_curr/why-are-teachers-leaving-profession.shtml.

6 Varathan, "The U.S. Is Having a Hard Time Keeping Teachers."

7 Desiree Carver-Thomas and Linda Darling-Hammond, "Teacher Turnover: Why It Matters and What We Can Do About It," Research Report, Learning Policy Institute, August 2017, https://learningpolicyinstitute.org/sites/default/files/product-files,Teacher_Turnover_REPORT.pdf.

8 Ibid.

9 Isabel Sawhill and Ron Haskins, "Work and Marriage: The Way to End Poverty and Welfare," Brookings Institution, 2003, https://www.brookings.edu/research/work-and-marriage-the-way-to-end-poverty-and-welfare/.; https://www.brookings.edu/opinions/three-simple-rules-poor-teens-should-follow-to-join-the-middle-class/

8. Focus on Instruction

1 American Council on Education, "To Touch the Future: Transforming the Way Teachers Are Taught," Washington, DC, 1999, http://education-consumers.org/wp-content/uploads/2018/01/To-Touch-The-Future-1999.pdf.

2 Daniel Gordon, "Pentagon's Schools Outrank Others in Academic Success," Wall Street Journal, December 1999, https://www.wsj.com/articles/SB945815431650916790; https://nces.ed.gov/nationsreportcard/.

3 Kate McGee, "What Really Happened at the School Where Every Graduate Got into College," nprED—*How Learning Happens*, November 28, 2017, citing research.

4 United States Department of Education, "Chronic Absenteeism in the Nation's Schools—A Hidden Educational Crisis," Washington, DC, June 7, 2016, https://www2.ed.gov/datastory/chronicabsenteeism.html#intro.

5 Inclass Today, Harvard University, Harvard Student Social Support R&D (S3R&D) Lab, 2016, inclasstoday.com.

6 Ibid.

7 Sean Covey, *The 7 Habits of Highly Effective Teens* (New York, Fireside/Simon & Schuster, 1998).

8 Charlotte Danielson, Framework for Teaching (Danielson Group of Princeton, New Jersey: 1996).

9 Utterback, Planning and Support Services Student Questionnaire, "Keys to Academic Success, General Findings for Grades 3–12, Howard County (MD) Public Schools, November 1994.

10 Ibid.

11 Ibid.

12 Brandon Busted, "The School Cliff: Student Engagement Drops with Each School Year," Gallup News, January 7, 2013, https://news.gallup.com/opinion/gallup/170525/school-cliff-student-engagement-drops-school-year.aspx?g_campaign=tiles.

13 Ibid.

14 Richard DuFour, "What Is a Professional Learning Community?," *Educational Leadership*, Association for Supervision and Curriculum Development, 2004.

15 "The 40 Developmental Assets," Search Institute, Minneapolis, MN, 1997, www.searchinstitute.org; https://www.search-institute.org/our-research/development-assets/developmental-assets-framework/.

16 Howard County (MD) Public School System, Alternative Education Programs, Tier 1, In- School Programs, https://www.hcpss. org/academics/alternative-education/.

17 Ibid.

18 Afterschool Alliance in Partnership with MetLife Foundation, "Keeping Kids Safe and Supported in the Hours After School," Issue Brief No. 65, May 2014, http://afterschoolalliance.org/documents/issue_briefs/issue_KeepingKidsSafe_65.pdf.

19 Afterschool Alliance, "America After 3PM: The most in-depth study of how America's children spend their afternoons," Washington, DC, 2009, http://www.afterschoolalliance.org/AA3_Full_Report.pdf.

20 Council for a Strong America's Fight Crime: "Invest in Kids," Washington, DC, 2003.

21 Robert Balfanz, "Putting Middle Grade Students on the Graduation Path: A Policy and Practice Brief, National Middle School Association, Westerville, OH, June 2009, http://new.every1graduates.org/wp-content/uploads/2012/09/policy_brief_balfanz.pdf.

22 "California's After-School Choice: Juvenile Crime or Safe Learning," as cited by Carla Rivera, "Hours After School Are the Riskiest for Youths," *Los Angeles Times*, September 2004.

9. Focus on Continuous Improvement

1 *Education Week*, "Continuous Improvement: A Closer Look," June 22, 2018, https://www.edweek.org/ew/collections/continuous-improvement/index.html.

2 American Society for Quality. (n.d.). Continuous Improvement. Retrieved from http://asq.org/learn-about-quality/continuousimprovement/overview/overview.html, as described by Jane Best and Allison Dunlap, "Continuous Improvement in Schools and Districts," McRel International, Denver, CO, https://files.eric. ed.gov/fulltext/ED557599.pdf.

3 G. Gorenflo and J.W. Moran (2010). *The ABCs of PDCA*. Washington, DC: Public Health Foundation. Retrieved from http://www. phf.org/nphpsp/ViewResourceLink.aspx?source=http%3a%2f%2fwww.phf.

org%2fresourcestools%2fPages%2f The_ABCs_of_   PDCA.
aspx&title=The+ABCs+of+PDCA, as cited by Jane Best and Allison Dunlap, "Continuous Improvement in Schools and Districts,"
McRel

4 Andreas Schleicher, "What Makes High-Performing School Systems Different," in *World Class: How to Build a 21st-Century School
System*, Chapter 3, 63, Organization for Economic Cooperation
and Development (OECD) Publishing, Paris, 2018, access complete publication at: https://doi.org/10.1787/9789264300002-en.

5 Tom Loveless, "Searching for a Way to Close the Achievement
Gap," Brookings Institution, October 22, 2000. Note: The author
used this reference, as he was unable to retrieve original Brookings study.

6 Schleicher, Chapter 3.

7 Jack Welch, with John A. Byrne, *Jack-Straight from the Gut*, New
York: Warner Business Books, An AOL Time Warner Company,
2001.

10. A Culture for Teaching and Learning

1 Angel Gurria, OECD Secretary-General, PISA 2015, Results in
Focus, Organisation for Economic Co-operation and Develop-
ment (OECD) Programme for International Student Assessment,
PISA, "Policies and Practices for Successful Schools," "What the
Data Tell Us," 10, https://www.oecd.org/pisa/pisa-2015-results-
in-focus.pdf.

2 Charles Krauthammer, *Things That Matter* (New York: Crown Forum, 2013).

3 Li Cohen, "Federal Court rules that transgender students must be
allowed to use bathrooms that match their gender," CBS News,
August 9, 2020,https://www.cbsnews.com/news/federal-court-
rules-that-transgender-students-must-be-allowed-to-use-bath-
rooms-that-match-their-gender/.

4 Ty Tagami, "Complaint says transgender bathroom policy led to
kindergarten assault," *Atlanta Journal-Constitution*, October 4,
2018, https://www.ajc.com/news/state--regional-education/
child-sex-assault-case-decatur-schools-touches-national-de-

bate-over-gender-identity/SKG4vOR4BCFpdrkynKSRyH/.

5 Christopher Bergland, The Athlete's Way, "Music Participation Linked to Teen Academic Achievement," Psychology Today, June 2019, https://www.psychologytoday.com/us/blog/the-athletes-way/201906/music-participation-is-linked-teens-academic-achievement.

6 Martin Guhn, Scott D. Emerson, Peter Gouzouasis. "Population-Level Analysis of Associations Between School Music Participation and Academic Achievement," *Journal of Educational Psychology* (First published: June 24, 2019), DOI: 10.1037/edu0000376.

7 Stephen Covey, *The 7 Habits of Highly Effective Teens* (New York: Fireside/Simon & Schuster, 1998).

8 The Temptations, "My Girl," *The Temptations Sing Smokey*, Songwriters Smokey Robinson and Ronald White, Gordy (Motown), Hitsville USA (Studio A), Format: 7-inch single, Genre: Soul-R&B, Detroit, MI, September 25, 1964. https://www.youtube.com/watch?v=swSytFVMHuU.

9 Eileen Kennedy-Moore, "They Call That Dancing?!" *Psychology Today*, February 18, 2013, https://www.psychologytoday.com/us/blog/growing-friendships/201302/they-call-dancing.

10 National Center of Education Statistics, U.S Department of Education, *Digest of Education Statistics*, 2017, https://nces.ed.gov/programs/digest/d17/tables/dt17_233.60.asp.

11 Ibid.

12 Noah Webster, *A Collection of Essays and Fugitiv Writings on Moral, Historical, Political and Literary Subjects.* Boston, 1790. Reprint. Delmar, NY: Scholars' Facsimiles & Reprints, 1977. Viewed via The Founders' Constitution, Volume 1, Chapter 18, Document 26, The University of Chicago Press, http://press-pubs.uchicago.edu/founders/documents/v1ch18s26.html.

11. A Focus on Partnership

1 Howard County (MD) Education Association, "Teachers Union Watchdog List," 2000, Ellicott City, MD.

12. Results

1 Stephen Wallis, "Then...," author's personal note made shortly after initial arrival, July 2000.

2 Wallis, Harper's Choice Middle School Improvement Plan, Needs Assessment, Data Analysis, February 2009.

3 Patricia Duffy, *Building Cougar Character*, Harper's Choice Middle School, September 2006.

4 Wallis, Harper's Choice Middle School Annual Report, "Content Area Academic Year Reports," 2004.

5 Wallis, *Cougar News*, Harper's Choice Middle School-Parent Teacher Association Newsletter, "Principal's Corner," October 7, 2003.

6 Nancy Grasmick, Maryland School Performance Recognition Program Letter to Principal Wallis, Harper's Choice Middle school, Maryland State Department of Education, January 2003.

7 Maryland School Assessment, Maryland Report Card, Maryland State Department of Education, 2003 www.mdreport.org.

8 Maryland School Assessment, Maryland Report Card, Maryland State Department of Education, 2004 www.mdreport.org.

9 Maryland School Assessment, Maryland Report Card, Maryland State Department of Education, 2009 www.mdreport.org.

10 National Parent-Teacher Association, "National PTA School of Excellence Award," Harper's Choice Middle School, 2003.

11 Lisa Magloff, "Job Satisfaction vs. Production." Small Business-Chron.com, http://smallbusiness.chron.com/job-satisfaction-vs-production-18821.html. Accessed 05 November 2019.

12 *HCEA Works* union magazine, Job Satisfaction Survey features Harper's Choice Middle among "Highest Overall Morale," Howard County Education Association, affiliate of MSTA and NEA, April/May 2009.

13 Lindsey Burke, "Unions Double Down on Inserting Critical Race Theory Into Education," *The Daily Signal*, The Heritage Foundation, July 6, 2021.

14 Joseph Staub, HCEA President, meeting at Howard County Teachers Association, Ellicott City, MD, July 2000; Ann DeLacy, HCEA President, Board of Directors & Representatives Dinner,

upon awarding author Howard County Education Association *Presidential Certificate of Merit*, June 9, 2009.

15 Jay Mathews, "Unstuck in the Middle," *Washington Post Magazine*, Education Review, April 15, 2007.

13. Leadership

1 Frank Sinatra, "New York, New York," *Trilogy: Past, Present, Future* album, 1979, written by Fred Ebb, composed by John Kander, for the 1977 Martin Scorsese Film, New York, New York.

2 Erik Engquist, "Bratton, Bidding Adieu, Says He Regrets Falling Out with Giuliani," CRAIN'S NEW YORK BUSINESS, September 12, 2016, https://www.crainsnewyork.com/article/20160912/POL-ITICS/160919981/nypd-commissioner-bratton-regrets-giuliani-falling-out.

3 Fortune Editors, "The World's 50 Greatest Leaders," March 2014, https://fortune.com/2014/03/20/worlds-50-greatest-leaders/.

4 Doug Pederson, coach, Philadelphia Eagles, *CBS This Morning* interview and article, citing his new memoir "Fearless: How an Underdog Becomes a Champion," August 24, 2018.

5 Madeleine Albright, "Commencement Address to the Class of 2015," Tufts University, Medford, MA, May 17, 2015, https://now.tufts.edu/commencement2015/speeches/albright.

6 Rudy Giuliani, with Ken Kurson, Leadership (New York: Hyperion, 2002).

14. School Safety and Security

1 E. Erin Artigiani Senior Research Analyst Center for Substance Abuse Research, University of Maryland, College Park, Maryland Research in Brief: HotSpots Community Initiative, Phase I, An interim report prepared for the Governor's Office of Crime Control & Prevention, August 2001, http://www.cesar.umd.edu/cesar/pubs/20010801.pdf.

2 Peter Hermann, "City, State Police join in 'Hot Spot' Patrol, Targeted Areas in State to Get Backup, Funds in Violent Crime Program," Baltimore Sun, March 14, 1997, https://www.balti-

moresun.com/news/bs-xpm-1997-03-14-1997073036-story.html.

3 Raja Mishra, Howard County "Hot Spot" Targeted, *Washington Post*, August 30, 1999, https://www.washingtonpost.com/archive/local/1999/08/30/howard-county-hot-spot-targeted/8ec8def1-4905-4498-b607-c76d451657d0/?utm_term=.3a3effe05fc9.

4 National Center for Education Statistics, U.S Department of Education, WEB TABLES, December 2016, https://nces.ed.gov/pubs2017/2017015.pdf.

5 YouthTruth Student Survey, "Learning from Student Voice," San Francisco, 2017–2018, https://youthtruthsurvey.org/bullying-today/.

6 Christina Whalen, "The Effects of Bullying," rethinkEd, October 12, 2017, https://www.rethinked.com/blog/blog/2017/10/12/the-effects-of-bullying/.

7 Gianluca Gini and Dorothy Espelage, "Peer Victimization, Cyberbullying, and Suicide Risk in Children and Adolescents," *Journal of the American Medical Association Network*, August 6, 2014.

8 Kelly Dedel, "The Problem of School Vandalism and Break-Ins," Center for Problem-Oriented Policing, Arizona State University, 2005, https://popcenter.asu.edu/problems/vandalism/#endref7.

9 U.S. Department of Justice, Office of Justice Programs, Office of Juvenile Justice and Delinquency Prevention, *Youth in Action*, December 1998, https://www.ncjrs.gov/pdffiles/94600.pdf.

10 Dedel, 1.

11 Handful of self-identified high school students and two staff members, unscheduled impromptu conversation on grounds of Columbine High School, Littleton, CO, July 17, 2001.

12 David Kohn, "Columbine: Were There Warning Signs? Should School Officials Have Known?" CBS News, *60 Minutes*, April 17, 2001, https://www.cbsnews.com/news/columbine-were-there-warning-signs/.

13 Andrew Pollack and Max Eden, "Why Meadow Died: The People and Policies That Created the Parkland Shooter and Endanger America's Students," New York: *Post Hill Press*, 2019.

14 "Job Corps Careers Begin Here," U.S. Department of Labor, Job Corps, Washington, DC, 2017, https://www.dol.gov/general/

topic/training/jobcorps.

15 Rachel Ponder, "Freestate ChalleNGe Academy Gives At-Risk Kids a Second Chance," APG News, United States Army, Aberdeen Proving Grounds, 2013, https://www.army.mil/article/100868/ freestate_challenge_academy_gives_at_risk_youth_a_second_ chance.

16 Lindsey Burke, "Father of Parkland Victim on What Could Have Stopped the Tragedy," *Daily Signal*, The Heritage Foundation, September 19, 2019.

17 Lauren Camera, "Did an Obama-Era Discipline Policy Contribute to the Parkland Shooting?" *U.S. News & World Report*, March 6, 2018, https://www.usnews.com/news/education-news/articles/2018-03-06/did-an-obama-era-school-discipline-policy-contribute-to-the-parkland-shooting.

18 The Parkland, Broward County, FL, "Collaborative Agreement on School Discipline," http://www.ncjfcj.org/sites/default/files/ Broward%20Co%20Collaborative%20Agreement%20on%20 School%20Discipline%20-%20MOU.pdf.

19 Curt Devine and Jose Pagliery, "Sheriff Says He Got 23 Calls About Shooter's Family, but Records Show More," *CNN Investigates*, February 27, 2018, https://www.cnn.com/2018/02/27/us/parkland-shooter-cruz-sheriff-calls-invs/index.html.

20 Ann Coulter, "The School-to-Mass-Murder Pipeline," distributed by Andrews McMeel Syndication, February 28, 2018, http://www.anncoulter.com/columns/2018-02-28.html.

21 Anna Deavere Smith, "The Myth of the School-to-Prison Pipeline," appearing in Robert Ward's *Rewarding Education* blog for Teachers and Parents, September 13, 2017. https://rewardingeducation.wordpress.com/2017/09/13/the-myth-of-the-school-to-prison-pipeline/.

22 Emelina Minero, "When Students Are Traumatized, Teachers Are Too," *Edutopia*, October 4, 2017, https://www.edutopia.org/ article/when-students-are-traumatized-teachers-are-too.

23 Betsy DeVos, U.S. Secretary of Education, and William Barr, United States Attorney General, Trump Administration 2018 Letter (signatories: Kenneth Marcus, Assistant Secretary for

Civil Rights, U.S. Department of Education and Eric Dreiband, Assistant Attorney General, U.S. Department of Justice), rescinding 2014 Obama Administration "Dear Colleague" letter on Nondiscriminatory Administration of School Discipline, Overview of the Supportive School Discipline Initiative, and related documents, Guiding Principles: A Resource Guide for Improving School Climate and Discipline, Appendix 1: U.S. Department of Education Directory of Federal School Climate and Discipline Resources, dated January 8, 2014; Appendix 2: Compendium of School Discipline Laws and Regulations for the 50 States, Washington D.C., and Puerto Rico, dated January 8, 2014; and School Discipline Guidance Package FAQs, dated January 8, 2014.

24 Francisco Vara-Orta, Chalkbeat, "It's Official: DeVos has axed Obama discipline guidelines meant to reduce suspensions of students of color," December 21, 2018.

15. Wokeness and Critical Race Theory

1 Rhona Shennan, "What Does Woke Mean," National World, June 17, 2021, JPI Media Publishing Limited, London, England https://www.nationalworld.com/whats-on/arts-and-entertainment/what-does-woke-mean-definition-of-woke-culture-in-2021-and-what-critics-mean-by-woke-police-3215758

2 Elliot Kaufman, "The 1619 Project Gets Schooled—The New York Times tries to rewrite U.S. history, but its falsehoods are exposed by surprising sources," Wall Street Journal, December 16, 2019, https://www.wsj.com/articles/the-1619-project-gets-schooled-11576540494.

3 Dennis Prager, "Most American Schools Are Damaging Your Child," Jewish World Review, March 9, 2021, http://www.jewishworldreview.com/0321/prager030921.php3.

4 Ian Rowe, "The Soft Bigotry of Anti-Racist Expectations Is Damaging to Black and White Kids Alike," USA Today, December 6, 2020

5 United States Department of Labor, Title VI, Civil Rights Act of 1964 statute, Office of the Assistant Secretary for Administration & Management, 1964 https://www.dol.gov/agencies/oasam/regulatory/statutes/title-vi-civil-rights-act-of-1964

6 Jonathan Butcher, "Rescuing Math and Science from Critical Race Theory's Racial Discrimination," Issue Brief, Center for Education Policy, The Heritage Foundation, July 13, 2021,https://www. heritage.org/sites/default/files/202107/IB5201.pdf?mkt_tok-=ODIoLU1IVCozMDQAAAFSk1zXZ8pp7YxpEfyM2zs8eDu8iRE-B5RR1ecV9cFhCxF18K59u3edJNrCcq1CfUlKU_wAwbwzrtMIM-0V888ra_Rmj1fZZXOUM82fk-vTDI_xyA

16. The Achievement Gap

1 Heather MacDonald, "Is the Criminal Justice System Racist?" *City Journal*, Spring 2008, https://www.city-journal.org/html/criminal-justice-system-racist-13078.html.

2 Robert J. Sampson and Janet L. Lauritsen, "Racial and Ethnic Disparities in Crime and Criminal Justice in the United States," 1997, as cited in MacDonald, Spring 2008.

3 Michael Tonry, *Malign Neglect—Race, Crime, and Punishment in America* (New York: Oxford University Press, 1995), as cited in MacDonald, Spring 2008.

4 National Center for Education Statistics, U.S. Department of Education, "Status and Trends in the Education of Racial and Ethnic Groups 2018," Washington, DC, 2018.

5 Ibid.

6 National Assessment of Educational Progress (NAEP), appearing in National Center for Education Statistics (NCES), U.S. Department of Education, "Status and Trends in the Education of Racial and Ethnic Groups 2018," Washington, DC, 2018.

7 Walter Williams, "Blind to Real Problems," *Jewish World Review*, June 20, 2018, http://jewishworldreview.com/cols/williams062018.php3#U5VtiAfuO2t19klt.99.

8 Thomas Sowell, "Race, Politics, and Lies," *Jewish World Review*, Creators Syndicate, May 15, 2015.

9 Marta H. Mossburg, "Reverend Wright Brings His Anti-American Crusade to Baltimore," Baltimore Sun, June 21, 2011.

10 Celeste Headlee, "What Is 'Acting White'?" National Public Radio podcast, *The Takeaway*, July 14, 2010, https://www.wnycstudios.org/podcasts/takeaway/articles/87969-what-acting-white.

11 Stuart Buck, *Acting White: The Ironic Legacy of Desegregation* (New Haven: Yale University, 2011).

12 Jason Riley, *Please Stop Helping Us* (Encounter Books, 2014, 2015).

13 Kareem Abdul-Jabbar and Peter Knobler, *Giant Steps: The Autobiography of Kareem Abdul-Jabbar* (Bantam Books, 1983), 16.

14 Felicia Lee, "Why Are Black Students Lagging?" *New York Times*, November 30, 2002.

15 John U. Ogbu, *Black American Students in an Affluent Suburb: A Study of Academic Disengagement* (Lawrence Erlbaum Associates, 2003), 35.

16 Ibid, 23.

17 Jack Fowler, "What Obama Didn't Say," *National Review, The Corner*, July 22, 2013, https://www.nationalreview.com/corner/what-obama-didnt-say-jack-fowler/.

18 Geneva Gay, *Culturally Responsive Teaching: Theory, Research, and Practice* (Teachers College Press, 2010), 23–24, 27.

19 James Samuel Coleman, "Equality of Educational Opportunity," U.S. Office of Education, Department of Health, Education, and Welfare, 1966, https://en.m.wikipedia.org/wiki/James_Samuel_Coleman#cite_note-5.

20 Phyllis Utterback, Planning and Support Services Student Questionnaire, "Keys to Academic Success, General Findings for Grades 3–12, Howard County (MD) Public Schools (HCPSS)," November 1994.

21 Ibid.

22 Tom Loveless, "Searching for a Way to Close the Achievement Gap," Brookings Institution, October 22, 2000 (as cited in the research of James A. Kulik, University of Michigan).

23 Utterback, Planning and Support Services Student Questionnaire, HCPSS, 1994.

24 George A. Akerlof and Janet L. Yellen, "An Analysis of Out-of-Wedlock Births in the United States," Brookings Institution Policy Brief, August 1, 1996, https://www.brookings.edu/research/an-analysis-of-out-of-wedlock-births-in-the-united-states/.

25 U.S. Department of Justice, Office of Justice Programs, National

Institute of Justice, "What Can the Federal Government Do to Decrease Crime and Revitalize Communities?" Panel Papers, "Trend Four: There Is an Increase in the Number of Fatherless Children, Who Are More Prone to Delinquency and Other Social Pathologies," 11–12, January 5–7, 1998, https://www.ncjrs.gov/pdffiles/172210.pdf.

26 Ibid.

27 Joseph Chamie, "Out-of-Wedlock Births Rise Worldwide," Yale-Global Online, Yale University, https://yaleglobal.yale.edu/content/out-wedlock-births-rise-worldwide, Chart Source: Organization for Economic Cooperation and Development.

28 Star Parker, "Urban Violence Begins in Broken Homes," commentary distributed by Creators.com, Center for Urban Renewal (CURE), August 15, 1918.

29 Gretchen Livingston, "About One-Third of U.S. Children Are Living with an Unmarried Parent," Pew Research Center, April 2018, https://www.pewresearch.org/fact-tank/2018/04/27/about-one-third-of-u-s-children-are-living-with-an-unmarried-parent/.

30 Ibid.

31 Chris Papst, "13 Baltimore City High Schools, Zero Students Proficient in Math," City in Crisis Town Hall, FOX45 NEWS and Project Baltimore, November 8, 2017, https://foxbaltimore.com/news/project-baltimore/13-baltimore-city-high-schools-zero-students-proficient-in-math.

32 Isabel Sawhill and Ron Haskins, "Work and Marriage: The Way to End Poverty and Welfare," Brookings Institution, 2003, https://www.brookings.edu/research/work-and-marriage-the-way-to-end-poverty-and-welfare/; https://www.brookings.edu/opinions/three-simple-rules-poor-teens-should-follow-to-join-the-middle-class/.

33 Sowell, "Race, Politics, and Lies," May 15, 2015.

34 David Autor and Malanie Wasserman, "Wayward Sons: The Emerging Gender Gap in Labor Markets and Education," The Third Way, Next, March 20, 2013, https://economics.mit.edu/files/8754 (accessed January 31, 2018); W. Bradford Wilcox and Nicholas Zill, "Stronger Families, Better Schools: Families and

High School Graduation Across Arizona," Institute for Family Studies, https://ifstudies.org/ifs-admin/resources/arizona-re-search-brief-final.pdf (accessed August 21, 2018); and W. Brad-ford Wilcox and Nicholas Zill, "Stronger Families, Better Schools: Families and High School Graduation Across the Sunshine State," Institute for Family Studies, https://ifstudies.org/ifs-admin/re-sources/florida-report-1.pdf (accessed August 21, 2018).

35 David Autor, David Figlio, Krzysztof Karbownik, Jeffrey Roth, and Melanie Wasserman, "Family Disadvantage and the Gender Gap in Behavioral and Educational Outcomes," National Bureau of Economic Research, Working Paper No. 22267, May 2016, http://www.nber.org/papers/w22267.pdf (accessed August 21, 2018); David Autor, David Figlio, Krzysztof Karbownik, Jeffrey Roth, and Melanie Wasserman, "Family Disadvantage and The Gender Gap in Behavioral and Educational Outcomes," Northwestern University, Institute for Policy Research, Working Paper WP-15-16, October 21, 2015, https://www.ipr.northwestern.edu/publi-cations/docs/workingpapers/2015/IPR-WP-15-16.pdf (accessed August 21, 2018); and Wilcox and Zill, "Stronger Families, Better Schools: Families and High School Graduation Across Arizona."

36 Lindsey Burke, W. Bradford Wilcox, and Derrick Max, "Educa-tion Choice and the Success Sequence: Adapted remarks from *The Heritage Foundation's* 2017 Anti-poverty Forum," September 12, 2017.

37 Larry Elder, *The Ten Things You Can't Say in America* (New York: St. Martin's Press, 2000), 156.

38 Armstrong Williams, "Last Dance: ESPN Series on Michael Jordan Full of Lessons on Life, Family," Daily Signal, May 15, 2020, https://www.dailysignal.com/2020/05/15/last-dance-espn-series-on-michael-jordan-full-of-lessons-on-life-family/?utm_source=rss&utm_medium=rss&utm_campaign=last-dance-espn-series-on-michael-jordan-full-of-lessons-on-life-family?utm_source=TDS_Email&utm_medium=email&utm_campaign=MorningBell&mkt_tok=eyJpIjoiWkdSbU5UVTVOV-GsxWXpjeiIsInQiOiJoQXJkNVF5UWdnXC9aQ3hVNDBBLenR lOHBRQodzdFJxUVwvNzlkZzlyVTlMMMHI1ZHNvTVc3MlNI RzBDdENGMDF5cEROTSs3ZTZsbVltMnZuODAxRHMxMF-c5N29CN3VwY2JOb3FhbkJnMVpncWh5M1FhVXlRUGpWYlV-

MaHVXRWJ5WDBxIn0%3D.

39 The Heritage Foundation, "Covid-19: Lessons Learned and Path Ahead" (accessed November 2020, https://www.heritage.org/covid-introduction.

40 U. S. Department of Health & Human Services, "Fact Sheet: Explaining Operation Warp Speed, What's the Goal?" (accessed November 23, 2020), https://www.hhs.gov/coronavirus/explaining-operation-warp-speed/index.html.

41 Paul Hannon and David Harrison, "A Covid-19 Vaccine Would Boost the Global Economy, but Not All at Once," *Wall Street Journal*, November 11, 2020, https://www.wsj.com/articles/a-covid-19-vaccine-would-boost-the-global-economy-but-not-all-at-once-11605087345.

42 *The Economist*, "What a Vaccine Means for America's Economy," November 14, 2020, https://www.economist.com/finance-and-economics/2020/11/14/what-a-vaccine-means-for-americas-economy39, Bureau of Labor Statistics, Employment Situation Summary, United States Department of Labor, Eugene Scalia, Secretary of Labor, Washington, DC, September 6, 2019, https://www.bls.gov/news.release/empsit.nr0.htm.

43 Bureau of Labor Statistics, Employment Situation Summary, United States Department of Labor, Eugene Scalia, Secretary of Labor, Washington, DC, September 6, 2019, https://www.bls.gov/news.release/empsit.nr0.htm.

44 Chris Isidore, CNN Business, telecast on record-low black unemployment, New York, September 6, 2019, https://www.cnn.com/2019/09/06/economy/black-unemployment-rate/index.html.

45 Dayna Haffenden, "Black Unemployment Rate Falls to a Record Low," *Black Enterprise*, September 10, 2019, https://www.blackenterprise.com/black-unemployment-rate-falls/.

46 United States Census Bureau, "Income and Poverty in the United States: 2018," September 10, 2019, https://www.census.gov/library/publications/2019/demo/p60-266.html, as cited in Associated Press, "U.S. Household Income Finally Matches 1999 Peak, While Poverty Rates Hit Lowest Point Since 2001," September 10, 2019, https://www.apnews.com/9e2a69b1728d4da99afb064d8f3

9f566.

47 News Clips, Economy and Job, "Americans of all Backgrounds Are Experiencing Economic Success in the Trump Economy," citing news clips underscoring the strong Trump economy creating an environment where job opportunities are plenty and Americans are lifted out of poverty, September 10, 2019, https://www. whitehouse.gov/briefings-statements/americans-backgrounds-experiencing-economic-success-trump-economy/.

48 United States Internal Revenue Service, "Opportunity Zones Frequently Asked Questions," Washington DC, August 23, 2019, https://www.irs.gov/newsroom/opportunity-zones-frequently-asked-questions.

49 Laura Clark, "What Are Title I Schools?" Student Debt Relief, October 3, 2019, https://www.studentdebtrelief.us/student-loans/title-1-schools/.

50 U.S. Department of Education, Fiscal Year 2018 Budget, Summary and Background Information, 3, https://www2.ed.gov/about/overview/budget/budget18/summary/18summary.pdf.

51 Andreas Schleicher, "What Makes High-Performing School Systems Different," in World Class/How to Build a 21st Century School System, OECD Publishing, Paris, 2018. Access the complete publication at: https://doi.org/10.1787/9789264300002-en.

17. Parents and Schools

1 William J. Bennett, *The Book of Virtues* (New York: Simon & Schuster, 1993).

2 Juliette Sivertsen, "The Importance of Parental Involvement in Your Child's Education," Washington Christian Academy, September 22, 2015, http://www.washingtonchristian.org/blog/the-importance-of-parental-involvement-in-your-childs-education.

3 LaurenTamm, "Boundaries, Routines and Early Bedtimes: 13 Habits That Raise Well-Adjusted Kids," *The Military Wife and Mom*, 2019, https://themilitarywifeandmom.com/raise-well-adjusted-kid/.

4 Michele Borba, "Want Happy, Succesful Kids? Teach Them Empathy," TODAY Contributor, NBC News, June 7, 2016.

5 Pamela Li, "Hugging—7 Benefits for You and Your Child (Backed by Science)," *Parenting for Brain*, November 8, 2019.

6 Lawrence Cohen, *Playful Parenting: An Exciting New Approach to Raising Children That Will Help You Nurture Close Connections, Solve Behavior Problems, and Encourage Confidence* (New York: The Random House Publishing Group, 2001).

7 Meryl Davids Landau, "Kids Should Play Outside 3 (!) Hours Every Day, This Expert Says. Here's Why—and How to Do It," *Huffington Post*, May 11, 2017.

8 Marty Rossman, "Involving Children in Household Tasks: Is it Worth It?" Research Works, College of Education and Human Development, University of Minnesota, Minneapolis, 2013, http://ww1.prweb.com/prfiles/2014/02/22/11608927/children-with-chores-at-home-University-of-Minnesota.pdf.

9 Liraz Margalit, "What Screen Time Can Really Do to Kids' Brains," Psychology Today, April 17, 2016, https://www.psychologytoday.com/us/blog/behind-online-behavior/201604/what-screen-time-can-really-do-kids-brains.

10 Sally White, "Reward Your Kids with New Experiences, Not Stuff," *Lifehack.org*, 2018.

11 John Duffy, as cited by Jaci Conry, "The Benefits of Slow Parenting," *Boston Globe*, May 2, 2016, https://www.bostonglobe.com/lifestyle/2015/05/10/the-benefits-slow-parenting/2LImOAIyqElORCStgOADSI/story.html.

12 Amy Joyce, "Why It's Important to Read Aloud with Your Kids, and How to Make it Count," Perspective, *Washington Post*, February 16, 2017. https://www.washingtonpost.com/news/parenting/wp/2017/02/16/why-its-important-to-read-aloud-with-your-kids-and-how-to-make-it-count/.

13 Melissa Locker, "This Is How Music Can Change Your Brain," *TIME*, December 16, 2014, https://time.com/3634995/study-kids-engaged-music-class-for-benefits-northwestern/.

14 Lily Garcia and Otha Thornton, "The Enduring Importance of Parental Involvement," *neaToday*, National Education Association, November 18, 2014, http://neatoday.org/2014/11/18/the-enduring-importance-of-parental-involvement-2/.

15 Sivertsen, "The Importance of Parental Involvement in Your Child's Education."

18. A Final Word

1 Carnegie Forum on Education and the Economy (USA). Task Force on Teaching as a Profession, "A Nation Prepared: Teachers for the 21st Century," a report by a task force assembled by the Carnegie Corporation of New York: 1986.

2 im Mullen, "Adulting 101," *Jewish World Review*, November 5, 2019, http://jewishworldreview.com/1119/mullen110519.php3.

3 Thomas Jefferson, "From Thomas Jefferson to Cornelius C. Blatchly, 21 October, 1822," National Archives, Founders Online, https://founders.archives.gov/documents/Jefferson/98-01-02-3106.

4 Thomas Jefferson, "Autobiography by Thomas Jefferson," with the *Declaration of Independence*, 1821, cited in Yale Law School, Lillian Goldman Library, The Avalon Project, Documents in Law, History, and Diplomacy, https://avalon.law.yale.edu/19th_century/jeffauto.asp.

5 Samuel Adams, in a letter to James Warren, February 12, 1779, as cited by Ashley Thorne, "U.S. Founding Fathers on Education, in their Own Words," National Association of Scholars, July 2, 2010, https://www.nas.org/blogs/dicta/u_s_founding_fathers_on_education_in_their_own_words.

6 Wikipedia contributors. (2019, November 10). History of education in the United States. In *Wikipedia, The Free Encyclopedia*. Retrieved 19:47, November 12, 2019, from https://en.wikipedia.org/w/index.phptitle=History_of_education_in_the_United_States&oldid=925445841; "High literacy rates in America... exceeded 90 per cent in some regions by 1800." Hannah Barker and Simon Burrows, eds. *Press, Politics and the Public Sphere in Europe and North America, 1760–1820*. (2002), 141; for lower rates in Europe, see p. 9.

7 "A Practical Matter: Education in the Middle Colonies," "Education in the Colonies," Education World, 2000, https://www.education-world.com/a_lesson/TM/EducationInTheColonies.shtml.

8 Todd Kominiak, "In His Words: John Adams on Education and Democracy," trustED, K-12 Insight, 2019, https://www.k12insight.

com/trusted/words-john-adams-education-democracy/.

9 Johann N. Neem, "The Founding Fathers Made Our Schools Public. We Should Keep Them That Way," Perspective, *Washington Post*, August 20, 2017, https://www.washingtonpost.com/news/made-by-history/wp/2017/08/20/early-america-had-school-choice-the-founders-rejected-it/.

10 Edwin Feulner, "Haven't We Learned Our School Lesson?" Heritage Foundation, April 10, 2019, https://www.heritage.org/education/commentary/havent-we-learned-our-school-spending-lesson.

11 U.S. Department of Education, National Center for Education Statistics. (2019). *The Condition of Education* 2019 (NCES 2019-144), Public School Expenditures, https://nces.ed.gov/fastfacts/display.asp?id=66.

12 National Assessment of Educational Progress, NAEP Report Card Results, Office of Educational Research and Improvement, U.S. Department of Education, Washington, DC, 2017, 2019, https://www.nationsreportcard.gov/reading_2017/nation/achievement?grade=4; https://www.nationsreportcard.gov/highlights/mathematics/2019/.

13 "Skilled-Labor Shortage Exacerbates Irma/Harvey Rebuild Difficulties," Rentar Fuel Catalyst, October 31, 2017 https://rentar.com/skilled-labor-shortage-exacerbates-irmaharvey-rebuild-difficulties/.

14 SKILLSUSA.org, 14001 SkillsUSA Way, Leesburg, VA 20176-5494, 2021, https://www.skillsusa.org/about/

15 Mike Rowe Works Foundation, Mike Rowe, 2008, https://www.mikeroweworks.org/

16 National Center of Education Statistics, U.S Department of Education and the Institute of Education Services, "Trends in High School Dropout and Completion rates in the United States," 2017, https://nces.ed.gov/programs/dropout/ind_01.asp

17 Alliance for Excellent Education, "The High Cost of High School Dropouts: The Economic Case for Reducing the High School Dropout Rate," Washington, DC, https://all4ed.org/take-action/action-academy/the-economic-case-for-reducing-the-high-school-dropout-rate/